In this call for a "renewal" within the Latter-day Saint tradition that is as fervent as it is sincere, Nathan Kitchen has offered us a gift. This memoir provides a compelling glimpse not only into Kitchen's own moving experience, but into the world of paradoxes, pain, and progress inhabited by those who aim to balance both queer and Mormon identities.

—Benjamin E Park
author of *American Zion: A New History of Mormonism*

Like the prophet-historian Mormon, Brother Nathan Kitchen deftly chronicles the history of his people while standing as a witness to their labors, sufferings, miracles, and eternal worth in the eyes of God. Interweaving secular history, soul-searching religious memoir, striking anecdote, and Christ-saturated imagery, Kitchen keeps a fixed foot on the reality of the past, contextualizing the present while longing for yet more glorious and redemptive futures for the queer Latter-day Saint. His book is engrossed with such thoroughly Mormon concepts as covenant belonging, unmerited grace, the ongoing restoration, and the sacred—if not essential—nature of questions in our spiritual journeys. An act of holy consecration, *The Boughs of Love* is as much an accessible, sprawling roadmap of the pitfalls and progress of queer identity within the LDS tradition as it is a testimony of the expansive hope that the Restored Gospel of Christ can offer to all members of the family of God.

—Jaxon Washburn
Master of Theological Studies, Harvard Divinity School;
PhD Student, the University of California, Los Angeles

I was not prepared for how much I would enjoy reading Nathan's memoir. I prepared myself to feel pain, anger, and grief as I read his words. But I found something else in addition—joy. Nathan deftly braids together his experience as a gay LDS man, the history of the Church of Jesus Christ of Latter-day Saints with regards to gender and sexual minorities, and his time as the President of Affirmation. Nathan's stories, poetry, and reflections provide an important glimpse into the lives of individuals and families navigating the intersection of their LDS faith and their queer realities. Nathan shares his testimony and anguish as he experienced harmful LDS policies with respect to 2SLGBTQIA+ people while also leading an organization of people directly affected by those policies. Remarkably, Nathan's joy as a father, husband, and person constructing a life of authenticity also shines through the pages and rings of hope and possibility.

—Roni Jo Draper, Ph.D. (she.her)
Emeritus Professor, Brigham Young University

In the LDS world, thoughtful voices of LGBTQ+ members are too often vexingly dismissed as being activist, adolescent, or apostate. Nathan Kitchen's memoir should break through as a faithful, mature voice tracing the trauma of trusting in religious teachings that harmed him and thousands of others over his lifetime as a gay man. Kitchen describes these harms while maintaining respect for the faith that developed both his spirituality and his concern for all people impacted by them. His book details the psychosocial violence inflicted on individuals with testimonies of the gospel who desire to engage authentically in Church community while being married to a same-sex partner. Kitchen's message is that the joy of the gospel and a divinely-rooted desire to live in Christlike love with a deeply-cherished marriage partner are not exclusive to straight cisgender members of the LDS Church. His narrative illustrates how denying this basic human/spiritual connection continues to inflict harm on LDS individuals and families.

In the 50,000 sessions of mental health therapy I have conducted or supervised in the LDS LGBTQ+ community, I can validate that the psychosocial violence of LGBTQ+ individuals being ostracized by their Church for living authentically and pursuing healthy relationships is felt in thousands of faithful families, impacting every ward and stake in Zion. These families are recognizing that their LGBTQ+ children are not the enemy of righteousness, but messengers to all of us to rethink our assumptions about what constitutes a holy and faithful life.

Nathan Kitchen's book shows us why we should pay attention.

—Lisa Tensmeyer Hansen, PhD., LMFT
CEO and founder of Flourish Therapy, Inc.,
a 501(c)3 nonprofit outpatient mental health clinic
serving the LGBTQ+ community

Few have captured the complexity of the LGBTQ+ experience within the LDS Church as powerfully as Nathan Kitchen does in this compelling memoir. As the Church grapples with evolving policies that profoundly impact its queer members, The Boughs of Love offers an intimate and rare perspective on how these changes have shaped not only his life, but also the lives of countless others. With stories of resilience, Kitchen's memoir is both eye-opening and deeply inspiring. It illuminates the strength and love that endure even in the face of profound challenges, while offering a hopeful vision for a future where the Church embraces its LGBTQ+ members with genuine compassion, understanding, and inclusivity.

—Gerardo Sumano
Mormon Stories Podcast Producer

LO
VE

BCC
PRESS

BY COMMON CONSENT PRESS is a non-profit publisher dedicated to producing affordable, high-quality books that help define and shape the Latter-day Saint experience. BCC Press publishes books that address all aspects of Mormon life. Our mission includes finding manuscripts that will contribute to the lives of thoughtful Latter-day Saints, mentoring authors and nurturing projects to completion, and distributing important books to the Mormon audience at the lowest possible cost.

A MEMOIR

THE BOUGHS of LOVE

NATHAN KITCHEN

Navigating the Queer
Latter-day Saint Experience During an
Ongoing Restoration

The Boughs of Love: Navigating the Queer Latter-day Saint Experience During an Ongoing Restoration
Copyright © 2024 by Nathan Kitchen

All rights reserved. Printed in the United States of America. No part of this book may be used or reproduced in any manner whatsoever without written permission except in the case of brief quotations embodied in critical articles or reviews.

For information contact
By Common Consent Press
972 East Burnham Lane
Draper, Utah 84020

Cover design: D Christian Harrison
Book design: Andrew Heiss

www.bccpress.org

ISBN-13: 978-1-961471-14-6

10 9 8 7 6 5 4 3 2 1

"I always thought, I shall be the happiest person, if I could reach Zion, with all my children alive."

ANN JEWELL ROWLEY, surrounded by her seven young children near the fifth Sweetwater River crossing where the Willie handcart company had stalled from hunger, cold, and exhaustion.

October 19, 1856

For Matthew

CONTENTS

	Introduction	xi
	A Note to the Reader	xviii
	The Cherry Trees	1
1	Fear at the End of Parley Street	6
2	Swept and Garnished	17
	Prayer 26	
3	An Autumnal Grove	27
	Divorce 36	
4	A New Age is Upon Us	38
5	Wheels Down	56
6	Behold, Here Are the Waters of Mormon	65
	Barrenness 77	
7	The Peak of Champions	78
8	Confused at the Grace that So Fully He Proffers Me	93
	The Arrow of Time 103	
9	A Refuge to Share	104
10	A Call to the Board	119
11	A Salmon in the Desert	133
	The Voice 145	
12	Pressing Forward	147
13	The Family is Ordained of God	156
	Navigating Masculinity 161	

14	A Recension	163
	A bird is not an ornithologist 183	
15	Seatbelts, Please	184
16	World Pride	196
17	What is Love?	205
	That We Call Home 216	
18	The BYU	218
19	The Rainbow Stained-Glass Ceiling	232
	The Blessing of Waves 252	
20	Under a Lemon Tree	254
	For Matthew— 264	
21	The Hunted	265
22	Unto Dust Thou Shalt Return	279
23	Change without Change	290
24	When the World Shut Down	305
	State of Emergency 318	
25	Of Sand and Stone	320
26	The Hosts	331
27	A Light on a Hill	344
28	The Family Will Endure	355
	Our Family Proclamation 369	
29	In the Temple with an Apostle	370
30	The Gentleness of Love	381
31	Smoke and Oakum	388
32	The Stench of Lazarus	400
33	Sprint to the Finish	408
34	The Lifting of Samuel	421
	Afterword	432
	To My Children 435	
	Love, Returned 443	
	Acknowledgments	444

INTRODUCTION

In January 2015, I stood in an upper room of the Brooklyn Borough Hall in New York City to see the St. Francis of Assisi exhibition. This was the first time these documents had left Italy in seven hundred years. The Holy See arranged this exhibit as an advance party to Pope Francis's first visit to the United States in September. In that once-in-a-lifetime moment, I was surrounded by beautiful, illuminated, handwritten eight-hundred-year-old documents of Catholic governance and worship from the period of St. Francis. Latter-day Saints know St. Francis as the author of the hymn "All Creatures of Our God and King." However, it is not well known in Latter-day Saint circles that St. Francis was part of the great renewal of the medieval church.

At the exhibit, Dr. John Edwards from St. Francis College gave a short lecture about St. Francis, the Franciscan order, and their place in the Church's history. He taught that the Catholic Church has gone through cycles of decline and renewal for two thousand years. During periods of decline, saving monastic orders, such as the Franciscan and other mendicant orders, rose from outside the church hierarchy to lead the Church away from its intimate relationship with politics and wealth and to forsake the corrupt policies and practices that accompany such relationships—answers for God's people when the church had gone astray.

As I considered my own religion, his assertion struck me as much as it confronted me. I reflected on our history in the Church of Jesus Christ of Latter-day Saints. Organized in 1830, we were still a relatively young church, come lately to the historical record, yet despite this, we have had our share of decline and renewal, crisis and change. Two thousand years has provided the Catholic Church and her scholars enough maturity to look back with comfortable hindsight to identify and talk about periods of decline and renewal without such acknowledgments threatening the Church's identity. We barely have two hundred years of hindsight in The Church of Jesus Christ of Latter-day Saints. Because of this, our church is not at all comfortable identifying periods of decline and renewal at this stage. We are still too close to our founding to see such things objectively without threatening our identity or feeling attacked. We can't even apologize yet to those hurt by such cycles. In our short history as a church, we have already experienced two significant periods of decline and renewal. Both have left a deep and permanent imprint on the Church's identity. The first was polygamy, and the second was denying Black men the priesthood and Black families access to the temple.

For the rest of the day, I thought about the current crisis in our church centering on rejecting behavior towards queer Latter-day Saints. How do we reconcile a restored theology majestically rising on the world from First Vision to King Follett—fueled by the prophetic promise that "Our Heavenly Father is more liberal in his views, and boundless in his mercies and blessings, than we are ready to believe or receive"[1]—with policies and practices rooted in prejudice, harassment, and discrimination

---

1. History, 1838–1856, volume D-1 [1 August 1842–1 July 1843] [addenda], p. 4 [addenda], The Joseph Smith Papers, accessed July 21, 2024, https://www.josephsmithpapers.org/paper-summary/history-1838-1856-volume-d-1-1-august-1842-1-july-1843/285.

that have structured the everyday life of queer Latter-day Saints in their spiritual home for generations?

Today, we are right in the middle of a third major crisis of decline: the treatment of LGBTQ people and their families. The 2015 exclusion policy and its 2019 recension reminded us that we are nowhere near renewal. LGBTQ Latter-day Saints are being drawn and quartered, sliced in two like a Solomon baby. In these circumstances, as the queer children of God, we are denied a wholeness in the house of God. The resolution of the present decline will certainly come and undoubtedly leave another deep and permanent imprint upon our identity as a church, just as the renewals following its last two crises did.

When I was president of Affirmation: LGBTQ Mormons, Families & Friends, Blaire Ostler asked me to write the foreword for her book, *Queer Mormon Theology*.[2] It was 2021, and I was knee-deep in the absolute crisis within the queer Latter-day Saint community when lived experience meets theology. In the foreword, I shared my experience at the St. Francis of Assisi exhibit because it encapsulated the crux of what was occupying vast amounts of real estate in my head at that moment.

As I took on Blaire's project, I told her I would acknowledge the practical effects of lived religion so that our queer peers would know that an examination of queer Mormon theology was not an act of ignoring the flesh-and-blood reality of queer people experiencing their sexual orientation and gender identity. I take a very practical, Pauline approach to theology. It does not matter how beautiful its fruit looks within the boughs of

---

2. Ostler, Blaire, and Nathan Kitchen. "Foreword." In *Queer Mormon Theology: An Introduction*, ix-xii. Newburgh, Indiana: By Common Consent Press, 2021.

the restored gospel or how eloquently and neatly it is parsed within the pages of Latter-day Saint thought; if a queer person consumes it and it causes harm, then it is bad fruit. In the lived experiences of queer Latter-day Saints, the Church's theology doesn't just stay in the realm of ideas and dogma. It has the flesh-and-blood effect of structuring our spiritual home through prejudice, harassment, and discrimination. But no one, it seems, wants to talk about the practical effects of such fruit in the lives of the queer children of God. Instead, the discussion stays maddingly centered on the fruit itself. In this, the discussion revolves around changing the queer person to be able to tolerate and even survive the beauty of a bruised fruit. Worse, some Latter-day Saints will observe the practical effects of this fruit on the queer children of God but then, like the priest and Levite, pass to the other side of the road and continue on their way to Jericho.

Today, more and more of the great houses of Zion are expecting an eternal life with their queer children by their side, nestling them here in mortality within their protective boughs, refusing to leave them behind. They are greeted by an institutional church ready to bat down this expectation of an exaltation with queer people. Latter-day Saints experience their queer children as part of their families, but the modern church experiences queer people as an ideology.

If we mark time according to Greg Prince's premise in *David O. McKay and the Rise of Modern Mormonism*,[3] the David O. McKay presidency marks the beginning of the modern church. This rise coincided with the rise of today's LGBTQ civil rights movement. The ideas that underpin the word "modern" and the word "movement" make both the *modern* church and the

---

3. Prince, Gregory A., and Wm. Robert Wright. *David O. McKay and the Rise of Modern Mormonism*. Salt Lake City, Utah: University of Utah Press, 2005.

LGBTQ civil rights *movement* social siblings who have grown up side by side. Although these siblings have now been in a long-term relationship of seventy-plus years—tirelessly meeting each other in the public square, the ballot box, city councils, legislatures, and even the courts—public engagement on an external social and political playing field is not what makes this relationship interesting. The heart of the story lies in the complex and evolving relationship between the modern church and its own queer population. Along with the rise of the LGBTQ civil rights movement came LGBTQ visibility. From those beginnings, the modern church has not only been anxiously engaged with a social movement requiring public policy but has also been increasingly confronted with the uncomfortable reality that LGBTQ Latter-day Saint humans exist and that they exist as born-in-the-covenant children of God, woven into the networking family branches of Zion.

This seemingly sudden visibility over seventy years ago set off a series of cascading events that compelled the modern church to develop a theology that could articulate a dominant narrative about queer people and their place in the plan of salvation. These actions then required the creation of a controlling set of policies specifically designed to manage its internal LGBTQ population according to this dominant narrative. In that moment of creation, the modern queer/Latter-day Saint intersection was born, and generations of queer Latter-day Saints have been navigating their personal intersection with the Church ever since. The most frustrating part of this long, drawn-out conflict is the realization that at any time, with a bit of revelatory husbandry, the fruit could be made accessible to the queer children of God with the same healthy results available to the general population of the Church.

While I appreciate and gladly participate in examining theology and doctrine, exploring the majesty of God's relation to the world, I realize that within my spiritual home, our conclusions in this exercise are limited by the final arbiter of theological and doctrinal identity: the Church. Too much exercising in this realm, especially at the borders where the brethren have not gone, can land us living an eleventh Article of Faith religion, where we are worshiping how, where, or what we may—just not the authorized Latter-day Saint way. In addition, doctrines of the Church change. Practices change. Cycles of decline and renewal are a reality. When the institutional church makes changes and announces old doctrinal positions irrelevant, all the arguments of dogma and theology it used to forcefully support those now abandoned positions are rendered immediately impotent. "We don't think that way anymore" is the frustrating conclusion to theological tensions in a church that once dug its heels in over such conflict. Once a part of the theological tussle, the Church simply moves on without apology, as if nothing ever happened. But something *did* happen. And that is what I want to convey in this book: what is happening right now as the modern church rides the arc of the moral universe, kicking and screaming at times, as it bends towards queer equity and justice.

When I wrote the foreword to Blaire's book, I had no intention of writing a book of my own. As I approached my final months as president of Affirmation, I realized that over four years, I had accumulated a unique library of experiences from my work in the queer/Latter-day Saint intersection. My work was immediate and practical. I was shoulder to shoulder with remarkable leaders, right in the middle of thousands upon thousands of queer lived experiences, rushing to render aid and build communities of safety, love, and hope. It was a time we were shouting affirmations as loudly as we could while empowering each queer soul as they claimed their space to confidently and authentically stand in places that felt safe and healthy for them. It struck me that if we leave the discussion about queer people in the realm of nameless, faceless ideology and dogma, when the Church rises from this current cycle of decline and embraces the queer children of God within its theology of exaltation, marriage, gender, and family, so much will be lost in the category of "We don't think that way anymore."

In this book, I invite you, the reader, to come down from the clouds and feel the soil and earth in corporeal space. I invite you to witness the courage of the queer children of God as they stand their bodies in front of the Church, look it in the eye, and ask for bread. This bread they ask for is the Bread of Life. They seek to authentically partake of it with you, in community, in the household of faith and family. In this book, you will, at times, be uncomfortable as you witness the relentless number of stones the queer children of God receive in this process, where lived experience meets theology. Let us not separate from one another as we work together to address these issues. It is my deep and abiding hope that this book will spur reflection and action. Instead of asking where the answers are for God's people, realize that *you* are the answers for God's people.

A NOTE TO THE READER

1. Although I had the absolute honor to serve as Affirmation's elected president from 2019 through 2022, this book is not an official publication of Affirmation. It does not represent Affirmation, nor do the views and analysis I present reflect an official position of Affirmation in any way. Affirmation is defined by its mission and vision,[1] not by its presidents—past or present. The governing documents of Affirmation explicitly state, "Affirmation does not take official positions on Church doctrine."[2] And it doesn't.

During my four years as president of Affirmation, I held this essential characteristic sacred as I faithfully fulfilled my duties. Contrastingly, in this memoir, I do take positions on Church doctrine as related to my lived experiences as a queer Latter-day

---

1. "Charter & Bylaws." Affirmation: LGBTQ Mormons, Families & Friends, February 8, 2022. https://affirmation.org/about/charter-bylaws/.

1.2 - MISSION Affirmation creates worldwide communities of safety, love, and hope and promotes understanding, acceptance, and self-determination of individuals of diverse sexual orientations, gender identities and expressions. We affirm the inherent self-worth of LGBTQIA+ individuals as complete, equal, and valuable persons and support them as they define their individual spirituality and intersection with The Church of Jesus Christ of Latter-day Saints. 1.3 - VISION To be a refuge to land, heal, share, and be authentic.

2. "1.4.6 - Principles and Values." In *Charter & Bylaws*. Affirmation: LGBTQ Mormons, Families & Friends, February 8, 2022. https://affirmation.org/about/charter-bylaws/.

Saint. It is essential that you do not conflate Affirmation with my personal story. Within Affirmation, each member assigns meaning to their own experiences, making decisions about how and where to navigate toward joy. With this latitude, I share my experiences, my choices, and what they mean for me and my family as we claim the joys available in abundance from our heavenly parents.

2. I will primarily use the terms "queer" and "LGBTQ" interchangeably as synonymous inclusive community identifiers. These are not the only inclusive identifiers in use today. In the future, a single standard may emerge, but for now, my use of either "queer" or any combination of the LGBTQ letters is a matter of writing convenience. It is not meant to be exclusionary or a statement about identity politics.

The 2SLGBTQIA+ letters represent sexual orientation and gender identity. These are not the same thing. The experiences and circumstances surrounding gender identity are different from those of sexual orientation. I will be clear when I am speaking about sexual minority experiences, gender identity experiences, or experiences that affect the collective queer community. Additionally, "heterosexual" or "straight" refers to men who are attracted to women and women who are attracted to men. "Cisgender" refers to a person whose gender identity corresponds with the sex assigned to them at birth.

3. My use of the word "church" refers to "the organized body of believers who have taken upon themselves the name of Jesus Christ by baptism and confirmation."[3] Additionally, because The Church of Jesus Christ of Latter-day Saints refers to itself

---

3. "Bible Dictionary." In *The Holy Bible*, 645. Salt Lake City, Utah: The Church of Jesus Christ of Latter-day Saints, 1979.

as "the Church," I will follow its lead and do the same. My specific use of the word "modern church" refers to the bureaucracy of Latter-day Saint church government, administration, and political machinery in the Church's current era of wealth and corporate power that came of age after the David O. McKay administration in the 1950s. This is the institutional church in the modern era.

PROLOGUE

The Cherry Trees

O ye mountains high, where the clear blue sky
Arches over the vales of the free,
Where the pure breezes blow and the clear streamlets flow,
How I've longed to your bosom to flee!
O Zion! dear Zion! land of the free,
Now my own mountain home, unto thee I have come;
All my fond hopes are centered in thee.

Charles W. Penrose
"O Ye Mountains High"

My heart stopped, mid-gasp, at the sudden, life-changing news staring me directly in the face. I put my phone down, momentarily disoriented, before I gathered myself together to process what 23andMe had just served up. This was a moment I had hoped for my entire life, but I never really thought about what to do if I actually caught this fish. For years, email notifications from 23andMe were just scores of unhelpful third- and fourth-cousin information. But this time, it was gold—a genetic uncle. By now, my heart began pounding out of my chest as I sleuthed out the details of this revelation. Our maternal genetic lines were the same, linking my mother with his. I stared at his name, now made flesh through genetic code. Here was the brother of my birth mother. What do I do now? I really wanted to reach out, but knowing almost nothing about the circumstances of my birth, I hesitated. I wondered how I would be received. Might contact open long-forgotten trauma?

As a closed adoption, the only information transmitted from Relief Society Social Services to my parents about my birth mother was that she was "a beautiful person, inside and out, and wanted the very best for her son." Weighing what I knew against the unknowns, I determined to handle this information with graciousness and pen a short "hello" to my uncle, a "please let her know that I am well and very grateful to her for life and much happiness," and then be okay if there was no response. I nervously emailed him, attached a few pictures of me from baby to adulthood, and waited. And waited. And then her response:

> I didn't know my brother had been searching on 23andMe for information about our mother. So, when he told me about being contacted by you and that I might be your birth mom, I went into emotional shutdown. I didn't know how to feel or how in the world I would respond! A few days later, my brother sent me your email and photos—then came the flood of emotions, memories, recognition, and a heart bursting with love.
>
> There are many different kinds of love and reasons for love, all as important as the next. The first thing I want you to know is that you were given in love.

After their wedding, my parents rented a home in the center of Orem in Utah Valley as my father began his lifelong career in the construction industry and my mother attended BYU. They wanted to start a family right away, but as the years passed, no children were coming. As they approached year five of being childless, they contacted Relief Society Social Services about adopting. They were vetted, approved, and told the next step was to wait for a phone call. There was no way to estimate when that call would come or even if there would be a call at all.

One mid-August afternoon after her shift at the BYU Bookstore, my mother stopped by the fabric store to pick up some cloth to make a baby quilt. She hoped that at some point, they would have a baby to wrap up in it. She had no reason to hurry home; the house was empty. My father was the Scoutmaster and had just left that morning with a dozen scouts for a week-long summer camp on Lake Powell. She stopped by her parents' house for a visit. As soon as she approached the front porch, my grandpa Rowley flung the door open, wagged his finger, and in his trademark humor said, "Boy, you are in trouble!" He couldn't sustain his faux-concerned look for long, and it immediately gave way to smiles as my grandparents excitedly pulled my mother into the house. Relief Society Social Services had been trying to reach my parents all afternoon and, in their search, had just called my grandparents. My mom used their phone to return the call. They had a baby boy, four days old, ready to join the Kitchen household. The only problem was that my mom needed to find my dad ASAP. He could be anywhere on that lake. This wasn't going to wait a week. When my mother got off the phone, she was not messing around. She immediately called the Utah Highway Patrol and put out an all-points bulletin to find Fred Kitchen at Lake Powell.

My father was launching the final boat at Bullfrog Marina when he saw a forest ranger driving down the road toward them. Everyone stopped what they were doing as the ranger parked at the top of the crowded boat ramp and loudly announced he was looking for a Fred Kitchen. After pushing to the front of the crowd, the ranger locked eyes with my father and said, "You, sir, need to get home. You have a baby boy waiting for you." After cheers, handshakes, and a few arrangements, my father jumped into his truck and made the four-and-a-half-hour drive home. My parents arrived at the Relief Society building on East Main in Salt Lake the following morning. As they entered, the Relief Society social workers brought them into a room where they met me for the very first time. At that moment, in the arms of my parents, I was received in love.

As a child, I lived on the edge of what felt like an endless orchard of cherry trees. On the periphery of our yard stood the peach tree and the apple tree, sentinels before the network of irrigation ditches and orderly rows began to stretch into infinity. Planted in the early 1940s, these were the Rowley orchards belonging to my mother's family, descendants of Ann Jewell Rowley, who arrived in the Salt Lake Valley by handcart in 1856. My father started working in these orchards when he was twelve, picking cherries every summer. Over the years, the oldest Rowley brother, Alvin, and his wife, Myrtle, took a liking to my father, and he became like family to them. As soon as the dust settled from my adoption, my father paid a visit to Alvin and Myrtle. He shared with them that he wanted to build a house for his young family and asked if they would sell a building lot, parceled from the northern edge of their cherry orchards. Their love for my father had not faded over time. He was not only like a son but was now family by marriage. They agreed and sold my parents a half-acre lot and a half-share of water. My father purposely retained several towering cherry trees on the property and built our home under their boughs.

During the summer evenings, I would climb the tallest cherry tree next to our carport and wedge myself among its branches to face Mount Timpanogos. I would feast on sweet cherries—spitting pits as far as my lungs could propel—and listen to the crickets sing. I learned in school to tell the temperature by counting a cricket's chirps—fifteen seconds of chirping plus forty. At dusk, the cricket chirps would slow as the winds rushed down from the canyons, breathing cool mountain air over the valley floor, hot from the summer sun.

I always felt wonder in the boughs of those cherry trees in my mountain home. But I also felt love. At that moment, I could not articulate all the circumstances that had brought me to these boughs, nor could I comprehend the interconnectedness of earthly and heavenly parents who had given and received me in love. I could not yet see the love that flowed through these immense branches of my family tree, hearts connecting and turning towards one another, infinitely expansive as the seemingly endless orchards behind my home. Yet still, I experienced love. Such is the mystery of love. Love is not an instrument of measurement, like a thermometer of steel and glass. No, love is not the thermometer. It is the experience. Just as one does not need a thermometer to experience the temperature, one does not need to comprehend the reasons, complexities, or depths of love's gentle presence to recognize and experience it. Any words we accumulate over a lifetime to describe the phenomenon of love only enhance and expand this human experience, which is the greatest of all. It is in the gentle chirps of life, counted over time, that tenderly confirm love is indeed present in your life.

And so it was—in the household orchards of my mother's family, nestled in the very cherry tree my father picked in his youth, given and received in love—that I was surrounded by people who loved me, a family of many parts and in many places who brought me there to experience joy with them, within the boughs of love.

CHAPTER 1

Fear at the End of Parley Street

> We agreed to leave the country for the sake of peace, upon the condition that no more vexatious prosecutions be instituted against us. In good faith have we labored to fulfill this engagement.
>
> The Nauvoo High Council
> January 20, 1846

I slumped my fifteen-year-old frame deep into the bench seat of the U-Haul as my father wound through the Rocky Mountains toward Illinois. As we passed the sign welcoming us to Colorado, I snatched my journal from the door pocket and dramatically wrote, "Today is the 4th of July. We have just left Zion." It was Independence Day in reverse, and I was trekking backward in an ominous direction.

At the end of my sophomore year, my parents called a family meeting. The world was in recession, and the impact on the construction industry in Utah was so severe that new projects were impossible to find. My father was able to secure work in Illinois, and we would be gone in a month. I was stunned. I had just made next year's Acapella choir. Such an honor was not simply posted on a hallway bulletin board. Instead, the choir came to my home one morning and "kidnapped" me, whisking me off blindfolded to the city park for a breakfast welcoming the incoming choir members. My older classmates that I looked up to and admired, were now flipping pancakes and cooking eggs for me. I felt immense pride. I was now one of them. I had been chosen.

With my parent's announcement, not only were all my future plans shattered, but it ignited a low-key sense of danger within me. We were moving to the "mission field"—lands far outside the mountain valleys of Utah where people did not live the standards of the Church. Living under the boughs of the Rowley family orchards may have framed my early life, but growing up cradled in the arms of Utah Valley framed how to live life. Utah Valley held the highest concentration of members of the Church per square mile of anywhere in the world. It was the exact opposite of the "mission field." Everyone and everything I encountered every day of the week—at home, at school, at play—all had the same frame of reference: the Church.

Most significantly, this was Illinois we were driving toward. It was there, at the end of Parley Street in Nauvoo, that my family's ancestors gathered at the ferry terminal in February of 1846 on the banks of the Mississippi to head west, forced from their homes by their Illinois neighbors. In their crossing, they recorded that a "filthy, wicked man"[1] spit tobacco juice into the eye of one of their oxen, plunging it into the ice-filled river,

---

1. Black, Susan Easton. "Thomas Grover." Doctrine and Covenants Central, August 16, 2021. https://doctrineandcovenantscentral.org/people-of-the-dc/thomas-grover/.

dragging their wagon and another ox overboard with it. The oxen drowned, and the damaged ferry sank to the bottom of the Mississippi. Mercifully, all my family was rescued, pulled from the bitterly cold water, clothes frozen stiff. They spent the next day sheltering behind a makeshift canvas windbreak on the Iowa side of the river, wrapped in quilts while their clothes dried by the fire—all in full view of the Illinois homes they had left behind in Nauvoo.

As we approached Denver, I looked at the mountains we were leaving behind. In my move to Illinois, I would be crossing the river the wrong way. The "mission field" carried the risk of continual temptation and negative peer pressure. Who and what awaited me that my ancestors fled from? I picked up my journal again and began to furiously pen a list of the "vexatious prosecutions" I imagined lay ahead.

My mother drove me by my new high school the week we arrived in Illinois. It was intimidating, larger than any high school I had ever known. At Orem High, I didn't know a single nonmember. At my new school, I would be one of five Latter-day Saints—and one of those was my sister. My mother, who had also lived in Orem her entire life, made an off-the-cuff remark that having some football friends at a school this size might be nice. I was way ahead of her. I had already decided that football friends at this place would be happening for my safety. I was not a football player. Even though I had an ideal build for an offensive lineman, I disliked the violent physical contact required to be successful on the line. At Orem High I spent the season on the sidelines cheering everyone else on. This was not an issue for either coaches or teammates. As a team, we were a band of brothers. Not only did I have a great group of friends, but the social cred of being on the football team was substantial. I figured transferring my previous football experience to my new school would replicate a huge social payoff, help me find friends, and, most importantly, mitigate being othered and bullied as the new Mormon kid in town.

I discovered that a returned missionary in my new ward had played football for the team. I asked him if he would make introductions. Soon, I was on the field running drills and being evaluated. I had a solid 40-yard dash and performed well enough on the skills, and when Monday came, my first time practicing with the team, the posted lineup listed me as first-string offensive tackle as a walk-on, bumping down legacy football family kids. I looked the part, a strapping offensive lineman, but by week two I was last-string tackle, because of how poorly I played the part. My teammates loudly noted my sudden fall from grace. I began to be relentlessly teased and bullied, but I kept at it, week after week, because I desperately wanted to fit in. It wasn't supposed to be like this. I was relegated to carrying the water bottle ice buckets to the field and made a part of the B-team "meat grinder" defense squad that functioned as practice fodder for the offensive starting lineup, endlessly getting hit for hours on end—but then, finally, mercy. In the intense Southern Illinois summer heat and humidity, we quickly stopped caring whose water bottles were whose. Soon, we were sharing more than water bottles. I got mono; no kissing required. It was the best day of my life when the doctor told me I could no longer play football. My spleen was so swollen that one direct hit would burst it wide open. She drafted a note, and I took it to the head coach the next day. He looked at it and dryly said, "We're sorry to see you go." He followed me out of his office and announced to the team as they were suiting up for practice, "Nate here is cleaning out his locker. He is leaving the team." He stepped back into his office, leaving me to face that locker room alone.

"So soon?" one of my teammates jeered as everyone laughed. They continued to taunt me, pelting me with unkind words as I emptied my locker. My face was hot, my insides burning in waves of shame. The very thing I desperately wanted to avoid in my move to Illinois was happening in real time. This moment was the end of Parley Street in my personal Illinois. Finally, as I folded my team jersey, one of my biggest bullies yelled out, "Yeah, you are not even worthy to wear that shirt." This prompted laughs from the crowd, but I was too emotionally exhausted to let it humiliate me. It just didn't matter anymore. None of these people were my friends. It had become a hostile environment for me, but somehow, it still profoundly hurt to leave the team. Hard lesson learned: not every community is supportive, no matter how desperately you want it to be.

"What about choir?" my mother asked the high school counselor as she reviewed my old transcripts to register me for classes. "Even though he made his audition choir in Utah, I can't just register him in ours," the counselor explained as she jotted down the director's phone number. "Hopefully he can still audition. I can't promise anything." I slouched in my chair. This news was just another gut punch in the summer of my Illinois move. At this point, football was already going south, a continual source of stress. I was the only person my age at church and missed Utah terribly. I was a fish out of water, wondering when my Mormon perseverance would finally pay off. I was too young to be at the "endure to the end" phase of life.

A few days before school started, I nervously walked into the choir room and met with the director. This was where I really wanted to belong, but would this be another rejection in Illinois? The director sat at the piano, smiled, and handed me some sheet music. "Melody, please," he said, looking at me over his reading glasses to bring me into the first verse. By the end of the audition, he not only invited me to join the choir but also to be a part of the school's Swing Choir ensemble. I beamed ear to ear, not believing my good fortune. That ensemble represented the best the school had to offer in musical performance. It was the musical equivalent of the varsity football team's first-string lineup. It was a dream I didn't dare think possible in my move to Illinois.

I was now a fish in water, swimming and thriving. Swing Choir was my instant friend group. This was the belonging I had craved in my move to Illinois but didn't know precisely how to accomplish. Moreover, the fabled widespread wickedness of the mission field was nowhere to be found. My friends offered me grace, values, acceptance, and support. Once they became familiar with my beliefs, they helped me live my standards and practices. Another lesson learned: Christ-like values and attributes exist abundantly in those not of my faith, even in Illinois. My life felt whole. I didn't have to live a double life, for I could openly have a busy social life and a rich religious life simultaneously without shame. I felt an intense happiness I hadn't thought possible outside of Utah. I had come to Illinois in fear, and the very people I feared melted away that fear.

By the middle of the first semester, the trauma of integration had subsided. I had found my best friend in choir. I admired him and was excited that he wanted to be friends with me. We were inseparable. One evening, as we sat in front of my house, I felt a tension while we talked. It was intoxicating. I innately knew what it was but hadn't formed the words to discuss it, especially in this context. I had a crush on him. It took over an hour for us to get to the point where we could talk about it. I felt such a rush when he told me he had a crush on me, too.

Curious about this part of growing up, I started researching about what I was feeling. I had always turned to the prophets and apostles for comfort and guidance, so who better to trust at this moment? As I scanned my parent's bookshelves, my eyes rested upon a book by Spencer W. Kimball: *The Miracle of Forgiveness*. This looked interesting. I grew up with President Kimball. He was the only prophet I had ever known. He seemed kindly and his plucky "do it" slogan inspired my approach to life. I pulled it off the shelf and began reading. Sitting cross-legged on the couch as the afternoon light streamed from the south-facing window, my sincere search for wisdom being given liberally was instead answered with a liberal, relentless upbraiding. I started sweating, heart racing, as I realized what a predicament I was in. I was a filthy homosexual. I was horrified at what I was. President Kimball laid out every sordid detail concerning the depravity of the homosexual, plainly declaring, "Homosexuality is an ugly sin, repugnant to those who find no temptation in it."[2] I put the book down and closed my eyes. The only thing I wanted now was forgiveness. I wanted to be clean and right in the sight of God. Despite never having acted upon these feelings, I wanted so desperately to repent of my homosexuality.

I spent countless hours soaking in all the information I could from the Church about homosexuality and how to get rid of it. I sincerely believed that I was unworthy of God's love. I now hated myself. I feared myself. Despite the peace in my social/religious intersection, this new intersection involving my sexuality and the Church was an absolute train wreck. My

---

2. Kimball, Spencer W. "Crime Against Nature." In *The Miracle of Forgiveness*, 78. Salt Lake City, Utah: Deseret Book, 1969.

world went into a tailspin. Something was awakening inside me that was forbidden within the one and only true church on the face of the Earth. It was abundantly clear in my readings that homosexuality would separate me from God, the Church, and my family. It was a one-way ticket out of Zion. With resolve, I was absolutely prepared to shut down every part of me and shut out anyone who might endanger my return to live with God and my family again in the eternities. I needed to feel some control in a body that was pumping out teenage levels of testosterone until I could sort out what to do. From all I could gather in my reading, I was having "homosexual temptations" like all men do, and the answer was that I must remove myself from temptation. I knew where that needed to start.

On a late autumn afternoon, as I walked with my best friend-turned-crush to his car after class, I blurted out that what was happening between us was wrong. I couldn't be his friend anymore. This was not a mutual feeling, but I refused to talk it out when he asked why. As we sat in silence, my mind grasped for any kind of context, only able to relate my feelings to the story of Joseph and Potiphar's wife: "How then can I do this great wickedness, and sin against God?" (Genesis 39:9). Deep down, I knew this was inaccurate, for I had freely given him the garment of my heart. And this was what I had to guard against, my own heart.

After pondering this matter for the better part of the year, a prophet of God answered my prayers during General Conference. During April's satellite broadcast of the opening session in 1986, Ezra Taft Benson stood and forcefully declared repentance. He endorsed the words found in *The Miracle of Forgiveness* and announced that it was time for the Saints to lengthen their stride.

To do so, "we must first cleanse the inner vessel by awaking and arising, being morally clean."[3] President Kimball told me what I was, and now, President Benson told me what to do about it. The instant that Saturday morning session ended, I made a beeline for the bishop sitting across the chapel. I told him I needed to see him. He invited me to come to his office the following evening. It was time to confess my homosexuality and lay myself at the mercy of the Church. My burden would be lifted and my homosexuality taken from me. I would be a clean vessel for the Lord.

When I left the house the next night, I didn't tell my parents or siblings where I was going. I entered the dark and empty meetinghouse foyer, trembling. I couldn't find the light switches, so I sank deep into the couch, resigned to the shadows. The interview before mine was going long. The darkness I sat in mirrored my emotions. I was acutely aware of another teen in our stake who had recently been kicked out of his home for being gay. I genuinely feared for my future, housing, and belonging. The longer I waited, the more my body began to shake. I drew from the very depths of my faith the confidence that my bishop would have the answers for me. I told myself to be brave. Despite any harsh repercussions that would come from discovering a homosexual in the fold, I would be made a clean vessel for the Lord, no matter the immediate consequences. This was the most courageous thing I had ever done in my young life. Eventually, the bishop opened the door. As light poured out into the hallway, he emerged with his arm around a sister from my ward who was crying. He seemed so compassionate as he gently told her, "It will be alright. It will be alright."

Seeing me hunkered down on the couch, the bishop invited me into his office and asked me what was on my mind. With

---

3. Benson, Ezra Taft. "Cleansing the Inner Vessel." *Ensign* 16, no. 5, May 1986. https://www.churchofjesuschrist.org/study/general-conference/1986/04/cleansing-the-inner-vessel.

all the courage I could muster, I poured out my heart concerning my feelings about boys. I felt completely vulnerable as I threw myself upon the mercy of the Church at the invitation of a prophet. And then the unexpected. He stopped me mid-sentence and told me I was being too hard on myself. He didn't want to hear any more. I should remain faithful and obedient, serve a mission, marry a woman in the temple, and, "it will be alright. It will be alright." Waves of relief washed over my body that this was all it took to cleanse my inner vessel of homosexuality. As he stood to show me out, he put his arm around me and told me never to tell anyone about these feelings. He paused at the door and continued his train of thought, "I am not going to tell your parents about our visit tonight. Such news would be a disappointment to such faithful parents." Message received. This information about me would deeply hurt others, even those closest to me, if they knew.

I walked out of the bishop's office with religious conviction that I would trust and obey my bishop's counsel with exactness. I knew precisely what to do. I was to push all these feelings out and never think or speak of them again. Just as they were unimportant to the bishop, they were to be unimportant to me. I now had a promise and a clear path forward, complete with the milestones I was to reach so that, in the end, it would "be alright." This felt like a covenantal moment. I was born again, and I had a fresh start in life. It was crystal clear that blessings of the gospel and the love of God all depended on my obedience with exactness to my bishop's counsel.

This was no "Hugh B. Brown cutting the currant bush to a stump" moment.[4] This was a "dig the root ball out of the ground and set the pit aflame so that nothing could ever grow

---

4. Brown, Hugh B. "God Is the Gardener." BYU Speeches, May 31, 1968. https://speeches.byu.edu/talks/hugh-b-brown/god-gardener/.

there again" moment. I knew the conditions of my cleansing. That night, when I returned home and retired to my bed, I received a confirmation about my standing before God. It was a message of forgiveness and redemption that I wanted to hear, and I wrote it in my journal:

> Nathan, look back on this day for all eternity. Know ye that all thy sins are forgiven, that thou standest pure in the sight of God. Let this day be a standard for all the rest, for Satan shall surely try to deceive your soul again. Now, therefore, press forward in light and truth, knowing that the Lord thy God has shaped and is guiding your destiny. The important purposes for you that are known unto the Lord shall be fulfilled! Remember and forgive yourself. Stay repentant and stay close to the Lord, even so, Amen.

CHAPTER 2

Swept and Garnished

> 43 When the unclean spirit is gone out of a man, he walketh through dry places, seeking rest, and findeth none.
>
> 44 Then he saith, I will return into my house from whence I came out; and when he is come, he findeth it empty, swept, and garnished.
>
> 45 Then goeth he, and taketh with himself seven other spirits more wicked than himself, and they enter in and dwell there: and the last state of that man is worse than the first.
>
> Matthew 12:43-45

I did not misunderstand what was being asked of me the night of the great cleansing. I did not misunderstand church teachings that homosexuality was a temptation. As far as I was concerned, my job now was to forget that this whole thing ever happened and faithfully follow the milestones my bishop laid out for me the night I walked out of his office, inner vessel cleansed. I may have heard my bishop's spoken words loud and clear, but the unspoken words continued shouting at me long after I left his office: "What you are experiencing is a profoundly shameful thing that we don't talk about." Meeting with my bishop did not absolve my shame. It magnified it. Shame was now attached to me like training wheels, keeping me from tipping over on the covenant path out of sheer terror of losing everything and everyone I held dear. Fear was no longer paralyzing my journey back to God. It was fueling it.

Just as my bishop swept aside my confession, I swept my emerging sexuality from my house and into the dry places. Jesus taught me that I needed to fill my newly cleansed inner vessel, or temptation would return seven times stronger (Matthew 12:43–45). I created detailed lists in my journal of physical and spiritual controls that would scrupulously keep me from ever letting anything homosexual enter my house again. The devil was not welcome here. Despite such vigilance, I could not understand why this banished problem wouldn't just stay away. I wasn't letting it in. I made no room for it to return, but why was it still just outside my door, lying on my threshold, crying? I didn't want to hear it or be reminded of its presence. I wanted it quiet. It was the enemy of everything I knew about love, belonging, and safety. Unable to silence the voice outside my door, I began to turn off parts of myself so I wouldn't be able to hear it. As its crying faded from my consciousness, it was not gone; I was gone. I traded myself for a pottage of silence, and I began to feel some measure of warmth and euphoria, hopeful feedback that these were the same sensations everyone else was receiving along the covenant path.

Once I hit the sweet spot between forced forgetting and obedience with exactness, the milestones were not that hard to achieve. All I had to do was willingly stick my toe into the river, and the powerful social current in the Church would pull me in and deliver me from milestone to milestone with riptide force.

I embarked on this endeavor with complete sincerity and absolute trust. I had a burning desire to serve God and felt his call to the work. In humility and without guile, I approached the riverbank, gently held my nose, and submitted my soul supinely into the currents, immersed in the work and glory of God.

Dutifully, I hit each milestone with deliberate earnestness. I served a mission, married in the temple, graduated from BYU and dental school, and had five wonderful children. I served in two bishoprics, as the stake Young Men president, and was on the stake high council. I was living every straight Mormon man's dream. I was in a state of forgetting in the stream. The internal controls and shutdowns I had installed as a young man seemed to be working perfectly—which is why I could not understand why I was starting to hollow away from the inside as the years rolled along. Little pieces of me were dying. My inner vessel was collapsing despite the great cleansing.

President Benson may have set me on my path in 1986, but twenty years later, Elder Richard G. Scott kicked me out of orbit. After dental school, my wife and I moved to Arizona to raise our children. As we established our roots, growing our family and my dental practice, Elder Scott attended our stake conference. He said he would speak from his heart instead of his prepared remarks. He felt prompted that his extemporaneous message was one someone needed to hear that day. He spoke of the damage and self-harm that is done when one lives a double life and the peace that comes when two halves of ourselves meet and become one. He then invited anyone living a double life to find the peace of the Savior, repent, and live as one whole and complete person. Unexpectedly, my heart burst open as the spirit declared: "You are living a double life inside your own soul, and it is causing you harm." I did not immediately understand what this meant until, in the stillness of that moment, I once again began to hear cries emanating from behind a door I had ignored for so many years. It wasn't the cry of wickedness but of woundedness.

This thing I had swept from my house was not temptation. It was an inherent part of me: my sexual orientation. I might have left no room for it in my house, banishing it to the dry places, but it still came to lie down outside my door, not because it was an evil spirit trying to return, but because it was *me* trying to return. This self-dissection was not cutting me off from the devil; it was cutting me off from myself. It prevented me from existing as a whole and complete child of God. I realized that the years of harboring subconscious internal strife and unrecognized self-hate were now bleeding out into the external aspects of my life. People closest to me, including my wife, noticed that something was eating away at me, and until this moment, I didn't have the words to articulate why. In a stake center pew, I once again faced what I was. Only this time, the stakes were much higher. I was an adult with a wife and children. No one save me and my bishop of twenty years ago knew about the homosexuality I had confessed to him. In all the ensuing years, I never once allowed myself the courtesy to even consider that I just might be gay—until that moment. By now, adrenalin was coursing through my body. This all seemed too much to bear. Things were not alright.

My wrestle with revelation slowly turned to introspection in the weeks following stake conference. How could I go twenty years without ever acknowledging my sexual orientation to the point that my inner vessel was now dangerously imploding amid great cachexia of my soul? In this moment of reflection, I remembered my great-great-grandfather John Rowley who, as a teen, sat down at the side of the Mormon trail in Wyoming to die. He was so cold, drowsy, and sick that he told his mother he was never going to rise again. Seeing him down, "Captain Willie whipped him, to make him go on."[1] I do not know why Captain Willie did what he did or if he even had a clue about what was happening internally to John's hypothermic body, but these handcart companies faced a cold, harsh fact out on the frozen plains of Wyoming: stationary pioneers will die.[2]

John's story resonated deeply with me. Keeping my inner vessel "cleansed" for twenty years was not some story of Herculean strength or gritty pioneer fortitude but of a wounded soul that had stopped moving even though his body was still walking the path his bishop had laid out for him. I was experiencing hypothermia of the soul. In sub-zero weather, the longer the hypothermic remain stationary, the faster their core body temperature plummets. In response, in its last act of self-preservation, the body reflexively opens its peripheral blood vessels, flushing what warmth is left within its organs out to the skin to warm the extremities. Paradoxically, this flush makes the hypothermic feel very warm and euphoric as they lose consciousness—so warm that the dead are often found in various stages of undress, their last act in this life removing their clothing in sub-zero weather to cool down.

Despite my obedience with exactness and an exterior flushed with the warmth of success, my core had been cooling for quite some time from the trauma of self-separation. I could no longer determine the truth between dangerous cold and euphoric warmth. And now, I had just met this part of myself, something I had hoped I would die before experiencing again. This desire

---

1. Rowley, Ann Jewell. *Autobiography of Ann Jewell Rowley*. Unpublished Family Document, n.d. http://aprilsancestry.com/files/AnnJewRowAuto.doc.

2. Richardson, Frank D., and Deane Johnson Cook, eds. "The Camp Rolled On." In *Rowley Family Histories*, 62-63. Fruit Heights, Utah: StoryWorks Publishers, 1992.

to die on my trek through life manifested itself in my slow collapse on my own trail, disoriented, sluggish, and tired. Ever so tired. Now, the Spirit had shaken me awake, pulling me up off the trail. It felt harsh to leave the warmth and euphoria of the frozen ground, but it was a lifesaving moment for me like it was for my great-great-grandfather. I determined to stop harming myself and live. I would not be stationary.

I instinctively knew that the healing of my soul from over twenty years of wounding would take time. I cautiously opened the door of my inner vessel and gently scooped up that wounded piece of me—my sexual orientation—and welcomed it back in with a healthy embrace. This was not a moment of coming out of the closet. This was a moment of self-acceptance. Over time, I got to know that part of me I had banished so many years ago, pulling back the curtain to understand there never was a devil involved in this inner city of Oz. Under no timelines or pressure as I warmed a wounded soul in chrysalis, I was kind to my younger self, understanding that I had been making the best decisions in life with the information I had at the time. And now I had new information.

All this was happening within my soul when California Prop 8 and Arizona Prop 102 became state ballot initiatives in 2008. One Sunday, the bishop asked me to train the ward council on the Church's efforts with Prop 102. As his counselor, I was a company man, complete with charts and Church talking points. I explained that Prop 102 would amend the Arizona State Constitution, recognizing only the union of one man and one woman as a valid marriage. It had the same end goal as the more famous California Prop 8. I shared a letter from the First Presidency concerning the politics of same-sex marriage,[3] not-

---

3. "California and Same-Sex Marriage." newsroom.churchofjesuschrist.org, June 30, 2008. https://newsroom.churchofjesuschrist.org/article/california-and-same-sex-marriage.

ed that the Church wanted members to volunteer in call centers to urge voters to support the proposition, highlighted that the Relief Society was spearheading this effort in our ward, and discussed holding a special combined Priesthood/Relief Society lesson on this issue. As I concluded my remarks, I looked up from my notes and summarized the campaign: "Look, we have to stop 'these people' from marrying." The hypocrisy of my words choked me. Time seemed to stand still, uncomfortably magnifying the silence I allowed to linger at the end of my presentation as I faced the ward council in the quiet realization of my double life, and the safety of the closet I existed in. I was one of "these people."

I do not know the lesson the ward council took away from my presentation, but it was a watershed moment for me. Many years ago, I was taught how to harm myself. Now, I was teaching others how to do it for me. Moreover, I realized the extent to which the Church had woven anti-gay political advocacy into the fabric of worship. Political advocacy had come to the pews as an uncomfortable pressing, involving members like fish in a barrel, permeating every corner of my spiritual home. When I searched the public databases following the money supporting Prop 102, I discovered dozens of leaders and fellow members surrounded me in my stake who had donated five, ten, even fifteen thousand dollars apiece[4]—all personally invited to do so by my stake president, under assignment from Salt Lake. I was surrounded by fellow citizens in the household of God financially invested in denying queer people, like me, civil rights.

I loved the Church with all my heart, might, mind, and strength. Even so, after having a front-row seat while still in the closet, watching how the sausage was made during Arizona

---

4. OpenSecrets. "Proposition 102 Top Supporting Donors." PROPOSITION 102 - FollowTheMoney.org, 2008. https://www.followthemoney.org/entity-details?eid=10246666.

Prop 102, I was not convinced that the feeling of love was mutual or that the Church had my best interest in mind as a sexual minority. My church ward had been turned into a political ward, and I was on the ballot.

Three different pieces of spiritual counsel from my leaders were now in motion within my life, becoming what physics calls a three-body problem, where no solution exists. This created a highly chaotic system within my soul, for it was not possible for all three to exist together: President Benson's cleansing of the inner vessel, Elder Scott's invitation to wholeness, and my bishop's admonition not to share my sexual orientation with anyone.

As I stitched myself back together, warming to the idea that I was a sexual minority in the Church, I assumed that once I came out to myself and accepted my sexual orientation, I would achieve the full blessings of wholeness and life would continue as usual. Telling people about this, even those closest to me, was not part of my bishop's calculus for me the night of the great cleansing. The closet may have been a necessary space of healing and protection but the longer I stayed there, conscious of my wholeness, the more I felt a hypocrite. My bishop's invitation was not just a life plan for a seventeen-year-old boy. It *was* the life of my wife and children. I was not alone on this journey. This no longer felt like protection, it felt like deception. I was now conscious, but my wife was not, that I was in a mixed-orientation marriage. This seemed abjectly wrong to withhold now that I had come to terms with it. It was time to jettison the counsel from my bishop, which I had considered the voice of God for so many years.

But this is the thing about the voice of God, it will not, it cannot, erase human agency. Even our first parents in the garden faced the direct voice of God, yet they made their own decisions about their lives—and that of their family and future children—that they determined were safe and healthy for them. In eating from the tree of knowledge of good and evil, they owned the consequences of their decisions in both joy and sorrow. It was time to tell the person I loved most in this world, and I knew that it would change everything—absolutely everything.

PRAYER
For Emily

"When thou prayest, enter thy closet and shut
 thy door."
So says Jesus.
But is this gentle Jesus holding a lamb,
Or the Jesus with a scourge of cords?

More often I enter, messy—
Violence matching anguish,
Feet stomping and shoulders bumping
The doorframe, hinge and molding.

He doesn't say how to enter,
Just that we enter.
So I come as I am
Trailing humanity into this godly space.

He doesn't say how to shut the door,
So, when I speak to God
And it's an emergency
It gets shut how I damn well please.

Then in secret I begin
To commune as Jesus taught,
In my closet, with door shut tight.
He doesn't care how I got there.

Only that I have entered
Only that I have shut the world behind me,
And made this space holy
To converse with God.

CHAPTER 3

An Autumnal Grove

> 7 Whither shall I go from thy spirit? or whither shall I flee from thy presence?
> 8 If I ascend up into heaven, thou art there: if I make my bed in hell, behold, thou art there.
> 9 If I take the wings of the morning, and dwell in the uttermost parts of the sea;
> 10 Even there shall thy hand lead me, and thy right hand shall hold me.
>
> Psalms 139: 7-10

Approaching midnight, our children were finally asleep. I sat on the bed, determined that tonight would be the night I came out to my wife. Earlier that day, I had packed a small suitcase with a few essentials—stashing it behind the laundry basket in the walk-in closet—and had made a reservation at a local hotel in case she asked me to leave.

As she walked into the room, I immediately looked down at the carpet, unable to meet her gaze. She knew something had been eating away at me for a while and asked what was wrong. I was back to my teenage self in that dark Illinois foyer the night I was waiting to talk with my bishop, trying to pull courage from the depths of my soul. That was easy compared to this moment. Stumbling over my words, I watched her face change from compassion to shock. I wasn't just coming out to her; I had just murdered the very person she thought she knew and had built a life with right in front of her eyes. This moment was the death of my identity as a straight Mormon man in our marriage, and it completely unmoored the both of us as we experienced it together on the edge of the bed. She gathered the comforter up in her arms and, through quiet cries, said, "Don't follow me." She disappeared into the dark hallway, and I was alone, where I lay on top of the bed, still in my clothes, until morning, drowning in shame, guilt, fear, and loss.

That night began a multi-year dialogue between us, processing information, re-negotiating relationships, and having difficult conversations about the life we had built together and whether it could or should continue with this new information. Over time, such conversations between ourselves or with therapists led to decisions—such as separation and divorce—with friends, family, and church leaders believing they were entitled to every detail. We employed boundaries respecting each other's privacy as people began to rubber-neck our marriage.

It is really easy to get married. It is extremely complicated to get divorced. Intersecting with the law to get married involves a twenty-minute visit to the courthouse for a license and then an officiant's and witnesses' signatures. That's it. Marriage law seems almost inconsequential, a blip in this event never talked about in the romanticized eternal love taught in my young men's classes. But upon divorce, I learned that while eternal marriage may have its head in the heavens, its feet are firmly planted in the cold, hard ground of earthly marriage law where marriage is an intricate legal business partnership with laws ruling the terms of dissolution. Love has nothing to do with it.

By the fall of 2013, I was in the middle of the discovery phase of my divorce. In encountering the legal landscape of marriage law, I felt like Dante entering hell under the inscription, "Abandon all hope, ye who enter here."[1] The entire marriage was being painfully and methodically reduced to debts, assets, and parenting—laid bare in filing after filing. The legal system efficiently dissolves a marriage according to the rule of law, not emotions. This does not mean that this process is void of emotions. Justice may wear a blindfold, but my entire family's eyes were wide open as we experienced every emotion of a process that began long before the filing and continued long after the dissolution. In this "eyes wide open" experience, I was undergoing the intensely emotional and human aspects of coming out: the renegotiation process within my closest family relationships—self, spouse, and children. Each of these renegotiations involved the risk of loss, and it was frightening. My greatest fear was the loss of the relationship with my children, either temporarily, long-term, or permanently. These profound and ongoing accumulating changes and losses in my life began coalescing into three traumas surrounding my sexual identity, my faith, and my pending divorce. I collectively called these my "trifecta of trauma." This trifecta held all the stresses of every dialogue, every renegotiation, every loss, both present and anticipated. These traumas manifested themselves physically as day-to-day symptoms of unwellness.

---

1. Dante Alighieri, 1265-1321. *The Divine Comedy of Dante Alighieri: Inferno*. Canto III, line 9.

At the height of this trauma, the time of my greatest uneasiness, I flew to New York to attend a dental continuing education course in Woodstock. When I arrived at the education center, instead of feeling like a peer among my colleagues, I felt like an outsider in a room full of highly successful, happy healthcare professionals, and I immediately resented them for being so. The course was interesting, but in my emotional state, I didn't feel like interacting with the group. I sat in the back, took notes, and made no attempt to make any connection beyond offering my name and where I practiced. That evening, the group ate together at a local restaurant. I didn't have the bandwidth to be social and listen to everyone's success stories when I felt mired in intense loss. As I returned to my hotel, I stopped for Thai food and ate alone. On the last day, the seminar ended early. As everyone excitedly began to plan lunch together, I looked down at my phone and typed, "Sacred Grove." I could make it in just under four hours.

During my drive upstate, I reflected on what was happening to me and my family and why it was all happening in the first place. I had what seemed to be monumental questions that needed equally monumental answers. I was under intense pressure to return to the closet, encountering suggestions that I had done something selfishly wrong by coming out instead of quietly managing a religiously-prescribed double life for the rest of my existence. Amid my trifecta of trauma, I was grappling with what it meant to be a gay Mormon, a gay father, and an outcast in a faith tradition where I once felt privilege. The grove had been a pivotal spot at the beginning of the Restoration. Today, it would play a role in my life as I went to the grove to pray.

Religiously guided, mixed-orientation marriages bury irreconcilable differences that eventually sprout from under a rich topsoil of promise and fear. I didn't know, nor could I predict, if, when, or how the sprouting would begin. My wife and I, my children and I, had barely begun to even notice this sprouting as we were thrown through the mess of divorce. As a sexual minority in the Church, I became aware of what had been buried long ago in myself, something that horrified me. I had often hoped I might die before those seeds of irreconcilable differences made it to the sunlight.

I entered the Sacred Grove alone, the only person there that late fall afternoon. Periodically, the sun would peek out from behind the striated clouds of the overcast sky, and its light would stream through the yellowing leaves, lighting the trees in a brilliant reddish-gold hue, almost as if they were on fire. Under illuminated autumnal boughs, I asked my questions in prayer and received the answers I needed to hear that day. I had the distinct impression that I would not be alone in the challenging months ahead. I felt a spiritual assurance that God would not leave my soul in hell—that my heavenly parents would not only be with me as I pressed forward, but they would also be my rearward (Doctrine and Covenants 49:27) as life recalibrated around me. My thoughts then immediately turned to my children. They were hurting. They had questions themselves. I prayed for each one by name and vowed not to abandon them in this moment. As I gathered answers for myself, I gathered leaves for my children.

When I returned home from New York, I made five enlarged prints of the most brilliant picture I had taken that afternoon of the illuminated autumnal grove. I affixed the leaves I had gathered in the Sacred Grove onto the mat surrounding each print. I pulled out my calligraphy pens and wrote with a sweeping boldness, "God Appreciates Questions." I gathered my children together and presented each with this framed gift. I told them about my visit to the Sacred Grove. I let them know that even in the hardest of times, their hardest of questions would in no way turn God away from them. No, God welcomes and appreciates questions. Just as the Restoration began with a question, our personal questions can begin a restoration within our own soul.

Four months later, I was sitting in Paradise Bakery with my attorney signing divorce papers over a muffin or a pastry—or . . . it really doesn't matter what it was because the only thing I can remember is how imposing a fifty-two-page stack of legal papers representing the dissolution of a twenty-three-year marriage with children can be. My hands shook, and I had a hard time catching my breath as I held the document. My attorney knew what was happening. She took the stack from my hands and cheerfully kept me on track by placing each page in front of me, prompting me where to initial or sign. When I first met her and told her I was a gay Mormon man with five kids who had just come out of the closet, she was not shy in telling me that, sexual orientation aside, Mormon divorce is the hardest to represent and hardest to keep focused. "It's a mess, and you're a mess. I am here to keep you on track."

As I pulled into the driveway of my rental home after the signing, I had recovered enough from the experience at the bakery to finally realize what had just happened. I was now officially alone. I opened the car door and vomited directly onto the driveway. This was paradise lost.

Learning that his father was gay and experiencing the slow dissolution of his parents' marriage threw a monkey wrench into the middle of my eighteen-year-old son's life. After the divorce, he was processing loss and anger on top of preparing for his mission. Eventually, he just put a pin in it, delaying his processing to focus on his upcoming missionary service. He sent me a letter laying out his grievances. He stopped coming over to the house along with his brothers, and made himself unavailable for family activities. I knew he was hurting. I knew we were in an "arm's length" relationship, but I felt it unwise to press for a resolution before his mission.

The day before my son departed to the Missionary Training Center, the stake president set him apart as a missionary. I knew in my heart that this was only one piece of the blessing of a missionary. I wanted him to enter the mission field armed with a father's blessing. Circumstances being what they were, I decided to write him a blessing. In 1844, Emma Smith desired a blessing from her husband. It was a turbulent time in Nauvoo. Circumstances made it impossible for Joseph to do this in person. He asked her to write the best blessing she could, and he would sign it upon returning from Carthage jail. He never returned, murdered while in the custody of his jailers, but the blessing Emma wrote for herself remains.[2] It is stunningly beautiful and hopeful. This was how I could bless my son, in the spirit of Emma, during this turbulent time of our relationship when circumstances did not permit otherwise.

The words flowed freely as I began to write out his blessing. I blessed him with wisdom, safety, humility, and the capacity to love the people he would be serving. I felt prompted to address the very thing he had wanted to avoid thinking about as he prepared for his mission. I blessed him that he would be able to let go of any anger, resentment, and disappointment he was harboring in the aftermath of the divorce. I reminded him that through it all, he had a loving mother, father, and siblings who supported him and were there for him: "Many things in life fade

---

2. Smith, Emma Hale, 1804-1879. Emma Smith Blessing. https://catalog.churchofjesuschrist.org/assets/855ea7b3-33a2-4b36-bd1a-720543d84a52/0/0 (accessed: July 21, 2024).

away, but your parents, brothers, and sister will not fade away. The very Eternal Father's purposes may not be clear at this moment in time, but I bless you with faith—faith that the unexpected threads that course through life will show to be a rich tapestry in the end."

I signed his written blessing by hand, and the following day, as he said his goodbyes at the airport, I handed him the envelope and asked him to read it on the plane. Written blessings sent my son out into the world with love. And within this love, a hope. The same hope that Joseph Smith wrote to Edward Partridge in 1834, that when we meet face to face again, "all matters between us will be fairly understood, and perfect love prevail."[3]

In my life, I have stood in person at river's edge at the end of Parley Street, and in the Sacred Grove. However, Parley Street does not have to be in Illinois nor the Sacred Grove in New York. They can exist within our own soul. Life may spit in my eye, but that doesn't mean I have to spend eternity drowned at the bottom of an icy Mississippi River because of it. It is not hope that is found at the end of Parley Street, but fear. Hope is the antithesis of fear. I found hope in my visit to the autumnal Sacred Grove during that intensive season of my life, and this gave me the courage to face grief, loss, rejection, divorce, and estrangement with my son without plunging overboard, dragging everyone and everything with me. Personal Sacred Groves are portable. Long after I left New York, I continued to find answers in my personal Sacred Grove, illuminating hope directly into my soul. Hope is protective of well-being. To abandon hope

---

3. Letter to Edward Partridge and Others, 30 March 1834, p. 35, The Joseph Smith Papers, accessed July 21, 2024, https://www.josephsmithpapers.org/paper-summary/letter-to-edward-partridge-and-others-30-march-1834/6.

is the great lie of hell, written above its very entrance. Hope does not eliminate our sorrow or problems but it lifts our chin to the future. In the spirit of the Psalmist: Weeping may endure for a night, but hope is the taste of coming joy (Psalms 30:5).

Divorce.

It is undiscovered country.

Bourn.

It is nailed colors to your mast.

Beat to quarters.

It is death before the resurrection.

The lingering taste of Lazarus stench

Remains upon your lips

Long after the stone rolls away.

Born again.

You emerge transformed,

Permanently.

Yet still the same.

Success and failure in quantum state, but
Schrodinger's cat's gone wrong here.

No matter how much looking inside the box

The waveform won't collapse

Into one reality.

You learn to live duality.

Joy despite sorrow.

It is why we are.

To live it all

That we might

Have

Joy

!

CHAPTER 4

A New Age Is Upon Us

> The world is changed. I feel it in the water. I feel it in the earth. I smell it in the air. Much that once was is lost; for none now live who remember it.
>
> Galadriel
> *The Lord of the Rings: The Fellowship of the Ring*

I am one of the last members of the generation of Latter-day Saint young men officially taught to get married to a woman as a remedy to overcome "homosexual inclinations."[1] I did not come to understand this until I was president of Affirmation and had a bird's eye view of all the activity that had been going on in the queer/Latter-day Saint intersection over the history of the modern church. During my second term, I noted that throughout my presidency, a noticeable uptick of queer Latter-

---

1. Hinckley, Gordon B. "Reverence and Morality." *Ensign* 17, no. 5, May 1987. https://www.churchofjesuschrist.org/study/general-conference/1987/04/reverence-and-morality.

day Saint voices, almost exclusively single, openly gay men, had been given access to the official channels of church communications. In these spaces (be it Deseret Book, church magazines and websites, or conferences), they shared their heartfelt experiences and wisdom on platforms that would have been unthinkable for queer Latter-day Saints for decades after *The Miracle of Forgiveness*—vilifying and threatening queer people—began to be sold at Deseret Book in 1969.

As I compared the characteristics of these two populations that stood at either end of the modern church, I thought about how my experience as a gay father fit into the picture. It felt like we were all one population of Latter-day Saint sexual minorities going to the same school but in different classes. However, the term "classes" seemed too rigid a definition, holding strict criteria for inclusion determined by our birthdate. We were actually "generations," with looser time borders defining membership, but still holding unique characteristics that made us clearly identifiable. I was not only a part of a generation, but different generations of Latter-day Saint sexual minorities surrounded me. Something was pressing each new generation into existence in the modern church. It had an engine: the force of a dominant narrative.

The dominant narrative is the official, approved narrative held by the Church. In a 2016 fireside, Richard Bushman introduced the "dominant narrative" concept concerning church history, saying that "for the church to remain strong, it has to reconstruct its narrative. The dominant narrative is not true; it can't be sustained."[2] From his historian's lens, church history did not occur as taught in Sunday School. Like church history,

---

2. "Richard Bushman States the Dominant Church History Narrative Is False." YouTube, July 14, 2016. https://youtu.be/uKuBw9mpV9w?si=m9XFw4i4o7ojfXxJ.

the modern church also holds a dominant narrative about queer people. This dominant narrative consists of three parts:

- What the Church thinks about queer people
- What the Church teaches others about queer people
- How the Church talks to queer people

The dominant narrative defines the queer person's place and identity in the Church's theology. It instructs Latter-day Saints how to understand queerness in the context of God's plan. It shows Latter-day Saints how to treat and speak to their queer neighbors and children. It tells queer people what God thinks about them and how to think about themselves. The execution of the dominant narrative is accomplished by deploying an entire ecosystem of policies meant to manage its queer population. The dominant narrative does the thinking, teaching, and talking. Policies are the practices, actions, and implementations that support and enforce the dominant narrative. Both the dominant narrative and its accompanying policies outline what one must do to be an acceptable queer in the kingdom. The primary purpose of the dominant narrative is to protect the doctrine from queerness.

A single dominant narrative does not contain the energy required to churn out generation after generation of queer Latter-day Saints. A new generation means a new engine driving this process. Clearly, the dominant narrative in force for queer Latter-day Saints in the days of *The Miracle of Forgiveness* is not the same dominant narrative in force today that tolerates openly gay Latter-day Saint authors on the shelves of Deseret Book. If changing dominant narratives is the force behind the creation of new queer generations, then what is the force that changes dominant narratives? It couldn't be a random force. The groupings of Latter-day Saint sexual minorities were too distinguishable to be random. The creation carried a sense of direction, not the blindness of organic evolution. They were not being introduced and discarded merely on the preferences of whoever was presiding. These generations were being pruned and shaped with a degree of sophisticated husbandry. The motivation to change dominant narratives was not coming from God; it was coming from society. The motivation for change was a response to what society values and tolerates.

The dominant narrative is constructed from prejudices and misconceptions about queer people. Because some prejudices and misconceptions are eliminated over time as the children of God learn and grow as they lean into the second great commandment, the dominant narrative does not age well and periodically collapses. These collapses occur when the public, healthcare professionals, parents, church members, and outside organizations no longer tolerate the immorality, harms, and outcomes of the dominant narrative and its accompanying policies, finding no value in them. Such a failure requires the modern church to then construct a revised dominant narrative with new policies, crafted to keep queer exclusion relevant and palatable for as long as possible until the next inevitable collapse. As long as the dominant narrative is derived from prejudices and misconceptions, these cycles of "collapse and rebuild" will continue. As long as the Church feels that it must protect its doctrine from queerness, a dominant narrative about the queer children of God will exist, and each successive revision of the dominant narrative will press a new generation of queer Latter-day Saints into existence. This is the arc that queer Latter-day Saints ride as it bends towards equity and justice.

Cycles of dominant narratives and queer generations go hand in hand. Because they are inexorably linked, it is helpful to examine them individually as well as their cause-and-effect relationship. In light of seventy years of data concerning the relationship between the modern church and its sexual minorities, and drawing on my lived experience as a member of a sexual minority in the Church, we can look at the population of Latter-day Saint sexual minorities to illustrate the phenomenon of generation-specific narratives changing over time.

Roughly four generations of sexual minorities exist in the modern church. The first generation has the largest class size. The dominant narrative for this generation declared that there are no acceptable homosexuals in the kingdom of God, putting anyone it deemed homosexual in its crosshairs. It was heavily focused on gay men, light on lesbians, and essentially nonexistent for the rest of the sexual minorities. This is the "Miracle of Forgiveness" generation, named after Spencer W. Kimball's book. This book was the inaugural address to this first class of gays and lesbians in the modern church, introducing in graphic detail how the dominant narrative would be executed for their generation.

This execution was absolute and complete rejection. It was a generation of erasure and ejection from Church, church education, and family. They were mocked from the pulpit.[3] Their parents were blamed for causing their "condition."[4] They were told their very presence contaminated all those around them.[5] They were shocked at BYU with electricity to cure their so-

---

3. Featherstone, Vaughn J. "'Charity Never Faileth.'" BYU Speeches, February 27, 1979. https://speeches.byu.edu/talks/vaughn-j-featherstone/charity-never-faileth/.

4. Brown, Victor L. "Two Views of Sexuality." *Ensign* 5, no. 7, July 1975.

5. Wilkinson, Ernest L., "Make Honor Your Standard." *Deseret News*, Church News supplement, p 11-12. November 13, 1965.

called "weakness."⁶ The collateral damage to this first generation, lasting for several decades, was severe. We must never forget those who were caught in this moment, who spoke up in this moment, and who perished in this moment. Filled with godly integrity, they were brave in the face of such ugliness and rejecting behavior. This era of outright violence and hostility didn't age well. Today, as we look back on the "Miracle of Forgiveness" era, it is unquestionably an aggressively violent and prejudiced moment in church history that created a hostile environment in both the Church and the home life of gay and lesbian Latter-day Saints.

As it became more unsustainable to outright reject and harass its sexual minorities, the modern church began to focus on the use of silent shame to quietly manage its next generation of gay and lesbian Latter-day Saints, especially those who were newly coming out and seeking support. Management efforts now supported an updated dominant narrative—the unsustainable premise that if you can get homosexuals to act like heterosexuals, they won't be homosexuals anymore. This created my generation, the second generation of sexual minorities in the modern church. We are the silent generation.

What I didn't realize as a vulnerable seventeen-year-old young man walking out of my bishop's office the night of my cleansing was that I had just been ushered into the modern Church's revised management of the Latter-day Saint homosexual. I was part of a generation of thousands upon thousands of trusting young men and women being silently shuttled into

---

6. McBride, Max Ford, *Effect of Visual Stimuli in Electric Aversion Therapy*, PhD Dissertation, BYU, August 1976.

mixed-orientation marriages under the cover of shame with the promise that "of course, it will work out if you are strong enough, and if it doesn't work out, then you weren't strong enough." We were the generation of Latter-day Saint gays and lesbians purposefully hidden from the rank-and-file members of the Church—made invisible so others wouldn't be ashamed or alarmed by us. We were the generation that was hidden from ourselves, surrounded by shame-filled effigies designed to terrify us from ever crossing into visibility. We were pressed into silence in exchange for acceptance and belonging.

As a gay man, I am part of a particular subset of the silent generation that experienced the entire scope of straight privilege, access, and power in the Church right alongside our straight male peers. You knew us and looked to us for leadership. We were your bishops, in your bishoprics, high councils, and stake presidencies. We extended callings to you and issued your temple recommends. We taught your young men and gospel doctrine classes, organized your ward Christmas parties, and pulled handcarts alongside you on your stake pioneer treks. We gave you comfort and aid as we magnified our callings. We blessed you and set you apart—all this while managing our sexual orientation in ways that a straight person never has to do and will never understand. Today, we are none of those things, many of us now divorced and flung to the margins of the faith after years of being at its center. The dominant narrative of our day could not sustain us as we stepped out of the closet, many of us later in life, to rise from under the silence and shame of our generation into an authenticity we were denied as young men.

This collapse is especially grievous for my generation because we were programmatically shuttled into making very serious commitments with a straight spouse in a very serious eternal and legal institution without any informed consent about the risks, heartbreaks, or long-term viability of such an arrangement. Just get them married, and "it will be alright." Most mixed-orientation marriages and families built on this foundation of secrecy and sand did not survive the collapse of the dominant narrative of the silent generation. The modern church abandoned my generation when the deep flaws and real failure of using straight marriage and straight spouses as a chronic conversion therapy for homosexual people manifested great harm in the ensuing years. This gave rise to the next generation.

The widespread use of the term "same-sex attraction" (SSA) characterized the modern church's management of the third generation. The modern church encouraged this generation not to identify as gay or lesbian but as SSA. This generation was openly introduced into the church ecosystem as those managing a great but admirable struggle. Bishops and stake presidents would identify and work with sexual minorities "struggling" with same-sex attraction, taking on an AA sponsor-like role.

Realizing that managing homosexuals was made easier with the help of other homosexuals, the Church turned to Evergreen, a now-defunct Church-approved organization that gathered gay and lesbian Latter-day Saints together for conferences where General Authorities were present, encouraging everyone along in the updated dominant narrative. Evergreen assembled a group of people from the gay and lesbian Latter-day Saint population who were cast as the rockstars of the SSA generation, claiming to have overcome homosexuality. These SSA celebrities stated they understood "the way" to successfully manage SSA. They taught other sexual minorities in the Church that if they wanted it bad enough, they, too, could overcome their homosexuality.

With such a hope spread among this generation of Latter-day Saint gays and lesbians, those who identified as having same-sex attraction often turned to programs and conversion therapies that utilized non-evidence-based methods to cope with and diminish same-sex attraction. Many felt this was the ticket to belonging in the Church and returning to live with God again. Because the Church characterized those in this process as "struggling with same-sex attraction," the chronic inability of those who faithfully tried to overcome their "struggles" caused much distress for the sexual minorities in the Church.

In February 2000, Stuart Matis expressed this distress in a letter published in BYU's student newspaper, *The Daily Universe*. After explaining his "tortuous path of internalized homophobia, immense self-hatred, depression and suicidal thoughts,"[7] he lamented that he continually failed to attenuate his homosexuality despite the calluses on his knees, frequent trips to the temple, fasts and devotion to his mission and church callings. Three days later, Matis died by suicide on the steps of his church building. He left a note stating, "I am now free ... I am no longer in pain, and I no longer hate myself. As it turns out, God never intended for me to be straight. Perhaps my death might become the catalyst for some good."[8] Disturbingly, Matis is not the only Latter-day Saint sexual minority to die by suicide under the dominant narrative of their generation.

In the third generation, mixed-orientation marriages continued as they had in the past, but with a wink and a nod because in 1987, Gordon B. Hinckley forbade leaders to outright

---

7. Matis, Stuart. "Letter to the Editor: Don't Stereotype Gay People." *The Daily Universe*, February 21, 2000. https://universe.byu.edu/2000/02/21/letter-to-the-editor-dont-stereotype-gay-people/.

8. Associated Press. "Gay LDS Man Leaves Suicide Note Behind." *Deseret News*, March 3, 2000. https://www.deseret.com/2000/3/3/19555219/gay-lds-man-leaves-suicide-note-behind/.

guide members into such marriages carte blanche as a remedy for homosexual inclinations. Now the fiancé with same-sex attraction and the straight fiancé would work together with their lay priesthood leaders to give the appearance to all parties that the same-sex attraction was under control or "gone" before the wedding. Even though both spouses were aware that they were entering a mixed-orientation marriage, for many, nothing could prepare them for the real-world conflicts and unmet needs in mixed-orientation marriages that would begin to pile up as weeks turned into months, which turned into years. Any struggle or quiet desperation was cast as heroic in the halls of the Church, even as the mental health of both spouses often suffered.

While not widespread among Latter-day Saint mixed-orientation marriages, a dark underbelly exists in the third generation where a loose confederation of married men in such marriages attempt to meet their sexual needs with other men in a prescribed manner "acceptable" to both wife and Church. This practice involves organized, married "same-sex attracted" men's cuddle groups meeting in various stages of undress, even complete nudity, to hold and touch each other "skin to skin" to work out their urges and attractions for men—who were then told not to tell their wives about what they did.[9] It involves weekend retreats in the woods to get naked, where they cuddle each other in the nude and reenact past sexual abuse.[10] They will openly talk about their attraction to other men in front of their

---

9. Dehlin, John. "'North Star' & Mormon-Approved Gay Cuddling Parties - Kyle Ashworth." YouTube: Understanding Mormonism with Dr. John Dehlin, June 9, 2021. https://youtu.be/eLEuAYnzdoM?si=ghoXUucFNNoirgJs.

10. Potok, Mark. "Quacks: 'Conversion Therapists,' the Anti-LGBT Right, and the Demonization of Homosexuality." Southern Poverty Law Center, May 25, 2016. https://www.splcenter.org/20160525/quacks-conversion-therapists-anti-lgbt-right-and-demonization-homosexuality.

wives, rating men on a danger scale from one—meh—to four—requiring restraints because he is so attractive.[11] Participating in these types of non-evidence-based behaviors billed as being "therapeutic" puts an exhausted straight wife in the unenviable position of chronically policing that "acceptable" boundary in fear that those unmet needs might get out of control. And sometimes they did—repeatedly. These chronic cycles of slip-ups and resolutions to do better are a known feature of a mixed-orientation marriage of the third generation. It's a version of marriage foreign to rank-and-file straight Latter-day Saints.

After I divorced and came out publicly, members of these unofficial Latter-day Saint groups approached me to participate. The idea repulsed me. These men were practicing ritualistic cheating on their wives, all to be able to "live the gospel." I had worked so hard and lost so much to claim my authenticity, choose honesty, be courageous, and stand with my family as life recalibrated around us. It was not easy. Like chemotherapy, the process took me to the brink of death so that I might heal, but it is the path of integrity. I know that the fear of loss—both of spouse, children, church, and even eternal life—drives this behavior done in the shadows. This fear is real. But if you are going to be married to a woman, respect her as a woman, as a daughter of God, and respect the rules and fidelity of the temple marriage you agreed to. If you cannot cleave unto her, forsaking all others (Genesis 2:24) as you covenanted to do when you knelt across the altar from each other in the sealing room, hands clasped in front of those infinity mirrors stretching off into eternity, then you are but a hypocrite, sneaking around the shadows of Zion a shell of a man.

---

11. TLC Presents. "My Husband's Not Gay." YouTube, January 13, 2015. https://youtu.be/ZqTuKyqav7w?si=nMnF2wem-4yV-7jf.

Tragically, even though some sort of informed consent and transparency was involved before marriage, mixed-orientation marriages in this third generation still failed at an alarming rate. Between the SSA generation and the previous silent generation, while I was president of Affirmation, at any one time we provided intense peer support for over 600 sexual minorities a year whose mixed-orientation marriages (as well as their wellbeing) did not survive the failed policies and practices of the dominant narrative that marked them. In the wake of this collapse are the broken bodies of the gays and lesbians of the Church, the corpses of dead marriages, and the tears of innocent children. What is the scope of the failure here? Each queer member had a spouse, and with an average of three children per mixed-orientation marriage, this totals 3,600 people each year during my presidency that Affirmation was directly aware of, who experienced life-altering adverse conditions under the collapse of the pastoral promises and systemic management of the second and third generation of sexual minorities in the Church. This is approximately the size of two stakes. This is a staggering number, and that is only those we knew about who made it through alive and wanted peer support in a Mormon cultural context.

Like all human endeavors, some mixed-orientation marriages do work out, but they comprise a minority.[12] It is pastoral malpractice to look past those lives destroyed by a dominant narrative, blame those who failed, and then hold up this minority of currently working mixed-orientation marriages to legitimize the dominant narrative and policies of the second and third generation.

---

12. Dehlin, John P., Renee V. Galliher, William S. Bradshaw, and Katherine A. Crowell. 2014. "Psychosocial Correlates of Religious Approaches to Same-Sex Attraction: A Mormon Perspective." *Journal of Gay & Lesbian Mental Health* 18 (3): 284-311. doi:10.1080/19359705.2014.912970.

With this kind of wholesale failure of the dominant narrative over the past three generations, the modern church once again rebuilt its dominant narrative, marketing a new and improved management of the homosexual population in the Church, pressing yet a new generation into existence: The celebrated celibate and single sexual minority. It was time for the modern church to put down its pom-poms for mixed-orientation marriages. This is the generation about which we can now comfortably use the term sexual minority because, over the ensuing years, the understanding of sexual orientation in the modern church has become more inclusive of all people who are not heterosexual, including those who are bisexual.

For this generation, an unofficial celibate monastic order was established for sexual minorities. It may have been created on purpose, but it is more likely an unintended consequence of the new policies that manage this generation of sexual minorities. In this age the modern church is walking out from behind the interview desk, and instead of finger-wagging, it sits side-by-side this new generation of sexual minorities with tears of sympathy and folksy wisdom. It is now okay to identify as gay, lesbian, or bisexual! This would have been unthinkable in the "Miracle of Forgiveness" generation. Instead of rejecting exclusionary language, this generation is greeted with messages such as "We celebrate you," "We see you," and "We want you to talk about your identity and feelings." We will put your story on our website. We will publish your experiences and put them on the shelves of Deseret Book and in our official magazines. You can serve a mission and go to BYU. We have callings for you.

The challenge of this new management system is that it not only needs to carefully capture Latter-day Saint sexual minorities when they reach marrying age, separate them from their straight peers, and funnel them into the newly constructed celibate monastic order of the Church—but it must do so while avoiding the failed tactics used on the three previous generations. No public hostility, no name calling, no harassing speech. No ignoring identity, no physical violence, no conversion therapy, and no longer "officially" directing gay or lesbian minors into mixed-orientation marriages—consensual or not. All the hallmarks of the past are turned on their ear because neither Gen Z nor their parents will put up with this nowadays. For this generation, it is now about "belonging." The draw of belonging to Church, family, and God is a critical factor in the stability of a young queer person's life. This draw is so strong that the modern church can use belonging as a motivator to influence behavior. To do this, the elements of belonging are made conditional—as long as they remain single and celibate, they will be celebrated and accepted as a part of the community of Saints and their family and able to see their heavenly parents again.

Today, it is the practice to never threaten a sexual minority, only threaten their "belonging." We witnessed this during a Young Adult devotional in February 2021. There, Elder Jeffrey R. Holland addressed the issue of sexual minorities in the Church and adamantly told the young adults, "We absolutely don't make any judgments about feelings or attraction. We don't make an ecclesiastical judgment or a disciplinary decision on the basis of what someone feels or attractions that they have." Yet Elder Holland articulated a "but" clause as he continued his train of thought: "but rather on behavior and what one actually does."[13] Let's be clear about exactly what Elder Holland

---

13. Gibson, Rachel Sterzer. "Elder Holland and 3 General Church Leaders Answer Young Adults' Questions about Dating, Marriage and Other Issues." Church News, February 16, 2021. https://www.thechurchnews.com/2021/2/16/23218290/elder-holland-alliaud-craig-budge-ysa-dating-lgbt-love-of-god/.

is communicating. First, this is a complete 180 from how sexual minorities were managed in the first generation, where one absolutely received church discipline because of their feelings and attractions. Second, the Church is not just asking sexual minorities to refrain from sexual relations before marriage as they ask of straight members. This is not what Elder Holland is inferring at all. Instead, he is threatening the very belonging of sexual minorities in the Church if they act like their straight peers, claim equality, and legally marry according to their orientation. Elder Holland's message to the sexual minorities of the Church is an expectation of celibacy—never marrying, in contrast to practicing abstinence until marriage, which is the expectation for straight Latter-day Saints. The difference between abstinence and celibacy can be confusing because they look and feel the same in practice as a young adult. Most queer Latter-day Saints discover the difference when abstinence begins converting into marriage for their straight Latter-day Saint peers, and they realize celibacy does no such thing for them. Simply put, abstinence is waiting to have sexual relations until marriage. Celibacy is the discipline of waiting forever because marriage is not approved for them on Earth or in heaven.

Celibacy is the new "mixed-orientation marriage" of the modern church. And just like Evergreen had with mixed-orientation marriages in the third generation, Latter-day Saint celibacy and singleness in the fourth generation has a cast of public-facing single and celibate rockstars proclaiming, "This is the way." Strictly speaking, this is not a forced celibacy, but for orthodox, believing gay and lesbian Latter-day Saints who desperately want to belong, live with God again, and be with their families for eternity, it is as close to "forced" as possible. It is terrifying to see a new generation of youth and young adults preparing for a life of singleness and celibacy, stepping into the space that mixed-orientation marriages once occupied within the Church. This is not a group of religious elites as in Catholicism, where the celibate order holds power and runs the Church. This is a second-class subgroup under the suspicious gaze and supervision of the straight majority. Celibacy is a discipline, not a virtue. Celibacy cannot be maintained by platitudes alone.

The modern church struggled to manage all the players in its now abandoned mixed-orientation marriage strategy. Today, it is even more ill-equipped to support the long-term mental and emotional health of a gay celibate order because singleness in the plan of salvation is set up theologically and socially to be a temporary condition. If the modern church is serious about lovingly committing every one of its sexual minorities to the discipline of lifelong singleness, it must put in the work and resources to deliver an effective support system of lifelong care amid the financial, social, relational, and professional ramifications of a partnerless life.

It is impossible to foresee what the future holds for this rising generation, but the allure of celibacy is already starting to lose its luster as more and more Latter-day Saint sexual minorities and their families begin to understand precisely what is being asked of them in this life and in the theology of the eternities. Despite the general rule to still excommunicate married same-sex Latter-day Saints—adopted in the early days of the 2015 Obergefell ruling legalizing marriage equality—we are starting to see such couples spared from excommunication occasionally. This may signal the birth of the next generation of sexual minorities in the modern church. Only time will tell.

At this moment, I feel a bit like Moroni, as if I am speaking out of the dust to the newest generation of sexual minorities: My age of mixed-orientation marriage is diminishing. Like Galadriel, I stand at the shores of the Great Sea, ready to depart for the Land of the Undying, and pensively reflect that, indeed, the LGBTQ Latter-day Saint world is changed. However, with wisdom, I see that all things are still the same. The age of the celibate single sexual minority is rising in the Church. You feel strong, committed, and celebrated. You are not the first generation to feel this way in the newness of your era. Even in this rise, within a space of belonging specially made for you, you still feel the sting of prejudice and misunderstanding from the dominant narrative that rules you. You are not the first generation to walk with faith, hope, and commitment under a new dominant narrative. Do not think of my age as weak because our mixed-orientation marriages failed. Do not judge the previous generations' actions as the dominant narrative of their day collapsed upon their heads. Do not shun the generations that have gone before you. The wreckage of each dominant narrative scaffolding still exists in the Church and occupies the same landscape as subsequent narratives, including the one presently in use. We were once you.

You are now us.

Although this generational examination was specific for the sexual minorities in the modern church, it is essential to note that sexual minorities are not the only Latter-day Saint queer population that exists in generations. At the beginning of the modern church, the entire family tree of queer people sat within the dominant narrative trunk of the harsh "Miracle of Forgiveness" generation. As time progressed, the modern church became savvier to sexual orientation and gender identity, creating specific narratives and policies that decay, collapse, and are rebuilt independent from the other branches of the Latter-day Saint queer family tree, creating a diverse landscape of unique generations for each specific letter of 2SLGBTQIA+ Latter-day Saints.

Today a towering queer family tree of various dominant narratives and policies stands directly in the center of Zion. It is breathtaking in size and the amount of husbandry required within the generational branches to keep its roots of inequality and exclusion alive. It cannot be sustained.

CHAPTER 5

Wheels Down

> Fitting in is about assessing a situation and becoming who you need to be to be accepted.
> Belonging, on the other hand, doesn't require us to change who we are; it requires us to be who we are.
>
> Brené Brown
> *The Gifts of Imperfection*

"What is your calling in the Church, Doctor?" This is a common question many of my new patients ask as I lean them back in the chair to begin their exam. Whether this is meant to be a conversation starter or an evaluation, this information about their healthcare provider matters in the heart of Mormon Mesa. I was never bothered by this question before my divorce. I admit that it even evoked a slight sense of validation from their nod of approval as I revealed my current leadership calling—as if this somehow made me a more capable dentist. But now, it was a query into a part of me that was a minefield.

As an active Latter-day Saint family, we had just navigated a separation and divorce over four years without activating the Mormon gossip network. There should be some kind of medal for this. Despite the intensity, tension, and emotions inherent in the legal process, no one involved in the divorce proceedings attempted to out me to the Church. Of course, our ward and stake knew we were divorcing, but no one knew why. I am a very private, introverted person, and as a member of the silent generation, I didn't need them to know why. Growing up in a church that never wanted me to talk about my sexual orientation, I didn't feel the urge to begin doing so now. For me, it was enough, more than enough, now that I had come out to myself, eliminated a religiously-prescribed double life, and sat with my immediate family through change and loss. I was content to live the rest of my life outside the spotlight in the Church I loved, where, despite divorce, I was still sealed to my children for the eternities and practiced dentistry in mortality.

Although I no longer subscribed to the dominant narrative in my own life, I knew it still posed a very real-world danger for me. During Arizona Prop 102, I learned firsthand what many of my fellow saints thought about people like me. Knowing this prejudice and seeing how it could be mobilized to harm gay people, I concluded that I would lose patients if I were out at church, tanking my ability to meet my financial obligations that the court had figured into the divorce decree—ultimately harming my children. It's a small world in Mormondom. The networks are so incredibly tight, and news travels fast. Mormons seem to understand divorce; it may carry a stigma, but they understand it—even Brigham Young was a divorcé. In Mormon networks, it is not a professional dealbreaker. Conversely, I saw that Mormons had no capacity to understand a divorced gay Latter-day Saint father of five children. This would be a professional dealbreaker. A gay brother Kitchen would not elicit an approving nod.

Initially, I didn't navigate my coming out with poise and composure. Instead, I came falling out of the closet, dripping in fear and shame, awkwardly tripping over the threshold, experiencing that unsettling step into nothingness like when you think you've reached the bottom of the stairs but haven't—there's one more left. I didn't just miss a stair; the entire landing was gone. My closet door was on the edge of Mount Everest, and I was in free fall, flames on fire, wildly spinning movie stunt-double style in a process that was lasting much longer than I thought it should.

Worst of all, I was falling in isolation. I wanted to feel a community of love, where being an LGBTQ person was not a sacred loneliness but an affirming connection. I was a refugee now from my church. My authenticity did not feel safe in the pews of my spiritual home nor in the broader Mormon community where I lived. Church was now a place where I was continually assessing myself to ensure that I was presenting in a heteronormative, Mormonormative manner to be accepted. Instead, I desperately wanted people to reach for my reaching, catch me, and hold me close, saying, "We see you. We love you. You belong with us just as you are. We're going to be right here to help." I craved a safe place to land, and until I did, I was just perpetually falling into loss—and that is incredibly disorienting. For me, a safe landing was three points of ground contact, like landing gear on an airplane: community in family, community among friends, and a community of LGBTQ Mormons. All three wheels needed to be firmly planted before I considered myself landed. Unsettled and rolling back and forth, I determined it was time to execute the landing checklist until all wheels were on the ground. I felt the end of the runway coming up fast.

I determined that the first wheel to set down was my extended family. Coming out to myself was hard enough. Now it was time to navigate this with my entire orthodox Mormon family. The dominant narrative in the Church about gay people may have profoundly affected me, but it was like kudzu in the branches of my family tree. I learned about kudzu on my mission in Alabama. As a new Elder, I was mesmerized by the dense, lush vines covering the woods in flowing robes of green as far as the eye could see. Locals told me that kudzu was introduced to the southern United States from Asia to prevent soil erosion, especially along railroad and highway embankments. In the mid-1940s, the Kudzu Club of America planted kudzu wherever it could throughout the South. After planting a half million acres, foresters and highway engineers began sounding the alarm about kudzu's dark side. It does not just stay where planted. Kudzu is a dangerously invasive vine that grows so quickly and climbs so efficiently that it smothers the native trees—blocking sunlight and taking nutrients, killing them as it coils from bough to bough through the immense network of Southern roadside forests.[1]

Over the decades, the dominant narrative, directing families how to treat and reject their gay children and siblings, had been zealously planted under the family trees in Zion in the misplaced hope of preventing the erosion of the family. These vines scattered about Zion did not stay where planted. They grew upward and outward, climbing the branches of the great

---

1. Loewenstein, Nancy J. "History and Use of Kudzu in the Southeastern United States." Alabama Cooperative Extension System: Alabama A&M and Auburn University, March 12, 2022. https://www.aces.edu/blog/topics/forestry-wildlife/the-history-and-use-of-kudzu-in-the-southeastern-united-states.

family trees in the Church, suffocating entire families with LGBTQ children, all while giving the counterfeit appearance of health by covering these dying boughs in a lush green veneer. To set my first wheel down into the belonging of my own family would take a steady hand. They would be confronting a dominant narrative—hanging from the branches of our family tree—about their son and brother. I immediately knew whom I would talk with first in my family.

Before I could get a word past "Hello," my sister enthusiastically jumped in, "I'm so glad you called. I was just thinking about you. What are you doing for Christmas?" Annette is two and a half years younger than me. She was also adopted, and my earliest memory was being with her at the altar in a sealing room, dressed in white in the Salt Lake Temple, as she was sealed into our family for the eternities. For many years, we were the only children before the arrival of our five other brothers and sisters in rapid succession, a happy surprise in the Kitchen household. Annette and I had always been each other's trusted confidants, no matter the subject. Our connection was a safe space of no judgment. In high school, she was a vocal LGBTQ community supporter. At this moment when I did not feel very strong, I needed a known family ally. Two years ago, she was the only one in my extended family whom I had told that I was separated and divorcing. I hadn't told her why, and true to form, she didn't press me for details. Now, she was first on my landing checklist. Although I knew that she would take my sexual orientation to the grave if I asked her to, that wasn't my goal. Authenticity was the goal. Inviting others in with trust and respect was the goal.

"The kids are at their mom's the last week of December, so I haven't anything planned," I replied. "Well, you do now! Come up to Seattle. I have extra miles on Delta, so pack your bags. I'll send you a ticket, and come spend some time with us." Her planning superpowers running at peak levels, she excitedly made detailed plans on the spot that ended up with us staying the last few days in the mountain village of Leavenworth, where she would put me on the Amtrak back to SeaTac for my flight home. "You have to take the train back. They call it the Polar Express because you wind through the snowy mountain pass, and it is absolutely beautiful winter scenery. It will take your breath away." That settled it. I would be in Seattle to ring in 2012 in just three weeks.

On my second day at Annette's Washington Adventure Week, we headed out early to the store to pick up a few groceries in Issaquah. I always liked time alone with Annette because we could dig into serious conversations about life, family, and the Church. As we climbed the hill to return home, I turned the conversation to what brought me to Seattle. "Can we talk about why I wanted to come see you?" She nodded. I paused to look at her, and, as she navigated the twists and turns of the hillside neighborhood, I said in almost a whisper, "I am gay." She didn't even blink. Not an eyebrow raised. No shocked expression. It was as if I had just said something as uncontroversial as "water is wet" or "the sky is blue." She immediately turned the blinker on to go left instead of right to return to the house.

"First of all, you just need to know that I love you. I am proud of you and always will be. Second, would it be okay if we take a drive together before going back to the house with everybody? I want the time to listen to you." By this time, she had a few tears starting from the corners of her eyes but held a gentle smile. I nodded as we headed away from the house and into the morning banks of fog covering the hillside. She shared that she had been preparing ever since her first child was born—how she would react and what to say if one of her children told her that they were gay—so that even her expression would not show anything resembling disappointment. "Now I know I have been practicing for my big brother." In her words, I felt care way beyond that of a traveler being tended to by a good Samaritan. This was pure and gentle love flowing across the boughs of our eternal family tree, and I felt an indescribable joy. At that moment, the groceries in the back of the car no longer mattered—ice cream melting and milk warming—as we spent the next hour driving, talking, listening, and affirming in a space as sacred as a sealing room.

A few weeks later, I confided in my sister that I felt stuck about how to share my life with my other brothers and sisters, especially my mother and father: "You know it will come as a shock when I come out to them. Some will immediately begin preaching fire and brimstone. I don't know if I am ready for that kind of family rejection."

"Listen," she began, "This is not a Chicken Little 'the sky is falling' moment. You know that I am here for you. Let's figure this out together." My parents were finishing their mission in Moldova, and my siblings were scattered around the country, so we settled on a "two shoe drop" approach. I would send an initial email to everyone stating that I was separated and divorcing, and when that dust settled, I would contact each of them to tell them why. Knowing her role in the family dynamics, she noted, "Everyone is going to contact me after the first shoe drops. I'll put out the side fires and address the questions that no one will dare ask you." I liked this strategy. It would give me the space to not feel overwhelmed. "I won't out you," she added. "That will be your job after I talk everyone off the ledge."

With plans made and my sister at my side, I sent the first email in "Operation Shoe Drop," letting my parents and siblings know I was separated and would be divorcing, citing "irreconcilable differences." I immediately received replies of sadness and sympathy, followed by admonitions to try and work things out. My very concerned father wrote, "There is no such thing as an irreconcilable difference. I don't know what the problems are that you choose to categorize in this way, but I know that every mortal problem we can possibly face in this world has a solution within the bounds of the eternal covenants we make with God." Although it seemed safest for me to deliver my news in two parts so as not to take my medicine all at once, when I received this letter from my father, I realized the downside of making my announcement in two stages. It left a very concerned family in the dark, grasping at straws about why this was happening. The dust would not settle until I dropped the other shoe.

When I contacted my brothers, sisters, and parents to come out to them, it was not just "the other shoe dropping." It was a bomb dropped directly into the middle of our family's orthodoxy. With this news, I now represented a broken link in our eternal family tree and the prospect of losing me and me being lost caused much sorrow and fear. Some of my siblings were supportive. Some took it hard. I gently engaged their many questions and feelings as they tried to make sense of what was happening. For my parents, the concept of being gay as a sexual orientation was extremely hard for their generation to understand. Being gay was never a part of their religious culture or society they grew up in. For them, homosexuality was truly a temptation to overcome, like all temptations in this mortal life. My mom was candid about where she was, saying that while she didn't understand it, she understood that she loved me and that wouldn't go away. She explained that my father was having a very hard time with this. I already knew this because he had been sending me letters—epistles really—by mail and email, talking about my great wickedness. It got to the point I didn't even want to go to the mailbox anymore. I started putting his letters in a drawer and archiving his emails. Though we were doing it in very different ways, both my father and I were aching about the same thing: family.

I continued to hold steady in this process with my siblings and parents through the weeks and months. Belonging and acceptance within my family were so important to me that when I began this process, I pledged to myself that I would always be available to them as they got to know the "new to them" Nathan. I held to mild words and gentle expressions in our conversations to advance respect and love rather than fear and anger. I was not confronting my family. I was confronting a dominant narrative. Slowly, our conversations began to change from intense admonitions to supportive communication. After sitting with one of my sisters as she sorted out her emotions and understanding of the situation, she emailed, "I really appreciated our conversations letting me openly ask questions and express my feelings. I apologize for my harshness through this process." And then, after I responded to his many missives with many soft answers (Proverbs 15:1) over the months, my father asked me to destroy all the letters he had previously written because they no longer accurately represented how he felt. This was huge. We had not given up on one another, and that made all the difference. Together, the entire Kitchen family was casting down entire swaths of kudzu from off the branches of our family tree, replacing a dominant narrative with a family narrative. The boughs were quickly becoming uncovered, filled with light and full of love. Two more wheels to go.

CHAPTER 6

Behold, Here Are the Waters of Mormon

> Here beside the waters of Mormon,
> Here we come to witness our God.
> Here is love in fountains o'erflowing,
> Waters as pure as the love of God.
>
> We will bear our burdens together,
> Lifting as one that our labors be light.
> Here we comfort the lowly in spirit.
> Here we mourn with loved ones who mourn.
>
> Heidi Rodeback

Still not out to the world, I considered it my guilty pleasure to secretly follow Joanna Brooks on Facebook. Although I didn't know her personally, we graduated from BYU the same year. Now on the faculty at San Diego State University, she was a well-known advocate for minorities in the Church, including LGBTQ people. Her posts drew a large cross-section of Latter-day Saints. As I felt marginalized in the Church and isolated as life recalibrated around me, her voice reminded me that the landscape of Mormonism was dotted with people who wanted me to belong. One day, I felt brave enough to comment on one of her posts. This seemed harmless, but even the most innocuous post on social media can be a beacon. Within an hour, I received a friend request with this message: "Facebook should be numbered among our latter-day blessings for its ability to restore friendships once lost. I treasure such happy memories made with you and Emily at BYU and am truly glad to have bumped into you here." It was from Heidi, one of my best friends when we were freshmen twenty-six years earlier.

My freshman year was a moment of personal renaissance. I had one year before my mission, so I didn't need to think about the marriage milestone yet. Best of all, I was back home in Utah Valley, a salmon triumphantly returning to its spawning grounds after a valiant fight up the runs and ladders. For the first time in years, I felt free and unencumbered. I enrolled in a six-credit Colloquium designed by Eugene England that met in the Maeser building's beautifully appointed two-tiered lecture hall. Colloquium was not "answers to gospel questions" but "questions to gospel answers."[1] It was not only an invitation to learn but permission to inquire and wonder. It was filled with more insights than a freshman had any business knowing, but that was the point. Those Colloquium seeds planted in our minds were intended to sprout over a lifetime, informing us how to approach ideas, discover truth, embrace knowledge, and understand the gospel—all while practicing charity for another's observations.

---

1. Lundquist, Suzanne. "Learning How to Learn." The Eugene England Foundation, 2011. https://www.eugeneengland.org/eugene-england/remembering-gene-project/st-olaf-college-to-early-byu-career/learning-how-to-learn.

After meeting Heidi and Emily in Colloquium, we became inseparable. We studied together, wrote together, and experienced campus together. We held impromptu "Conferences of Truths" where we would stay up all night, covertly commandeering one of the giant lecture halls in the Jesse Knight Humanities building, filling the huge sliding chalkboards with ideas, poems, scriptures, and cartoons—no tangent too obscure as we pursued truth. More than once, the early morning custodial crew would find us in the middle of our thoughts and shoo us out of the building so they could clean.

As close as we were, our first year at BYU could not last forever. In the end, Heidi was engaged, I was headed home to Illinois to submit my mission papers, and Emily was staying at BYU to continue her education. This moment marked the end of the period in my life that I felt I could freely program for myself. As a freshman, I may have been a triumphant salmon returning to the waters of my childhood, but horrifyingly, such a return meant death—the end of the lifecycle for the salmon. I was now entering my programmed senescence, succumbing to the freshwaters of milestones. I accepted this loss with a stiff upper lip as a shedding of "childish things." It was time to get serious about two huge "inner vessel protecting" events: mission and marriage. Those and church callings were the adult roles that would offer me God's promised protection for the rest of my life. I traded away my best friends for milestones. I threw away my Colloquium notebooks to make room for a correlated curriculum and abandoned this flourishing identity I really loved and nurtured into existence my freshman Camelot year. Decades later, I was spat ashore from the fish's belly, half-digested—a Jonah with no memory of who he was now that he was no longer a role. My innocuous message on a Joanna Brooks post became a beacon for two angels on this side of the veil. Heidi and Emily had found me. We had much catching up to do. I lamented that I had thrown my Colloquium library away, to which they excitedly exclaimed, "We have it all. We have the Colloquium files." Ever the archivists, they sent me file after file. It was like downloading an operating system after a hard drive wipe. Documents and friendship restored a wholeness lost in the collateral damage of dividing myself in two for decades.

As we got to know each other again, I wanted to include Heidi and Emily in every part of my life, just like they were doing with me. I decided to come out to Heidi first. Over the years, she had made a substantial difference in her community. Having been elected to the American Fork city council, she wasn't just about sidewalks and libraries. In 2011, she wrote American Fork's first nondiscrimination ordinance for LGBTQ people.[2] After taking in my news, she asked, "How *are* you? Peak or valley? Turmoil or peace?" I shared that I was currently all those things at once, "Pressing forward in Christ even as I encounter the innumerable inhabitants of the great and spacious building pointing and mocking as I pass. Trusting the iron rod again after those closest to me broke it to beat me with its pieces." Understanding my Nephi references, she responded in kind: "I do not know the meaning of all things. Nevertheless, I know that God loveth his children."

I was unsure how to proceed with Emily. A returned missionary, she had earned an MBA and was now a highly successful senior-level executive. She wore her testimony proudly on her sleeve—genuine, open, and honest. I worried how the Church's dominant narrative about LGBTQ people would affect our reconnection. Hurt was already simmering just below the surface. When I abandoned Heidi and Emily after freshman year, it was

---

2. Fidel, Steve. "American Fork to Consider Sexual Orientation Ordinance for Housing, Employment." *Deseret News*, December 11, 2011. https://www.deseret.com/2011/12/11/20390407/american-fork-to-consider-sexual-orientation-ordinance-for-housing-employment/.

hardest on Emily. She didn't understand how I could just be done—door-slammed done—with such a meaningful friendship. As I crafted my coming out message to her, I likened our reconnection to that of Alma and the sons of Mosiah. Part of their great joy in reunion was openly sharing the circumstances of their individual journeys. "Likewise, I want to share my journey with you even though it is something that still feels fragile to talk about: I am gay." I revealed my silent sorrows at BYU and addressed my abandonment of her after our freshman year in the misguided effort to keep my eye single to my bishop's salvific milestones: "I make no excuses for how I acted. I am sorry. I do not want to dash this healing and joyous occasion, but I also do not want to hide information from you."

Unbeknownst to me, Emily was sitting in Relief Society when I hit send. Within minutes, she messaged back, "If I could write it in giant letters, please know of my love and regard. I am in RS. Totally should not be texting." My heart flooded with joy and relief. "Just one more quick thing. I feel such a warm spirit of love to you—to Nathan, my friend. Grief at pain you have suffered. But want to send you love without condition. So, now, someone I love is gay. I welcome learning how to show the love I always hoped I would show in that case." I put my phone down and marveled at such belonging amid friendship. I began to feel the weight of steel and wing set down upon my second wheel, stabilizing this 747 coming in to land after a turbulent flight. In the coming months, one final experience would firmly plant my final wheel on the ground, confirming that I had finally come to rest after seven years of falling.

During my reconnection with Heidi and Emily, I contacted Wendy and Tom Montgomery. I had been following their public story as an active Latter-day Saint family supporting and protecting their teenage son after he came out. After sharing my story, Wendy excitedly said, "I know just where your people are." Unbeknownst to me, she sat on the Board of Affirmation, and immediately added me to Affirmation's main Facebook page. Over the next few days, I devoured every bit of content Affirmation had published. I discovered a rich library of voices openly speaking about life in the queer/Latter-day Saint intersection from a place of pride, not shame. Many of these stories were told by people who represented demographics that were not my own. They not only spoke about their sexual orientation and gender identity but shared how this was experienced in every corner of the Church around the world.

I learned that before Affirmation was founded in 1977, many groups of gay Mormons informally met together in secret because it was dangerous to do so otherwise. One of these groups was made up of BYU students. Between 1976 and 1977, two of these students submitted to electroshock therapy to cure their orientation. During their shock therapy, ecclesiastical leaders counseled both men to cut off contact with all gay friends as part of their "recovery" process—thus cutting themselves off from any sort of supportive network that might have been able to help prevent their deaths. When the therapy failed, they became overwhelmed by feelings of unworthiness, which they felt they could only resolve by taking their own lives. Upon learning of their deaths, this group of friends at BYU determined that a formal support network providing affirming connection in community was essential for gay and lesbian Mormons—and Affirmation was officially born.[3] In the ensuing decades, Affirmation grew in size and scope around the world because wherever the Church

---

3. Mortensen, Paul. "Our History." Affirmation, July 4, 1987. https://affirmation.org/about/history/.

is, queer people are also. Now encompassing sexual orientation, gender identity, and gender expression, Affirmation was still about friends looking out and caring for friends. This was the kind of community I wanted to be a part of.

I was so intrigued by what I had learned that in the early months of 2015, I decided to attend Affirmation's May retreat in Palmyra, New York, to personally experience this remarkable community of mentors and peers. As I approached the front doors of the Palmyra Inn, I took a deep breath before I walked into the lobby. This seemed a life-changing moment. Leaving me no time to feel alone, Ron and Sue Raynes were right there to greet me. "Welcome, we're glad you're here, Nathan," Ron said as he extended his hand, pulling me in for a hug. "We have several other guys in or just out of mixed-orientation marriages coming, and we can't wait to introduce you." Ron and Sue had just formed the mixed-orientation marriage support group within Affirmation. They named the group MOFIA—Mixed Orientation Families in Affirmation—because a mixed-orientation marriage affects a family, not just a husband and wife. I found this acronym incredibly clever and the premise absolutely true. Ron asked me if I was a singer and invited me to join the weekend's Affirmation retreat choir.

I experienced connection the moment I walked through the front doors of the Palmyra Inn. It was incredibly healing for me to meet others from around the Church who were like me. This community building continued and expanded as the weekend progressed. By the end of the retreat, I made meaningful friendships with people across the entire LGBTQ spectrum. I was connected and plugged into a diverse community. It was a remarkable feeling of belonging. That first evening, as Jim Carlston, vice president of Affirmation, welcomed us all with his trademark humor, I held my program close, reading and rereading the events planned for the weekend. One of

Affirmation's purposes printed in the program was to "Provide support and opportunity for social interaction, intellectual development, emotional stability, and cultural exposure with those of similar heritage and background." Affirmation was not just an observer of the queer Latter-day Saint falling out of the closet. Affirmation didn't just talk about it on a podcast or pontificate about the experience on a social media post. Affirmation provided a physical place to land among friends.

※

In The Book of Mormon, we read that two hundred and four souls gathered with Alma on the banks of the Waters of Mormon. Surrounded by thicket and forest, Alma began preaching, stacking a series of compelling observations one upon another—each rhetorical layer teaching what it means "to come into the fold of God" (Mosiah 18:8). I believe this to be the most beautiful commentary in all scripture about the second great commandment—how to love your neighbor: willing to bear one another's burdens that they may be light, willing to mourn with those that mourn, willing to comfort those that stand in need of comfort. To this day, we receive these by covenant upon baptism and renew this willingness each time we partake of the sacrament. The second great commandment is about being willing.

In this story, we often focus on Alma's masterful teaching, but if we also consider the community that had gathered at the Waters of Mormon—its demographics, why it formed, and why it was in the forest of Mormon in the first place—we come to appreciate and understand the fullness of "willingness." This was a radically supportive community considering the political and religious atmosphere during the time of Alma. This band of souls lived in an enclave nation surrounded by a people who desired to harm and enslave them. In addition, their leader, King

Noah, had pillaged the poor to fund the government's laziness, idolatry, and whoredoms. His example "did cause his people to commit sin, and do that which was abominable in the sight of the Lord" (Mosiah 11:2). Most horrifying, their king had just killed Abinadi, scourging "his skin with faggots" (Mosiah 17:3), violently setting God's prophet on fire. Considering the exclusion, tension, and fear in their homeland and the hostile nation that surrounded them, it is no wonder that they "clapped their hands for joy" when Alma invited them to join this new supportive community at the Waters of Mormon, exclaiming in one voice: "This is the desire of our hearts" (Mosiah 18:11).

Abridging these events, Mormon observed that "these things were done in the borders of the land" (Mosiah 18:31). Those who gathered at the Waters of Mormon were refugees. This was a supportive community in the margins. Their community was lifesaving and life-giving. LGBTQ Latter-day Saints know this status all too well. Queer Latter-day Saints continually experience exclusionary events in government and religious spaces they have no control over, which may make them refugees. Sometimes, circles are drawn to exclude them from full participation or membership. Sometimes, definitions of acceptability change, and they suddenly find themselves an "other" where they once found belonging.

As a people on the borders of the land in the latter days, we look for our Waters of Mormon, a radically supportive community that will recognize the authenticity of our humanity, support our wellbeing, see and love us as the queer children of God we are, and in empathy mourn with us, comfort us, and help bear our burdens. Our personal Waters of Mormon provide immediate safe harbor to strengthen and heal us during difficult times. When we feel we cannot go on any longer, supportive communities nurture us, lift the hands that hang down and strengthen our feeble knees (Hebrews 12:12). Most importantly, these supportive communities are there to experience joy with us! Supportive communities can be a group of friends, an organized support community, a civic community, a religious community, a partner, your marriage, your family—anywhere you feel love. There is no rule that you can only have one supportive community. If you feel love in multiple places, that's okay. You can never have too much love. Science shows that supportive communities are both lifesaving and life-giving.[4] It is essential as a queer person to find supportive communities. Being part of a supportive community is the most powerful predictor of increased health, lifespan, and happiness.[5] It is life-threatening when an LGBTQ person is pushed to the margins—or worse, pushed entirely out of their spiritual home, their family, schools, workplaces, or even the heavens.

Often when Latter-day Saints see queer people seeking supportive communities outside their spiritual home, they will ask, "Why isn't the Church enough for LGBTQ Latter-day Saints?" This question ignores the reality that having a network of supportive people and communities is healthy. It also assigns blame in the wrong direction: to the refugee. Queer people navigate to supportive spaces that feel safe and healthy for them. This migration is a Waters of Mormon moment for queer Latter-day Saints, just as it was anciently for those refugees who gathered with Alma. If you look around and can't see queer people surrounding you in church spaces, this moment says more about you than it does about queer people. As Elder Patrick Kearon observes, "This moment does not define the refugees, but our

---

4. Holt-Lunstad J, Smith TB, Baker M, Harris T, Stephenson D. "Loneliness and Social Isolation as Risk Factors for Mortality: A Meta-Analytic Review." *Perspect Psychol Sci.* 2015 Mar; 10(2):227-37. doi: 10.1177/1745691614568352. PMID: 25910392.

5. Pinker, Susan. "The Secret to Living Longer May Be Your Social Life." TED Talk, April 2017. https://www.ted.com/talks/susan_pinker_the_secret_to_living_longer_may_be_your_social_life.

response will help define us."⁶ Rather than ask where all the queer people are, instead ask, "Why are they not with us? What can I do to help my queer neighbors feel safe and healthy in our spiritual home as a community of Saints?"

When LGBTQ Latter-day Saints deal with the challenges of coming out, their most urgent need is safe community. Communities where individuals feel unconditionally loved, wanted, and needed are one of the strongest protective factors against depression and suicide. A Waters of Mormon community provides a sounding board where queer Latter-day Saints can work through the difficult questions they face as they figure out how to navigate coming out, faith, and family. As queer persons, often the decisions we make in our most vulnerable moments are some of the most incredibly difficult ones we will ever make. Do not let us make these decisions alone in grief.

It is the vision of Affirmation "to be a refuge to land."⁷ There is not a word in English that can fully express this phenomenon of landing in the context of what a queer person needs as they are falling out of the closet seeking community. But there is in Portuguese. Affirmation's leaders in Brazil translate the word "land" not as *cair*, which is the act of falling into something, but as *pousar*, meaning "to rest." This beautiful rendering envisions that in all your falling, Affirmation is a refuge where you may rest, just as you would rest your head on the shoulder of a loved

---

6. Kearon, Patrick. "Refuge from the Storm." *Ensign* 46, no. 5, May 2016. https://www.churchofjesuschrist.org/study/general-conference/2016/04/refuge-from-the-storm

7. "1.3 - Principles and Values." In *Charter & Bylaws*. Affirmation: LGBTQ Mormons, Families & Friends, February 8, 2022. https://affirmation.org/about/charter-bylaws/.

one at the end of a long day. Instead of just "falling into something," you are doing so much more. It is the act of your soul coming in for a rest after a long journey. I experienced this as my third and final wheel touched down there in Palmyra, bringing my entire soul to rest. It was that gentle moment in my life where I found my *refúgio para pousar*.

A year and a half prior, I had entered an autumnal Sacred Grove isolated, alone, and in distress—leaves falling from the boughs, creating a barrenness that matched my soul. As I entered the Sacred Grove during the weekend of Affirmation's retreat, the boughs were a luscious green, heavy with new growth. This time, I was surrounded by friends who understood me and affirmed the difficult choices I had faced over the past seven years. I felt seen. I felt loved. I felt affirmed. All these remarkable people created a supportive community—*my* supportive community. After a while, I told my friends I was going to walk a side trail in the grove to be alone for a bit. As I rounded the bend of my chosen path, the trail unexpectedly straightened out as far as I could see, much like a runway. The pathway and surrounding trees became vanishing lines that seemingly converged into eternity. Within this beauty, I paused to utter a prayer of complete gratitude that God had indeed not left my soul in hell. I had landed. I had shed my personal autumn just as the grove had done in its spring. Amid the birdsong, walking under the boughs of a mid-May Sacred Grove was a testament that life will indeed spring forth out of barrenness.

BARRENNESS

In loneliness
Barrenness collects upon your person,
Carried on your soul,
Attached to you like whale and ship
As you slice through desert oceans.
It weighs the buoyant, tender heart:
We hunker to survive, not live.

The laugh of Sarah at the thought
That I am worthy to bear connection
With another,
And in such fullness, end.
Barrenness scraped away,
Life transformed
Forever.

Nourished in wholehearted love.

CHAPTER 7

The Peak of Champions

> 13 And they brought young children to him, that he should touch them: and his disciples rebuked those that brought them.
> 14 But when Jesus saw it, he was much displeased, and said unto them, Suffer the little children to come unto me, and forbid them not: for of such is the kingdom of God.
> 15 Verily I say unto you, Whosoever shall not receive the kingdom of God as a little child, he shall not enter therein.
> 16 And he took them up in his arms, put his hands upon them, and blessed them.
>
> Mark 10: 13-16

My marriage of twenty-three years did not survive my second coming out. But my children did. They may have survived the reconfiguration of their family, but surviving does not mean an absence of trauma. They, too, were falling into loss. Understanding how critical supportive communities were for me, I was determined to create a healthy, supportive family in the wake of divorce—a refuge of trust, security, acceptance, and love where they could come in for a rest after a long night of falling.

On Thanksgiving morning 2011, I gathered my young sons for a pre-Thanksgiving dinner hike in Usery Park. Usery is sandwiched between the city of Mesa and Tonto National Forest, a vast swath of desert foothills encompassing the western edge of the Goldfield Mountain Range. A month earlier, my children experienced their parents' separation. Today, their emotions were still raw, with the youngest ones wondering if this meant an eventual parent/child separation as well. It broke my heart to watch my children anticipate abandonment. This was not a fear I could just reassure away with words. It would require daily actions and relationship-building to demonstrate that I was not going anywhere.

We navigated the desert floor to the base of Cat Peaks, two sister peaks that tower over the park, providing a sweeping view of the entire valley to the west and the desert forests to the east. After making the ascent through the pass, we stopped at a crop of boulders, perfect for a rest. I noticed a wide, well-traveled trail leading to the northern peak. However, no clear path existed to the southern peak. One of my boys scampered over the boulder fields to the south and returned, excitedly telling us he had found a small trail. Feeling adventurous, we headed towards the imposing rocky peak ahead. The navigation challenged us. The trail was steep and, at times, hugged the ridgeline where cactuses and drop-offs surrounded us. Once we reached the peak, we found a huge palo verde tree clinging to the side of the mountain, growing out of a rock. It was an impressive sight. It seemed impossible for a tree to grow from a rock, but desert plants are known for the impossible. Just south of the tree, someone had planted a banner on a wooden staff—and even attached a Sharpie—so fellow travelers could sign their name commemorating having reached the peak. We felt accomplished. This was a special place.

I gathered my boys in to come sit with me under the shade of this remarkable tree. Knowing that each of us was experiencing trauma from the recent events, I told them that this tree, springing from a wall of rock, was an example for each of us: "Just like this desert tree, we can find strength and growth—we can even flourish—during the rockiest parts of our lives." I recalled the hard parts of the trail—the occasional slips and falls—but through it all, we were there for each other and encouraged one another along. I noted the times during our hike when one of the brothers would scout out ahead to find us the best path forward and observed, "This is an example of making the road easier for those who follow. It is our great gift to all those on the trail behind us."

I reflected that, in the end, we all made it. We accomplished this together because we helped one another. This is what families do, even in the hardest of times. We can make it because we are there for each other as we reach our peaks in this life. I paused, voice cracking in emotion as I looked at my young sons huddled under the sweeping boughs of this remarkable tree, and concluded: "And in this, we become champions in our lives." By this point, the ground we were on was no longer just Cat Peaks. As we began our descent off the mountain, I christened it "The Peak of Champions." I determined to make the hike to The Peak of Champions a new Thanksgiving tradition. It would be an annual marker amid our day-to-day healing as a family, one of the gentle chirps in life counted under a palo verde tree growing from a rock, tenderly confirming that love was indeed present in our lives.

The Church was one of the subjects we broached as a family during this time. My children held strong testimonies of the gospel. For them, church was a place that felt safe and healthy as they met their spiritual needs. I shared with them that I was a spiritual refugee from the Church at the moment, vacating the pews because it was not a safe place for me to be during my second coming out. Pondering my status as a refugee, I attended my first Affirmation International Conference in Provo, Utah, in September 2015. For several years, Affirmation's messaging had been optimistically and unashamedly knitting LGBTQ Latter-day Saints into the fabric of the Restoration—you can be Mormon and gay, you don't have to choose[1]—and it was on full display in Provo. The entire weekend, I felt part of a glorious Waters of Mormon community as I connected with LGBTQ Mormons from around the world and listened to Affirmation leaders deliver powerful and confident talks.

Popular Church songwriter Michael McLean came on stage during the evening plenary and sang to us. It was absolute chills in the hall as he performed his "Together Forever Someday." When I was a missionary in Alabama, I first heard this song on a Church video that I played countless times to teach investigators about forever families. It called down the Spirit every time. Now, at Affirmation's International Conference, he was personally telling LGBTQ Mormons that he knew *our* families would be together forever someday:

> Thank the Lord above
> Who showed us the way
> That we can be together, forever someday
> We will be together forever someday[2]

---

1. Thacker, Randall. "Happy New Year Affirmation Friends!" Affirmation, January 9, 2013. https://affirmation.org/happy-new-year-affirmation-friends/.

2. McLean, Michael. "Together Forever." YouTube, July 9, 2023. https://youtu.be/v7GFRENleK0?si=T7XyxOtQIZ8sA5xd.

Waves of electricity ran up and down my body as he sang that last line over and over again—the line I felt so profoundly as a missionary, only this time in the context of being a gay father: We will be together forever someday. This was my message to my children under the boughs of the palo verde tree on The Peak of Champions. This was the hope that remained my pole star as my life and my children's lives shifted around us amid change and loss. This was the message I was certain Christ had for us all. I asked myself if perhaps it was time for this spiritual refugee to cautiously return to church—the community of Saints and the faith I loved and believed in. Affirmation was undoubtedly there to support me in this decision if I chose to do so. I would soon learn what a difference forty-six days can make.

On Thursday, November 5th, 2015, I came across a story on my Facebook feed about a church handbook change. I read it with interest. With each word, my soul filled with enveloping darkness as curiosity turned to crushing disbelief. My church would never do this to children—to my children. This was not the church I knew and had a testimony of. I initially dismissed it as a cruel hoax. It wasn't scriptural. It wasn't kind. I had an instant testimony it wasn't true. But this was no hoax.

The handbook change was a new policy, stipulating that children who lived with a parent who was legally married to someone of the same sex or was cohabitating with —or had *ever* done so in the past—were prohibited from receiving a name and a blessing in the Church. If these children had already been blessed before the enactment of this exclusion policy, they were prohibited from being baptized, receiving the gift of the Holy Ghost, being ordained in the priesthood, or serving a mission until they turned 18, moved out of said household, and disavowed the practice of legal same-sex marriage to their priesthood leaders.[3] I felt a deep sense of grief on behalf of my children. My sons were preparing to be ordained in the priesthood, one a deacon and the other a priest. Both wanted to serve missions. It would be seven years before my youngest turned eighteen. If I were to marry again during that period, instead of being a joyous ceremony, the event would trigger, through no fault of their own, immediate damnation of their progress in the Church.

The part that bothered me most was that this new policy was a slap in the face to every child from a mixed-orientation marriage who had already endured the devastating collapse of their own families from the failure of the Church's old mixed-orientation marriage policy. They were now getting hit again, undergoing a direct frontal assault by the modern church as it punished them for the "sins of their fathers." The threat of abandonment by the Church in their journey along the covenant path now loomed large in their life. Under the exclusion policy, children would be forbidden to come unto Christ. Apostles seem to have a history of such a thing, no matter the dispensation.

The exclusion policy was a one-two punch. It not only came after the children; it came after the sexual minorities. Married same-sex Latter-day Saints were automatically branded apostates,[4] putting married same-sex couples in the same category as those who murder, rape, or abuse children. Family stability in a legally binding public commitment of fidelity and love was now a far more serious sin than wholesale promiscuity that was not considered apostasy. The world of morality had turned up-

---

3. "Policies on Ordinances for Children of a Parent Living in a Same-Gender Relationship." In *Changes to LDS Handbook 1 Document 2 Revised 11-3-15*. The Church of Jesus Christ of Latter-day Saints. 2015. https://www.scribd.com/doc/288685756/Changes-to-LDS-Handbook-1-Document-2-Revised-11-3-15-28003-29.

4. Prince, Gregory A. "The Policy." In *Gay Rights and the Mormon Church*, 257-58. Salt Lake City, Utah: The University of Utah Press, 2019.

side down. This felt like I was meeting a chess master who had already read the board and figured out every move to checkmate. If I married again, claiming marriage equality, I would incur a "no questions asked" excommunication as an apostate. This would force me to witness the damnation of my children's spiritual progress in the Church and their violent unsealing from me through my excommunication. As I built my family in this life, the Church was determined to destroy it in the next. But why now? Marriage equality had existed in countries around the world since 2001, yet it took the Obergefell ruling at the Supreme Court in June 2015—declaring marriage equality the law of the land in the host nation of the Restoration—to incite panic within the Church. Was the Church so afraid of same-sex marriage within the walls of Zion that they were prepared to sacrifice children to keep it out?

 I gathered my children in the living room and talked about what was happening. After I read the exclusion policy to them, my eleven-year-old looked at me in shock and said, "Dad, why do they want to do this to us?" I could only say through tears, "I don't know, son. I just don't know." I realized that my children needed a voice. They needed to be heard. The policy awoke within me the strength and courage to stand and protect my children from harm. I was no longer content living the rest of my life in the shadows. The day after the exclusion policy appeared, I took my sons to a Phoenix Suns game. As I snapped an obligatory dad selfie of us in our seats, I noticed that my ordinarily steady dentist hands were shaking. I sat down, unable to catch a full breath. It was a panic attack. My little family was being hunted.

Love, not the exclusion policy, shattered my Eden—the place I had planned to stay, content to live the rest of my life outside the spotlight with my children as I diligently practiced dentistry among the Saints, a refugee from the faith. The only thing that mattered to me now was that my children needed an advocate, and I would speak as loudly as I could so that it would reach Salt Lake. As I contemplated how to accomplish this, Wendy Montgomery called me out of the blue. Brady McCombs from the Associated Press was looking to interview a gay Latter-day Saint parent about the exclusion policy. Sensitive to my situation, she added that she understood if I wasn't in a place where I wanted to speak publicly. I didn't even pause at her query. I had already decided to stand up for my children.

My interview with Brady hit the AP news wire, appearing from *The New York Times*[5] to the community newspaper on Kauai, where one of my vacationing patients reading on the beach excitedly poked her husband, "That's our dentist! All the way out here in the little local paper. Imagine that!" The AP story led to an invitation to speak with *The Phoenix New Times*[6] and Channel 12 News. In each interview, I stood as a voice for my children and expressed the injustice and harm this policy posed to my family and me in our spiritual home. After my television interview, the reporter shared that the Church had just announced it would be making a statement about the policy the next day. She didn't know what it would entail, but something was coming.

---

5. McCombs, Brady. "Gay Mormons Distressed by New Rules on Same-Sex Relationships." *The New York Times*, November 7, 2015. https://www.nytimes.com/2015/11/08/us/gay-mormons-distressed-by-new-rules-on-same-sex-relationships.html.

6. Hogan, Shanna. "LGBTQ Mormons Lose Faith in Church After Announcement of Anti-Gay Policy." *Phoenix New Times*, November 27, 2015. https://www.phoenixnewtimes.com/news/lgbtq-mormons-lose-faith-in-church-after-announcement-of-anti-gay-policy-7811861.

Sure enough, on Friday the 13th, the Church announced it had modified the exclusion policy. The policy would now only be applied to children in families where the same-sex parent is the primary residence of the children. This clarified nothing in the practical world of divorced parenting. On paper, the policy might affect far fewer children than how it was initially written, but for children from failed mixed-orientation marriages, divorce law does not deal with "primary residences." It deals with parental custody, parental decision-making, parenting time, and which parent claims the child tax deductions. This modification pulled the determination of "primary residence" away from the law and placed it directly into the roulette of local leader—and general authority—interpretation, an especially sticky determination when most mixed-orientation divorces are arranged as joint custody and 50/50 parenting time. Despite this "clarification," the violent spiritual consequences of excommunication in my life and that of my children remained. This threat of eternal separation from God and family through marriage equality loomed large, the ultimate existential threat for queer Latter-day Saints and their family.

Less than a week after my interviews, I received this text at midnight: "Hi Nathan, I don't know if this is still your cell phone or not but just wanted to reach out. I would love to have a chance to visit with you." I will never know if my words reached headquarters in Salt Lake, but they reached my stake president. I felt an immediate pit in my stomach as I read his message. I had just publicly expressed dissent in a church I considered the only true and living church on the face of the Earth. We arranged a time when the kids would be over at their mom's, and at the appointed hour, he arrived alone at my home. We were friends, having served together for many years in the stake. During the process of my divorce, he had been called to be the stake president. He indicated that he knew I had divorced but didn't know why until he caught my interview on the news. As the evening progressed, we reminisced about the old times. I remembered the gentle spirit that he had exhibited in his ministry since the earliest days I had known him.

At the end of our conversation, he asked me how I could retain my testimony if I did not attend my church meetings. I answered that the exclusion policy may have made me a refugee from the faith, but I knew that Christ was present in the margins with me. After Arizona Prop 102 and this new policy, the Church didn't feel safe for me as a Latter-day Saint sexual minority. But I felt a hope of return when the hostilities were resolved. Until then, I stood firmly planted in the hope that Christ would not abandon me in the crossfire happening above my head between the modern church and the LGBTQ civil rights movement.

As my stake president prepared to go, he asked how he could help my spiritual home feel safer. I told him, "I just don't want to feel like I am being hunted." The spirit in the room suddenly changed. He looked me in the eye, hunter to the hunted, and said, "If you ever marry a man, I will excommunicate you." The verdict had been pronounced before the deed in my living room. He continued, "Please don't make me do that to you. It would be easier if you just resigned instead." The irony did not escape me. My son was out on a mission inviting souls into the Church at the very same time my stake president was in my home inviting me out of the Church. I was doing what I could to hold my family together, and the exclusion policy threatened to tear it apart.

That year, our Thanksgiving hike to The Peak of Champions happened twenty-one days after the exclusion policy appeared.

Our emotions and questions seemed too big to contain under the boughs of that palo verde tree growing from a rock. But I had an idea. Instead of a single tree, this moment required a grove. I told my kids that it was time to start thinking about what we would do for their spring break in March. Thinking locally, they started suggesting Arizona destinations. I chimed in, "How would you feel about going to New York?" I now had my boys' complete attention. "We'll spend some time in the city, then drive upstate and spend a few days in Palmyra visiting the church history sites."

Voicing excited surprise, my sons immediately started making a list of things to do: *Wicked* on Broadway, the Statue of Liberty, the Empire State Building, the Museum of Natural History—the list went on and on. Most exciting for me was introducing them to the church history sites for the first time in their lives and seeing the places where the beginnings of the Restoration happened. I anticipated that this would be a time they could contemplate what their faith meant to them amid the new challenges that had just appeared in their spiritual home. I hoped that such a moment would become a touchpoint they could return to throughout their lives. Twice, I experienced revelation and comfort in the Sacred Grove during pivotal moments in my life, and now I desired this for my children.

After three eventful days exploring Manhattan, we were ready to get out of the city. We picked up a rental car, found a Walmart off I-80, and stocked up on snacks for the drive upstate. We got to Palmyra just as the sun was setting and stopped at the temple before checking into the hotel. The last rays of light had cast Moroni in a brilliant golden glow, and the stained-glass windows depicting the Sacred Grove were brilliantly illuminated in gold as if by a pillar of light, contrasted against the evening woods. Parking lot empty, we stood alone as a family next to this temple on fire, directly under the stone inscription, "HOLINESS TO THE LORD, THE HOUSE OF THE LORD."

The following morning, we talked about the Sacred Grove over hotel waffles drenched in maple syrup. "You know," I began, signaling some dad facts coming their way, "Joseph Smith never recorded the exact day he had the First Vision. All we know from his account is that it was a 'beautiful, clear day early in the Spring of 1820'" (Joseph Smith—History 1:14). I reminded them that "early spring" could very well be in March, a time when the Sacred Grove wouldn't have been all leafy and green like we see in church videos. This morning, they would experience the Grove like Joseph did, in hat and coat, trees without leaves, but still a place of solitude and wonder. "And perhaps today, for you," pointing to them as I finished my last bite of waffle, "Answers."

We arrived at the Sacred Grove just as it opened. No one else was there. I was secretly happy that we would have the Grove to ourselves, at least for a while. My kids wanted to walk the Grove alone first and explore the reality of this place, which, up to this point, had only been an abstract idea learned about in Sunday School and seminary. In true dad fashion, I insisted that we first take a photo together by the entrance sign, proud of my boys in their coats, hats, and gloves, ready to take on the reality of their own sacred groves that cold midweek morning in March. "Don't worry about getting lost," I said, "The Sacred Grove has many different trails, and you will often come across a fork in the path as you walk the Grove. Your walk is not about the path but your experience: what you are bringing in and what you hope to bring out. There is no 'one' true path in the Sacred Grove. Follow the way that looks most interesting to you and where you feel prompted to go. When you are ready to return, signs will point you back to me at the entrance."

I sat on a bench as they disappeared into the grove and reflected on this moment. This is where it all began, a sacred spot of beginning for Mormons, the place where a fourteen-year-old boy knelt in prayer, perplexed about religion. Three and a half years earlier, I had come to an autumnal grove alone and very much perplexed. Through that experience, I realized that as the children of God, we not only bring our questions to God, but in turn, God appreciates these questions and answers them in wisdom. The God of the Restoration is an appreciative God. From this example, I strive to be an appreciative parent to my own children. When I returned to the Sacred Grove eighteen months later, I found my supportive community in Affirmation—my personal Waters of Mormon, where I clapped my hands with joy as the desires of my heart were fulfilled. Now at the Grove for a third time, armed with the wisdom from my previous visits, my role was not that of questioner but appreciative parent. I eagerly awaited my children's return—prepared to answer questions and talk about what they experienced. And then we would walk the Grove together, greeting it as a family in the state Joseph encountered it 196 years ago on a beautiful, crisp March day.

Through no fault of their own, my children experienced trauma at the hands of their church because they had a gay Latter-day Saint father. Be it under a palo verde tree, in the Sacred Grove, or in our home, my work as their father was to help them walk out from under trauma and towards their joy. What do we do as a family about trauma? If there is one thing I know with certainty, it is that God is not a God of trauma. God is a God of love (1 John 4:8).

As humans, our wellbeing comprises many parts. These parts (such as physical, mental, emotional, and spiritual health) are not independent; they are connected like a web. A point of trauma in one of these components can affect the entire web. Our web of wellbeing also relies on components that stand outside of ourselves. Humans are social creatures. We know that close relationships and social integration are the highest predictors of longevity, having the most significant influence on our overall health. We are connected to the health of the communities we are a part of. The family is one of the primary social units that healthcare professionals identify as an integral part of our wellbeing.[7]

The exclusion policy was a trauma that cut into the families of the Church, including mine. The Church suddenly held a sense of danger about it in my life. It was an odd, unfamiliar feeling, as if strangers had nestled between me and the walls of my spiritual home, preparing to enucleate me from God, family, and the church I loved. My children also felt danger from the exclusion policy, a threat to their eternal connection to their father. Despite their strong testimonies of the gospel, they were starting to look at the Church differently. Their questions about the status of our family in God's eyes were beginning to raise trust issues in some of the Church's truth claims. Determined to meet this acute trauma head-on, I created and maintained healthy boundaries between my family and those who sought to invalidate it through rejecting language and exclusionary behavior. I established a house where my children could grow, explore, question, and build their own spiritual wellbeing in a way that felt safe and healthy for them—in a way they felt supported and not upbraided.

I knew three things for certain: our family was ordained of God, God is not a God of trauma, and the exclusion policy was

---

7. White, Sarah C., and Shreya Jha. 2023. "Exploring the Relational in Relational Wellbeing" *Social Sciences* 12, no. 11: 600. https://doi.org/10.3390/socsci12110600

trauma for my family. In these three truths, we could separate God from the exclusion policy and protect ourselves as a family from all things exclusion policy while wholly embracing God. We could connect our family to God without trauma being an intermediary. Trauma no more defined our family than the exclusion policy did. At this moment, my mission was to build my house to be a well of continual support and love that would be a positive flow throughout the web of our individual wellbeing. Ours would be a house impervious to traumas and exclusions that attempted to separate us from one another and the love of God.

CHAPTER 8

Confused at the Grace That So Fully He Proffers Me

> But all is not lost. The grace of God is our great and everlasting hope.
>
> Dieter F. Uchtdorf
April 5, 2015

Coming out is always a process. As I sat with my family through change and loss, I became more comfortable with who I was. I began to look beyond this inner circle for those to invite into my life. Amid the various social groups I needed to come out to, I always felt that I needed to reach out to my high school best friend. I had hurt him, but until now, I didn't have the emotional tools or resources to overcome this hurt through a conversation.

We had previously reconnected through Facebook in my earliest days of coming out to myself. My account was a superficial skimming of a curated life because I was not at all comfortable being absolutely public with my sexuality. I saw that since high school, he had lived his life authentically. Three days after my divorce was final, I picked up the phone and came out to him. We finally finished the conversation we had begun in his car in the high school parking lot thirty years earlier. I apologized for how I had treated him and for the hurt I knew I had caused. Now, I had the maturity and the words to articulate how wrong I was to treat him so poorly. When he expressed his hurt and confusion as a teen over my actions, it stung deep. I told him I had always admired that he chose the brave path towards authenticity when we were younger, and now in my life, I was just at the beginning. He reflected that we had both come to learn much about ourselves. High school was a hard time for both of us but in different ways. After our conversation, he sent an email, showing incredible grace: "I am proud of you. I know you still have challenges facing you with the family, and I hope they all learn to accept and love you for who you are and have always been—a loyal, loving father and son."

This was the first moment I experienced unexpected grace from another in my long process toward wholeness, and I felt incredibly unworthy of being extended such a gift. I had spent years believing that shame and condemnation were the only fruits of sharing my sexuality with others. On the contrary, authenticity was allowing grace to fill my life. Until that moment, I did not understand that grace was even possible for me or how healing such a gift would be.

It was easy to feel lost in the sea of bulk email recipients in my son's missionary correspondence from England. This feeling was magnified by how we left our relationship when he went on his mission. I wrote him weekly, but receiving no reply to my letters, I would end up scanning his "Dear Family and Friends" emails for any sign of connection. This was me planespotting barren skies with no sign of an aircraft approaching. Was it a mistake that I had not pressed for a resolution before his mission? Nagging thoughts that this might become a permanent relationship loss began to take over. In the lingering stasis of our unresolved concerns, my hands began to hang down and my knees to be feeble. My friends in Affirmation sat with me through this time as my supportive community, helping me work through the trauma of this situation. It was incredibly protective for my soul to not have to experience this alone in isolation. As the months turned into years, a personal email came just weeks before my son was to return home:

Dad,

My mission is coming to an end. I wanted to thank you for the support you have given me while I've been out.

I want to put anything that has been between us behind. I also want to say I'm sorry. I haven't treated you as I ought. I wrote you a very unkind letter before my mission, and I have kept you at a distance since then. I want you to know that I do love you, and I care about you. I know you do love me, as you do all the kids in our family, and that you would only want the best for us.

I want anything that has been done to stay in the past because I want to have a good relationship with you. I would love to see you at my homecoming.

Elder Kitchen

I could not stop the tears as I read and re-read his short and tender letter. Like a pilot calling the control tower, my son was coming in for a landing. It was a moment of grace like I had never felt before. It was as stunning as watching the majesty of a

British Airways Dreamliner approaching the runway after hours of planespotting the garden variety of domestic flights. Three months after returning home from his mission, my son climbed The Peak of Champions with his brothers and me for our annual Thanksgiving morning hike. After years of estrangement, this was his first time making this journey to see the impressive palo verde tree growing from a rock. In my heart was the joy of Lehi, to have all my sons with me under these boughs of love.

Grace is the gift of deep healing of the soul. Supportive communities, especially supportive families, are protective for LGBTQ people.[1] Grace and supportive communities have a symbiotic relationship. Coming to rest within my community of family and friends centered my soul away from trauma. My friends in Affirmation encouraged me to hold open hope, providing unconditional support so that I could locate my soul in a space where it could acknowledge and receive grace. Grace may be an unearned gift, but trauma can roil the soul, making it unreceptive to grace. In such a state, grace can go unrecognized and unappreciated.

The third week of June in 2017 was record-setting hot in Arizona. Pictures of street signs melting and eggs frying on the sidewalk flooded the Internet. This also happened to be the week my daughter was getting married. The Monday before her wedding, she hosted a barbeque for all the family who had come into town for the event. I was very aware that "all family" included my former in-laws and my former wife's sisters, all of

---

1. Ryan, Caitlyn, and Robert A. Rees. *Supportive Families, Healthy Children: Helping Latter-day Saint Families With Lesbian, Gay, Bisexual & Transgender Children*. Family Acceptance Project. Marian Wright Edelman Institute, San Francisco State University, San Francisco, CA. 2012.

whom had held significant resentment towards me after I came out. Except for a series of angry texts one of the sisters sent to me after I had spoken publicly about the exclusion policy, I had not spoken with them or been in the same room with all of them since the divorce.

In the hustle and bustle of picking up my parents and sister from the airport, I inadvertently left my car in the sunny driveway during the hottest part of the day. My family graciously endured the drive to the barbeque in this mobile oven. When we arrived, I noticed my former father-in-law sitting on the bench on the front porch of the house. Outside. On the porch. In 112 degrees. As we filed by him, fleeing the heat for the air-conditioned indoors, he motioned to me and said, "I'd like to talk to you." I felt an immediate rush of anxiety as I made a U-turn at the door and walked towards him. It was not lost on me that here I was, a father wanting happiness and security for my daughter at the beginning of her marriage, now sitting down with another father who had witnessed his own daughter's loss and sorrow at the end of hers.

As I sat next to him, he began to recount how he felt during my coming out, the separation, and divorce: "I admit that I had some very hard feelings towards you when you broke your family." That one sentence stung me to the core. "You broke your family" is the most common censure levied against a gay divorced Mormon man instructed in his youth to marry a woman—piercing judgment that you were not strong enough spiritually—deficient in some manner. I felt the familiar walls start to rise around me that I had built over the past seven years to protect myself from personal attacks and judgment, and had only recently begun to dismantle. Then, inexplicably, they stopped rising. My mind focused on the words of Pahoran to Moroni, "You have censured me, but it mattereth not; I am not angry, but do rejoice in the greatness of your heart" (Alma 61:9).

It no longer mattered to me that his narrative was harsh. It was his truth, and he was a grieving father who loved his daughter with all his heart. Despite his censure, I could appreciate his burden because I understood a father's love for his daughter. Instead of a wall that hot Arizona night, a bridge was extended as my soul spoke to this moment with empathy: "I do not joy in your great afflictions, yea, it grieves my soul" (Alma 61:2). We sat in silence for what seemed an eternity. Then, with his burden noticeably lifted from his shoulders, he turned directly towards me on that bench in the heat of the Arizona evening and said, "Nathan, I want you to know that I forgive you. I unconditionally forgive you." He grasped my hand and held it gently. The time to protest his censure was no more, forever, no more. The only appropriate words to offer were a humble and sincere "Thank you." It was a moment of unexpected grace.

It was also a moment of realization. No matter how closely we observe, we can never truly know another person's narrative. Our lenses and judgment will always color our perceptions of their journey. No matter how selfless we become, we will write ourselves into the experiences, intentions, and choices of others. No amount of work, observation, or explanation will bridge our understanding to their experiences. No matter how close we get to one another, there will always be a chasm. And it is there, at the edge of our chasms, that grace makes the connection. Grace does not change the other person. Grace does not fill in the gaps. Through grace, we overcome ourselves and discover within it, a mystery—indescribable, inexplicable connection.

Through his atonement, Christ took upon himself every mortal experience of the children of God so that "his bowels may be filled with mercy, according to the flesh, that he may know according to the flesh how to succor his people" (Alma 7:12). Because of this, only Christ can fully understand our journey and our hearts. Being human, we fall very short of such godly understanding towards others. But it is grace for one another that connects us despite our shortcomings. Recognizing this human shortcoming, Christ reminds us, "I, the Lord, will forgive whom I will forgive, but of you it is required to forgive all men" (Doctrine and Covenants 64:10). So, there we sat, his hand in mine, two fathers who might never understand the other's narrative in mortality, basking in forgiveness in 112 degrees. As I reflect on this moment, as well as the many other instances where grace was present in my life, afforded by others at unexpected times and in unexpected ways, I am left only to be amazed at such a gift and marvel at the lessons of such care. When grace appears in our lives, gratitude is all we can adequately give in such a moment of connection.

As I entered 2017, two years into the exclusion policy, I realized I was stuck in my forward movement in life. I was experiencing the haunting absence of a companion. But I was also still experiencing the vehement resolve of my seventeen-year-old self at the end of Parley Street, where I would not let anything or anyone into my life that might endanger my return to live with God and my family again in the eternities. Activating the exclusion policy by finding love and marrying again would incur the wrath of God, violently stripping me of hope and my children of a father for the eternities.

The Church had now become the gatekeeper of love for queer Latter-day Saints. It declared my love for the gospel of Jesus Christ apostasy if I declared my love for another in a "same-orientation" marriage. As I yearned for remarriage, the Church stood between the love of my children and the love of a spouse—forcing me to choose. If I married again, I would automatically be excommunicated as an apostate, which would unseal my children from me. The chess master was attempting to hold me in a cruel theological checkmate, utilizing my absolute love for my children to control my behavior and choices in love for another so I would not lose them. It was dictating the terms of the second great commandment. I was being managed by a policy not meant to support me or my family but to support the dominant narrative. As I churned through this predicament, I pulled the lounger out to the back patio to enjoy some January Phoenix sunshine and let my mind wander. I recalled the moments when grace had appeared in my life. Enveloped in gratitude at the grace others had so fully proffered me, I realized that grace flows into our life from multiple springs. The problem I was facing now was not the exclusion policy. The problem was that I had shut my life off from two sources of grace, preventing it from cascading freely into my soul: grace towards myself and the grace of God.

When it came to grace, I was a true blue, through and through, all you can do Mormon. I grew up in a generation in the Church taught from The Book of Mormon that I was saved by grace only *after* I did everything that I could possibly do to qualify to be saved (2 Nephi 25:23). Therefore, from the moment I walked out of my bishop's office as a queer teen, milestones, not Christ, became my protector and savior. For years I had been doing all that I could do, qualifying myself in a transactional life of accumulating straightness to purchase exaltation. I was confused at the grace that so fully God proffered me. The exclusion policy was just another reminder of the extraordinary qualifiers within my spiritual home that queer people must achieve to earn acceptability to God and belonging within the Church. But was God ruled by the exclusion policy?

This much I knew about the nature of grace: It is not tethered to policy, dominant narrative, what we do, or even the law. I realized that the presence of grace would not remove the exclusion policy, nor would it stop the execution of its violent actions upon me and my family, for that is not its purpose—I would need to be brave when those things came for me. Instead, grace would be my healing companion in life's travels—that giver of hope that connects me to God and acknowledges the dignity of my queer soul in the face of difficult and consequential decisions as I navigate to joy. Hope is part of Paul's great triad of things that last forever: Faith, hope, and love (1 Corinthians 13:13 NIV). The continually changing dominant narratives and policies about queer people built from prejudice and misunderstandings actively attempt to kill our hope, but from grace springs hope eternal. It was time to have the faith to proffer grace towards myself as I made decisions that were safe and healthy for me, especially those that, on their face, contradicted dominant narratives and policies. I realized that my stuckness was an absence of hope where I had been denying God's grace within my life. And there, in the warmth of a January sun, the voice of God: *Give yourself grace so you can finally accept mine.*

As a queer Latter-day Saint, you can experience the abundant blessing of God in your life right now, not at some distant time, and not dependent on policy, heteronormative or gender-normative standards, hierarchical approval, who your local leaders are, whom you love, whom you marry, your relationship with the closet, or if you transition. As a queer child of God, do not fear that you will miss out when you make the best decisions for your health and happiness—even if it appears to contradict the Church's current dominant narrative about you. Doing your best to follow where the Spirit leads you by personal revelation is your healthiest and happiest outcome, even when authoritative voices loudly tell you otherwise. Keep yourself open to grace, for hope grows from grace.

Today, we have come to better understand what The Book of Mormon is teaching us about grace. The phrase "after all we can do" that Joseph Smith used in his translation was in wide circulation in the early nineteenth century. Whenever it was utilized in the context of grace, it "was always used to mean 'despite all we can do'."[2] As a nineteenth-century translator, Joseph knew exactly how to render what Nephi was teaching about grace. Grace truly is a gift freely given. You do not earn it through any merit of your own. Grace is not transactional. **You** are sufficient to own, to redeem, and to justify, *despite* all you can do. When you face the ugliness of the dominant narrative, all is not lost! Step back and identify the moments of grace in your life. Remember to proffer yourself abundant grace as a queer child of God. Know that when our heavenly parents see you, a beloved queer child of God, appear from the barrenness of the skies, coming in to land into their outstretched arms that have always been open for you, the grace of Christ in the family of God extends through both your salvation and your exaltation—and does so in ways that the traditional "after all you can do" crowd on earth denies and cannot explain through the prejudice of the human lens. Christ will always say, "Let the queer children come unto me; forbid them not." Be confused no longer by the grace that so fully God proffers you.

---

2. McClellan, Daniel O. "2 Nephi 25:23 in Literary and Rhetorical Context." *Journal of Book of Mormon Studies* 29 (April 1, 2020): 1-19. https://hcommons.org/deposits/item/hc:43493.

THE ARROW OF TIME

Don't drive your mirrors,
Look ahead, not behind.
You can't change your history,
So make it.

Time flies as an arrow,
And forward it flows—
Death fixed at the feather,
Life springs from its point.

You are so meant to fly,
To become, to choose.
And that's the point, to be at the point
And not drive your mirrors—

Live forward.

CHAPTER 9

A Refuge to Share

> I testify that as each of you reach out to help others, you will find your true selves and bless greatly the world in which you live.
>
> Teachings of Presidents of the Church: Gordon B. Hinckley

"How would you like to help me create a father's support group in Affirmation?" Troy Mitchell caught up with me in the hall after the mixed-orientation marriage panel discussion at Affirmation's 2015 International Conference and asked me this intriguing question. Earlier, we sat together at the panelist table, tasked with representing the support of children during and after divorce from a mixed-orientation marriage. We had been ignored for the better part of the hour. I innately understood why, having been in a mixed-orientation marriage for twenty-three years. Just a year earlier, a published study indicated that almost 70% of mixed-orientation marriages fail.[1] Against these odds, understandably the overwhelming demand for support in mixed-orientation marriage spaces requires an almost singular focus on the survivability of the marriage itself. No one wants to talk about issues surrounding dissolution until it is happening to them. After spending six months in these mixed-orientation marriage spaces in Affirmation, sitting on this panel helped me realize that a critical support need was not being met: The queer parent.

For almost twenty years, a strong and vibrant father's group called Gamofites—a portmanteau of "gay Mormon fathers" and The Book of Mormon suffix "ites"—existed within the communities of Affirmation.[2] By 2012, Gamofites was no longer meeting. Troy shared how that group had been lifesaving for him when he came out as a gay father, and he felt it was time to bring this kind of support back into Affirmation for the next generation. Having worked alone through my own coming out and the subsequent life changes—only finding Affirmation afterward, I told Troy I was in. I never wanted a queer father to have to feel that he was alone and isolated at any point along his journey. To stand on the shoulders of the giants who built Gamofites and continue the tradition of supporting gay Mormon fathers with love and understanding offered me an opportunity to join the great generational process of queer Mormons supporting queer Mormons. I welcomed this opportunity to give back and share my time and talents to make the road easier for those who follow.

---

1. Dehlin, John P., Renee V. Galliher, William S. Bradshaw, and Katherine A. Crowell. 2014. "Psychosocial Correlates of Religious Approaches to Same-Sex Attraction: A Mormon Perspective." *Journal of Gay & Lesbian Mental Health* 18 (3): 284-311. doi:10.1080/19359705.2014.912970.

2. Burroway, Jim. "Today In History, 1977: Gay Mormon Group Affirmation Founded." Box Turtle Bulletin, June 11, 2016. http://www.boxturtlebulletin.com/2016/06/11/73017.

I wrote a letter to Affirmation's board requesting formal recognition of a support group I dubbed "Fathers in Affirmation." The board was responsive, and as we discussed the support needs of queer parents, it became readily apparent that queer fathers and queer mothers confront completely different social expectations and pressures within a patriarchal system such as the Church. This creates unique issues that warrant specific support communities. At this moment, Fathers in Affirmation and Mothers in Affirmation were born.

Fathers in Affirmation went live on November 4th, one day before the exclusion policy was leaked online. I do not doubt the hand of God in the timing of its formation. The immediate aftermath of the exclusion policy was rough on the fathers in Affirmation. I was unprepared for the sheer volume of community grief and anger the policy elicited. It plunged a dagger directly into the hope that many gay Latter-day Saint fathers held for their families, especially their children. One evening, I spent hours with a father considering suicide, just helping him to stay alive until we could find professional help. I choked back tears as I assured him, "There is always hope. You may not see it right now, but there is hope. I am here as an example that it does get better. I am here to remind you that you are surrounded by people who love and care about you." Later, I was flummoxed when another father in the group shared that his former wife had subpoenaed him back to court to begin an expensive fight to rearrange their divorce terms so she could be considered "primary residence" so their children could qualify for baptism. The exclusion policy was not just a theological exercise; it was costing gay fathers in the Church real time and money.

Blanket charges of apostasy and coming after our children was a level of harassment from the Church that gay fathers new to their authenticity had not encountered before. But this is the genius of assembling a group like Fathers in Affirmation. I was not just helping fathers from my own "recently out" generation. Fathers in Affirmation was like having a library of experience and wisdom at our fingertips. It was a multi-generational community of fathers populated with our elders who had been the bellwethers of their own generation, navigating complicated situations. They met this new generation of fathers with compassion and advice. They had earned their wisdom and were now passing it down through the generations. It was lifesaving, and I saw firsthand that Fathers in Affirmation was a critical component in harm reduction within the population of queer fathers in the Church. As the months under the exclusion policy rolled along, same-sex legally married Latter-day Saints were being rounded up by their stake presidents and summarily excommunicated. It is frightening when you are targeted with such spiritual violence. One of the significant benefits Fathers in Affirmation provides is support for gay fathers being pursued by their stake presidents for claiming marriage equality and marrying the love of their life. The tenacity of a stake president in this pursuit reminds me of the tenacity of a US Marshal pursuing our early polygamist apostles and prophets.

In 1887, apostle Wilford Woodruff, who had gone into hiding because of his polygamous marriages, wrote in his journal: "Marshal Armstrong arrived in the evening in St. George."[3] Feeling the pressure of federal law enforcement, he took his bed and luggage and fled to Atkinville, five miles west of St. George, to stop a while. There, Woodruff felt great support from the Atkin family. They offered him hospitality, dependability, and loyalty. Joseph Walker remarked, "It was no small honor, even as it was a heavy responsibility, to have such an eminent man's

---

3. Woodbury, Grace Atkin, and Agnus Munn Woodbury. "Wilford Woodruff on the Underground." In *The Story of Atkinville: A One-Family Village*, 26. 1957. Washington County Historical Society. https://wchsutah.org/documents/woodbury-atkinville-book2.pdf.

safety and welfare entrusted to this family."[4] Today, I feel much like Joseph Walker. It is an absolute honor to support the queer fathers in the Church, each one eminent and brave as they wend their way in this life with their children towards safety and joy.

In January 2018, the Board of Affirmation gathered from around the world in Mesa, Arizona to conduct a strategic planning session. I was invited to participate as a representative of Fathers in Affirmation and provide input to help direct Affirmation's work over the next few years. Rene Frost Singleton, the leader of Mothers in Affirmation, was also in attendance. We both represented unique populations within the LGBTQ Mormon community, and I was grateful that our voices were being heard. This was not my first invitation to participate in such an event. Two years earlier, I attended Affirmation's strategic planning session at Loyola Marymount University in Los Angeles. I noted that the mood and discussions among Affirmation's senior leadership experiencing a chronic exclusion policy in Mesa were completely different from what I witnessed at Loyola when the exclusion policy was hot off the press. I concluded that this was another example of Affirmation doing what it has always done: adapt to the ebbs and flows of dominant narratives and policies and center on the queer soul. This was but another chapter in the story of Affirmation's relationship with the modern church—and this chapter had its beginnings in California Prop 8.

Soon after becoming church president, Thomas S. Monson received from Affirmation a letter in February 2008 asking for dialogue. Affirmation leaders acknowledged that while many areas of hurt and disagreement separated Affirmation and the Church, many more areas existed where they could find agree-

---

4. Woodbury, *The Story of Atkinville: A One-Family Village*, 26.

ment.[5] The Director of LDS Family Services, Fred M. Riley, wrote back, indicating President Monson had directed him to meet with them. A meeting date was set for early August. The political backdrop at this time was California Prop 8, which had just received enough signatures in June to be included on the November ballot. In July, Director Riley sent Affirmation a letter indefinitely postponing their meeting. Disappointed, leaders in Affirmation asked to meet with a general authority instead, which was denied.[6] Not wanting to wait until the following year to meet with the Church, Affirmation held a press conference and brought their talking points to the public.

It was a stunning press conference. This was a time in history when the dialogue in the Church and Affirmation primarily focused on gays and lesbians, with the word "gay" encompassing today's gay and lesbian identifiers. From this lens, the senior leaders of Affirmation expressed well-prepared talking points, every single one still shockingly, if not unsurprisingly, valid today: safety in the Church for gay members, the reality of suicide in the gay population of the Church, the need to provide better training for local leaders, the need to hear more affirming words in General Conference, the recognition of the significance of committed long-term relationships for gay people, and the need for Church leaders to leave the door open to doctrinal change through revelation.[7] A few hours after Affirmation's press conference, the Church issued a terse press release in response,

---

5. Associated Press. "Gay Mormons Request Meeting with Pres. Monson." *Deseret News*. February 10, 2008. https://www.deseret.com/2008/2/10/20069740/gay-mormons-request-meeting-with-pres-monson/.

6. Associated Press. "LDS Agency Delays Meeting with Affirmation." *Deseret News*. July 27, 2008. https://www.deseret.com/2008/7/27/20266109/lds-agency-delays-meeting-with-affirmation/.

7. Penrod, Sam, and Mary Richards. "Affirmation Discussing Gay Issues without LDS Church." KSL.com, August 11, 2008. https://www.ksl.com/article/3987016/affirmation-discussing-gay-issues-without-lds-church.

scolding Affirmation for going public: "The issues surrounding same-gender attraction deserve careful attention, not public posturing. It appears from Affirmation's actions today that it has opted for a public rather than a private exchange."[8] In this very public tussle, the appetite for dialogue waned between the Church and Affirmation, each going its own way—Affirmation to its lifesaving mission of community building, and the Church off to face an intense backlash over its involvement and money spent in the California Prop 8 campaign.

In the aftermath of Prop 8, the Church lamented by press release that it felt it was "being singled out for speaking up as part of its democratic right in a free election."[9] Indeed, it faced a huge public image problem due to its high-profile involvement. The Church was positive that it did not have a doctrinal problem concerning LGBTQ people, only a messaging problem. To rectify this, it began to hone its messaging toward the outside LGBTQ community as well as toward its own LGBTQ population. Externally, this messaging needed to forge a friendly working relationship with the LGBTQ community, calling all sides to sit down together in good faith at a common negotiating table to hammer out constructive politics in the civil arena. Over time, this resulted in the 2009 Salt Lake City non-discrimination

---

8. The Church of Jesus Christ of Latter-day Saints. "Church Issues Response to Affirmation." newsroom.churchofjesuschrist.org, August 11, 2008. https://newsroom.churchofjesuschrist.org/article/church-issues-response-to-affirmation.

9. The Church of Jesus Christ of Latter-day Saints. "Church Issues Statement on Proposition 8 Protest." newsroom.churchofjesuschrist.org, November 7, 2008. https://newsroom.churchofjesuschrist.org/article/church-issues-statement-on-proposition-8-protest.

ordinance[10] and its crown jewel, the 2015 Utah Compromise.[11] Internally, this new messaging needed to create a bubble of belonging within a doctrine hostile to queer exaltation that could be a time-out space. This bubble would be a place of respect, recognition, understanding, and compassion for LGBTQ Latter-day Saints, giving members of the Church permission to love their LGBTQ children and fellow ward members within a narrow tolerance that would not counter the dominant narrative. Church Public Affairs began working behind the scenes to create this internal bubble inviting "gay and lesbian Mormons to stay in the church."[12] In December 2012, the Church rolled out a new website: mormonsandgays.org.[13] The product of public relations savvy, it included video messages from gay Latter-day Saints and pages of encouraging words—more encouraging than we had ever heard before—from church leaders.

While the Church was undergoing its multi-year effort to repair its public image, Affirmation's work of community building continued in earnest. A year before the Church unveiled its new Mormons and Gays website, Affirmation president David Melson stood and welcomed 110 souls to Cleveland, Ohio in

---

10. The Church of Jesus Christ of Latter-day Saints. "Church Supports Salt Lake City Nondiscrimination Ordinance." newsroom.churchofjesuschrist.org, November 10, 2009. https://newsroom.churchofjesuschrist.org/article/church-supports-nondiscrimination-ordinances.

11. Goodstein, Laurie. "Utah Passes Antidiscrimination Bill Backed by Mormon Leaders." The New York Times, March 12, 2015. https://www.nytimes.com/2015/03/12/us/politics/utah-passes-antidiscrimination-bill-backed-by-mormon-leaders.html.

12. McCombs, Brady, and Rachel Zoll. "Mormon Church Wants More Compassion for Gays." The Seattle Times, December 7, 2012. https://www.seattletimes.com/nation-world/mormon-church-wants-more-compassion-for-gays/.

13. Farrington, Dana. "Mormon Church Launches Website on 'Same-Sex Attraction.'" NPR, December 6, 2012. https://www.npr.org/sections/thetwo-way/2012/12/06/166687164/mormon-church-launches-website-on-same-sex-attraction.

2011 for an Affirmation conference.[14] It would be a remarkable Waters of Mormon experience for all who attended. On Sunday, Joanna Brooks spoke to Affirmation during the concluding session of the conference in the Kirtland temple. Later, she recounted that many Affirmation members were overwhelmed to be welcomed as gay Mormons into a sacred Mormon space, observing that "tears flowed freely when the Affirmation choir of gay and lesbian Mormons sang the stirring Mormon classic 'The Spirit of God Like a Fire is Burning.'" Legend has it that as this hymn was sung at the temple's dedication 175 years earlier, bystanders witnessed the temple bathed in celestial fire. Enveloped in both spirit and community, a young gay man from England named Liam stood, pointing west towards Salt Lake City, and through tears exclaimed, "Don't you think, if they could just see us—if they could just see us here, don't you think they would change their minds?"[15] This was the day the conference attendees clapped their hands in joy in the spirit of Liam's words and exclaimed in one voice, "This is the desire of our hearts." The Kirtland Temple experience awakened within Affirmation a yearning for belonging. In a high holy site in Mormonism, the first temple of the Restoration, this band in Affirmation not only asserted that they wanted to belong, but that "we *do* belong, and we belong in our authenticity." This movement happened independently, with no knowledge of the Church's internal movements to create a bubble of belonging for gay and lesbian Mormons.

---

14. Kent, James, and Hugo Salinas. "2011 Conference Report." Affirmation, October 3, 2021. https://affirmation.org/conference-archives/2011-conference-report/.

15. Brooks, Joanna. "LGBT Mormons Ask in Historic Temple: 'If They Could Just See Us, Don't You Think They Would Change Their Minds?'" Religion Dispatches, September 23, 2011. https://religiondispatches.org/lgbt-mormons-ask-in-historic-temple-if-they-could-just-see-us-dont-you-think-they-would-change-their-minds/.

When Randall Thacker took office as Affirmation's new president in 2013, these two forces coalesced "like a fire is burning." Randall's first message was the hope that filled this new bubble that the Church had created: "We are building a community where we don't have to choose between being Mormon or gay. We can be fully affirmed as both."[16] This was the optimistic message that resonated throughout Affirmation over the next few years. In its messaging, Affirmation was creating the terms of belonging from a queer-centric position within the permissions of this new bubble. Suddenly, Affirmation was no longer a drab social services matter as it was in 2008. In this "Mormons and Gays" era, Affirmation was now a valuable public affairs matter, so that in 2008, Affirmation was assigned a dedicated public affairs liaison to meet regularly and discuss LGBTQ issues within the Church.

The post-Prop 8 bubble the modern church had constructed was quickly filling with LGBTQ Latter-day Saints. This demonstrates that LGBTQ Latter-day Saints do want to belong and is proof positive that if you prepare a place—any place with even a hint of welcome—LGBTQ Latter-day Saints will gather. For the first time in the history of the modern church, LGBTQ Latter-day Saints felt wanted because they were hearing that they were wanted. Unfortunately, the long-term outlook about what happens after this "wanting" and "gathering" stage was never addressed. No one was talking about the elephant in the room: None of the Church's teachings or doctrines had changed one whit since the Prop 8 days. Flying in the face of "bubble belonging," the harsh theology that excluded queer people in exaltation, marriage, and family was still fully operational. The act of avoiding the realities of theology created a vacuum that

---

16. Thacker, Randall. "Happy New Year Affirmation Friends!" Affirmation, January 9, 2013. https://affirmation.org/happy-new-year-affirmation-friends/.

many LGBTQ Latter-day Saints filled with their hopes that once they were in the bubble and everyone got to know them, changes in the Church and their acceptance into the plan of salvation would surely follow.

Full steam ahead, I joined Affirmation here, at the crest of this optimism. It was infectious and on full display at the 2015 September International Conference where even Heidi and Emily came away from that experience on cloud nine, lifted by the feeling that something significant was just around the corner for LGBTQ Latter-day Saints. Forty-six days later, the exclusion policy dropped a bomb into the middle of it all, obliterating the tender words of Liam in the Kirtland temple, "Don't you think, if they could just see us—if they could just see us here, don't you think they would change their minds?" No amount of "seeing" had protected the LGBTQ Latter-day Saints.

Hours after the exclusion policy leaked, Affirmation was on the phone to Church Public Affairs. They seemed surprised that Affirmation even wanted to talk with them. Public Affairs had been caught unawares by the appearance of the exclusion policy.[17] It was in full damage control mode, preparing press releases while the managing director, Michael Otterson, was putting together a Q&A public relations video where he would interview Elder D. Todd Christofferson about the exclusion policy, formally introducing it to the members of the Church and the world.[18] In the immediate aftermath of the policy, Affirmation

---

17. Prince, Gregory A. "The Policy." In *Gay Rights and the Mormon Church*, 260. Salt Lake City, Utah: The University of Utah Press, 2019.

18. The Church of Jesus Christ of Latter-day Saints. "Elder Christofferson: Context on Handbook Changes Affecting Same-Sex Marriages." newsroom.churchofjesuschrist.org, November 6, 2015. https://

pressed forward with Public Affairs, communicating common ground and common goals. Regardless of the dialogue and the relationship built over the years, the exclusion policy had broken the optimism of the post-Prop 8 bubble, and neither Public Affairs nor Affirmation could put it back together again.

Notably, the exclusion policy caused a fissure in Affirmation's once united institutional voice. In the absence of a united front of optimism and facing the terror of full-on exclusion, the messaging was fractured. Affirmation's senior vice president, Todd Richardson, told the *Phoenix New Times* that any attempt the Church made to change its tone about the LGBTQ population had been thrown out the window. "The official church now seems hostile to me. When before it seemed there were glimpses of hope when it came to acceptance."[19]

Then, in December, John Gustav-Wrathall, board member and president-elect, seemed to button down the public-facing direction of the organization when he opined about the exclusion policy in a very different way to the *Deseret News*, "I disagree with the idea this is a retrenchment. I honestly believe the church has moved forward in terms of its engagement with us as human beings, as members of families, as members of wards. There is a deeper, more profound understanding. There has been more explicit talk from the highest levels of the Church about love and about acceptance and about listening. My perception is that members of the Church are taking that seriously."[20] As a gay Latter-day Saint father taking the exclusion policy serious-

---

newsroom.churchofjesuschrist.org/article/handbook-changes-same-sex-marriages-elder-christofferson.

19. Hogan, Shanna. "LGBTQ Mormons Lose Faith in Church After Announcement of Anti-Gay Policy." *Phoenix New Times*, November 27, 2015. https://www.phoenixnewtimes.com/news/lgbtq-mormons-lose-faith-in-church-after-announcement-of-anti-gay-policy-7811861.

20. Walch, Tad. "Elder Christofferson Explains Updated LDS Church Policies on Same-Sex Marriage and Children." *Deseret News*, November 6,

ly, I did not feel that it was a movement forward toward positive engagement, more less "love and acceptance." Unlike the LGBTQ-centered optimistic messaging of Affirmation's past, these new words from an Affirmation senior leader, soon to be its president, had an optimism, but an optimism that seemed to face the Church, not LGBTQ people. So many people in Affirmation were hurting from the engagement of the exclusion policy and they were feeling ignored.

At Affirmation's Southern California Conference at Loyola Marymount in January 2016, the program and speakers were well prepared, but I noted that it was missing that spark of queer optimism and pride that had been a part of Affirmation's trademark for the past few years. During the Saturday session, most attendees chose to sit in the commons area and talk with each other rather than go to the workshops. We needed the time and space to share and receive our stories of exclusion. We needed community. Even as some tried to find hope in the face of the exclusion policy, nothing could lift the melancholy. Several Affirmation senior leaders questioned themselves, wondering out loud if maybe they had been wrong to say that you could be gay and Mormon, too.

The policy was mentioned tangentially when I attended Affirmation's strategic planning session the day before the Southern California conference. The consensus communicated by the new executive committee was that Affirmation's relationship with the Church was as strong as ever. Affirmation's focus needed to strengthen that relationship while strengthening LGBTQ Latter-day Saints to endure the new realities of exclusion within their spiritual home. No one was talking openly about the long-term effects the exclusion policy would have on LGBTQ

2015. https://www.deseret.com/2015/11/6/20576211/elder-christofferson-explains-updated-lds-church-policies-on-same-sex-marriage-and-children/.

Latter-day Saints, especially those with children. It seemed to me that a chronic exclusion policy presented a danger of fracturing our beloved community of LGBTQ Latter-day Saints and allies along "faithfulness" and church loyalty lines judged by how you openly talked about the exclusion policy. I feared that if we didn't allow grace for one another's experiences, and if we let the exclusion policy divide us, the fracture would be hard to mend.

One PowerPoint slide in the strategic planning session summed up this entire affair: "Even if the policy doesn't go away, in the long run it won't matter if it means that we have enhanced opportunities to engage with the Church and foster an enhanced dialogue." I sat there stunned. It absolutely mattered if the exclusion policy never went away. Were we sacrificing queer people for dialogue? People were being harmed right now, this instant. I wrote in the margins of my notebook, "Do we really know what just hit us?"

For twelve months, the shattered optimistic messaging of a "pre-exclusion policy" Affirmation—you can be gay and Mormon too, you don't have to choose—lay in pieces amid the rubble of the exclusion policy wreckage. Amid it all, a hand had been quietly sweeping up the shards of Affirmation's once powerful mantra. On October 26th, 2016, almost a year into the exclusion policy, the Church replaced its four-year-old Mormons and Gays website with a new site and an updated URL with one significant tweak: mormonsandgays.org had become mormonandgay.org.[21]

Mormon *and* gay.

---

21. The Church of Jesus Christ of Latter-day Saints. "Mormonandgay.Lds.Org Provides Ministerial Materials for Members and Families." newsroom.churchofjesuschrist.org, October 25, 2016. https://newsroom.churchofjesuschrist.org/article/official-update-mormon-and-gay-website.

CNN reported, "Mormon and gay: Church says you can be both."[22] *The Washington Post* wrote, "Mormon and Gay? The church's new message is that you can be both."[23] It was Affirmation's message, but it wasn't the message of Affirmation. The modern church had asserted its dominance to become the sole gatekeeper of queer belonging. The ultimate messaging takeover had happened.

---

22. Jackson, Lauren. "Mormon and Gay: Church Says You Can Be Both." CNN, October 26, 2016. https://www.cnn.com/2016/10/25/living/mormon-gay-website.

23. Zauzmer, Julie. "'Mormon and Gay'? The Church's New Message Is That You Can Be Both." *The Washington Post*, October 25, 2016. https://www.washingtonpost.com/news/acts-of-faith/wp/2016/10/25/mormon-and-gay-the-mormon-churchs-new-message-is-that-you-can-be-both/.

CHAPTER 10

A Call to the Board

> I, Nathan Kitchen, understand that as a member of the Affirmation Board of Directors, I have a responsibility to ensure that Affirmation pursues its goals in the most effective way possible.
>
> "Affirmation Board Member Commitment Letter"
> February 2018

As the 2018 strategic planning session in Mesa progressed, I realized that Affirmation had become trauma-aware and was using that weekend to formally incorporate trauma-informed messaging and programming into its peer support efforts. This was a huge and welcome change from the messaging I encountered at Loyola Marymount in 2016. For the past two years, Rene and I had been exchanging notes regularly about what was happening in the queer mother's and father's groups since the exclusion policy was implemented. The trauma was high as we welcomed a steady influx of LGBTQ Latter-day

Saint parents, both in and out of mixed-orientation marriages, who were carrying immense amounts of grief and hurt. To see Affirmation acknowledge on an organization-wide level what we had been experiencing within our groups and then take specific actions to address trauma seemed a huge step forward. In addition, Affirmation had just elected a new president, Carson Tueller, who brought a fresh queer-centric perspective into the organization.[1]

That weekend, I sat enraptured as Laura Skaggs, a board member and marriage and family therapist, taught us that the highest priority of spirituality and wellness was keeping our LGBTQ members alive. To do so not only required us to acknowledge that we were leading a people in trauma but to be conscious that our messaging and actions did not exacerbate trauma within those who come to Affirmation's supportive communities. She indicated that suicide prevention would become a part of the fabric of Affirmation's program offerings.

Additionally, the mind of the board was moving towards acknowledging that for two parties to have a genuinely healthy collaboration, they must be able to speak to what is hurting them. If Affirmation cannot show up authentically in its collaborations with other organizations—including the Church—for fear of ruining chances of dialogue, then it is party to an unhealthy collaboration. Being privy to internal conversations that weekend, I noted that not everyone in the senior leadership was on board with implementing this kind of authenticity with the Church. This idea of healthy collaboration clashed with the long-standing communication culture that still governed the public voice of Affirmation, a holdover from the ground rules set in the pre-exclusion policy days with public affairs. Affirmation

---

1. McDonald, Joel. "Carson Tueller Elected to Serve as President of Affirmation for 2018." Affirmation, November 27, 2017. https://affirmation.org/carson-tueller-elected-as-president-of-affirmation/.

was still reluctant to publicly acknowledge actions and events that harmed LGBTQ Latter-day Saints—holding the Church accountable for the consequences of the exclusion policy—out of fear that it might hamper its opportunities to engage with the Church in enhanced dialogue. Public statements were meticulously reviewed and vetted to be as trauma-free as possible for the Church to hear.

Does publicly talking about the full spectrum of LGBTQ lived experiences—from harm and trauma to queer joy—and openly working through divine discomfort, hamper healthy collaboration with church leaders and members? Can believing, testimony-bearing queer Latter-day Saints have hard discussions about prejudice, harassment, and discrimination at the hand of the Church, or is that only an attribute of the angry and bitter queer anti-Mormon crowd? These questions and the conflict they incited within the senior leadership of Affirmation over how to interface with the Church in this exclusion policy era was a microcosm of what was playing out across the entire swath of Affirmation. At this moment, I was watching my fears of Loyola Marymount materialize. The exclusion policy was slowly starting to cleave the whole of the LGBTQ Mormon community in two along perceived lines of "faithfulness," determined by those who spoke out about how the exclusion policy was harmful and those who found such talk disrespectful towards the Church.

I did not like how this scenario was being painted in such a binary way, queer people judging one another as faithful or unfaithful, respectful or disrespectful, testimony-filled or anti-Mormon according to how one voiced their experiences with the Church. The current state of queer Latter-day Saint conversation seemed to be full of virtue signaling and walking on eggshells. I saw this as an unsustainable and unhealthy position under the weight of the spiritual violence of the exclusion policy. I did not know how this would eventually play out within Affirmation, but controlling the messaging under a chronic exclusion policy was becoming more difficult with the mounting trauma Affirmation was handling in-house from the exclusion policy. Hiding trauma—not acknowledging it and its source—was like a pressure cooker with no pressure release valve. An explosion seemed imminent.

January 2018 not only brought a new trauma-informed strategic plan to Affirmation, it also brought a new First Presidency to the Church. President Thomas S. Monson passed away on January 2. He was the president who presided over Prop 8 and then gave us the exclusion policy. These were significantly hefty bookends holding together his ten-year ministry. On January 16, newly called church president Russell M. Nelson held a press conference with his two counselors, Dallin H. Oaks and Henry B. Eyring. New first presidencies are important in the world of Affirmation because they set the tone and engagement for LGBTQ relations. In this new first presidency, Dieter F. Uchtdorf, widely known for his compassion and moderation during the Monson years, was out, and Dalin H. Oaks was in. Not only did the first presidency now hold the last two living authors of the Family Proclamation in Presidents Nelson and Oaks,[2] it was no secret that President Oaks was the mastermind driving the political and legal anti-LGBTQ initiatives in the modern church. In 1984, he delivered a confidential memorandum titled *"Principles to Govern Possible Public*

---

2. Turley, Richard E. "Public Affairs." In *In the Hands of the Lord: The Life of Dallin H. Oaks*, 215. Salt Lake City, Utah: Deseret Book, 2021.

Statement on Legislation Affecting Rights of Homosexuals"[3] to the First Presidency, kicking off his tireless anti-LGBTQ work as an apostle.

When the First Presidency began to take questions from the press, AP reporter Brady McCombs was first to the mic. He asked President Nelson, "How do you plan to approach LGBT issues?"[4] President Nelson answered that he knew there were challenges with the commandments of God, but God loves his children, "and we love them, and there's a place for everyone who wishes to do so, regardless of challenges, to be with us in The Church of Jesus Christ of Latter-day Saints." His message breathed hope into my soul. I was less concerned that he was articulating an old trope that being queer equates to having a challenge; I was excited by the possibilities of belonging for LGBTQ Latter-day Saints in his answer.

President Nelson hadn't finished putting the period on his last sentence when President Oaks picked up the conversation, "Surely, President, your statement of the love of God for all of his children is the pole star for our relationship to every living person on this planet." He continued, saying that because of this love, God gives commandments and a plan to achieve the highest blessings he has for his children. In turn, leaders of the Church have the responsibility to teach the commandments of God "and the high destination that he has prescribed for his children, all of which is embodied in the Plan of Salvation." I immediately understood what was happening. President Oaks was casting the law of the Lord in a facially neutral manner,

---

3. Oaks, Dallin H. "Principles to Govern Possible Public Statement on Legislation Affecting Rights of Homosexuals." Internet Archive, August 7, 1984. https://arks.org/ark:/13960/t1qg5c46j.

4. "First Presidency News Conference." The Church of Jesus Christ of Latter-day Saints, January 16, 2018. https://www.churchofjesuschrist.org/media/video/2018-01-2000-first-presidency-news-conference.

one that doesn't appear to be harmful or discriminatory but becomes so when applied to LGBTQ people. The "rule of law" and "justice" are not synonymous. The law, even if it is applied uniformly, does not in itself guarantee a just result: "A society that operates under the rule of law must also remain vigilant to ensure the rule of law serves the interests of justice."[5] Currently in the Church, the complete plan of salvation is not an equal opportunity employer. It terminates prematurely for those who are not allowed to pursue a temple marriage and those who transition. When the queer children of God claim marriage equality, the "high destination" and "highest blessings" of God that President Oaks referred to are simply "unavailable" under the law. And in this termination, the queer children of God face injustice in the law. As Martin Luther King Jr. wrote from a Birmingham jail, "Sometimes a law is just on its face and unjust in its application."[6]

The answer to Brady's question ended with a short sidebar conversation between Presidents Nelson and Oaks, seemingly hammering out LGBTQ policy before our eyes:

> **President Nelson**: "So we've got a love and law balance here that we have to consider."
>
> **President Oaks**: "Yeah, the love of the Lord and the law of the Lord."
>
> **President Nelson**: "Yeah."[7]

---

5. "What Is the Rule of Law." American Bar Association. Accessed July 24, 2024. https://www.americanbar.org/advocacy/global-programs/who-we-are/rule-law-initiative/what-is-rule-of-law/.

6. King, Martin Luther. "Letter from a Birmingham Jail." African Studies Center - University of Pennsylvania, April 16, 1963. Accessed July 27, 2024. https://www.africa.upenn.edu/Articles_Gen/Letter_Birmingham.html.

7. "First Presidency News Conference." The Church of Jesus Christ of Latter-day Saints, January 16, 2018.

I clicked away from the news conference and started mindlessly scrolling through Google News as I reflected on what I had just heard. For a lawyer and former Utah Supreme Court justice, President Oaks restraining love was sound legal thinking if you approach God, the great lawgiver, as a professional colleague. This was not a moment to broach the interests of justice, let alone mercy and grace. It was just made clear that in this administration, the management of queer Latter-day Saints would hang in an Old Testament love and law balance. A headline then caught my eye, snapping me back to the present moment: Donald Trump, President of the United States, had just proclaimed today, January 16, as Religious Freedom Day.[8] I had no idea the portent of stormy weather that lay ahead for LGBTQ Latter-day Saints, an amalgamation of religious dominant narrative and religious freedom foreshadowed by these two seemingly unrelated events by two different presidents happening on the same day.

A month later, I was honored to receive an invitation to join Affirmation's Board of Directors. It was important to me to have a voice in this distinguished body, to help direct the work of Affirmation, and to keep it aligned with its mission. Affirmation's communities directly impacted me and my children for good. I desired to spread its supportive communities far and wide, connecting more and more LGBTQ Latter-day Saints with their mentors and peers. My first board meeting in March

---

8. Trump, Donald J. "President Donald J. Trump Proclaims January 16, 2018, as Religious Freedom Day." National Archives and Records Administration, January 16, 2018. https://trumpwhitehouse.archives.gov/presidential-actions/president-donald-j-trump-proclaims-january-16-2018-religious-freedom-day/.

was a time to get my bearings. A few months previous, Public Affairs helped facilitate an application with the Church's LDS Foundation for a $25,000 suicide prevention grant. After hearing a report that our application was still in the queue for consideration, the board held a short discussion to help bring the newly elected executive committee and board members up to speed. This was a tip of the iceberg discussion, barely a mention that flew past my radar as Affirmation's newest board member.

When we met in April,[9] the spirituality and wellness committee recommended aligning ourselves with the well respected QPR Institute for our organization-wide suicide prevention training program. If we received funding, we would identify four in-house QPR trainers and have them ready to provide training at the July International Conference in Salt Lake City. Several board members then suggested that receiving funds from the LDS Foundation would be triggering for some in Affirmation. Others questioned if the Church might use this opportunity to tokenize Affirmation. One board member expressed discomfort with accepting a grant from the Church when there were no concrete actions by the Church to alleviate the wounding of LGBTQ people on the front end of the doctrine. To this, the executive director argued that this was a fundamental challenge in the queer/Latter-day Saint intersection because of the Church's doctrine on the family. Doctrine is the last thing to change. The Church was in a position with LGBTQ people where it had to find ways to be supportive but short of changing doctrine. This grant was a way it could be helpful.

The entire conversation instantly fell apart at this assertion, becoming heated with raised voices and cross-talk. From our perspective, the Church was the power center in this sce-

---

9. Affirmation: LGBTQ Mormons, Families & Friends. "Affirmation Board Meeting Minutes." April 8, 2018.

nario. Were the leaders really powerless, operating under the constraint of inviolable doctrine, making this gesture representative of all they could do in the way of help, or was this small gesture the sum total of the effort they were willing to expend on our behalf? None of us knew the rationale for the Church's implementation of the exclusion policy, but we did know the seventy-year history of the modern church with its LGBTQ population. It seemed to me that seventy years was an awfully generous amount of time to quietly extend grace to a church struggling to be helpful as it continued to exclude us from eternal life, our heavenly parents, eternal marriage, and our families. I felt that the only way we could ethically accept this suicide prevention grant was in tandem with Affirmation publicly acknowledging the wounding of the LGBTQ Latter-day Saint population by the Church, which, to that point, Affirmation had been reticent to do since the Prop 8 experience in California. I posited that none of us in the senior leadership had the power to change doctrine, dominant narratives, or policies. However, we *were* in a position to create a community to save lives in a conflict older than any of us in that meeting.

By now, Carson had lost control of the meeting. As the discussion intensified, some began to take it personally. Then, at the height of tension, Carson announced that before tonight's meeting, his executive committee had already decided that Affirmation would not accept the LDS Foundation's grant if awarded. The board immediately called for a point of order, inquiring where the wording for that power lies in the bylaws. A motion was made for a vote of confidence or no confidence in the executive committee's decision, followed by an intense discussion and more cross-talk about what a vote would mean and if it was even necessary. It was absolute chaos. The executive committee's decision and the motion for a vote of confidence had surprised many of us on the board. In the end, the motion carried and the board expressed confidence in the executive committee's decision not to accept the grant if it were awarded. I was the lone dissenting vote. In my mind, this was not a neutral organization granting money to a random nonprofit. This was a matter of the modern church intersecting with its LGBTQ population, and after seventy years of ongoing relationship, there were some very strong feelings. The entire scenario was thorny, no matter the decision to accept or decline the grant. Because of the gravity of the matter, I felt this needed to be a board decision, not an executive one.

Despite the vote, the matter was not settled in the mind of the board. Members continued to passionately discuss the grant amongst themselves over the following week. During these informal discussions, word came that Affirmation's suicide prevention grant application had been approved. Even before this news, the mind of the board was moving toward formally reopening the discussion. With the LDS Foundation awaiting a response to its decision, I called on Carson to convene an ad hoc board meeting to officially reopen discussion on this matter and call for a board vote. I noted that four of our board members had not been present at the last meeting. Except for one, these absent board members were from outside the United States. I felt it wise to get the perspective of queer leaders involved in the work of Affirmation in other countries. I contacted each one and asked them to attend this critical meeting to contribute their point of view.

On the evening of April 22, every member was present for our ad hoc board meeting.[10] Unlike the passion and cross-talk of our previous meeting, the mood was somber. Each member had time to clarify their thoughts and calibrate their feelings to the

---

10. Affirmation: LGBTQ Mormons, Families & Friends. "Affirmation Ad Hoc Board Meeting Minutes." April 22, 2018.

mission of Affirmation and our responsibilities to each member around the world. Carson asked that we go one by one and individually express our thoughts about the grant. The grace and wisdom each board member expressed about our fellow peers in Affirmation moved me deeply. This time, the Church was not the center of the discussion; it was an exclusively queer-centric moment. In the end, Carson called for an anonymous ballot so we could vote our conscience without peer pressure. We sat in silence as the secretary tabulated our emailed votes. After what seemed an eternity, she announced that fourteen voted to accept the grant, one abstained, and one voted "no." Affirmation would accept the suicide prevention grant. In my mind, it mattered that we collectively wrestled with this as an international board, considering all aspects of our worldwide network of mentors and peers, and in so doing, directed the organization not in the heat of the moment or from our own traumas but from the measured judgment of our own convictions cradled in our responsibility to the mission of Affirmation and for one another.

In this new initiative, I became Affirmation's first QPR suicide prevention trainer. It was the first time something like this had been offered on such a scale in the LGBTQ Latter-day Saint community. As I organized our suicide prevention training offerings for the International Conference, Carson—mindful that the decision to accept LDS Foundation money would be controversial for some—hosted listening sessions for members to voice their feelings. Almost immediately, the press picked up this story. Following her conscience, Affirmation's vice president publicly resigned over the grant acceptance in an op-ed in *The Salt Lake Tribune*,[11] and as anticipated, the intense and passionate discussion we had as a board was now taking place in the public arena. Because board meeting minutes are public, Affirmation started receiving requests for minutes from various sources to review the discussion and process.

Five days before our International Conference, Carson wrote an op-ed for *The Salt Lake Tribune*, posing the question: "Why collaborate on suicide prevention with an organization so many perceive to be the source of so many LGBTQ+ wounds?"[12] He spoke to the consensus that had risen from our discussions as a board: the power of connection can reduce suicide. He observed that over the past forty years of its existence, Affirmation may have witnessed the destructive effects of rejection, but it also saw the power and healing that takes place when those around us provide love and understanding. Since suicide is considered by healthcare providers an indicator of community disorganization and despair, Carson argued that effective suicide prevention programs reflect an integrated, educated, and caring community. In the acute needs of suicide prevention, saving lives must be a community endeavor. My heart cheered at this moment. This op-ed was a remarkable sea change for Affirmation: its president publicly recognizing and representing the wounding of LGBTQ Latter-day Saints while proposing solutions to come together as a community. I embraced this fledgling change of queer-centric candor and community-building, and let it inform my work within the senior leadership of Affirmation.

---

11. Stack, Peggy Fletcher. "Affirmation Veep Resigns, Calls Acceptance of Mormon Church Donation for LGBTQ Suicide Prevention 'Morally Reprehensible.'" *The Salt Lake Tribune*, July 18, 2018. https://www.sltrib.com/news/2018/07/18/affirmation-veep-resigns/.

12. Tueller, Carson. "Commentary: The Power of Connection Can Reduce Suicide." *The Salt Lake Tribune*, July 15, 2018. https://www.sltrib.com/opinion/commentary/2018/07/14/commentary-power/.

Amid this intense publicity, I felt immense pressure to prepare Affirmation's QPR programming. Press members had confirmed that they would be at this inaugural training. After I presented Affirmation's first suicide prevention training session at our International Conference, the weight of the past few months finally hit me. I found a spot in the great hall, away from everyone, and leaned against a column to recharge. As I let my mind wander, a person who had just attended my course approached me, obviously shaken. They reported that they had just done the QPR suicide prevention protocol with a fellow attendee at the conference and had connected them with professional support. Within an hour of Affirmation's first QPR training, we had already saved a life. I realized on a very practical level what we were accomplishing in Affirmation. It was the organization's founding principle of the lifesaving power of connection.

The exclusion policy was the most rejecting action undertaken by the modern church against its queer population to date. This ushered trauma into the fold, creating an unhealthy environment within the spiritual home of LGBTQ Latter-day Saints. This trauma from the exclusion policy was so pernicious it had even infiltrated the senior levels of Affirmation's leadership, kicking it off balance. I marveled that such an action by the Church had the power to shape the everyday lives of queer people in such a manner. Facing such community trauma, I felt somewhat powerless as a new member of the board. However, I understood that I was responsible for acting as a steward of the organization. Daily, I pondered what needed to happen within Affirmation to propel it forward, up and past trauma. One thing was for sure, amid rejection and exclusion—until spiritual equality was available for all queer Latter-day Saints in opportunity, outcome, and privilege, and until families could envision exaltation with their queer children—trauma would be a continual factor for all LGBTQ people who were navigating their intersection with the Church. Trauma must be addressed. You cannot ignore trauma. You cannot talk yourself out of trauma. You cannot bury trauma among fields of platitudes and stoicism. The thing about trauma is that when you bury it, you don't bury it dead. You bury it alive. Trauma had risen within Affirmation very much alive.

CHAPTER 11

A Salmon in the Desert

> Romantic love is not only a part of life, but literally a dominating influence of it. It is deeply and significantly religious. There is no abundant life without it.
>
> Boyd K. Packer
> November 3, 1963

I approached dating like a nerd missionary. Nearing my fifties, I didn't have time to date inefficiently. I knew I would not just wake up one day, and God would have fashioned a husband from a rib, and off we would go into the lone and dreary world. No, finding love would take effort. Gratefully, the Church had provided me with the skills to approach this task with missionary savvy and tenacity.

To fill my finding pool, I pulled from four dating apps. Then, to cut down on the time spent getting to know one another, I had a detailed bio on each app explaining who I was and my interests. A detailed bio is like the Great Filter in Fermi's

Paradox.[1] It wipes out unpromising prospects up front in the dating universe, so I'll never see them. Accommodating coy and sparse details in a dating profile takes up much of your precious time in the "get to know you" phase, leaving a high probability that a significant incompatibility will be uncovered after weeks of investment. My Great Filters were that I was a divorced father of five, a Mormon, and looking to find somebody to build a life with and get married to. I billed these as assets. If someone agreed, I'd hear from them. If they didn't, my inbox wasn't cluttered with non-starters.

The churn from the finding pool to the dating pool and back to the finding pool could get exhausting. I would run this process for about six months at a time before I had to take a break for my own sanity. Eventually, during a dating sabbatical, I would experience the haunting absence of a companion and head back out into the dating field. It was like finding a needle in a haystack, but the missionary commitment pattern was a genius way to move truckloads of hay out of the way in a short amount of time.

After I hit year three with no success, I wondered if I was destined to spend the rest of my life without a companion. I felt I needed to step away from dating for an extended period. I was mentally and emotionally exhausted and had become a bit jaded in the process. Then, one late November evening in 2017, before I headed to bed, I logged into OkCupid to see whom the algorithms had matched me with that day. The algorithm gods served up one Matthew Rivera from Seattle, Washington. I was immediately smitten by his pictures but reserved any judgment until I did my due diligence and perused his profile. He had just finished his Ph.D. in history and was adjuncting at a lo-

---

1. Hanson, Robin. "Are We Almost Past It?" The Great Filter, September 15, 1998. http://mason.gmu.edu/~rhanson/greatfilter.html.

cal university. He was well-traveled, a poet and writer, spoke several languages, including French and Spanish, and was an Episcopalian—this first impression was highly intriguing to me. I feverishly started scrolling his profile, tension building, to get to his Great Filter—would I make it through? And suddenly, there it was. "Doesn't have kids, might want them."

Might want kids.

That will do.

I learned over the years that a first message on a dating site does not have to be long. It just needs to indicate interest, then the profile will take over. If he made it through the Great Filters, he'd write back. I decided to take a chance and send a message to Matthew. Something short, sweet, not too forward, but something that would get the ball rolling.

"Hey there"

Two words, no punctuation.

My kids recently held an intervention with me about my texting habits. They told me never to end a text with a period. A period means that you are mad or something's wrong. No period means it's all good, leaving things open-ended and inviting a conversation. My Gen Z kids were making me a hip and savvy dater. I liked that. I really liked Matthew's profile. I wanted this to go somewhere, and I did not want to give the first impression that I was mad or that something was wrong. I didn't stop to think that I had just sent an unpunctuated, two-word message to a Ph.D. humanities college professor whom I was hoping to impress.

I woke the next morning to a notification from OkCupid. It was Matthew. He had responded with a well-crafted, well-punctuated message where, to my great happiness, he very clearly indicated he wanted to continue this conversation despite ending his own message with a period. This was a very comfortable connection and quickly grew into vulnerability. Soon, we were talking on the phone every day about anything and everything. When we would call, we would identify ourselves according to our area code:

"Hi, 425."

"Hey, 480."

It was a familiar playfulness and interaction I had missed when I was single. We established a standing conversation time every day after work. Matthew had just started a job at the Northwest African American Museum in Seattle, and since the end of my day with patients was variable, we decided I should call when I was on the road home. Remarkably, no matter what time I called, Matthew was just getting off the bus and available to talk. It took me a couple of weeks to figure out that he was getting off at the next stop to walk along the bus route while we talked and laughed about our day. When we were done, he'd hop back on the bus and continue the ride home to Queen Anne Hill.

"You're walking an hour in the cold rain just to talk to me," I protested when I figured out what he was doing, "we can always talk when you get home."

"I live in Seattle. It's always raining," he retorted. "You are important to me, and I can't wait to talk with you. Plus, every true Seattleite is always dressed for the rain, so don't worry about me."

"You are important to me too, Matthew. You are important to me, too."

We were making room for one another in our lives. As the Christmas holiday approached, we made plans for our first in-person date and picked the third weekend in January to meet. That Friday night, I shooed the kids out the door to their mom's and drove to the airport to be on time to pick Matthew up. Earlier that day, I had pulled out the multi-colored Sharpies and made a sign with his name in giant colorful letters surrounded by little hearts to greet him as he exited the terminal. I anxiously waited at the security exit of Terminal 3 as Matthew's plane began its final approach. This little spot had such meaning for me. Five months earlier, this was the place where my son and I held a long, welcoming embrace, not just celebrating the end of a mission but the end of estrangement.

Matthew texted me when he landed, "Just got off the plane. Can't wait to see you! I don't know why, but I'm really nervous." His confession of vulnerability was refreshing. I texted back, "I'm nervous, too. It's always hard meeting someone for the first time. We'll get through this together!" I readied my sign, holding it against my chest. I moved when the crowd shifted so I could always be in the direct line of sight of the exit. People kept coming through in waves, and my anticipation grew with each passing wave. And then suddenly, there he was. When he saw me, he made that cute face I would soon know as his trademark greeting and extended his arms as if to say, "Ta-da! I'm here!" I instantly fell in love with Matthew as he walked through that security exit. My brain was yelling, "Too soon, too soon!"—but it all faded behind the torrential tidal waves of the heart. It had never encountered a moment like this. I timidly held up my sign as we walked to one another and held a long embrace as if we had known each other for years. That spot at Terminal 3 now held two significant meanings for me.

We talked over spinach enchiladas at my favorite Mexican restaurant. Any nervousness had melted away. After dinner, I brought him to see the house he had only seen in pictures. It was a pleasant evening, as Januarys in Phoenix are wont to be, and I gave him a tour of the backyard surrounded by trees. The corners of the lot are anchored by two towering fifty-foot trees, a jacaranda to the east and a giant mesquite to the west. Grapefruit, orange, lemon, and lime trees line the south and west walls. Along the east wall is a bank of pomegranates and several queen palms. It was there—in the center of the backyard on soft winter grass, surrounded by the boughs of this desert oasis framing the star-filled Arizona skies—that we began to chart our course through the universe—together.

The next day, I asked Matthew if he would like to go for a hike in the Arizona mountains. Usery Park was close and would be a great representation of what the desert had to offer. Right in the middle of the park stands Merkle Hills. The hike to its summit would be gentler than a trip up Cat Peaks yet still provide a rewarding panoramic view—a perfect first-date hike. I planned to ask Matthew to be my boyfriend as we stood on the summit overlooking the valley below. I didn't have a plan for how things would look afterward; I just knew I loved him, and those plans were not mine to make alone.

As we rounded the mountain's base to begin our ascent up the trail, we faced the Usery Park covered playground. Matthew commented that it looked like a fun and interesting playground for young kids. Emotions immediately flooded my body and I froze. "Not now," I told myself. "I cannot do this now." I completely forgot that the playground was there. After we had moved to Arizona, my wife and I would come here as a young family, four little children in tow. After a homemade lunch and a family hike, we would sit under this veranda and watch the kids play. Somehow, I could hear my little kids laughing and yelling—joyous sounds of happiness that accompanied the promises of a young couple who realized they had much of their life ahead of them and an unbridled hope that the best was yet to come.

With Matthew by my side, I tried to shut these unexpected memories down but they kept coming. One giant wave after another, the emotions of a simpler time were washing over me. And then the waves stopped. It was quiet. Like looking into a box at Schrodinger's cat to see if it was dead or alive,[2] by observing this forgotten playground, the waveform of my life under this covered playground collapsed into reality. The possibilities of a young married couple held there for almost twenty years were dead. The playground was empty. Life and family looked very different in the future that had actually come to pass. A profound sadness swept over me. An emptiness of what had been lost began to envelop me.

As I gently held Matthew's hand, looking at this playground, a distinct voice from my heart rose above the sadness. It was louder than the grief of that moment. It said, "Nathan. It's okay to feel sad. It's okay to feel anger. Feel these emotions. Own them." And so I did. I relived a lifetime ago in those few traumatic seconds as I faced this playground. I allowed myself to feel the absolute sadness and the profound anger. As I did so, my loss and grief gave way to gratitude. Gratitude for what the past had given me, including the past that built me. And in this gratitude, grace. I extended grace towards myself as a young father watching his toddlers play there on a desert playground, privileged to enjoy such a time in life before I was shaken up off the trail. Allowing that space for my sadness and anger helped me realize that I was ready to let go—let go of the guilt and blame I had tethered myself to during the coming-out process. In doing so, as Matthew and I ascended the trail, I was not abandoning

---

2. Orzel, Chad. "Schrödinger's Cat: A Thought Experiment in Quantum Mechanics." TED. Accessed July 24, 2024. https://ed.ted.com/lessons/schrodinger-s-cat-a-thought-experiment-in-quantum-mechanics-chad-orzel.

the Nathan of the playground. He was coming with me to build new memories on top of a mountain.

Matthew and I made plans to travel to see each other, rotating weeks between Arizona and Seattle. Although I was saving introductions with my kids, he began to meet my friends and extended family, and I began to meet his. I learned from the fathers in Affirmation to never involve your kids in the dating churn: You figure it out, and once you are sure you have found the one, then make the introductions. After the introductions, he will need to build his own relationship with your kids. You can't force that relationship. If you force it, your kids will resent him, and that is a hard injury to recover from.

This advice hit home. Together, my kids and I had made a house our home. After the divorce was final, they came with me as my trusty companions to look at houses, and why not? It would be their home, too. They discussed the pros and cons of each property, negotiated bedrooms amongst themselves, and finally voted on the winner. This really was our home and our life. It would take someone special to join with us. Yes, I was looking for a companion, but he would also be coming into an established family. Someone for me and my kids was a tall order. In March, I invited Matthew to attend the Fathers in Affirmation retreat in Utah. This would not only be a great time for him to meet my friends in Affirmation but also give me the opportunity to introduce Matthew to Heidi and Emily—and, since we were in the Motherland, the Church.

Matthew's Ph.D. focused on the Catholic Reformation in France during the sixteenth and seventeenth centuries. While researching his dissertation, he spent time living with the Dominicans, an 800-year-old order of the Catholic Church, at the Saint-Nom-de-Jésus convent in Lyon, France. Matthew grew up a devout evangelical in the Assemblies of God. However, uncharacteristic of his Evangelical roots, he looked for truth wherever it was to be found among the many religious traditions of the world, finding great freedom through academics to do so.

While in Lyon, Matthew had growing concerns about why he had failed to make a romantic connection with women. He wrestled with the ongoing consequences of this social isolation, which was becoming more difficult to manage in his late 30s. He didn't know what prompted this awakening exactly, although he was familiar with the maxim that a new environment can spur questions thought too unsafe to ask in familiar surroundings. Matthew read every book in the convent about the subject of homosexuality. He filled his evenings listening to gay evangelicals online who had come out. Their stories resonated with him profoundly. In the spring of 2013, toward the end of his research trip in France, a visiting Dominican from Germany came to the convent and soon befriended Matthew. Matthew began to wonder if the invitations from his German Dominican friend to go to the park for long walks, engage in lengthy talks about life, or attend the Lyon Opera weren't just friendship but something bordering on "dates." Matthew was still deep in the closet and couldn't consider this romance. In hindsight, however, this friendship bordering on romance was an important step in his coming out because, for the first time, dating a man entered his vocabulary and the realm of the possible.

When Matthew returned from France, Northwest University, a well-known evangelical university, hired him for a tenure-track position. During the interview process, as Matthew and the university president walked the halls in conversation, the president suddenly pulled Matthew into a small prayer closet completely lined with pictures of past storied alums, faculty, and administrators. There, the president pointed to these pictures and pressed Matthew for a loyalty pledge to uphold the denomination's evangelical traditions and support its teachings in a way that would be faithful to the people pictured in this prayer closet, even if this meant sacrificing academic integrity. This moment shook Matthew, cornered in a prayer closet and expected to uphold the evangelical way at all costs.

During his first year at Northwest, the various conversation threads in his head that had begun in Lyon converged, leading him to come out to himself and his friends. The cleavage between the institutional culture and his integrity became too great to endure. He had begun dating men, which would have resulted in a messy, immediate termination had it come to the attention of administrators. He decided to leave Northwest University because there, life would be no bigger than a picture-lined prayer closet.

On the weekend of the Fathers in Affirmation retreat, Matthew and I met up in Salt Lake. I planned out the day to begin at Temple Square. There, I would proudly introduce him to the Mormon tradition, stopping for lunch with Heidi and Emily at the Garden Restaurant overlooking the Salt Lake Temple before heading down to the Fathers opening social that evening. I was the ultimate guide. Temple Square was my backyard, and I knew every inch and every story. Temple Square held three narratives unique to Mormonism: The Restoration, the pioneers, and forever families. I was an ambassador of the faith to a Ph.D. in religious history.

Matthew was particularly struck by the towering statues standing side by side near the South Visitors Center, one depicting John the Baptist restoring the Aaronic Priesthood to Joseph Smith and Oliver Cowdery, and the other depicting Peter, James, and John conferring the Melchizedek priesthood upon them. There, I commenced with the glorious story of the Restoration from First Vision to the conferral of priesthood keys.

Matthew squinted his eyes, "So, God just skipped over one thousand eight hundred and thirty years and brought the primitive church back through a parade of resurrected prophets and apostles to a New Yorker in the early 1800s? That's an efficient origin of power story." My complex, beautifully woven narrative and testimony of the restoration I had delivered in missionary fervor had just been summarized by a historian in one concise sentence. Then, obviously taken by the message these statues were broadcasting as he stood under the shadows of these larger-than-life apostles frozen in bronze, Matthew remarked, "Well, the iconography sure helps the narrative."

The Salt Lake trip was wonderful. Matthew met my friends in Affirmation, met Heidi and Emily, and met my testimony of the restored gospel, giving me space in my beliefs independent of academic and historical analysis. He understood that faith and belief are a personal and important part of the human experience, the substance of things hoped for, the evidence of things not seen (Hebrews 11:1). He understood the history of religion and the reason for religion—and gave grace for both.

By April, we realized that our love was expanding beyond long-distance limitations. Back in Seattle, as I sat at Matthew's kitchen table while he made us brunch, I looked out over Lake Union, past the Aurora Bridge. He was making oatmeal with blueberries, bananas, almonds, and real maple syrup, served with a stack of his perfectly buttered toast. This entire moment was a taste of what I wanted my future to look like. We began to chart our course together for the next part of the journey. As we discussed the possibilities, Matthew shared that his job prospects for a professorship in Seattle were slim due to the position pool/applicant ratio. Whether moving for a job or love, he would need to move. And he would much prefer to move for love.

A few months later, as Matthew was taking me to the airport after my last trip to Seattle before his big move to Arizona—preparations and plans complete—I acknowledged that such a move, even in the best of circumstances, would be stressful for him. He was leaving a home, a climate, friends, and memories of twenty years in the Pacific Northwest to move to a completely foreign landscape. Plus, he would be coming to Phoenix in July. No one is prepared for Phoenix in July. I knew full well that I was bringing a salmon to the desert. Matthew took my hand and gently told me to be troubled no more. He was making this move because he wanted to. This love that we had was his life's desire. "Mine too," I whispered as I looked at him through tears and vowed that I would forever make his deserts, both real and metaphorical, blossom and flourish.

THE VOICE

What makes the wind?
The unseen currents
That flow o'er Earth and sea—
The brushstrokes on a canvas globe,
That take no shape, no form, no hue,
Yet yields a pow'r
To change the world,
To lift the wings
That carry you home,
To cool my face
In desert sun.

Yet in its ebbs and in its flows,
It has no voice heard overhead.
A silent pow'r transforms, unheard
Until it meets corporeal space,
The marriage of earth and sky
That gives a voice unto the wind:
The whistles through the canyon bends
The rustling leaves in backyard trees
The wistful oboe's pensive tone
The words you breathe into my ear,
All nature makes it sing.

So, what of love?
Fools claim to know.
But love, like wind, will flow unseen
As currents o'er Earth and sea.
It takes no shape, no form, no hue
Yet yields the pow'r
To change my world.
To lift the wings

That carry you home,
To cool my face
In desert sun.

Like gentle winds, a gentle love
Will course without a sound,
Until it meets its canyon bend,
Its bough of backyard tree,
The oboe's wistful reed,
Or words you whisper in my ear.
What is this thing
Giving voice to love
As it passes through heart and soul?

I know.

It is you.

For you give voice to love.

CHAPTER 12

Pressing Forward

> If we are anxiously engaged in whatever we are inspired and called to do, we will be prepared for what the Lord has in store for us as we go through life. For some it may not be the conventional path. If we are diligent it will be the direction the Lord would have us follow.
>
> Elaine Michaelis
> BYU women's athletic director
> March 12, 2002

As a historian, Matthew was highly interested in the history of the Church, finding its claims bold and unashamedly peculiar in a restoration tradition that held a depth and richness just as interesting as its much older siblings within Christianity. But he was not prepared for the culture that came with it. It is all-encompassing and swallows you up in everyday life in a way that does not happen in the traditional faiths. Most intriguing to Matthew was the Mormon network. When we orchestrated his move from Seattle, he told me jokingly that he planned to "hire a thug" for the moving tasks. "No, no, —No." I retorted, "I'm going to activate the Mormon network." Matthew was skeptical. Imposing upon people's time without paying them?

My sister and brother, who live in Seattle, came with their families to load the moving truck on the Seattle end. On the Gilbert end, my network of friends from Fathers in Affirmation came together to help unload the truck—pizza and cold drinks provided to help everyone along. At the end of this kinetic chain of Mormon movement, Matthew watched with mouth wide open as people he did not know lugged his grandma's heavy oversized couch up three flights of stairs in 106-degree July weather. I loved this experience with Matthew, introducing him to the Mormon network. Most importantly, he was now in Arizona, just a half mile from my house, and we were ready to have him start getting to know the kids. This move was a defining moment in our relationship, a moment of vulnerability for us as we continued building a life together. But this move, as exciting as it was, was not the only thing on my mind.

After the moving van was unloaded and the Mormon network dispersed, I sat on the edge of Matthew's bed, folding clothes while he was out in the kitchen unboxing dishes. The workings and personal feelings between Affirmation's executive committee, board, and executive staff were still in disarray after the LDS grant discussion, and this created a dysfunction that arrested the organization's forward movement. I understood that the diverse coalition of experienced leaders assembled on Affirmation's board and executive staff would have intense ideas and opinions. I understood that it was healthy to discuss different points of view. I understood that disagreement can be healthy in the forward movement of an organization. I understood that Affirmation was a refuge for some who were experiencing trauma within their personal intersection with the Church. But what I could not understand was why a storied LGBTQ organization was in such a place that an action by the Church had the power to completely kick the institutional legs out from under our day-to-day executive functions and processes—and we were still face down in the dirt three months later, struggling to get up. Was this a leadership issue? Was this a governance issue? Was this a cultural issue? This felt like an organization in trauma. Were the exclusion policy and the Church's subsequent suicide prevention grant a perfect storm?

Now, just four months in as a board member, I had my first glimpse of the extent to which queer trauma is spread as it simmers within dominant narratives and policies. It was a phenomenon that extended beyond the exclusion policy. The policy may have been a set of rules to manage queer Latter-day Saints who strayed into marriage equality, taking their children down in the process, but that was not the limit of its reach. The policy was a reminder to all queer Latter-day Saints that the Church was not afraid to enforce queer exclusion in the plan of salvation—even if it meant coming after the children—as it reached into the great houses of Zion to rearrange and sever family relationships on an eternal scale.

During my hospital residency training, I witnessed physical trauma daily: broken teeth, fractured jaws, and teeth knocked out by drunken falls. Trauma care providers have training, protocols, and systems in place to prepare ourselves for whatever comes our way. Because of this, a trauma center does not grind to a halt because it experiences people in trauma. What could we do in Affirmation to not shut down because we experienced people in trauma? In trauma care, trauma is not the final destination. The journey to wholeness is the end goal. I did not want Affirmation beholden to trauma or the experiences of its members filtered through trauma. Yes, Affirmation needed to acknowledge trauma, but more importantly, it needed to lift the chin of all those who sought our communities so the ground was not the only thing in view. A supportive community will not hold you perpetually wounded. A supportive community knows where the inns are in our lives and is willing to transport us there so we may heal before we continue our journey in this life toward joy. It was time to stop focusing on what the Church thought about us—it was time to strengthen our beloved community, build our Mormon network, and navigate toward joy.

As I reached for the last box of clothes that needed hangers, I weighed my responsibility as a new board member. In my heart, I knew the kind of stability I wanted to see in this organization that was undergoing substantial worldwide growth. I knew the changes I wanted to see so that Affirmation might continue its rise. This was an election year for Affirmation. A presidential candidate had until the end of the first day of the International Conference to declare their intention to run. That was twenty days away. This would be the junction point to insert change into the organization. I hung the last of the clothes in the closet, picked up my phone, and asked Laurie Lee Hall to run for president of Affirmation.

I first met Laurie during the opening social at Affirmation's strategic planning session in Mesa. She exuded a grace and confidence I wanted to know more about. As she told me her story about being a transgender woman, the Church's chief architect who directed the design and construction of temples, and a stake president, I was impressed by her integrity as she transitioned while still working at headquarters.

Laurie had transitioned before the Church had a formal policy for transgender Latter-day Saints. Because of this, she was treated harshly. She was a pioneer in unashamed authenticity in the transgender Latter-day Saint community. The loss of her employment and her excommunication from the Church for no other reason than she transitioned was incredibly difficult for her. Yet, she rose above it, overcoming prejudice and discrimination to achieve an authenticity that cisgender people often take for granted.[1] Her story reminded me of the universal experience of loss and change that happens when we come out or transition. During this reconfiguration into authenticity, we search for our supportive communities. To see her volunteering her time now directing the mission of Affirmation as a member of the board brought me great comfort that the best of the best in the LGBTQ Mormon world were standing for me and my family in the queer/Latter-day Saint intersection. Through our conversations that evening, I was also taken by her New England dry sense of humor. I told myself I didn't care how or when it happened but I wanted to be her friend.

Now, after serving with Laurie as a fellow board member these past few months, I saw firsthand that she was a mover and shaker. She had been assigned to lead the governance committee, and with her organizational and management skills honed through years of church service and church employment, she accomplished the daunting task of revising the charter and bylaws that had been floundering as unfinished business in committee for years. She had executive skills in spades. I nervously laid out my invitation to Laurie to run for president of Affirmation. I spoke freely about what I observed during and after the discussions and votes surrounding the $25,000 suicide prevention grant. I shared how her leadership skills were not only needed to run a board, but having spent her career navigating a worldwide system, she had a particular skill set that would build and

---

1. Hall, Laurie Lee. *Dictates of Conscience: From Mormon High Priest to My New Life as a Woman.* Salt Lake City, Utah: Signature Books, 2024.

bless Affirmation for generations. In true Laurie fashion, this invitation began a conversation.

As we talked over the next few weeks, we shared our experiences as board-level leaders and our unique intersections with Affirmation. We talked about how the transgender moment was poised to soon consume the time and attention of the Church. Back in January 2015, Elder Oaks, then a senior member of the Quorum of the Twelve Apostles, told Jennifer Napier-Pearce in a Trib Talk interview that the brethren didn't have much experience with the "unique problems of the transgender situation." They had some unfinished business in teaching on the matter.[2] At the time of his interview, the Church was up to its eyeballs dealing with the gays and lesbians who were occupying a huge, earth-shaking piece of ecclesiastical and legal real estate now that Obergefell was on the Supreme Court's docket to decide the legality of marriage equality. Despite Obergefell's pressing, Elder Oaks was remarkably savvy in his observation about the need for the brethren to parse something entirely new to their experience—gender identity.

This "unfinished business" was quickly becoming finished. By 2017, the Church filed an amicus brief in the Gavin Grimm case before the Supreme Court, opposing transgender students using restrooms that corresponded with their gender identity.[3] In tandem with this moment, Laurie shared that the Church laid out its first attempt to manage its transgender population

---

2. Napier-Pearce, Jennifer, Peggy Fletcher Stack, and Robert Gehrke. "Balancing LGBT, Religious Rights Won't Be Easy, Mormon Leaders Concede." *The Salt Lake Tribune*, 2015. https://www.sltrib.com/news/mormon/2015/03/03/balancing-lgbt-religious-rights-wont-be-easy-mormon-leaders-concede/.

3. Winslow, Ben. "Utah, LDS Church File 'friend of the Court' Papers in Transgender Bathroom Case." FOX 13 News Utah (KSTU), February 18, 2017. https://www.fox13now.com/2017/02/17/utah-lds-church-file-friend-of-the-court-papers-in-transgender-bathroom-case.

through policies that specifically addressed the transgender experience: no self-determination of gender identity, no attending Relief Society or Priesthood meetings that aligned with their identity, no "cross-dressing" at church, and if someone had transitioned, they must detransition or resign their membership—or else be called in for church discipline. In effect, this was the first transgender generation to sprout out of the trunk of the "Miracle of Forgiveness" generation of the queer family tree in Zion. More generations were surely coming as the Church's transgender dominant narrative matured in cycles of collapse and rebuild. Finger to the wind, we both agreed that this would be the moment in Affirmation where the transgender experience was not an afterthought but a central thought.

During our last presidential exploratory conversation, we came down to the practicality of how this would all work. Having just led the revision of our charter and bylaws, Laurie was intimately familiar with every word, including the president's duties. She candidly expressed that although these duties may be good for Affirmation, they were perhaps not a good match for how she wanted to express leadership as an executive in Affirmation. We began to construct a plan, a pivot from the original, where we would team up to form a candidate executive committee, but she would serve as senior vice president, and I would run for president. The president of Affirmation methodically moves like a king on a chess board, one square to the left, right, or diagonal—dignitary duties, running a board, employee interface, trauma, and drama. Yet the Senior VP has the latitude and freedom to traverse the board in all strategic directions like a queen, and with this freedom, has the leeway to do an immense amount of good for both the people and outcomes in Affirmation.

We needed a vice president to round out our candidate executive committee. Considering the needs of Affirmation, we decided to ask fellow board member Jairo Fernando González Díaz if he would join our team as vice president. Like I had with Laurie, I met Jairo at the board's 2018 strategic planning retreat in Mesa. There, he gave an impassioned plea that it was time for Affirmation to create a financial and economic policy to manage its cash flows and control its money. Since the exclusion policy, Affirmation was receiving large donations in amounts never before seen in its history. Uniquely skilled in money management, Jairo spent a significant portion of his career as an auditor before founding an accounting and consulting firm that serviced companies in western Colombia and Ecuador. Jairo's expertise couldn't have been timelier. Financial savvy was not the only talent Jairo brought to Affirmation. Ever engaged with each Affirmation community throughout Latin America, he was not only an inspiring speaker at our regional conferences, but he effectively translated his good nature and wit across the diverse cultures of Latin America as he built the supportive communities of Affirmation. And could he ever spin a great story! With Jairo, you could not help but be fully engaged. He was a person who went about doing good, and you would run to keep up. Graciously, Jairo accepted the invitation to run with us on the ticket. I was excited about what each of us was bringing to the table.

In August 2018, I posted my presidential candidate statement for the members of Affirmation to consider. I laid out our vision for what was next in Affirmation and our commitment as a candidate executive committee to be community builders in the queer Latter-day Saint world. I outlined the power of being part of a supportive community. In community, we have a responsibility to become involved, share in ways that inspire us, and give voice to our thoughts and opinions. Calling back to the very spirit embedded within Affirmation from its founding, I concluded, "I want to convey that my first love is to you, the individual member of Affirmation. Affirmation exists for you. This space of love will be home base for me as president as we together create safe and supportive communities among friends."[4] On November 3, I was elected President of Affirmation. In response to my peers' trust, I posted a "thank-you" note on Facebook: "I ask for your support for me and my family during these upcoming two years. There is much to do around the world."

---

4. Kitchen, Nathan. "Nathan Kitchen - Presidential Candidate Statement." Affirmation, August 26, 2018. https://affirmation.org/nathan-kitchen-presidential-candidate-statement/.

CHAPTER 13

The Family is Ordained of God

> 11 ... We are witnesses! May the Lord make this woman who enters your house like Rachel and Leah, who together established the house of Israel ...
>
> Ruth 4:11 (ISV)

When Matthew first moved into his Gilbert apartment, he would ring the doorbell when he came over to the house even though he had a key. I asked him why he did this. "This is your and your kids' house, and I want them to know that I know that," he replied. "I get how important family space is, and I am coming into their space to be with you." The kids picked up on this, and instead of having to find room for Matthew, they started looking for ways to include him in our family activities. As we all started getting to know one another, we took many weekend trips, hikes, and adventures around Arizona. As the weeks rolled on, one of my favorite phrases of theirs was, "Where's Matt?"

"And hello to you too," I would tease, "I know you like him better than me." They would laugh but never deny it.

A few years earlier, with the kids getting older and their schedules more complex, we decided that Sunday dinner would be the one time, hard stop, when we would eat together as a family. It was an event we all looked forward to. One Sunday, as we sat around the kitchen table having the kids' favorite, Kings Ranch Casserole, my eighteen-year-old blurted out, "Where's Matt?"

"Well, I suppose he is at his apartment having dinner," I said.

"That's mean, making him eat alone. I can't believe you make him eat alone," he chided. He was partly joking but mostly not. The other boys chimed in in agreement.

"So, what should we do about this?" I asked, "Should we include Matt and invite him to Sunday dinner with us every week?" Not only were all the kids in agreement, but they made me put down my fork and immediately call Matthew to extend him a standing invitation to come and eat dinner with us every Sunday.

"Oh, and he needs to come over right now because we still have King's Ranch left for him," my eighteen-year-old shouted loud enough for Matthew to hear. Matthew chuckled, and at that moment, I realized that he had done the work to be a part of the children's lives, treating them with respect and building an individual relationship with each of them. It was how he wanted to start things off with the kids, and they loved him for it. I loved him for it.

By the fall of 2018, I had been dating Matthew for almost a year. My parents asked to meet him, knowing he had become integral to my and my children's lives. I called Annette to ask her how best to facilitate this, and of course, she had an immediate answer. "Everyone needs to come to my house for Thanksgiving!" She began to make her famous extemporaneous plans, fleshing them out in great detail. "I'll fly Mom and Dad out, and we'll see who else in the family wants to come...."

My mind wandered as she talked, contemplating what was about to happen. I was still beyond nervous about my parents meeting Matthew for the first time. Both my parents and I formed opinions about being gay from the same source, *The Miracle of Forgiveness*. Despite the work we had done overcoming what we had learned, our heavy lifting had been done before the exclusion policy. I didn't know exactly where my parents were at this point in their journey under its long shadow. It was evident that I was very close to bringing another person into the family, but apostasy by same-sex marriage was a whole other universe in Mormon theology than just identifying as gay. I took this as a hopeful moment—they had, after all, reached out to me first about meeting Matthew. I knew from experience that you can only know if someone will be your ally if you give them a chance to show you. Doing this is a very vulnerable action involving people you love deeply. Because of Matthew, I was ready to be vulnerable. I was sold on this Thanksgiving weekend idea to get us all together. It would be fun.

"... And we will definitely make time to tour the Seattle Underground and have lunch on the pier. Sound good?" My sister faded back into my consciousness, and I couldn't have loved her more in that moment.

"This all sounds so lovely. Let's do it!"

When Matthew and I walked into my sister's house on Thanksgiving afternoon, my parents immediately embraced him in a genuine and familiar way. It was that kind of guileless love and interaction I had witnessed them exude over a lifetime toward others they care about. My father greeted Matthew with his best dad joke, and my mom talked books and Latin with him throughout the night. As we gathered around my sister's kitchen island later that evening, my stress levels were already at zero. It was a lovely moment. My sister, her family, and two of my brothers and their families had joined us that weekend, and Matthew was holding his own with the Kitchen humor and competitive gameplay.

With Matthew occupied by my family, I took a moment to steal away into the backyard alone. I stood in the grass, looking in on the warm light streaming from my sister's kitchen windows as I watched my family gather around Matthew. And in that moment, I openly wept. How far we had come as a family. This light streaming such a scene from these immense windows reminded me of the light that streams through the stained-glass windows of temples, telling the story of what occurs inside. Only tonight, this light was not filtered through colored glass panels but through my family as a love that lit up the darkness of that crisp November night. I recalled standing with my children at the Palmyra Temple, flanked by the golden light streaming from its massive stained-glass windows, underneath the stone inscription announcing to all who approach: HOLINESS TO THE LORD, THE HOUSE OF THE LORD. The word "house" signifies not only a building but also lineage—family. The prophet Joshua proclaimed, "But as for me and my house, we will serve the LORD" (Joshua 24:15). The House of Israel becomes important to Latter-day Saints when our patriarchal blessings pronounce our lineage within this house upon us. It is through the love of the Lord that we are brought into this house, becoming spiritually-begotten children of Christ, the family of Christ, filled with his love.

Currently, thousands upon thousands of LGBTQ Latter-day Saints stand outside these temples, under this inscription in stone that identifies the building as the house of the Lord, yet they are barred from entering its physical space. Amid such religious exclusion, with many being called unclean to enter, softly and tenderly, Jesus is calling his children home. And in response, the great houses of Zion hear him, and with hope, gather their authentic and beloved LGBTQ children up into their family boughs in moments just like tonight, all across Zion—seeking wisdom from the appreciative God of the Restoration, the great parents of the Universe.

This moment marked that Matthew was part of the House Kitchen. And it indeed was holy. Matthew had been received in love throughout the branches of our family tree, from children to siblings to parents, carried up into the arms of so many who loved him. And to see us as a family, giving good gifts to one another, I asked myself, how much more shall our heavenly parents give good things to those who ask them (Luke 11:13)? Dare I ask for the greatest gift God can give (Doctrine and Covenants 14:7): eternal life with Matthew? Through tears, I had the presence of mind to snap a picture to capture this moment. It was a scene of intense happiness. I spoke aloud to God and asked that somehow, someday, we would all stand together under the boughs of eternal love.

On January 19, 2019, Matthew and I hiked to the top of a mountain, the same range that held the tree borne from a rock, branches reaching to the heavens on The Peak of Champions. Overlooking the Valley of the Sun, we asked for each other's hand in marriage.

NAVIGATING MASCULINITY
For Matthew

"You make me feel safe."
I never fully understood that phrase
When you said it to me
At the beginning of us.

Never fully understood
Because I was born into an expected masculinity.
A lonely, "Suck it up Buttercup" captain of a massive ship,
Christened to me when I should have been just an ordinary seaman.

Responsible for everyone else's happiness and health and needs and wants.

This was my masculinity, given to me.
Because I was a boy.

I was lonely in the wheelhouse.
The storms I navigated in dark, deep seas,
Charted while passengers dined
And played shuffleboard.

It is scary, but you can't talk about that.

Ever.

Outwardly calm through the shipwrecks
In my own soul
As I kept it all afloat
For everyone else.

And then one night,
White-knuckled,
My ship ran aground.
Lifeboats launched.
"Women and children first!"

And all I knew to do was stoically stand
On a lonely bridge,
Still in uniform, saluting.
Master and Commander of none.

Alone.

And then I heard you, calling.
You opened the door and entered my starving heart
You saw the tears I wasn't supposed to show
And held me in ways I wasn't supposed to be held.

And for the first time another stood
With me at the helm.
You took a watch and let me rest.

And I rested.

And for the first time, I felt safe.

And then I knew what you meant
By what you said
At the beginning of us.

CHAPTER 14

A Recension

> 1 By the rivers of Babylon, there we sat down, yea, we wept, when we remembered Zion.
>
> Psalm 137:1

On April 4, 2019, my alarm was set to go off at 6:35 a.m. like it was every Thursday. But this would turn out not to be just any other Thursday. Long before the alarm, my phone began buzzing incessantly. Like a dream that deposits you in the middle of a scene already in progress, I groggily tried to orient myself to time and place. Eyes still closed, I reached my arm over to the nightstand, blindly pecking about to find my phone, to see who or what was blowing it up at this hour. Phone located, I rubbed the sleep out of my eyes and scrolled to the top of the incoming messages. At the first sentence, I jolted up off the pillow and onto the side of the bed. It was Affirmation's rapid response team discussing pressing news. We had just received a tip that a major announcement on LGBTQ issues would be made from headquarters in Salt Lake in just a few hours—broadcast on the church newsroom website at 9 a.m. MDT. Still groggy—and as an Arizonan who never has to observe daylight saving time—I had to do a bit of math in my head to remind myself if Arizona was now on Utah time or California time.

California time. This meant the news would drop at 8, right in the middle of my clinic hours.

At the 2018 board strategic planning session in Mesa, Affirmation identified that an area of improvement the organization needed was to become faster and nimbler at responding to breaking news in the queer/Latter-day Saint intersection. With the help of the public relations experience that Bill Evans brought to the board, Affirmation created a small, experienced group of executive staff and board members to be a rapid response team. Its responsibility was to immediately digest information, contextualize events, and get a response out pronto that aligned with Affirmation's mission.

Bill's journey to the Affirmation board was the remarkable story of a changed heart. As a part of the Church's public relations department, he was integral to the Church's coordinated efforts in the California Prop 8 campaign in 2008. When he was recalled back to Salt Lake, his next assignment was to collaborate with LGBTQ community leaders to develop and promote a new civil rights ordinance in Salt Lake City. Bill was astonished by the graciousness of those activists toward him even after acknowledging his role in the Church's Prop 8 campaign.[1] His collaborative work with the LGBTQ community was life-changing for him. In 2013, he facilitated opening a channel of dialogue between Affirmation and the Church, being present in those meetings to help grease the wheels. After he retired from church employment,

---

1. Stack, Peggy Fletcher. "Retired LDS Church Lobbyist Joins Board of LGBT Mormon Support Group." *The Salt Lake Tribune*, August 30, 2016. https://archive.sltrib.com/article.php?id=3808850&itype=CMSID.

Bill was invited to join Affirmation's board of directors in 2016. As an ally, he was exceptionally well-connected and respected in the LGBTQ community and the Church. He brought his extensive public relations experience to Affirmation, which I heavily relied upon when I was president. This forthcoming announcement by the Church would be Affirmation's first real test of this new system Bill helped put in place.

Heart pumping, I got out the door faster than usual and rushed to the office. I called Laurie on the way. Typically, the president would quarterback this process from beginning to end. With a full schedule of patients on the books, I asked if she would take the lead on my behalf and then take the responsibility for writing the first draft of our response to get it on the table for revisions. I would find strategic times to participate, but since my first responsibility was to my patients, I should refrain from taking point on this time-sensitive matter, possibly slowing this critical process down. Laurie accepted the assignment, and by the time I got to the office, she had the team primed and ready to go. Curiously, the only person we couldn't reach was Bill.

I looked at my patient schedule and mapped out the flow of the morning procedures so that I would have a natural break point at announcement time. I sent a short message to the team, "Let us rise to the occasion and be the resource for comfort and comment," then went to meet my first patient—anxious for what lay ahead for LGBTQ Mormons. A little before announcement time, I went to my office, pulled up the Mormon Newsroom site, and started manually refreshing my browser. Refresh, nothing new. Refresh, nothing new. Refresh, nothing new. Refresh—and there it was.

My mouth dropped open not only because of the content but also because of who had been assigned to deliver it. President Oaks announced, "Effective immediately, children of parents who identify themselves as lesbian, gay, bisexual or transgender may be baptized without First Presidency approval."[2] In addition, LGBTQ parents could now request that their baby be blessed. Stunned, I felt like I did earlier that morning, frantically trying to orient myself to time and place. I pushed back from my desk. I could hardly see the screen now through uncontrollable tears as it began to sink deep into my soul that we were witnessing the dismantling of the exclusion policy. President Oaks was not done: "Previously, our handbook characterized same-gender marriage by a member as apostasy. While we still consider such a marriage to be a serious transgression, it will not be treated as apostasy for purposes of Church discipline. Instead, the immoral conduct in heterosexual or homosexual relationships will be treated in the same way."[3]

By this time, my phone started blowing up again as the rapid response team furiously typed out their astonishment: "Are you seeing this?" "Is this what I think it is?" I grabbed a tissue to clear my eyes so I wouldn't alarm my patient when I returned to finish their procedure. I had so much to personally unpack before I could put on my president hat and help contextualize this for the LGBTQ Latter-day Saint community. This meant no more scarlet "A"s for apostasy affixed to our married Latter-day Saint same-sex couples. The threat of apostasy that lay over my head after I married Matthew was now gone. But what in

---

2. Oaks, Dallin H. "Details Shared by President Oaks." In *First Presidency Shares Messages from General Conference Leadership Session*. newsroom. churchofjesuschrist.org, April 4, 2019. https://newsroom.churchofjesuschrist .org/article/first-presidency-messages-general-conference-leadership- session-april-2019.

3. Oaks, Dallin H. "Details Shared by President Oaks." April 4, 2019.

the world did President Oaks mean when he said, "Immoral conduct in heterosexual or homosexual relationships would be treated in the same way?" That sentence sounded deceptively equal, but I could not imagine that this was the moment of equality in the Church for queer Latter-day Saints.

Such an about-face reinforced in my mind and heart that none of this had been revelation.[4] It was just another failed policy in a long line of collapsed dominant narratives about queer Latter-day Saints and their children built on prejudice and misunderstanding—and possibly fear. By now, I was going through all the emotions as a sexual minority in the Church, including anger when President Oaks observed that these "very positive policies" would help affected families, telling members to show more understanding, compassion, respect, and love towards others. "We want to reduce the hate and contention so common today."[5] I was stunned at the disconnect between how the power center was painting the policy and how it had been experienced in the margins of the Church. As a gay Latter-day Saint father who had just lived through the spiritual terror of what felt like a hateful policy, the call for compassion, goodwill, and love was years late.

---

4. Nelson, Russell M. "Becoming True Millennials." Homepage - The Church of Jesus Christ of Latter-day Saints, January 10, 2016. https://www.churchofjesuschrist.org/study/broadcasts/article/worldwide-devotionals/2016/01/becoming-true-millennials.

At the Worldwide Devotional for Young Adults broadcast from BYU-Hawaii in 2016, President Nelson taught the following about the 2015 exclusion policy: "The Lord inspired His prophet, President Thomas S. Monson, to declare the mind of the Lord and the will of the Lord, each of us during that sacred moment felt a spiritual confirmation. It was our privilege as Apostles to sustain what had been revealed to President Monson. Revelation from the Lord to His servants is a sacred process, and so is your privilege of receiving personal revelation."

5. Oaks, Dallin H. "Details Shared by President Oaks." April 4, 2019.

I was now through a half dozen tissues, mad at myself that I could not get it together to put on a professional face for the clinic floor. However, the tears now were not for me. They were the tears of a president. I was not crying because the policy had been rescinded. I was crying because the full weight of the pain, trauma, rejection, and suicides of my LGBTQ peers over the past three and a half years pierced my soul. All this suffering had been so very unnecessary. Who and what had been lost that we will never regain? I messaged Laurie my initial impressions as source material for her first draft, concluding, "I do think we need to give the church the grace and room as they begin this process of walking back the policy." Laurie responded, "I'm writing a very strong first draft; it will need tempering."

I finally pulled myself together and returned to the clinic floor. Over the next hour, I moved the patient schedule along, popping back into my office at pre-planned times to interface with the rapid response team. After Laurie posted the first draft template and our edit suggestions started coming in, the honesty of the immediate reactions struck me. They came in like rapid fire as we furiously typed out our first impressions exactly as they fell out of our heads and burst from our hearts. Our task in this new Affirmation communications initiative was not to edit down a first draft to milquetoast but to hone the institutional message so that it would boldly stand up for the community in a queer-centric manner and not reopen trauma in our peers.

As we approached Arizona's ten o'clock hour, only a few minor details remained, mainly what the headline should be. We were now beginning to get calls from the press and the Human Rights Campaign asking for Affirmation's response. By this point, I had kept my next patient waiting for over twenty minutes, so I asked Laurie to bring this process home and get it out to the press ASAP. Making the final touches, Laurie messaged the group: "We have an exceptional and timely statement on the table now. Thanks to our combined efforts. Let's move to get it released." This was an intense moment in a short amount of time. As I walked in to see my patient, he commented about me being late. I apologized for keeping him waiting, and then it dawned on me. The Church's announcement that morning lacked one critical component: an apology.

Affirmation's response went out under the headline, "Affirmation Applauds Reversal of the November 2015 Policy on Gay Families, Acknowledges Continuing Pain."[6] Within minutes of posting our official statement, we began to receive a substantial number of comments from many in the LGBTQ Mormon community who had been searching for a response—any response—that resonated with them after this surprise announcement. Many shared that they felt seen and heard by Affirmation. We were able to put into words how they felt but couldn't fully articulate. We had struck the balance of acknowledging the positives of walking back the harmful exclusion policy while realistically representing the depth of pain that LGBTQ Mormons had experienced over the past three and a half years.

I was intensely proud of our collective effort, working together to be a beacon of hope for the queer Latter-day Saint community. I also liked that we furthered the objectives that the board had charted as our member support needs moved from "pre-exclusion policy" messaging to "post-exclusion policy"

---

6. Affirmation: LGBTQ Mormons, Families & Friends. "Affirmation Applauds Reversal of the November 2015 Policy on Gay Families, Acknowledges Continuing Pain." Affirmation, April 4, 2019. https://affirmation.org/affirmation-applauds-reversal-of-the-november-2015-policy-on-gay-families-acknowledges-continuing-pain/.

messaging. In this, we unashamedly provided an institutional voice that acknowledged the lived experience of queer Mormons, contextualizing what was happening from a queer-centric position, and acknowledging progress and improvement towards queer people. At its end, our statement cast the hope of the refugee. Affirmation would provide safe spaces of unconditional acceptance for all LGBTQ Mormons and former Mormons while it continued to work towards the time when every individual who chose to worship God could do so with full acceptance, fellowship, equality, and love. During lunch, I drove to a nearby park, where I took calls and answered emails from reporters asking for comment. That afternoon Bill called me. "Nathan Kitchen! Great statement. So well done." His feedback meant a lot to me coming from a career public relations guy. He explained that Thursdays were the days he worked in the Salt Lake Temple. When he walked out after his shift, he was not only greeted by a hundred rapid-response team messages but by a very different world for LGBTQ Mormons than the one he left behind earlier that morning. "Talk about a surprise," he quipped.

When we met as an executive committee later that day, I contrasted Bill's feedback with the feedback we had received from the Church that our statement sounded "harsh." Laurie countered that there were a lot of hugely harmed people out there who did not see any magnanimity in the Church reversing what was so horrible in the first place. This observation kicked me back to a conversation I had with Bill and Greg Prince over breakfast at the Coffee Shop in Little America a month earlier when Greg was in Salt Lake preparing to launch his book *Gay Rights and the Mormon Church*. Between bites, he leaned over his plate, looked me in the eye, and asked, "What are your plans for Affirmation as you begin your presidency?" I led off with the thought that, like my predecessors, I would continue strengthening Affirmation's relationship and dialogue with the

Church. Greg looked at me and point-blank said, "Don't focus on the men in the red chairs. Lobbying the brethren is a waste of time." He noted that there was nothing that I, Affirmation, or any LGBTQ individual or group could say that would change the minds or course of the men in the red chairs. Giving advice between bites, he reminded me that the Church is very self-conscious about its image. "The best thing you can do is focus on building strong, visible LGBTQ communities that show happiness and success, the kind of vibrant public success that embarrasses the Church for holding harmful, exclusionary stances about LGBTQ people." This point of view stunned me. I looked over at Bill, who looked just as surprised. I remembered that Greg sat on the board during Affirmation's successful Thacker administration before the modern church enacted the exclusion policy, when the idea was that our relationship, dialogue, and reconciliation with the Church was seen as a critical part of the identity and success of Affirmation and LGBTQ people in general.[7] Greg holds a unique "insider" vantage point as an ally. His privilege allows him access to the same circles as the men in the red chairs while at the same time lets him see the "behind the scenes" discussions held in queer-led Mormon spaces. As Bill pressed Greg about his position, I pushed my breakfast potatoes around my plate, wondering what Greg had witnessed in the modern church and the changing landscape of the queer/Latter-day Saint intersection over the past six years that led him to draw such conclusions. Finishing his last few bites, Greg summed up his observations, reiterating them in a follow-up email: "It will take twelve years and two funerals before any substantial changes occur for LGBTQ members."

---

7. Prince, Gregory A. "Bridges to Somewhere." In *Gay Rights and the Mormon Church*, 213-14. Salt Lake City, Utah: The University of Utah Press, 2019.

I shared with the executive committee that during breakfast, Greg predicted the exclusion policy would eventually be walked back to neutral like the Church's position on birth control was. Now, a month later, here it was. I observed that from a queer perspective, even neutral was still deeply embedded in prejudice. So, what to do now in neutral? Laurie, Jairo, and I shared our observations about the state of the queer/Latter-day Saint intersection. We discussed the merits and possible blind spots of Greg's observations. I proposed our forward movement at the dawn of this post-exclusion policy era, noting that the Church may enact the policies, but it has no claim on how people experience those policies. We must be able to name our hurts and share our experiences if we ever expect to rise out of trauma and move towards queer joy. We must be able to talk about this publicly. We must also give space for grief. Grieving is not a sign of weakness or unfaithfulness. Anyone, anywhere on the faith spectrum, has a human right to express the depth of pain they have experienced at the hands of another. We cannot abandon our peers at this moment, hide their voices, or move along as if nothing had happened. This was not a time for us to shrink ourselves small to placate the feelings of an institution that had exacted the harshest exclusion to date upon its own LGBTQ members and their children.

Within hours after the recension, LGBTQ Mormons started sharing their experiences about life under the exclusion policy. I noticed that some of these experiences were being discounted or gaslit: "You are exaggerating," "You are being overly dramatic," or "It wasn't really that bad." The greatest betrayal to LGBTQ Latter-day Saints concerning this vulnerable moment eventually found its way into *The Routledge Handbook of Mormonism and*

Gender, casting the public sharing of our experiences under the exclusion policy as "overwhelmingly rehearsed stories of pain and trauma."[8] I was deeply concerned by the queer-erasing language appearing just hours after the recension. Personal experiences were being quieted and discounted so that a power structure's dominant narrative might prevail. My biggest fear was that, at some point, the Church itself would enter the chat and try to downplay, or worse, erase the entire queer experience and assign its own meaning to the event. What could Affirmation do? Whatever we did would be tricky, considering the culture of dialogue that had risen within Affirmation during the post-Prop 8 bubble of the early 2010s.

I took a moment to step back and give myself a bird's eye view of the historical landscape of Affirmation that had brought us to this juncture where it was "OK" to challenge, discount, and even hide another queer person's experience in the queer/Latter-day Saint intersection. It hadn't always been this way. I remembered that when my friend, Dennis Kelsch, was researching Affirmation's publicly archived newsletters of the 80s and 90s for an article he was writing, he shared with me that he had originally hypothesized that Affirmation's historical attitude towards the Church was like a pendulum swinging back and forth between favorable and unfavorable depending on who was in control of the leadership. This should have been reflected in what made it to print and what was censored. He was surprised that the data showed otherwise. No matter who was in charge, "the newsletter was willing to print opposing viewpoints right alongside each other at the same time." He concluded that as an organization, "Affirmation has regularly been sought after as a safe avenue for ALL to express feelings towards the church;

---

8. Gustav-Wrathall, John Donald. "Mormon LGBTQ Organizing and Organizations." In *The Routledge Handbook of Mormonism and Gender*, 233. Edited by Amy Hoyt and Taylor Petrey. Abingdon, UK: Routledge, 2022.

both pro and con. There have been petitions for ALL thoughts and feelings to be openly expressed so that members can form and congeal their own opinions."⁹

Outside of Dennis's analysis were the 2010s. Affirmation's tolerance for the entire spectrum of queer Mormon expression cooled once the Church created its post-Prop 8 bubble and introduced the "Mormon and Gays" website in December of 2012, advertising "belonging." Brand new generations of queer people, their parents, and allies were now flooding into this new space in record numbers and became interested in Affirmation, attracted by its 2013 motto: "You can be gay and Mormon too—you don't have to choose." Many had no knowledge of the historical conditions that their queer elders of the Church experienced, and assumed that the Church had always been this reasonable. They did not have the tools to contextualize or even recognize the shoulders of the queer giants that they were now standing on, who for decades paved the way for this remarkable moment of "bubble belonging" in the Church. This was also the moment the Church became interested in Affirmation. Dialoguing with the Church about this new LGBTQ belonging became a priority for Affirmation. The Church made it clear it was amenable to dialogue provided that Affirmation cool any harsh public messaging that might embarrass the Church.

This new public face of Affirmation was confusing for some of Affirmation's queer elders who had been hugely harmed by past Church actions and had something to say about it, loudly. They now not only felt silenced but with generational wisdom, they saw right through the post Prop-8 bubble to see it for what it was: a portent of impending harm. Their vocal pushback fueled a growing internal "us vs. them" binary narrative

---

9. Kelsch, Dennis. "The Mormon and Affirmation Relationship: It's Complicated." Affirmation, July 22, 2019. https://affirmation.org/the-mormon-and-affirmation-relationship-its-complicated/.

that persisted through the first few years of the exclusion policy. Younger generations, and even some of our leaders, unfairly cast the older generations as angry, bitter ex-Mormons who had driven Affirmation to the brink of bankruptcy, requiring a reboot of the organization in order to save it.[10] This binary narrative of the "good" happy queer Mormon vs. the "bad" angry queer ex-Mormon greeted me when I entered Affirmation in 2015. Affirmation's executive director, John Gustav-Wrathall, instrumental in perpetuating the "us vs. them" strategy to favor dialogue with the Church, told *The Salt Lake Tribune* in 2017 that Affirmation determined "we couldn't be the angry ex-Mormon organization anymore."[11]

Now, here I was, in 2019, president of Affirmation, knee-deep in the immediate aftermath and queer trauma of the recension of the exclusion policy, having inherited the binary scripts of an Affirmation past. I realized the irony of John's statement. Affirmation's greatest attribute was indeed that it is *always not its past anymore*. This is a feature, not a bug. As previous Affirmation administrations courageously confronted the consequences of the Church's post-Prop 8 bubble in 2013 and then the implementation of the 2015 exclusion policy, they rode the crest of the current events of their day in the queer/Latter-day Saint intersection, needing to let go of the past ways of doing things while staying laser focused on Affirmation's mission. The art and science of change is to do this without disenfranchising your elders, and admittedly, Affirmation had not done a good

---

10. Stack, Peggy Fletcher, and Jennifer Dobner. "Affirmation, the Gay Mormon Support Group, Has Seen a 'Sea Change' in Its 40 Years." *The Salt Lake Tribune*, September 23, 2017. https://www.sltrib.com/news/2017/09/23/affirmation-the-gay-mormon-support-group-has-seen-a-sea-change-in-its-40-years/.

11. Stack, Peggy Fletcher, and Jennifer Dobner. "Affirmation, the Gay Mormon Support Group, Has Seen a 'Sea Change' in Its 40 Years." *The Salt Lake Tribune*, September 23, 2017.

job with this. It was time to engage with the executive committee about how to implement our mission under these new circumstances in a post exclusion policy world. One thing was certain, when previous generations of Affirmation leaders deliver the organization to a new leadership team, they are handing you their precious and meaningful work that they dedicated their life to accomplish. They don't hand it to you so that you can coast along on their coat tails in the status quo, they hand it to you with the expectation that you will grasp this baton, hit the ground running, and continue to raise Affirmation. And this means daring to lead in the face of change.

As I prepared to discuss our path forward with the executive committee, I realized that the answer had been in front of me the whole time. During his lunchtime lecture at the 2015 St. Francis of Assisi exhibition in Brooklyn, Dr. John Edwards demonstrated that Catholic scholars explore and acknowledge their church's periods of harmful behaviors, decline, and renewal without it becoming a "belief" issue. He candidly acknowledged the reasons why St. Francis of Assisi needed to save the Medieval Church but never once insinuated that the Catholic Church herself was anything less than the beloved bride of Christ, worthy of the dignity and respect that such a holy position holds. He respectfully communicated a great sadness in the wounding of the Church at the hands of those who were ordained to lead her on Earth, calling St. Francis of Assisi and the Franciscans the answer for God's people when the Church went astray. This very healthy way to look at a church was missing in Mormonism, especially in queer Latter-day Saint spaces. Every discussion about our church immediately gravitates to either supporting or denying its truth claims. We lack the space and expansiveness to explore different faith narratives or talk about the harmful attributes of the Church, its declines, or prejudices, without others immediately viewing such talk as an accusation that the Church is not "true."

It was time as a community to practice the ethics of moral conversation, dialogue, and disclosure. As a healthcare provider, I have been trained in the art of ethical dialogue, which surprisingly mirrors how Dr. Edwards conducted his ethical and moral discussion about cycles of decline and a church going astray. The healthcare professional is morally bound to speak the truth and ethically obligated never to hide information from a patient, no matter how difficult the conversation. We have open, honest dialogue with the patient about their condition and then collaborate on a solution without ever questioning the dignity of the patient. Likewise, it was time to instill such ethics in the queer/Latter-day Saint intersection. It was time to return to our roots in Affirmation and acknowledge, affirm, and give space for the exploration of the entire queer experience but with one critical change from our immediate past. We needed to remove the culture of institutional gatekeeping—judging stories as either supporting or challenging the truthfulness of the Church. Hard conversations and even venting about the queer Latter-day experience is not inherently an "angry ex-Mormon trait." Affirmation existed to create communities of safety, love, and hope. It did not exist to prove or disprove the Church. Such judgments are statements of belief and very personal for each queer person to decide for themselves. Every queer soul has the right to speak up about their experiences, their joys and harms, and their personal beliefs or non-beliefs about the Church. If we cannot freely speak to this, or extend such courtesy to our queer peers, then what in the world have our queer elders been fighting for since Stonewall? It was time to fully embrace the concept of healthy collaboration in how we dialogue with others and the Church. We must be able to freely speak about what is harming us. I remembered that this idea had been simmering just below the surface with the board since Affirmation's 2018 strategic planning session in Mesa. It now needed to be fully implemented.

As I had forecast at Loyola Marymount in 2016, the exclusion policy had been highly effective at splitting the queer Latter-day Saint community into binaries of faithful and unfaithful, casting anyone who named their hurts and wounds as being "angry" or "bitter" and anyone who professed belief in the Church as "misguided" or "naïve." It was time for Affirmation to do a very healthy queer thing: reject binaries and demonstrate unity in our diversity, including our spiritual diversity. We must embrace the morality of engaging in ethical dialogue about the queer experience, including our experiences with prejudice, harassment, and discrimination in the Church, without everyone immediately retreating to team "Church" or team "Queer." You can be just as Christ-centered flipping tables in a temple as you can by participating in quiet devotional activities. You can be a queer person of faith and still explore the harms and prejudice of your spiritual home. You can affirm another's testimony and faith without it threatening your own beliefs or invalidating your own experience. Such positions were not possible in an "us vs. them," Mormon/ex-Mormon narrative. But now, the landscape had changed, it was time to change the narrative. It was time to embrace the morality and expansiveness of ethical dialogue, accounting for our history and our queer elders, while remaining true to the diverse experiences, belief, and faith nuances of queer Latter-day Saints today. This is the beautiful messiness of queerness.

When I got home after work, I opened the Doctrine and Covenants, turned to section 123, and read this admonition in the section heading: "The Saints should collect and publish an account of their sufferings and persecutions." It was an imperative duty that we owed to the rising generation. "Let no man count them as small things" (Doctrine and Covenants 123:15). This was the answer for Affirmation, the Latter-day Saint way forward in fostering ethical conversations, first given to Joseph Smith while he was held prisoner at the Liberty Jail in Missouri. This was how we could begin to reclaim one of the defining characteristics of Affirmation since its founding: its tolerance for publishing the entire depth and breadth of the queer experience within the queer/Latter-day Saint intersection. I proposed to the executive committee that Affirmation gather up the stories of any queer Mormon or former Mormon who experienced life under the exclusion policy and share them on our extensive social media platforms. We would retain these stories as a permanent repository on our website—a site that the United States Library of Congress has been continually archiving since 2002 as a matter of public interest.[12]

In doing so, I wanted to ensure that this call for personal stories was a queer-centric event, not a church-centric one. This would be a healing event to address trauma, not bury it. It would not be a free-for-all "bash the church" venture but a trauma-informed invitation to speak from personal experience. I pulled out some scratch paper and began to flesh out my invitation to all in Affirmation: "We do not want to hide your story. Name your hurts, call out those who have harmed you, tell of your triumphs, and speak to your queer joy, but whatever you do, don't suppress your experiences. Assign meaning to them, record them, and publish this authenticity to the world." This was a moment to take Joseph Smith at his word. If any of this sharing of our stories made one appear angry or unfaithful,

---

12. Library of Congress. *Affirmation: LGBTQ Mormons, Families & Friends.* United States, 2001. Web Archive. https://www.loc.gov/item/lcwaN0028631/.

then the entirety of Doctrine and Covenants 123 was a recipe for anger and a toxic guide. But it is not. After any traumatic event, anger is not the destination. You can't stay in anger and ever expect to heal. The final admonition in section 123 is the great key to this process of collecting and publishing an account of a people's sufferings and persecutions: "Cheerfully do all things that lie in our power, and then stand still with the utmost assurance" that God will take care of the rest (Doctrine and Covenants 123:17).

The next morning, I published the call for personal stories about people's experiences under the exclusion policy: "This event belongs to all of us."[13] The floodgates were open, and we started receiving story after story. One man lamented that he was a poor writer and had hoped for some editorial help. At the same time, Kristine Haglund, a former editor at *Dialogue: A Journal of Mormon Thought*, contacted me and offered her editing skills. It was humbling to see fellow Latter-day Saints answer the call and come together to gather up these important stories. To capture the immediacy of our feelings, I kept the submission window for stories short. Like our immediate reactions as a rapid response team, I wanted to capture the immediate emotions of those who lived under the exclusion policy. Over forty thoughtful stories were submitted and published, each a powerful reflection of this moment.[14]

The day after our call for stories, Elder Neil L. Andersen stood at General Conference and observed that "a chaste gay

---

13. Kitchen, Nathan. "A Call for Your Stories: Reversal of the November 2015 Policy." Affirmation, April 5, 2019. Accessed July 28, 2024. https://affirmation.org/a-call-for-your-stories-reversal-of-the-november-2015-policy/.

14. Affirmation: LGBTQ Mormons, Families & Friends. "Stories and Reactions to Reversal of the November 2015 Policy on Gay Families - Affirmation: LGBTQ Mormons, Families & Friends." Affirmation, April 6, 2019. https://affirmation.org/tag/nov-15-policy-gay-families-reversal/.

man can have a fulfilling, even noble life."[15] It is always so fascinating to me to see a man so abundantly blessed by the institution of marriage try to sell celibacy to the homosexual population in the Church.[16] This was not breaking news. Of course, gay Latter-day Saints can live a fulfilling life even in celibacy. I know some who do. I also know straight Latter-day Saints who live incredibly fulfilling chaste lives as single people. This is not the issue. The issue is the inequality of treatment between a gay or lesbian Latter-day Saint and a straight Latter-day Saint when they choose to marry according to their orientation. That's the news. And it's not good news. After listening to Elder Andersen, I now understood what President Oaks meant earlier when he said that immoral conduct in heterosexual or homosexual relationships would be treated in the same way: Everyone would be treated equally under a law of chastity that, in practice, was not equal for queer people. His was a tricky way to cast this to not facially appear discriminatory, indicating that the sole configuration of marriage approved by the Church is available to everyone regardless of sexual orientation or gender identity. Everyone would be judged equally according to how they obeyed or disobeyed the chastity rules currently interpreted as one-man/one-woman marriage. Lucky for you if you happen to be heterosexual and cisgender.

My last interview about the recension was with Samantha Allen at the Daily Beast. As a trans woman with Mormon heritage, she

---

15. Stack, Peggy Fletcher, and Lee Davidson. "Gay Latter-Day Saints Can Live a Fulfilling Life Even in Celibacy, Apostle Says." *The Salt Lake Tribune.* https://www.sltrib.com/religion/2019/04/06/practicing-your-faith-not/.

16. Andersen, Neil L. "The Eye of Faith." *The Ensign*, May 2019. https://www.churchofjesuschrist.org/study/ensign/2019/05/25andersen

was interested in what was next for LGBTQ Mormons. It was a moment I could sum up my thoughts about the entire experience. I acknowledged that this event had changed us as a community. And in this change, we would move forward—stronger, more resilient, and more aware of ourselves. This was a time to be proud of what we had endured and to realize that we could personally move forward regardless of what the Church said or did. I wasn't pinning my hopes on policy change or church LGBTQ reforms, but instead on the community of LGBTQ Mormons I wanted to keep building. I didn't want to just sit around and wait for change. Church leaders are responsible for getting that answer about change and reform. "Meanwhile, I'm going to be me," I told Samantha. "I'm going to draw my friends, my family, and my community into my circle of love. That's where I focus."[17]

---

17. Allen, Samantha. "The LGBT Mormons Pushing the Church to Accept Equality." The Daily Beast, April 13, 2019. https://www.thedailybeast.com/the-lgbt-mormons-pushing-the-church-to-accept-equality.

A bird is not an ornithologist.

It just is.

Living life as itself

Basking in the sun and eating a morning meal

And singing.

Oh, the singing!

Being.

Despite book, proclamation, and policy

Being!

Naming does not confine nor words control—

Neither two farthings.

For the thing jotted in a field notebook is nothing for the bird in the field.

Both man and God watch the sparrow fall

But in the watching

It is still a sparrow.

CHAPTER 15

Seatbelts, Please

> We firmly believe that Affirmation had a place in the plan of our Father in Heaven and His Kingdom and that the Holy Spirit is still with us, as individuals and as a group of His Children, guiding us in what we are seeking to accomplish. His Spirit is most reflected when we are working toward our goals, ever mindful of the needs of our sisters and brothers, ourselves, and the working of our Savior in our lives and in our hearts.
>
> Matt Price
> Founder of Affirmation
> June 1977

The day before Affirmation's International Conference in June 2019, I sat face-to-face across the table from the Church's religious freedom specialist in the Joseph Smith Memorial building. It was but another complete surprise in what was turning out to be a six-month baptism by fire as president of Affirmation.

When I hit the ground running at the beginning of my term, I was immediately immersed in my behind-the-scenes duties of running a board, assessing employment structure and financial controls, and nurturing the health of our communities. However, the position also explicitly sets the president out in front of the curtain as its official spokesperson to dignitaries, the press, and the public.[1] This is the institutional voice of Affirmation and this unique role came into sharp focus during the unexpected recension of the exclusion policy. While I was president of Affirmation, I had the rare opportunity most members of the Church do not get: to not only be an institutional voice but experience the institutional voice of the Church. This is an entirely different animal than how members typically interact with the Church as a spiritual home. It is a competitive church-ball experience of elbows and uncalled fouls, far from the gentleness of love experienced in a pastoral worship setting.

The institutional church is outward-facing, and tussles in politics, social issues, and government matters around the world. It also forges relationships with other religious and social organizations to create beneficial coalitions. It draws from its long institutional history of tussles and relationships—some dating back two hundred years to its founding—to inform its modern-day social awareness and political savviness. One notable long-standing tussle is the Church's institutional relationship with the LGBTQ civil rights movement. Affirmation not only has an institutional voice as well, but it also has an institutional history. In short order, I needed to plug myself into this history and become socially aware of just how special and important Affirmation had been in the lives of so many LGBTQ people. I had the responsibility to honor the work and lives of my queer elders who, for decades, delivered Affirmation to the

---

1. "Charter & Bylaws." Affirmation: LGBTQ Mormons, Families & Friends. Section 4.1.4. February 8, 2022. https://affirmation.org/about/charter-bylaws/.

next generation in the hope and trust that it would continue being just as special and important for those who followed.

Because of this trust of continuance, I also had the responsibility to keep Affirmation and its communities relevant in the rapidly changing landscape of LGBTQ civil rights, meeting the needs of queer people in real time. The Church also exists in this changing landscape and makes strategic moves to protect its religious freedoms amid such change. In those changes, Affirmation creates communities to support queer people and their families through dominant narrative collapses, rebuilds, and policy enactments. The relative speed at which this all happens means that even a span of three or four years can mean a completely different landscape for Affirmation to navigate. An example of how interconnected the LGBTQ civil rights movement, the modern church, and Affirmation are to one another would be the Supreme Court's 2015 Obergefell ruling recognizing marriage equality in the United States. This huge win for the LGBTQ civil rights movement meant an immediate response by the Church to protect itself by issuing the 2015 exclusion policy. In turn, Affirmation shifted focus according to the needs of queer Latter-day Saints to more trauma-aware support for LGBTQ people and their children, becoming a place of refuge for the policy's spiritual refugees as well as providing community-focused lifesaving measures against spiritual violence.

Today, every Affirmation president walks into a program already in progress. This is why it is imperative to assemble a trusted team, identify what is happening now, forecast what is on the horizon, and continue the rise of Affirmation for that moment in history. It's how we honor our past and build our future. One of my first orders of business in 2019 was to drink from a firehose to get up to speed on the landscape I was navigating. One thing I knew for sure: Affirmation was encountering a new phenomenon in the modern church's relationship with the LGBTQ civil rights movement, and I had only just begun putting the pieces together.

※

After watching the new First Presidency roll out its "love of the Lord and law of the Lord" narrative,[2] hearing President Nelson tell young adults in Las Vegas that Satan tempts us to "love as we should not love,"[3] reading his admonition to the Saints in Chile to eat their vitamin pills because more change was coming in this ongoing restoration,[4] and then experiencing the dismantling of the exclusion policy, I had a pretty good idea that wherever the Church was going next in its relationship with its queer population, it would be running, not crawling, to get there. It was time to put on a seatbelt. The Church was terraforming the landscape for queer Latter-day Saints, and we would be off-roading for a while.

One of the impacts Affirmation immediately felt with a new First Presidency was the dissolution of the Office of Public Affairs, folding it into a new entity, the Church Communication Department. Affirmation had long enjoyed a relationship with Public Affairs. We had each other on speed dial. We were consulted on the Mormon and Gay website, and they facilitated the application and approval of our suicide prevention grant with

---

2. "First Presidency News Conference." January 16, 2018.
3. Mims, Bob. "Satan Tempts Us to 'Love as We Should Not Love,' LDS Prophet Russell M. Nelson Warns Mormon Millennials." *The Salt Lake Tribune*, 2018. https://www.sltrib.com/religion/2018/02/19/satan-tempts-us-to-love-as-we-should-not-love-lds-prophet-russell-m-nelson-warns-mormon-millennials/.
4. Staff, Church News. "Video: 'Eat Your Vitamin Pills. Get Your Rest,' Says President Nelson on the Future of the Church." Church News, November 29, 2018. https://www.thechurchnews.com/2018/11/28/23264563/video-eat-your-vitamin-pills-get-your-rest-says-president-nelson-on-the-future-of-the-church/.

the LDS Foundation. Not only did we have an open door with Public Affairs, but for years, during Affirmation's International Conference, we would bring in LGBTQ people from around the world to meet with them. At headquarters, Affirmation members would share their personal stories. For these meetings, Public Affairs asked everyone to bring a second copy of their stories so they could keep one in their binders for possible inclusion in a packet for the brethren. Typically, there was not a dry eye in the room when these stories were shared. The Public Affairs employees were attentive, asking follow-up questions and making everyone feel heard. For years, this kind of engagement brought some hope that such relationships and efforts at headquarters would soften hearts and help remove homophobia and transphobia. This was the long-haul strategy for Affirmation, held before and into the exclusion policy. However, as the exclusion policy wore on, it felt more like we were flying in a holding pattern rather than being given permission to come in for a landing among the Saints.

When Public Affairs was dissolved, we not only lost those hard-won relationships but also lost contact. Since Bill still had connections at headquarters, I asked him to make some inquiries. We were told that everything was in flux and that we would eventually have a contact again. After some time, we were assigned a liaison with government affairs. As our International Conference approached, I called our point of contact and introduced myself. I shared that in the past when Affirmation held its International Conferences in Utah, we would traditionally meet with our contacts at headquarters for dialogue. I asked if he would be open to meeting with us. He was affable, and we made an appointment to meet at the Joseph Smith Memorial Building in Salt Lake. I asked Laurie and Bill to come with me as we established initial contact.

On the day of our meeting, we were ushered into a meeting room in the JSMB. When our contact entered the room, he was flanked by one of the Church's religious freedom specialists. In this display, it no longer felt like a collaborative public affairs moment. It was a brand-new twist in the forty-year relationship between the modern church and Affirmation. I felt like we were being looked at through a new lens. The immediate incompatibility with this new dynamic was that religious freedom and "fairness for all" politics were not in Affirmation's wheelhouse. They never have been. Since our beginnings, we have been singly focused on the individual needs of our queer peers, supporting them in their personal intersection with the Church while creating safe and supportive communities to accompany them as they navigated towards queer joy. In this context, with the Church as a collaborative partner, we were highly invested in supporting queer Latter-day Saints who called the Church their spiritual home. Yet, that was not how the Church now wanted to interface with us. I wondered if it had put any kind of thought into this pairing. Had they not drawn from our shared institutional history to inform this decision? And then I came to the realization that perhaps they had.

The clue about this shift happened a year earlier when, in that very same building, Elder Christofferson hosted the NAACP. Over lunch, he spoke with NAACP leaders about religious liberty, LGBT rights, and fairness for all. He talked about pluralism being the best solution in society to protect both LGBT rights and religious rights. Throughout his remarks, he spoke of the "religious community" and the "LGBT community" as wholly separate from one another, binaries in identity. He observed that both sides want many of the same things: affirmation of their basic dignity, social respect, freedom to live life according to the dictates of conscience, and social and legal equality: "These are the core interests animating both religious believers on one hand and LGBT people on the other."[5]

My jaw dropped as I watched Sistas in Zion livestream Elder Christofferson's remarks on their Facebook page. Religious believers on one hand and LGBT people on the other? As a gay Latter-day Saint, I very much experienced a space in the overlapping center of these two spheres, making this a Venn diagram, not two separate, unconnected orbs. He was completely ignoring the concerns and experiences of LGBTQ people within the faith.

Elder Christofferson argued that in a fairness-for-all approach, neither side should face an existential threat to its core rights and interests: "Each side should do everything possible to avoid conflicts that the other side has to win in order to survive."[6] His assertion frustrated me. A major—if not *the* major—core interest for LGBTQ Latter-day Saints is exaltation—not being excluded from their heavenly parents, spouses, or families for the eternities. Current Latter-day Saint doctrine means queer erasure, which is an absolute existential threat to the queer soul. In the case of comparing existential threats, the Church will absolutely survive full-equality LGBTQ Latter-day Saint inclusion. It will 100% survive and even thrive. However, LGBTQ people will not survive the loss of eternal life. This kind of separation from God is the very definition of spiritual death. In the queer/Latter-day Saint intersection, only one existential threat exists, and it is for queer Latter-day Saints. What were the "everything possibles" the Church was doing to avoid this existential threat for LGBTQ Latter-day Saints?

---

5. Sistas In Zion, 2018. "Elder Christofferson's address to the NAACP livestream." *Facebook*. May 18, 2018. https://fb.watch/tySm8ON4VD/.

6. Sistas In Zion, 2018. "Elder Christofferson's address to the NAACP livestream." *Facebook*. May 18, 2018.

I certainly did not feel any kind of avoidance of conflicts on the Church's part under the weight of the exclusion policy still in force at that time.

After Elder Christofferson finished his remarks, my mind turned to my peers in Affirmation around the world. I knew them and knew their hearts. Queer Latter-day Saints were not asking to come in and burn everything down. No, as integral parts of their families, they desired spiritual equality in both privilege and opportunity to equitably access the law of chastity, marry the love of their life, and live their gender as they experienced it—to rise along with their straight/cisgender peers in the plan of salvation. We are *not* on one hand or the other. We are directly in between these two outstretched hands that Elder Christofferson spoke of—in between and at the center—being at the heart of the matter.

During our meeting, I tried not to be upset that religious freedom was in the room. It was more than a reminder of the power imbalance that exists in the spiritual home of queer Latter-day Saints. It was a display of strategy in the Church's ongoing post Prop 8 efforts, where it held separately an external focus on the LGBTQ community and an internal focus on its own LGBTQ population.

Externally, the Church highlights its desire to find common ground with the LGBTQ community so that they can work together. Finding common ground is essential in this scenario because both parties compromise when they work together. However, internally, LGBTQ Latter-day Saints exist on church ground, not common ground. We are the prize to be won in the Church's external religious freedom endeavors, to be managed at the sole discretion of the Church as a sincerely held religious belief without threat of government civil rights interference. In this strategy, our civil rights interests as LGBTQ Latter-day Saints are to be represented by our LGBTQ community leaders in a pluralistic society, while our eternal life interests are to be represented solely by the Church acting as a benevolent dictatorship—no compromises, no negotiations. This leaves us vulnerable to prejudice, policies, dominant narratives, and doctrine interpreted as having no place for us in our authenticity. Vigorously protecting religious liberty ensures that these two interests, external and internal, never meet under the law or the Civil Rights Act. Religious liberty in the queer/Latter-day Saint intersection means prejudice and acts of prejudice within our spiritual home.

It is difficult for some LGBTQ Latter-day Saints to fully appreciate the vast amount of ground the Church covers in the LGBTQ world. For most people, church offers an experience to feel the spirit as a community, where our neighbors are called to shepherd and serve for a while. Because we are part of a family, it is easy to project this feeling of family onto how the Church operates. The cold, hard reality of church government is often missing in this pastoral scene. Church government is the complex hierarchical system of power that maintains order, administers the ordinances, and protects the doctrine. Church government is the power center of the Church. But unlike a democratic system of government, you, as a queer person, are not allowed into the decision-making room of the power center nor afforded any ability to negotiate or change the system when you feel it unjust. This power center of church government is protected by the right of religious freedom. The Church has utilized this right in the past to defend its practice of polygamy and its priesthood/temple ban on Black people. Today, religious liberty broadcasts that you have no power here if you are authentically queer.

As the meeting wound down, I indicated that both Affirmation and the Church have a shared mutual interest in the wellbeing of LGBTQ Latter-day Saints. LGBTQ people do not live in a vacuum. They are surrounded by a family that loves them—and these families are eternal. In this family-centered/Church-supported era, families in the Church with LGBTQ children need critical support. When I suggested various ways to make the Church safer for LGBTQ people that didn't require a change in doctrine, I was met with several counter reasons why the way things were working now was just fine. I was most alarmed when I highlighted the different ways LGBTQ Latter-day Saints were being treated and disciplined around the world, some harshly. I suggested that a worldwide leadership training could calibrate local leadership on the Church's official stances for ministering to LGBTQ Latter-day Saints. This would protect those who lived in less affirming wards and stakes, saving lives. Without comment, this was countered with the observation about how wonderful it was that local leaders have the latitude to make specific decisions that are right for their particular location. This praise of leadership roulette was the praise of prejudice, where queer people are highly vulnerable to the preferences of whoever happens to be leading their ward or stake. By the end of the meeting, I realized the sea change that had happened here, moving from a public relations relationship to a religious freedom relationship. There would be no relationship building or collaboration on the scale that we had enjoyed with the public relations department. Later, as Laurie, Bill, and I stood on the sidewalk on South Temple reflecting on our experience that morning, Bill—a coalition builder by profession and skilled at finding common ground—wondered aloud what had just happened, noting the Church's change in tone, direction, and engagement.

Maybe Greg Prince *was* on to something during our breakfast at Little America. The previous rules of engagement with public affairs tolerated dialogue within an agreed-upon "time out" space where the Church would not focus on the boundaries in its doctrine, theology, or practices that excluded queer people in exaltation, marriage, and family. In turn, Affirmation would not press the Church on these topics. This timeout space created a bubble within a doctrine hostile to queer exaltation to dialogue about respect, recognition, understanding, and compassion to the degree that such things never challenged the doctrinal premise, dominant narrative, or policies. Amid a new administration and department reorganization, the modern church had just shattered its "gentleman's agreement" of engagement with its queer population. What it now brought to the table was a bold declaration of its rights under the law to manage its queer population in the Church, the brandishing of religious freedom, and a bright light that called attention to precisely where the boundaries were in the law of the Lord that would enable someone to remain an acceptable queer in the kingdom. This was now an institutional display of power, probably a valuable tactic to carve out its place in this world of increasing LGBTQ civil rights, but a soul-crushing power imbalance for the queer children of God in the kingdom. The existence of boundaries, exclusions, and rights was no longer the elephant in the room; the modern church was now evangelizing them. These boundaries were now the focus. Any conversation now was filtered through religious freedom with a baseline understanding that the Church was just and right in both human law and God's law for behaving as it did. The focus now was on the law, not on love.

The post-Prop 8 timeout was over. We were now in regulation play. Religious freedom was in the room. In the ebbs and flows of the shared history between the modern church and

Affirmation, we had entered new territory in the Church's relationship with its queer population. This was a territory that President Oaks lamented during a BYU-Hawaii devotional just two weeks earlier, one where religious freedom would be fiercely utilized as both shield and sword, simultaneously protecting and defending itself from the "increasing frequency and power of the culture and phenomenon of lesbian, gay and transgender lifestyles and values."[7] The landscape had definitely changed, and the territory toward which the Church was pushing its queer population was entirely uncharted. There was no knowing what lay ahead.

---

7. Oaks, Dallin H. "Anxiety in Stressful Times." BYUH Speeches, June 11, 2019. https://speeches.byuh.edu/devotional/anxiety-in-stressful-times.

CHAPTER 16

World Pride

> Pride is the opposite of shame.
> I hope that every person, especially those who have been previously weighed down by shame, feel an overwhelming sense of dignity, self-respect, and honor.
>
> Ben Schilaty
July 2, 2019

The arrival of June 2019 meant it was time for the Affirmation International Conference! This would be my fifth International Conference and first as its president. These gatherings always recharge my batteries as I spend the weekend with some of the best people I know.

Before Friday evening's opening session, the Board of Affirmation met in the Utah Valley Convention Center's Boardroom in Provo, windows opening to the mountains in panoramic view. Since we typically conduct Affirmation's business over Zoom, this was our first time together in a year. Board members pepper the globe and are vital in linking the worldwide LGBTQ network of mentors and peers. The wellbeing of each board member is critical to the entire organization. Meeting face-to-face is a time for the senior leaders to feel uplifted, appreciated, recognized in community, and enveloped in the excitement of our work.

Saturday evening, as I addressed Affirmation's members during the plenary session, I reflected on what it meant to be a global organization. Wherever the Church is, queer people are also. Outside the Intermountain West, Affirmation is often the only support system available for queer people navigating their intersection with the Church. This crucial lifesaving link provides connection within a community. "No matter where you are in this world," I confidently declared, "Affirmation is reaching for your reaching." Drawing from my experiences with Affirmation—remembering the different lifesaving roles it played during pivotal moments in my life—I introduced a vision for Affirmation: We are a place to land among friends, heal through connection, and serve one another. These aspirations resonated with my peers. When the Board of Directors met the following year to create Affirmation's next strategic plan, they built upon this presidential vision and created Affirmation's first organizational vision: To be a refuge to land, heal, share, and be authentic.[1]

Our June conference was an invaluable moment of connection we had created for one another at the shared intersection of self and Mormonism. The following weekend, Affirmation

---

1. "Charter & Bylaws." Section 1.3. Affirmation: LGBTQ Mormons, Families & Friends, February 8, 2022. https://affirmation.org/about/charter-bylaws/.

turned right around and joined the entire LGBTQ community to participate in World Pride in New York City. June 2019 marked the fiftieth anniversary of the Stonewall riots. The modern LGBTQ civil rights movement rose from this moment in history. Stonewall inspired Pride marches and events across America and other countries. In the LGBTQ community, religious LGBTQ organizations have long been recognized "in the family of things"[2]—to quote the poet Mary Oliver—as a critical component in the wellbeing of queer people. As such, they are celebrated in the community for standing in deeply rejecting territory, creating lifesaving spaces for queer people in their chosen spiritual homes or those of their birth.

During World Pride weekend, Affirmation planned a special Saturday conference before marching together on Sunday. Finding real estate to hold a conference in the Manhattan area during the largest World Pride event on record seemed impossible. However, Affirmation has a standing invitation that can make the seemingly impossible possible. Community of Christ has welcomed Affirmation to use their facilities when we meet as LGBTQ Mormons. When we talked to our contacts about our plans for World Pride weekend, they offered us the use of their Ridgewood congregation building in New Jersey. Ever the consummate host, Apostle Lachlan Mackay greeted us as we arrived and, along with the local leadership, made sure we had everything we needed for the day.

After the program ended and everyone went into the city to gather at an ally's home for dinner, Matthew and I stuck around at the church to help clean up. As Matthew and I left to take the train back to Paramus to change before dinner, Lachlan asked if he could drive us, as it would be faster and less hassle than

---

2. Oliver, Mary. "Wild Geese." Poem. In *Devotions: The Selected Poems of Mary Oliver*, 347. New York: Penguin Press, 2017.

taking the train. I had only just met Lachlan. Yet in my short interactions with him, as he helped set up and clean up, he exuded a sense of humility and hospitality that radiated Christ-like behavior without needing any formality or honorifics. He was like no apostle I had been with before. He came to the church ready to work in Levis and soccer slides. When he said "Welcome" you could feel it in your soul that this was a genuine, unconditional welcome—no agenda—just Christlike service for the sake of Christlike service.

As we pulled out onto Lenox Street, I knew I only had about fifteen minutes with an apostle. What could I ask him? What should I ask him? I decided to go for the jugular, "How did you all do it? How did you get to a place of LGBTQ acceptance within Community of Christ?" He smiled, probably because he knew the answer would take much longer than the short car ride we would have together, but he was very forthcoming in the Cliff Notes version.

Lachlan recalled that in 1984 President Wallace B. Smith presented an inspired document announcing that women could be ordained to the priesthood, admonishing: "Therefore, do not wonder that some women of the church are being called to priesthood responsibilities."[3] For many rank-and-file members of Community of Christ, that announcement caught them by surprise, deeply contradicting their understanding of the priesthood and the order of God that had been taught to them for generations. This created upheaval within the church, causing schism to spawn a significant exodus of members. I sat there imagining the schism the Latter-day Saints experienced when our leaders announced—and then enforced—the end of the practice of polygamy in our church. That announcement seemed to fly in the face of what members had been taught about marriage

---

3. Section 156:9c (Doctrine and Covenants) Community of Christ.

the previous fifty years. Disagreeing over this, two apostles were removed from the Quorum of the Twelve, and breakaway fundamentalist groups began forming, whose communities still dot the borders of Zion today.

Lachlan went on to say that when the leaders of their church reflected on what had happened in 1984, they realized they had not prepared the Saints to receive continuing revelation from God on women's ordination. Almost three decades later, the church leaders humbly began the process of preparing its members to extend the sacraments of ordination and marriage to LGBTQ people. He recalled the invitation church president Stephen Veazey gave to the members in 2010—Section 164 in their Doctrine and Covenants—that opened this period of preparation by inviting members of the church to consider the inclusion of LGBTQ people as part of their baptismal covenants. I had to look this up later, but it is a lovely set of verses that called upon the members to understand that through their baptismal covenants, old prejudices melt away. In their place, a new community of tolerance, reconciliation, unity in diversity, and love is born.

President Veazey noted that God is ultimately concerned about behaviors and relationships that uphold the worth of all people and protect the most vulnerable: "Such relationships are to be rooted in the principles of Christ-like love, mutual respect, responsibility, justice, covenant, and faithfulness, against which there is no law."[4] He promised that if the church would more fully understand and apply these principles, questions concerning responsible human sexuality, gender identities, roles, relationships, and marriage may be resolved according to God's divine purposes. This invitation to understand LGBTQ inclusion in light of one's baptismal covenants was an invita-

---

4. Section 164:6a (Doctrine and Covenants) Community of Christ.

tion to participate in the life and mind of Christ. In Lachlan's estimation, this participatory preparation made all the difference, allowing the Spirit to move upon the church. This time, the members formally asked leaders for LGBTQ inclusion in the sacraments of the church, which the president of the church presented for a sustaining vote, paving the way for marriage and ordination of LGBTQ members. They didn't lose many members over this important doctrinal change concerning a hot-button social issue.

As we pulled into the hotel parking lot and said our goodbyes, I was struck by the contrast. Of the major denominations in the Latter Day Saint movement, Community of Christ had thoughtfully worked through the inclusion of same-sex married couples and their families proactively before Obergefell. At the same time, my church waited until after Obergefell to react wildly to the ruling by rolling out a very punitive and harmful exclusion policy.

To this day, I wonder what participatory preparation might look like in our church if the brethren invited the membership to consider LGBTQ inclusion as part of their baptismal covenants. Considering recent General Conference talks and amicus briefs, it is not happening currently, nor does it seem likely to be happening anytime soon. But if not now, when? These are issues that will never go away for the modern church. Queer Latter-day Saint children are continually being born into the families of the Church. Sexual orientation, gender identity, and marriage equality are not matters we can ignore as the queer children of God continue to pile up out on the Mormon Trail, stalled on the frozen banks of their personal Sweetwater crossings.

The following day, Matthew and I caught the train into New York City to meet up with Affirmation at our staging area just off Fifth Avenue. When we arrived, my friends excitedly pulled me in and stenciled rainbows on my face and arms. I wore my rainbow Converse shoes with "Affirmation" embroidered on the side, ready to carry me along the route. Since we came out later in life, Matthew and I had not participated in a Pride march before, so I had not expected the level of excitement and energy I was drawing from the crowd. Affirmation was just a tiny fraction of the 150,000 participants and 750 groups marching that day.[5] The World Pride march was so big that it lasted twelve hours. Luckily, we were assigned an early spot, leaving us the rest of the day to enjoy the festivities.

When we were directed out onto Fifth Avenue to begin the two-and-a-half-mile march through Manhattan, the acoustics alone were unbelievable. World Pride organizers said five million people were there that day to cheer us on.[6] I have no words to describe what it feels and sounds like to encounter five million friendly faces of enthusiastic support joined together to be proud of you. I had been in many packed stadiums, but this far surpassed anything I had experienced before. The noise from the crowds rose from the streets, bouncing off the skyscrapers, turning them into towering amplifiers, filling a city the size of New York with joy.

For most of the route, we were so close to the sidewalks that the crowds became individual people. People we would never meet again stood in what felt like an endless reception line,

---

5. NYC Pride. "NYC Pride Gears Up for 2019 - 2020 Season." NYC Pride, December 9, 2019. https://www.nycpride.org/news-press-media/nyc-pride-gears-up-for-2019-2020-season.

6. Allen, Karma. "About 5 Million People Attended WorldPride in NYC, Mayor Says." ABC News, July 2, 2019. https://abcnews.go.com/US/million-people-crowed-nyc-worldpride-mayor/story?id=64090338.

reaching to clasp hands, give a hug, or slap a high five. I didn't expect this kind of intimacy and closeness with the crowd. Despite being surrounded by millions of people, time and again, the world around me would go silent, and I would have a personal interaction with a stranger. These strangers-turned-friends would look me in the eye and say, "I am so proud of you," "I support you," "Happy Pride!" and "Hey, I am Mormon too! You are my people!" I was getting hugs from moms along the route, and one person yelled out, "What? Gay *and* Mormon? I didn't know that was possible, but I support you!"

As we approached the First Presbyterian Church and the Church of the Ascension along 5th Avenue, clergy and members ran to greet us, carrying trays of water cups. Yes, they ran to us. It was a hot afternoon, and the cool water was so very welcome. The scene reminded me that just as Peter and John ran to an empty tomb on resurrection morning, running towards others is an attribute of pure love in discipleship. When I thanked a collared pastor holding a trash bag for empty cups, he looked at me and said, "You are so loved. Don't ever forget that." As I tossed my white paper water cup, I noted that it was the same kind but a larger version of the paper cups in our own sacrament trays, a symbol of remembering Christ, the living water. It was a stunning reminder of Christ's love and acceptance.

As I marched hand-in-hand with Matthew, I was acutely aware that an incredible band of people in Affirmation surrounded me. We were doing incredible things creating loving and affirming communities as we worked to keep our families and loved ones together in this life and in the next. When we reached the end of the route, World Pride volunteers stood on the side of the street holding signs that said, "Please Keep Marching." Logistically, I understood why this was necessary. If everyone immediately stopped at the end of the route in

Chelsea, it would disrupt the flow for those following, bringing the entire operation to a standstill in grave dysfunction.

Affirmation kept marching right off onto a side street, where we stopped to take a group picture gathered around our pride banner, leaving one another with hugs and goodbyes before going our separate ways. The following day, as Matthew and I sat on the plane waiting to take off to Phoenix, I reflected that I was leaving Pride and returning to a less affirming world. But in the end, I didn't need a crowd of millions cheering me on. I had the personal communities I was helping build in places like Affirmation. This circle of love and support was cemented by personal connections that were even stronger than World Pride. It was the kind of community building that Mormons were known for.

Before turning my phone off for departure, I wrote my thoughts to Affirmation on my Facebook page, inviting everyone to join me in building communities of safety, love, and hope. As I reviewed my post, I thought about the signs that greeted us at the end of the march at World Pride and added one final line: "We may be at the end of Pride month, but personal Pride isn't over. That lasts all year long. Keep marching. Please keep marching."

CHAPTER 17

What Is Love?

> No, I don't know why you're not fair
> I give you my love, but you don't care
> So what is right and what is wrong?
> Gimme a sign.
> What is love?
> Oh baby, don't hurt me
> Don't hurt me
> No more.
>
> Haddaway
"What is Love"

I almost didn't catch President Nelson's September 2019 BYU devotional live. I had a last-minute patient cancellation, so I pulled up the broadcast and prepared to be fed by a prophet. I was not only listening for myself, but I was listening as a president.

Since their calling, the Nelson/Oaks duo had been injecting change into the queer/Latter-day Saint intersection frequently in their public addresses. If it wasn't direct change, then their words clarified the dominant narrative, disclosing the most up-to-date information about what the modern church officially thought about queer people. Despite the modern church's long-standing policy of civility towards LGBTQ people, when such change and clarification came, it was a shock every time to hear that the modern church still held very harsh, rejecting, and prejudiced views about the queer children of God—and said so aloud.

I settled in my chair, not knowing what to expect. President Nelson began the devotional stating that he felt impressed to discuss five truths.[1] As he spoke about our divine nature and the nature of truth and love, I pulled my chair closer, shoulders now relaxed. Three truths in, and I felt a great sense of relief that he was leaving the queer Latter-day Saints alone in his address. This was great! We needed a break. He then began his fourth point, introducing the relationship between the love and the law of the Lord. Recalling the sidebar conversation that President Nelson and Oaks had at their first press conference, I became uneasy. This was a moment where I was now standing in the batter's box, trying to anticipate what the pitcher had in store.

He began his wind-up, "Sometimes we are accused of being uncaring as we teach the Father's requirements for exaltation in the celestial kingdom." He then observed that their commission as apostles did not give them the authority to modify divine law but to adjust policy when the Lord directed them to do so. Nervously eyeing the pitcher, I muttered: divine law unchangeable, check. Policies changeable, check. Pitch in motion, he continued, "Perhaps I can illustrate this through policy adjustments regarding those who identify themselves as lesbian, gay, bisexual or transgender and their children."

---

1. Nelson, Russell M. "The Love and Laws of God." BYU Speeches, September 17, 2019. https://speeches.byu.edu/talks/russell-m-nelson/love-laws-god/.

He then released a curve ball towards the plate, delivering a well-crafted spin, creating the pitch's famous illusion that the ball is not where you think it is: "The 2015 and 2019 policy adjustments on this matter were both motivated by love—the love of our Heavenly Father for His children and the love of the Brethren for those whom we serve." Love? I did *not* see that one coming.

Just six months earlier, I was sitting in this very same chair in my office digesting a very unexpected exclusion policy recension, running through a box of tissues under the full weight of three and a half years of unnecessary queer Latter-day Saint suffering. Now, in the space of a thirty-minute devotional, we had all just been told how the brethren—from a position of extreme privilege—had experienced suffering under the exclusion policy. We learned of their grieving and weeping about a policy that they had enacted but didn't have to live. In a church founded upon the bold concept of continuing revelation to bless the Saints, not the status quo, hearing about the tears of a power center did not console me.

President Nelson's admission that the First Presidency had continually overruled the policy, allowing almost all children of LGBTQ parents to be baptized, surprised me. What, then, was the real purpose of the exclusion policy if the power center that made it didn't even follow it? This information would have been lifesaving for the general queer population of the Church to know; they had no choice but to take the policy at face value as they made decisions about their lives while it was in force. I recalled that the Board of Affirmation faced the same realization with the Church's suicide prevention grant: A church that was finding ways to be helpful while still holding a doctrine hostile to queer exaltation.

This was also the moment my biggest fear about the recension materialized. The modern church had just entered the chat, assigning its own meaning to the experience. The possibility that this might eventually happen was what prompted me to collect and publish a queer account of life under the exclusion policy back in April. In laying out the duties of the Saints concerning their persecutors, Joseph Smith taught, "There is much which lieth in futurity, pertaining to the saints, which depends upon these things" (Doctrine and Covenants 123:15). As for LGBTQ people, that futurity was now, and it came much sooner than I had anticipated in the form of a BYU devotional address. The Church had inserted itself into the conversation to tell us this was love. I don't know a lot of things in this life, but having lived in that moment of the exclusion policy, I know that it was not love. I recognize it as a lot of other things—concern, fear, managing an unknown, or as a response to the 2015 Obergefell ruling—but I do not recognize it as love. My entire life, I have been taught that every good tree bears good fruit, but a bad tree bears bad fruit. "A good tree cannot bear bad fruit, and a bad tree cannot bear good fruit" (Matthew 7:28 NIV). When I reflect on my lived experience as a gay father in the Church and read the stories Affirmation collected from queer Mormons about their personal experiences under the exclusion policy, I do not discern the fruits of love. It was dark irony to be told the fruit of the exclusion policy tree was love. It had been a mere five months since we had all witnessed the exclusion policy tree hewn down and cast into the fire. You don't do that to trees that bear good fruit.

Each queer person owns their intersection with the Church. They are the ones who are navigating it. They get to define it and assign meaning to their experiences there. In this intersection, we, as queer people, understand what we experience, even when authorities tell us that we really don't. No matter how authoritatively or forcefully someone is saying that they are loving us, if we say we did not experience love in the exclusion policy, then love was not present. Simply put, love is experienced. I know this deeply, for I was given and received in love. In my earliest memories, I experienced love within the boughs of the cherry trees surrounding my childhood home. Love shaped my life in meaningful and profound ways. With my life enveloped in the gentleness of this love, I recognize love when it is present because it has been abundant in my life. You can tell someone you love them, even mean it sincerely with all the good intentions of your heart, but if that person does not experience love in the actions backing up those words, such words are wasted. This was what was happening over the pulpit at a BYU devotional. I am convinced that some of the most profound harm we experience in this life happens at the hands of well-meaning individuals. It is especially difficult when they tell us they did what they did to us out of love. Just because someone claims to have acted in love, even if they are a prophet, does not make it true. It is up to us to assign meaning to what we experience and determine what love is and what hurts us.

Almost immediately, my phone began to chime. Reporters were contacting me for comment. I looked at the incoming emails anticipating what they would be asking me. I realized the predicament President Nelson presented when he concluded his speech with the invitation: "I plead with you to seek earnestly a confirmation from the Spirit that what I have told you is true and is from the Lord . . . Ask your Heavenly Father if we truly are the Lord's apostles and prophets. Ask if we have received revelation on this and other matters."[2]

Melissa Wei-Tsing Inouye writes, "To me, the way truths become manifest in lived experience is a more valid measure of what is real or divine. Who cares whether something is 'true' by any abstract measure, including intellectual or theological argument, if it cannot be realized in our daily work, bodies, or, most importantly, relationships with fellow beings?"[3] Why ask to know if the exclusion policy was true when I had lived it and tasted its bitter fruit with my own lips? In my own life, the exclusion policy was not just some abstract intellectual or theological argument. It was absolutely realized in my daily life in corporeal form—shaping, through prejudice and acts of prejudice, my relationships with others: Matthew, my children, my extended family, my fellow saints, and even my heavenly parents. But most importantly, my relationship with myself. No matter how much truth is attributed to doctrine—even the doctrine of marriage—if it cannot afford the lived experiences of the queer children of God the same access to the law as their straight/cisgender peers enjoy, then it is prejudice. Prejudice springs from the human mind, not from God. Prejudice prevents the queer children of God from coming unto Christ and justifies such action by the law.

Most disconcerting, President Nelson had just tightly tied the dominant narrative about LGBTQ people to the doctrine. He had just performed some boundary maintenance for Latter-day Saints. No "true" Latter-day Saint would declare a dominant

---

2. Nelson, Russell M. "The Love and Laws of God." September 17, 2019.

3. Inouye, Melissa Wei-Tsing. "Faith Is Not a String of Christmas Lights." In *Crossings: A Bald Asian American Latter-Day Saint Woman Scholar's Ventures through Life, Death, Cancer, and Motherhood (Not Necessarily in That Order)*, 48. Provo, UT, Salt Lake City, Utah: Neal A. Maxwell Institute for Religious Scholarship; Deseret Book, 2019.

narrative about queer people untrue because it is the teaching of a prophet, which is truth—and prophetic truth is doctrine. Was it even possible now to hold a testimony of the Church and the restored gospel but not subscribe to the Church's dominant narrative about queer people? The queer population in the Church has had seventy years of experience with rising and collapsing dominant narratives about us. We have the collective lived experience to know that dominant narratives are built from prejudice and misunderstandings. We know that they are not true and cannot be sustained. We know that even the Church abandons them over time. Yet now, in this moment, we had an administration that was tying faithfulness to subscribing to the Church's dominant narrative about queer people.

For a long time, the Church considered its dominant narrative about church history tightly bound to doctrine. Historians and scholars deviating from the dominant historical narrative were seen as attacking the doctrine and the Church itself. They were excommunicated, fired from BYU and positions at headquarters, or blackballed from working in any Mormon Studies position; their character was often besmirched publicly.

Sometime after the 1993 "September Six" excommunications of scholars and historians, the Church began to soften somewhat as it began slowly professionalizing its historical efforts.[4] More comfortable with historical truth, warts and all, the Church began uncoupling the dominant historical narrative from its doctrine. By 2016, the Church historical landscape was safe enough—or perhaps it was safe enough because he got old enough—that church historian Richard Bushman could publicly proclaim that the dominant historical narrative was "not true.

---

4. Mason, Patrick. "The September Six and the Lost Generation of Mormon Studies." *Dialogue Journal*, November 14, 2023. https://www.dialoguejournal.com/articles/the-september-six-and-the-lost-generation-of-mormon-studies/.

It can't be sustained,"[5] and still be considered faithful and not threatening to the doctrine or the brethren. Currently in the modern church, the dominant narrative about anything queer has been so tightly bound to the doctrine that they are treated as one and the same. Calling out this dominant narrative as not true is considered an attack upon doctrine. It used to be like that for historical narratives, too, and the modern church's response to such criticisms—even if they were true—was forceful.

Without question, the institutional voice of Affirmation at this moment would unequivocally be queer-centric, stand up for queer Latter-day Saints, and acknowledge their lived experiences. It would amplify their voices and validate the meaning they assigned to those experiences. However, behind the institutional voice was a person: Brother Kitchen. In countering the power center's narrative with a queer narrative, the ecclesiastical arm of the Church would rip past the institutional voice and focus on me. I knew that when I stood as a voice for my queer peers—remembering their lived experiences and pointing out the untruths of the dominant narrative about the exclusion policy—I would not have the latitude of a Bushman.

The following two days, I answered reporters' emails and provided comment, not shying away from the hard questions as I stood up for my fellow queer Latter-day Saints. It was a moment of lived experience confronting power. The evening after my last press interview,[6] I sat exhausted on my couch to rest both

---

5. "Richard Bushman States the Dominant Church History Narrative Is False." YouTube, July 14, 2016. https://youtu.be/uKuBw9mpV9w?si=m9XFw4i4o7ojfXxJ.

6. Kuruvilla, Carol. "Queer Mormons: Church's Exclusion Policy Did Not Feel like 'Love.'" HuffPost, September 19, 2019. https://www.huffpost.com/

body and spirit. I felt exposed. As I scrolled through my phone, YouTube served me up Gladys Knight and the Be One Choir singing "More Than I Can Bear." I watched Gladys confidently stroll up to the center of the platform in the Conference Center, surrounded by pianos, bass, guitar, and drums. She then led the Be One Choir to stand, and they served up the word of God:

> I've gone through the fire
> And I've been through the flood.
> I've been broken into pieces
> Seen lightnin' flashin' from above.
> But through it all, I remember
> That He loves me
> And He cares,
> And He'll never put more on me
> Than I can bear.[7]

I wept uncontrollably as Sister Knight and the Be One Choir centered my soul and spoke to my heart in song. It gave me strength. It was the message I needed to hear, and I considered it no accident to have stumbled across this music. It was the hand of God for me at that moment. Filled with the Spirit, I asked God, "What are we doing to one another here on this Earth? What are we doing to one another in the name of love?"

The exclusion policy was but a symptom of an exclusionary doctrine. It will take the hard work of the entire body of Christ, culminating in a revelation on the scale of Peter's vision concerning the cleanliness of the Gentiles, to affirm same-sex marriage in the Church. Despite the misconception that doc-

---

entry/mormon-church-lgbq-policy-love_n_5d823b52e4b0849d4721ba88.

7. The Church of Jesus Christ of Latter-day Saints. "Be One - a Celebration of the Revelation on the Priesthood." Song: More than I Can Bear. Timestamp 30:12. YouTube, June 4, 2018. https://youtu.be/52-y98r2ZYs?si=soiaBIIBNOcexnVa&t=1812.

trine never changes, it most certainly does. But it is always the last thing to change after all dominant narrative and policy options are exhausted. Today, LGBTQ Latter-day Saints and their families are vulnerable to this policy/dominant narrative churn towards doctrinal change. Those caught in this churn as the brethren work things out have the continued and real possibility of facing harm as they stand at the intersection of their identity and their faith. And this, right in the middle of the churn, is where I proudly stood during my season as president of Affirmation, shoulder to shoulder with a team of leaders just as invested in supportive community building for our queer peers.

The Psalmist asks the question that burns in the hearts of LGBTQ Latter-day Saints who look for a day of full inclusion and acceptance: "How long, Lord God Almighty, will your anger smolder against the prayers of your people?" (Psalm 80:4 NIV). This is a question with an unknowable answer. It took Peter ten years after the organization of the primitive church to receive the revelation extending the fullness of the gospel to the Gentiles. In the modern church, since our visibility at the beginnings of the LGBTQ civil rights movement, on the specific question of extending the fullness of equality and exaltation to queer people, we are now in year seventy and counting. But one thing I knew for sure in this uncertainty: this beloved global network of LGBTQ Mormons that often operates unseen in the margins will continue to care for one another in the face of intimidating prejudice and rejecting behavior for as long as it is needed. We do not belong to prejudice; we belong to each other. And in this belonging, we are a lifesaving and life-sustaining community, affirming the inherent self-worth of our queer peers as complete, equal, and valuable persons, supporting them in the godly act of claiming joy as they navigate their life and their faith to places that feel safe and healthy for them.

In the moment of empowerment and healing that Gladys Knight sparked within my soul, I reflected that during the intensity of these past few days—through it all—something so pure and wonderful had happened. We had welcomed an addition within the boughs of love in our family. My first grandson was born into this world. Four weeks early and oh so tiny, he was having a hard time breathing on his own, so he was beginning life in the NICU. I called my daughter in Provo, now a worried mother full of love for her son, and listened as she expressed her concerns about the future. I told her we were family and would get through this together. My heart was full of so much love for my daughter's little family and my tiny grandson, who was born into this world too early. "He is part of a huge and loving family," I said, "Tell him, 'You got this.'" I loved him, and I had not even met him yet.

THAT WE CALL HOME

Beyond Laniakea, the immense heavens,
Galaxies cluster by the billions.
Each a steward
Of one hundred thousand million stars.

Each night we look into the sky
But cannot comprehend
A system greater than the limits
Of this, our earthly place.

And in the morning's gentle light
Upon the leaf, ten drops of dew
Hold molecules equal to
Each star that's ever been.

Breathe—

We are surrounded by vastness!
Both high and low!
We look,
But cannot see.

We were not born to fit this scale
To comprehend the suns and atoms
More numerous than grains of sand,
The dust from whence we came.

We are the dust,
Sandwiched;
Between expanses, swallowed.
But yet we still feel rev'rence.

We send our Gods into those spaces
To be the understanding,
To tend their own creation
They spoke into existence.

And then we cluster,
Together in love,
Celestial nebulas, but human–
So that we are not alone
In a universe of stars and quarks;
Calling ourselves the children of God
While cradled in Orion's arm,
Trav'ling a million miles an hour
Through immense heavens
That we call home.

CHAPTER 18

The BYU

> Then cheer anew for the BYU
> We've come to work, to live, to do;
> We'll raise our standard—bear it through;
> Our hearts are true to the BYU
>
> Annie Amelia Pike Greenwood
"College Song", 1899

When the opening session of Affirmation's June 2019 International Conference concluded, it was time for pictures, hugs, and reconnecting with friends old and new. As everyone filed out of the ballroom and into the east hall, two BYU professors appeared from the crowd to greet me. They had contacted me a month earlier, sharing that they had just registered for the conference, and asked if I might be available to meet with them after the first night's session. I was excited to do so.

After handshakes and a bit of small talk, I invited them to the boardroom, where we could visit away from the noise and crowd. As we sat down, one of the professors shared an interesting bit of news about BYU. In April, the Classical Association of the Middle West and South (CAMWS) had just withdrawn its invitation to BYU to host its annual conference on campus.[1] The professors explained that this was a significant and embarrassing loss for the university. The withdrawal centered on serious concerns that could not be resolved over eighteen months of ongoing dialogue with BYU concerning the Honor Code as it pertained to LGBTQ students, the absence of sexual orientation and gender identity protections in the university's nondiscrimination policy, and the restrictive speaker policy and public expression policy that limited LGBTQ academic freedom.

In the face of this loss, the classicists at BYU saw an opportunity for faculty and administration to become better educated and learn to foster respectful dialogue between visiting scholars and the university regarding LGBTQ issues. The BYU professors indicated that the College of Humanities had invited Professors T. H. M. Gellar-Goad of Wake Forest University and Christopher B. Polt of Boston College—the very professors who spearheaded the successful effort to move the CAMWS meeting off campus[2]—to come to BYU for a mini classics conference. This was an effort to show hospitality despite the conflict and provide these LGBTQ community leaders the opportunity to facilitate a roundtable discussion with faculty, administration, and students about ways BYU could improve relations with the LGBTQ community.

---

1. CAMWS Executive Committee. "New CAMWS Statement on Provo." CAMWS, April 20, 2019. https://camws.org/node/1386.
2. Gellar-Goad, T. H. M., and Christopher B. Polt. "Blog: CAMWS and BYU: Background, Reflections, and Next Steps." Society for Classical Studies, April 22, 2019. https://classicalstudies.org/scs-blog/thmgg/blog-camws-and-byu-background-reflections-and-next-steps.

When I heard this I sat back in my chair and smiled. It was a refreshing move in the face of loss—a way I had not expected this story to end. One of the professors then turned to the other and said, "Should we continue to . . . ?" The other said, "Sure, I think we should." They then floated the idea of inviting me to participate in this historic meeting and speak at the roundtable. "We will need to discuss this with the department chair and dean before it's official," they cautioned. "But we just wanted to gauge your interest."

"I would be honored to be a part of this if everything works out," I answered.

A few weeks later, I received an official invitation. BYU would fly me up, host me, and provide an honorarium for my time. I was grateful to be a part of this conversation and exchange ideas on how to better build relations between BYU and the LGBTQ community. As the plane made its final approach to Salt Lake International on the eve of the roundtable, I looked out the window at my mountain home below me—the lights of Zion spread out along the Wasatch Front for as far as the eye could see. I considered the long, complicated history of LGBTQ student treatment at BYU. I was not sure what to expect when I arrived on campus.

The conference began downstairs in the Joseph F. Smith Building, where the visiting professors presented their scholarship to faculty and students. Notably, Professor Geller-Goad enjoyed full academic freedom as he delivered his classics paper about the houses of sex-laborers in the works of Plautus and Terence,[3] possibly the first time this subject had been taught at BYU. Later, after I introduced myself, they expressed their genuine surprise that BYU wanted to understand better why

---

3. Gellar-Goad, T.H.M. "Looking at Life behind the Scenes: Houses of Sex-Laborers in Plautus and Terence." *Brigham Young University*. Lecture, October 10, 2019.

the issues that led CAMWS to withdraw its invitation were important to queer students and faculty, as well as other academic institutions.

After lunch, BYU arranged two opportunities for dialogue: a meeting with the Honor Code Office and a meeting with BYU's General Counsel. Even though it had been almost thirty years since I was a student at BYU, I was surprised at the visceral feeling of doom as we approached the Honor Code Office. Even though I was nowhere near being out when I was a student at BYU, the office's reach through surveillance—as well as its connection to the police department and our bishops and stake presidents—was well known. The thought of interacting with the Honor Code Office over *anything* was a fearful thing when I was a student. As we walked past the huge painting of Del Parson's "Lost Lamb" hanging at the entrance of the Honor Code Office, we were ushered into an office where I was happy to see a familiar face. Ben Schilaty had just been hired as an Honor Code administrator that August. He was also an out gay man. As a fellow Arizonan, I knew him from his University of Arizona student days, during which he was doing great things building the LGBTQ Latter-day Saint community in Tucson. We were of different generations of gay men in the Church, but we had both faithfully embraced the dominant narrative of our generation. Now, I was working through the collapse of the silent generation, and he was rising with the single and celibate generation.

Soon, Kevin Utt joined us in Ben's office. Shortly after Utt was hired as director, BYU students held a highly successful protest over the Honor Code Office's tactics.[4] Part of their

---

4. Eaton, Daysha. "A Rare Sight at Brigham Young University as Students Protest The Honor Code Office." NPR, April 16, 2019. https://www.npr.org/2019/04/16/714056430/a-rare-sight-at-brigham-young-university-as-students-protest-the-honor-code-offi.

success was owed to creating a public Instagram account where students could anonymously share their horror stories with the Honor Code Office.[5] These disturbing stories helped prompt BYU to change how the Honor Code Office did business, and Utt was leading this transformation.

Utt began our meeting by introducing the Honor Code Office to the visiting professors and summarizing the changes he spearheaded. He indicated that to protect student privacy, he had ended the practice of sharing information disclosed in confidence to the Honor Code Office with the student's ecclesiastical leaders—which had been standard practice when I was a student at BYU. In addition, he refused to accept anonymous tips, or Honor Code violation reports from bishops and stake presidents. He also walked us through the separation of the Title IX Office from the Honor Code Office, where the only connection now was what was mandated by federal reporting laws.[6] He pointed out that most Honor Code violations were now self-reported because of these changes. He emphasized that he had worked hard to make the Honor Code Office a place where students could feel comfortable dropping by to ask questions. Moreover, with Ben on board, the Honor Code Office had a friendly face for LGBTQ students. As a 1993 BYU alum, I perceived an Honor Code Office completely made over. As a student, I would have never gone to the Honor Code Office just to talk.

But then Professor Polt politely interrupted, seeking to clarify language in the Honor Code. Referencing the "Homosexual

---

5. honorcodestories. Instagram. Accessed July 26, 2024. https://www.instagram.com/honorcodestories/.

6. Evans, Whittney. "BYU Separates Honor Code, Title IX Offices, Provides More Support for Sex Assault Victims." KUER, October 26, 2016. https://www.kuer.org/public-safety/2016-10-26/byu-separates-honor-code-title-ix-offices-provides-more-support-for-sex-assault-victims.

Clause,"⁷ he asked for a list that outlined specific forms of physical intimacy that would be Honor Code violations. Salient to Polt's question was the real danger he perceived lurking behind vague language. With suspension or expulsion a possibility for running afoul of an ambiguous Honor Code, queer students are at a disadvantage when opaque codes of conduct subject to interpretation and uneven implementation are in place.

Utt explained that the Honor Code Office didn't have a written list because such things are considered on a case-by-case basis, depending on student intent. Surprised, Polt questioned how intent was determined. He observed that the ambiguity in the Honor Code discriminates against LGBTQ students because, presumably, the Honor Code Office doesn't need to determine intent when an opposite-sex couple holds hands on campus. When asked about BYU's transgender students, Utt explained that the Honor Code provided no guidance about gender identity. Each report of a transgender student was looked at on a case-by-case basis. Polt responded, "Exactly what are those transgender issues that may arise?" Again, the treatment would be case-by-case. As Utt and Schilaty defended the office's ability to accurately determine the intent of LGBTQ BYU students, Polt expressed his doubts. He challenged BYU to

---

7. The Church of Jesus Christ of Latter-day Saints. "Church Educational System Honor Code." Wayback Machine - Internet Archive: Church Educational System Honor Code, Archived February 14, 2020. Accessed July 27, 2024. http://web.archive.org/web/20200214105302/https://policy.byu.edu/view/index.php?p=26.

Before it was removed on February 19, 2020, the "Homosexual Clause" in the BYU Honor Code read: "One's stated same-gender attraction is not an Honor Code issue. However, the Honor Code requires all members of the university community to manifest a strict commitment to the law of chastity. Homosexual behavior is inappropriate and violates the Honor Code. Homosexual behavior includes not only sexual relations between members of the same sex, but all forms of physical intimacy that give expression to homosexual feelings."

clearly state the university's expectations of LGBTQ students' behavior since such expectations were extraordinarily particular compared to those for non-queer students. He expressed concern that ambiguous policies gave the Honor Code Office extraordinary power over LGBTQ students. Such uncertainty not only stokes LGBTQ fears but also unfairly burdens LGBTQ students.

The visiting professors did not like the lack of written behavioral guidelines for LGBTQ students. I could see that the deeply held Latter-day Saint belief of "the mantle"[8] and governing by the "unwritten order of things"[9]—where people in power determine intent according to an often subjective and opaque personal preference—was impossible to translate into any reasonable scenario outside Latter-day Saint culture. After we left the Honor Code Office, the visiting professors had many questions, not about the words they had just heard but about the culture they were encountering. For the rest of the weekend, I became an interpreter of culture, translating the BYU and church ecosystem to help them understand "peculiar."

We had an hour before our scheduled meeting with BYU's general counsel. I wanted our guests to connect with known faculty allies, so I called my friend Dr. Roni Jo Draper to see if

---

8. Packer, Boyd K. "The Mantle Is Far, Far Greater than the Intellect." Homepage - The Church of Jesus Christ of Latter-day Saints, August 22, 1981. https://www.churchofjesuschrist.org/study/manual/teaching-seminary-preservice-readings-religion-370-471-and-475/the-mantle-is-far-far-greater-than-the-intellect.

9. Packer, Boyd K. The Unwritten Order of Things. Accessed July 26, 2024. https://emp.byui.edu/ANDERSONR/itc/Teachings/chapter2/The_Unwritten_Order_of_Things.htm.

This is a transcript of Elder Packer's "The Unwritten Order of Things." BYU devotional address, 15 October 1996, used at BYU-Idaho in "The Teachings of the Living Prophets" course, REL 333. The original has been removed from the BYU *Speeches: Devotionals, Forums, Commencement Addresses* catalog.

we could come visit her in her office. Roni Jo is an amazing supporter of all things LGBTQ. Not only was she the faculty advisor to BYU's off-campus LGBTQ group, USGA (Understanding Sexuality, Gender, and Allyship), but she had created an unmistakably safe and affirming place in her office for LGBTQ people on campus. We asked a passing faculty member for directions as we approached her office. With a smile, they said, "You'll know when you get to it." Of course we would. As we turned the corner, it was the only door completely covered—every square inch—in rainbow colors and decorations. She had a comfy couch in her office, and as we faced her desk, I noticed she had arranged all the books on her wall-to-wall bookshelves by color. We were surrounded in rainbow. As she welcomed us in to visit, this had all the makings of "coming in for a rest." Until that moment, I had not realized how much I needed this space and how vital such spaces were for LGBTQ students. When I was a student, I was deeply in the closet and did not experience campus life as a visible queer person. Now, thirty years later, I was experiencing queer visibility on campus, and the inherent pressure was inescapable. I had not even been through one day yet. I could not begin to imagine how out LGBTQ students managed the system under the obligations of an "unwritten order of things" Honor Code.

After our visit, we hiked to the administration building to meet with BYU's general counsel, Steve Sandberg. There, in a board room overlooking the Quad, Professor Gellar-Goad asked why the university's nondiscrimination statement did not include sexual orientation and gender identity. Such an absence exposes LGBTQ students and visiting faculty to harm, which had been a primary objection of many in CAMWS concerning their safety. Mr. Sandberg explained that BYU's sponsoring organization, The Church of Jesus Christ of Latter-day Saints, receives Title VII, Title IX, and Utah State protections to create a university space that gives preference to members of the religion and allows them to make decisions that are in alignment with doctrine. What may be seen as inequitable to others is protected religious belief. He reminded us that all religious universities in America have the protection to create nondiscrimination policies that align with their doctrine as long as they do not conflict with federal, state, and local laws. Currently, BYU's management of its LGBTQ population did not run afoul of the law.

Gellar-Goad noted that BYU Law School had sexual orientation and gender identity protections[10] while BYU-Provo did not.[11] "This would seem to indicate that such protections have been worked out on a part of campus," he observed. Mr. Sandberg responded that much of this has to do with housing issues, which are an integral part of the university but not an issue for the law school. Mr. Sandberg then recalled that one of CAMWS's objections was BYU's visiting faculty speaker policy.

---

10. "Policies & Procedures, I. General Policies, L. Policy on Non-Discrimination." BYU Law School. Accessed July 26, 2024. https://law.byu.edu/explore/about/policies-procedures.

"The Law School provides equal opportunity in legal education for all persons, including faculty and employees with respect to hiring, continuation, promotion, and continuing faculty status, applicants for admission, enrolled students, and graduates, without discrimination or segregation on the basis of race, color, ethnicity, religion, national origin, sex, gender (including identity and expression), sexual orientation, age, disability, or military status."

11. "Nondiscrimination and Equal Opportunity Policy." BYU University Policies. Accessed July 26, 2024. https://policy.byu.edu/view/nondiscrimination-and-equal-opportunity-policy.

"Brigham Young University prohibits unlawful discrimination in employment, education, and all university-sponsored programs and activities. This prohibition applies to acts of unlawful discrimination by or against university employees, students, and campus visitors—including applicants for employment or admission—and it includes unlawful discrimination on the basis of race, color, national origin, religion, sex (including pregnancy), age (40 and over), disability, genetic information, or veteran status."

He argued that the current policy's intentions are not as restrictive as CAMWS has interpreted them and that BYU was currently clarifying this policy to eliminate any confusion. "Such a clarification would be helpful," Professor Gellar-Goad replied. "Policies are messaging tools. They broadcast values and practices." He pointed out that the values that BYU's policies and Honor Code broadcast to LGBTQ people indicate that the campus is not safe for them nor conducive to academic freedom. Gellar-Goad's conclusion struck me. When LGBTQ prejudice underpins a policy, even if protected by religious freedom, an organization that wants to project a welcoming stance towards LGBTQ people must spend considerable time, money, and energy to counteract the message that its policies are broadcasting for free.

As we concluded, I asked why there was still no on-campus LGBTQ support organization. Professor Polt interjected, "What is the university's anxiety about this?" Mr. Sandberg reported that the university had spent considerable time and resources creating a faculty-run, on-campus LGBTQ support organization. The president of BYU approved the plan, but the Board of Trustees returned the proposal with a one-word answer: "No."

When I left campus that afternoon and reflected on the day's events, I sensed that I had been dropped into an underlying tension between the administration, its queer students, and the university's professional affiliations. It simmered just below the surface. I wasn't sure where my place as president of Affirmation was in all of this, but I was glad that I could represent the needs, hopes, and desires of queer people as a queer BYU alum.

The following morning, Professors Gellar-Goad, Polt, and I met with the USGA presidency. We requested no allies or university chaperones be present at this meeting so that it would be an exclusively queer space to speak openly and candidly. This was my favorite of all our meetings. As an off-campus student-led LGBTQ organization, USGA was building community one relationship at a time. One aspect of their efforts surprised me. These leaders expressed great loneliness in their work at BYU. They went about it with no support from the administration, under the suspicious gaze of the Honor Code Office, and among a student body that had been taught its entire life about the wickedness of LGBTQ people.

Organized in 2010, USGA has attempted many times to become an official on-campus organization, working through administrative channels. Eventually, Sandberg told USGA that "BYU had no intention of letting USGA on campus. If a BYU LGBT group was ever to exist, it would be one the university created themselves."[12] After the Board of Trustees shut down the university's efforts to create and oversee its own on-campus LGBTQ group, USGA leaders concluded that BYU was incapable of meeting the community and support needs of LGBTQ BYU students. The path forward was clear. A student-led group, not a university-led group, was the healthiest way forward for queer BYU students. We spent over two hours listening to these queer student leaders tell their stories and describe their intersection with the Honor Code. I recognized the work they were doing because it mirrored the work of Affirmation in many ways. We were colleagues working in different realms of the queer/Latter-day Saint experience.

---

12. Hall, Hayden. "History of USGA." USGA home, May 7, 2021. https://www.usgabyu.com/single-post/history-of-usga.

The day's activities ended with a roundtable discussion that included faculty, department chairs, USGA leaders, the BYU general counsel, and students. I gave the opening remarks of this session, welcoming everyone in before the visiting professors led the discussion. Although I knew that most of the faculty and administration were there to learn how to better their relationship with the LGBTQ community and create safe spaces for LGBTQ students on campus, I realized that many of the queer students at the roundtable would be there for themselves, seeking safe and supportive community at their university.

My goal was simply to empower my LGBTQ Latter-day Saint peers in that room who were navigating their intersection with the Honor Code. Much of the roundtable discussion would follow Elder Christofferson's NAACP "two-hand" template, with the LGBTQ community on one hand and the BYU community on the other. I was not there that afternoon to stand on the right hand or the left. I would be addressing my LGBTQ Latter-day Saint peers who exist between the hands— the heart of the matter. I scanned the room to see where the students were so that I could connect with them as I spoke.

I began by thanking everyone at BYU for their attentiveness and hospitality that weekend. I shared a bit of Affirmation's beginnings at BYU in 1977 and reflected that those early founders would surely be proud of the progress that had been made in society and church concerning LGBTQ people. I observed that we had come a long way from those early days when Affirmation leaders had to use code names at BYU for their safety.[13] Contrastingly, today the president of Affirmation can come to campus and speak openly about LGBTQ issues.

---

13. Melson, Dave. "Affirmation Is Turning Thirty!" Affirmation: Gay & Lesbian Mormons: Archived, June 2007. https://web.archive.org/web/20100920063440/http://affirmation.org/news/2007_058.shtml.

I turned to the USGA leaders in the room and acknowledged that they were doing very meaningful, lifesaving work as they built community through their principled LGBTQ leadership. I pledged Affirmation's support in their community-building efforts, and as part of this effort, I would donate the entirety of my speaker's honorarium to USGA. "You are the angels of this LGBTQ/BYU intersection," I candidly observed. I shared that Elder Holland taught that not all angels are from the other side of the veil: "Some of them we walk with and talk with—here, now, every day. Indeed, heaven never seems closer than when we see the love of God manifested in the kindness and devotion of people so good and so pure that angelic is the only word that comes to mind."[14] Angels can come in times we are afraid, in our anxieties and trauma. In the scriptures, when angels appear, they have two messages. Be it for Zacharias in the temple, Mary with child, the Marys at the tomb, or the shepherds abiding in the field, the first message is "Fear not!" and the second is a message of good tidings of great joy. In this, angels teach us that fear robs us of our joy. I concluded with this challenge: "Find your angels who not only admonish you to fear not but also to have joy! Be those angels who minister in times of fear and are anxiously engaged in bringing about joy and doing good."

When the roundtable finished, and I was standing among BYU's queer leaders and students, I realized the space I was in. I was among queer people who were creating supportive communities within the BYU ecosystem under the crossfire going on above their heads between BYU, its professional affiliations, and federal education civil rights laws. I might have questioned my place yesterday, but now it was clear. My place as Affirmation president was right here, under the tussle, among

---

14. Holland, Jeffery R. "The Ministry of Angels." *Ensign* 38, no. 11, 2008. https://www.churchofjesuschrist.org/study/ensign/2008/11/the-ministry-of-angels.

my queer friends. I was not going to change the world of education; I had no power in such things. But I did have the ability to build community, stamp out isolation through connection, and support my queer peers as we navigated our intersections with the Church. In Mormon-speak, it was a call to serve.

As I left campus that evening, I drove past the sign at the entrance of BYU's campus: "Enter to learn, go forth to serve." Many years ago, I had entered BYU to learn—wide-eyed and inner vessel cleansed. And today, after all my learnings and all my "going forths," Alma Mater's son had returned to serve.

CHAPTER 19

The Rainbow Stained-Glass Ceiling

> Perhaps no issue has provoked more debate within the Church than its treatment of LGBTQ people. For decades, the Church was an uneasy partner in the religious right's crusade against same-sex marriage—united in a shared orthodoxy.
>
> [In] recent years the Church has taken a more conciliatory approach... Still, the Church has not changed its prohibition on same-sex relationships and gender transitions. Nathan Kitchen, the head of the Mormon LGBTQ group Affirmation, calls this "the rainbow stained-glass ceiling" in the Church.
>
> McKay Coppins
"The Most American Religion."
The Atlantic, January/February 2021 Issue

Today when queer Latter-day Saints come out and begin navigating their intersection with the Church, and when new allies start their work in Latter-day Saint spaces, they do so in a landscape that has been carefully crafted for them by the modern church. They are entering a program already in progress, like joining a TV show after a breaking news story. Both generational awareness and historical knowledge help clarify what the landscape is and what the tolerances are in our spiritual home within the Church. We are not just part of a church guiding us back home to the heavens. We are part of a church that is extremely politically active in governments around the world, anxiously defending itself against what it considers the "increasing frequency and power of the culture and phenomenon of lesbian, gay, and transgender lifestyles and values."[1]

Although queer people have always existed in the human population, including in the Church since its restoration, the concept of sexual orientation and gender identity is a relatively new understanding of the human experience that began to develop in the nineteenth century to explain the lived experience of sexual and gender minorities.[2] By the middle of the twentieth century, the various communities coalescing around sexual orientation and gender identity became large enough to draw the prolonged attention of government and society. This awareness was often not kind to those in these emerging minority populations, and prejudice, harassment, and discrimination shaped their everyday lives. In the face of increasing government and public harassment, LGBTQ people began to resist. By the time of the Stonewall Riot of 1969, LGBTQ people were front and center in the public's consciousness. This era was when the sweeping gay liberation movement began, emphasizing unashamed and unapologetic visibility. Amy Hoffman, a lesbian

---

1. Oaks, Dallin H. "Anxiety in Stressful Times." BYUH Speeches, June 11, 2019. https://speeches.byuh.edu/devotional/anxiety-in-stressful-times.

2. McClellan, Dan. "The Bible Never Addresses Homosexuality as an Orientation." YouTube, March 29, 2024. https://youtu.be/BwOuNnTs7S8?si=cUqFEPGVCSC1nKgZ.

activist and staff writer for the *Gay Community News* during the peak of the gay liberation movement, writes that the movement always included LGBTQ people. As activists added letters over time to the "gay" community identifier, they also worked to transform old insults into words of power. In those days, "some of us wished we could just say queer . . . we all liked it, but we knew it would never happen. It was the final frontier."[3]

The gay liberation movement was the beginning of the modern LGBTQ civil rights movement,[4] and for much of the public, it seemed to burst onto the scene ex nihilo after Stonewall. It rose alongside the counterculture of the 1960s and 1970s, advocating radical politics common to counterculture, such as feminism, anti-racism, and anti-capitalism. These stances were antithetical to the modern church's stances at that time, especially the gay liberation movement's proposals of legitimate alternatives to the nuclear family.[5] In response, the Church met the counterculture movement head-on, and the gay liberation movement was chief in its crosshairs. Queer Latter-day Saints felt extreme pressure as the Church pushed back hard against the entire counterculture movement. Dr. Neil Young observes that this historical moment was not unique to Mormonism. It was happening across the entire swath of American Christianity.

---

3. Hoffman, Amy. "The Swan Princess." In *An Army of Ex-Lovers: My Life at the Gay Community News*, 79–80. Amherst, Massachusetts: University of Massachusetts Press, 2007.

4. Davidson, Jon W. "A Brief History of the Path to Securing LGBTQ Rights." American Bar Association, July 5, 2022. https://www.americanbar.org/groups/crsj/publications/human_rights_magazine_home/intersection-of-lgbtq-rights-and-religious-freedom/a-brief-history-of-the-path-to-securing-lgbtq-rights/.

5. Downs, Jim. "The Radical Roots of Gay Liberation Are Being Overlooked—Red-Hot Gay Marriage: Gay Liberation Didn't Begin with Marches and Political Rallies, but with a Revolution in Thought." Edited by Sam Haselby. *Aeon*, April 19, 2016. Accessed July 29, 2024. https://aeon.co/essays/the-radical-roots-of-gay-liberation-are-being-overlooked.

Young argues that this emerging LGBTQ visibility "was causing religious groups to articulate and develop a theology that for most of them wasn't there or certainly wasn't developed."[6]

Confronted with what seemed to be the sudden appearance of LGBTQ people in the middle of the ongoing restoration, the modern church had no framework in place to specifically explain the existence of LGBTQ people within its theology. The theology that emerged in this process is underpinned by three pillars: doctrine, dominant narrative, and policy. In this framework, the doctrine did not change. Instead, the dominant narrative was tasked with the heavy lifting to protect the doctrine from queerness, articulating how a queer person fits into the existing doctrine of eternal marriage, gender, and exaltation. Then, policies were deployed not only to ensure queer people stayed in their place but also to control their behavior in conformity with the dominant narrative's standard of what defined an acceptable queer in the kingdom. Even though dominant narratives and policies change over time in response to internal and external tolerance of queerphobia, the doctrine remains heavily protected by one unchanging premise.

Elder Vaughn J. Featherstone articulated this doctrinal premise at a BYU devotional in 1979: "To condone homosexuality is not an act of charity. Perversion is perversion. All the reasoning of the greatest minds in the world cannot change the seriousness of the transgression. Worlds without end, *the homosexual cannot be exalted.* That is it—as plainly, simply, and clearly as one can state."[7] In 2020, Church Education System

---

6. Young, Neil J. "D. Michael Quinn: The Life and Times of a Mormon Historian." Conference at "D. Michael Quinn: The Life and Times of a Mormon Historian." Timestamp 29:54. Salt Lake City, 2022. https://youtu.be/WZHP_-1glu4?si=u-TUnyzEXR3IbRoZ&t=1794.

7. Featherstone, Vaughn J. "'Charity Never Faileth.'" BYU Speeches, February 27, 1979. https://speeches.byu.edu/talks/vaughn-j-featherstone/charity-never-faileth/. Emphasis added.

Commissioner Elder Paul V. Johnson reiterated this doctrinal premise when he explained the updated Honor Code at BYU: "*Same-sex romantic behavior cannot lead to eternal marriage* and is therefore not compatible with the principles included in the Honor Code."[8] During the leadership training session of the October 2019 General Conference, President Oaks instructed the General Authorities and General Officers of the Church that the intended meaning of "gender" in the family proclamation and as used in church statements and publications since that time was biological sex at birth.[9] From this springboard, he issued a trans-inclusive doctrinal premise at April's General Conference in 2022: "Fundamental to us is God's revelation that *exaltation can be attained only through faithfulness to the covenants of an eternal marriage between a man and a woman*. That divine doctrine is why we teach that 'gender [i.e., biological sex at birth] is an essential characteristic of individual premortal, mortal, and eternal identity and purpose'."[10]

This doctrinal premise has been consistently articulated ever since the modern church encountered queer visibility at the beginnings of the modern LGBTQ civil rights movement: Queer people, in their authenticity of sexual orientation, gender identity, and gender expression, cannot be exalted. More clearly articulated over the years to accommodate any form of queerness that presents itself to the Church, the doctrinal

---

8. Matsuura, Alicia. "CES Letter Addresses BYU Honor Code Updates." *The Daily Universe*, March 4, 2020. https://universe.byu.edu/2020/03/04/ces-letter-addresses-byu-honor-code-updates/. Emphasis added.

9. Oaks, Dallin H. "General Conference Leadership Meetings Begin." newsroom.churchofjesuschrist.org, October 2, 2019. https://newsroom.churchofjesuschrist.org/article/october-2019-general-conference-first-presidency-leadership-session?cid=HP_NWSRM_10_2_19.

10. Oaks, Dallin H. "Divine Love in the Father's Plan." *Liahona*, May 2022. https://www.churchofjesuschrist.org/study/liahona/2022/05/51oaks. Emphasis added.

premise remains unchanged and is the keystone of authorized Latter-day Saint queer theology.

Queer people are not the first people to encounter discrimination and exclusion in the Church. In the primitive church, a doctrinal premise was that the Gentile was inherently unclean and could not be baptized. It took a revelation (Acts 10) to correct the premise that doctrine was ethnically-based. Earlier in the restoration, a doctrinal premise was that a Black man could not receive the priesthood, and Black families could not enter the temple. It took a revelation (Official Declaration 2) to correct the premise that doctrine was race-based. Because of these revelations, the doctrine became accessible to all people without regard to ethnicity, race, or color. When the modern church "discovered" LGBTQ people and joined the rest of American Christianity in working out a theology to incorporate their presence in the plan of God, it faced the same question the Catholic Church did when it arrived in the New World and encountered indigenous populations of which it had no previous knowledge or experience: "Do they have rational souls?"[11] After wrestling with this question for years, the Catholic Church, through the 1537 papal bull *Sublimis Deus*,[12] finally affirmed that the Indians were capable of receiving the Catholic Faith.

---

11. Lantigua, David. "'By What Right and Justice?' The Legacy of the First Dominicans in the New World." The School of Salamanca. University of Notre Dame. December 18, 2011. https://sites.nd.edu/schoolofsalamanca/2011/12/18/by-what-right-and-justice-the-legacy-of-the-first-dominicans-in-the-new-world/.

12. Pope Paul III. "Sublimis Deus on the Enslavement and Evangelization of Indians." Papal Encyclicals, January 31, 2024. https://www.papalencyclicals.net/paul03/p3subli.htm.

The point at issue for the modern church was this: Are covenants inherently heterosexual and cisgender based? To work through this issue, the question was essentially, "Do LGBTQ people exist as a 'thing', and if so, do they have souls worthy of exaltation?" Instead of a *Sublimis Deus* moment, the modern church determined that LGBTQ identity was an ideology. LGBTQ people were not a thing. The children of God must be protected against subscribing to the ideology, identity, and lifestyle of queerness, for it was considered an incompatible belief system with the beliefs of the Church. What do you do as a human being when you are reduced to someone's sincerely held religious belief? As illustrated by President Oaks' latest articulation of the doctrinal premise given over the pulpit in 2022, the doctrine of marriage, gender, and exaltation for all human beings remains firmly based on heterosexuality and cisgenderism. Because this premise is a sincerely held religious belief, a correction will need to be recorded in the religious texts of the Church.

Because the modern church paints a scenario of a rising ideological power of lesbian, gay, and transgender culture marching as if to war upon the Church, it obfuscates what is really happening with queer Latter-day Saints. Such fear-mongering is entirely counterproductive within the Church, creating fear and anxiety about its own LGBTQ brothers, sisters, and siblings, creating enmity between the Church and its queer population. No matter how many acceptability standards queer Latter-day Saints meet, no matter how obedient queer people are, no matter the reality that the queer children of God are actually "the least of these," not anywhere near a power center, queer Latter-day Saints will always be seen as a danger, a rising power, handled with suspicion and as a threat, not a fellow citizen.[13] The practical effects of enmity towards queer Latter-day Saints are exclusion from the privileges afforded the general population, separate accommodations in their spiritual home, and punishment for attempting to claim equality. In this we all lose, because enmity is antithetical to Zion, for with a Zion people, there is no division among them (1 Corinthians 1:10).

It is a misunderstanding to assume that queer Latter-day Saints do not respect the gospel of Jesus Christ. In the spirit of Justice Kennedy,[14] they respect it so deeply that they desire its fulfillment within their own lives as a queer person. They are asking for equal dignity in the eyes of the law of the Lord to authentically seek access to the law of chastity, eternal marriage, and to experience their gender without the prejudice of a doctrinal premise that does not recognize the existence of queer people as anything other than an ideology. Theirs is the pleading of the importunate widow (Luke 18:1-8) in love and earnestness that they may rise alongside their straight/cisgender peers into "ultimate exaltation in the presence of God to share in his glory and life,"[15] without the covenant path prematurely terminating for them. Until such a day, queer Latter-day Saints will contin-

---

13. Schilaty, Ben, Charlie Bird, and McKay Bryson. "Is There a Place for Me in the Church?" Timestamp 7:50. Questions from the Closet, December 8, 2020. https://questionsfromthecloset.com/episode/?s=1&e=37.

14. Obergefell v. Hodges, 135 S. Ct. 2584 (2015)

"No union is more profound than marriage, for it embodies the highest ideals of love, fidelity, devotion, sacrifice, and family. In forming a marital union, two people become something greater than once they were. As some of the petitioners in these cases demonstrate, marriage embodies a love that may endure even past death. It would misunderstand these men and women to say they disrespect the idea of marriage. Their plea is that they do respect it, respect it so deeply that they seek to find its fulfillment for themselves. Their hope is not to be condemned to live in loneliness, excluded from one of civilization's oldest institutions. They ask for equal dignity in the eyes of the law. The Constitution grants them that right."

15. Bradford, M. Gerald, and Larry E. Dahl. "Doctrine: Meaning, Source, and History of Doctrine." Entry "Doctrine." In Encyclopedia of Mormonism,

ue to navigate a spiritual home that embraces their exclusion from the privileges and exaltation of the plan of salvation.

The spiritual home for queer Latter-day Saints does not look the same as it does for the general population in the Church. It is a very different experience, with different rules and different expectations. From lessons learned during California Prop 8, the modern church strategically divorced the LGBTQ community from LGBTQ Latter-day Saints. It deals with each group independently. While it may have some tolerance for equal rights for LGBTQ people in a pluralistic society, it considers queer Latter-day Saints an internal matter. Queer equality is an unauthorized internal "idea." This "idea" is managed by the Church's dominant narratives and policies about queer Latter-day Saints. This narrative/policy duo creates the landscape of a queer person's spiritual home, and is called the queer/Latter-day Saint intersection when queer Latter-day Saints interact with it. For queer Latter-day Saints, policies create an elaborate management mechanism to prevent equality or get rid of those who demonstrate equality. Because the dominant narrative changes over time, the policies also change to accommodate the Church's current thinking. This change is forceful enough that it creates identifiable generations of queer people who must navigate different waters than their predecessors. Although the modern church started in its newly articulated triad of queer theology by wholly rejecting LGBTQ Latter-day Saints, it slowly began to accommodate belonging—just as long as it did not contradict the doctrinal premise. In the wake of California Prop

---

edited by Daniel H. Ludlow, 394. Macmillan, 1992. https://lib.byu.edu/collections/encyclopedia-of-mormonism/.

8, the modern church put lots of thought into how to control belonging and make itself welcoming, while firmly asserting the Church's sole right, protected by religious freedom, to determine the conditions of belonging in a queer person's spiritual home. It is important to note that no matter how much time, energy, and money the modern church puts into this process so that it may own "belonging," queer people will always own the intersection. It is ours to navigate, talk about, and assign meaning to according to our experiences there.

Any examination of the conditions found in the queer/Latter-day Saint intersection must begin by acknowledging that a rainbow stained-glass ceiling exists in the Church. Most people are familiar with the term "glass ceiling," which refers to a real but invisible barrier that prevents women from rising beyond a certain level in a company hierarchy. Similarly, the rainbow stained-glass ceiling in the Church is firmly in place to prevent queer people from rising alongside their straight/cisgender peers in privilege and opportunity. Queer Latter-day Saints bump up against this ceiling when they participate in marriage equality or claim self-determination of their gender and transition. The rainbow stained-glass ceiling is central to the queer/Latter-day Saint intersection. It is what every queer Latter-day Saint is currently aware of, fearful of, navigating under, crashing against, or navigating away from. It determines how far belonging can be extended before policies kick in to quash queer equality or remove the queer Latter-day Saint altogether. Above the rainbow stained-glass ceiling is the privilege of eternal marriage, being sealed to one's children and family, authentically living one's gender identity, and exaltation. On a more earthly level, privilege includes access to the power centers of the Church and to civil marriage without fear that it will jeopardize one's church membership. Below the ceiling is where queer Latter-day Saints are held—and told continually that they are lovingly held there. It is a spiritual home where they are infantilized and segregated both culturally and theologically.

Each year, the modern church must work harder and harder to sustain this system of structural inequality. Queer children are born into Latter-day Saint homes, not into the modern church. When the modern church continues to offer Latter-day Saint families with queer children less protection and equality in their spiritual home than what is granted them under the law, it doesn't matter how politely and eloquently the modern church paints the terms of belonging under the rainbow stained-glass ceiling. Today's parents want their queer children to have the same opportunities and happiness that they have experienced in life and are promised in the heavens.

Instead of confronting the doctrinal premise about the potential exaltation of the queer soul, the modern church instead presents a life of belonging under the rainbow stained-glass ceiling in the most appealing way it can: by example. It needs spokespeople. It needs stories of queer Latter-day Saints, and lots of them. Not every queer story is useful to the modern church. The modern church has a specific story that it traffics in, one that requires a particular set of skills. Every story must come from someone under the rainbow stained-glass ceiling who can tell the story that they are faithfully managing life under it. Using the stories of a mix of rugged, good-looking, smart, athletic, relatable, heteronormative, Mormonormative, single, non-transitioned, queer Latter-day Saints, the Church builds an unsustainable model to show parents and their queer children—as well as other queer Latter-day Saints—that, "Look! All the popular kids are doing it!"

The problem with this strategy is that these queer Latter-day Saint stories typically have a short shelf life. The churn of queer spokespeople is significant. Most eventually navigate themselves out from under the restrictions of the dominant narrative towards joy and equality. The moment a queer spokesperson transgresses the dominant narrative, their church videos come down, articles are erased, books get pulled off the shelves of Deseret Book, and church membership is withdrawn. The modern church then conducts another star search to find the next generation of queer stories to support its dominant narrative. The dominant narrative holds unreasonable expectations that even queer spokespeople cannot sustain for long. Capturing a snapshot of a queer person and freezing them in one moment of time broadcasts a false hope in the efficacy of the dominant narrative to sustain a queer person throughout their life—and then provide an eternal happiness without exaltation. When a queer Latter-day Saint appears on an official platform of the Church, it isn't their authentic words that are powerful, it is the inequality they represent that makes their words powerful to the modern church.

The truth about the queer children of God is not found in dominant narratives or policies. It is not found in the prejudice of a doctrinal premise about queer exaltation. The truth about the queer children of God is found in the entire collective spectrum of the lived experience of each queer soul who is navigating or has navigated their personal intersection with the Church. It is important to acknowledge that at any one time, there are LGBTQ Mormons who are living a self-determined life that aligns with the Church's current dominant narrative. However, this phenomenon is more a testament to how far we have come in society to allow visible queer people spiritual freedom and choice than it is an indicator that the dominant narrative of a religious power center is "true" or "just." Queer "dominant narrative congruent" stories hold immense value. The modern church treats such stories like currency, carefully pulling them from the rich tapestry of the entire spectrum of LGBTQ Latter-day experiences. It then "spends" these carefully curated queer stories to broadcast its queer acceptability standards and advertise belonging under the rainbow stained-glass ceiling. In so doing, it is utilizing what Chimamanda Ngozi Adichie refers to as the phenomenon of the single story: "Show a people as one thing—as only one thing, over and over again—and that is what they become."[16]

With the modern church loudly advertising its dominant narrative about queer people as doctrinal, how can someone come to know for themself the truth about the nature of the queer soul, queer joy, the queer experience, and queer belonging? My husband, Matthew, is a historian. As he moves his world history students at Arizona State from the sixteenth century to modern history, he comes to a point where history stops, and the course is over because they are to the point where current events begin. Current events are not for history. Current events are for journalism. But where is that inflection point where journalism becomes history? It's not a point, really; it's a zone of transformation dependent on a couple of factors: First, the passage of time permitting the identification, gathering, and archiving of materials, reports, and documents. Second, the changing politics in which issues that formerly concerned the power structures under study have become irrelevant and their influence diminished. In some cases, the power structure

---

16. Adichie, Chimamanda Ngozi. "The Danger of a Single Story: Ted." YouTube, October 7, 2009. https://youtu.be/D9Ihs241zeg?si=p8Uo9OlbBRPAYyot.

under study no longer exists, rendering former controversies irrelevant. The passage of time provides enough distance from a power structure's influence to allow historical objectivity.

When historians move backward in the timeline, journalism gives way to history. Archived stories and experiences become primary sources for analyzing and producing accurate accounts of the past. No credible historian writes a history and then goes looking for primary sources to support it. Instead, primary sources independently reveal the history. Knowing this, how do we approach today's huge pool of contemporary queer stories with the tools of a historian if we are still living in a journalistic present? How do we build an accurate account in a journalistic present?

First, remember that organizations wield immense power to reframe and restructure a current narrative. In the journalistic present, the modern church as a power structure has already written a dominant narrative about queer people. It is now out looking for queer stories to sustain its narrative. To counteract such power, don't approach a queer story as if it is true or false. Do not analyze it as either sustaining a power structure's dominant narrative or contradicting it. Instead, consider queer people reliable reporters of their own experience. Second, uncouple the queer story from the dominant narrative. Allow yourself to sit with and accept each story as a valid experience. Do not be intimidated by the diversity of queer stories coming from the queer/Latter-day Saint intersection. Listen to as many queer stories in as many different and diverse places as you can. Like a historian, gather, listen to, catalog, and organize each experience to build an accurate account of queer people's experiences as they navigate their intersection with the modern church. Let the diverse stories show you an accurate account, and do not be influenced by the pressures of a power structure advancing a dominant narrative.

The lived experience of a queer person creates authority which creates an accurate narrative. Enough of these narratives reveal the wholeness and inherent worth of the queer children of God. On the other hand, "authorities" create a dominant narrative, which creates an artificial experience. Notably, authorities are subject to human prejudice and misunderstanding. Prejudice's parasitic ability to comfortably latch onto people in authority is why it is critical to understand the queer/Latter-day Saint intersection from a queer-centric position of lived experience. Trying to overlay the heterosexual/cisgender experience over top of the queer experience only hides and erases queer people. To say that everyone is just a child of God navigating their way back to their heavenly parents downplays the inequality that exists for queer Latter-day Saints in the opportunities and privileges of the plan of salvation otherwise abundantly afforded their straight/cisgender peers.

Being queer-centric is about queer self-determination. It is centered on how we, as queer people, experience this world with our friends, families, and communities. It is centered on how we experience God and our spiritual home. It is centered, as the psalmist writes, in the desires of our heart (Psalm 37:4). No longer is the question, "What does the Church think about queer people?" but "What do queer people think about the Church?" When we are queer-centric, we see and understand the spiritual equality of the queer soul in the family of God—that Jesus is not wiping away our queerness but is instead the Christ who experiences queerness with us.[17] "Queer-centric" does not mean "Christ-displaced." When we acknowledge the dignity of others—including the queer children of God—and provide them care, we center ourselves on the Savior. Christ teaches that

---

17. Ostler, Blaire. "Concerning Christ." In *Queer Mormon Theology: An Introduction*, 37-38. Newburgh, Indiana: By Common Consent Press, 2021.

when you see the least of these, his brothers, sisters, and siblings, you see him (Matthew 25:35-40). Being queer-centric is being Christ-centric.

Queer people are making impossible choices in a plan of salvation not built for them. When we allow a structure such as the rainbow stained-glass ceiling to define queer people as they navigate their intersection with the Church, we enable an instrument of prejudice to work among the Saints. Do not give prejudice this power. This is our intersection as a queer people, and we are giving others the gift of our stories to understand it as it really is and how it really feels—and that is the power of the queer story. It is the power of intersection ownership. It is a power that absolutely threatens the power center's dominant narrative. Our collective lived experiences build an accurate picture of unashamed authenticity and absolute queer joy, even in the face of prejudice, harassment, and discrimination. Thousands of compelling stories exist of queer people who are or were Latter-day Saints. Many who are no longer members of the Church didn't leave because they no longer believed. The modern church forcibly removed them because they refused to be managed by acts of prejudice. Listen to the voice of the refugee. You cannot just focus on church-approved, "safe" queer voices. You will miss the complete and accurate picture of the queer children of God. You will miss the depth of queer joy.

As I sat in the rubble of the collapsed dominant narrative of my generation in the Church with my children and family, I sat amidst broken promises and shattered hopes in a construct that no longer existed. In time, all queer Latter-day Saints from collapsed generations drain into the newest dominant narrative and policies governing queer Latter-day Saints. We are not coming in wide-eyed and fresh-faced. As elders of previous generations, we are battle-weary, infused with earned wisdom that comes from being a seasoned navigator of the treacherous seas of the queer/Latter-day Saint intersection of our day.

As a sexual minority, I was part of a cohort of thousands upon thousands of gay and lesbian members whom the Church had introduced into mixed-orientation marriages through policy decades before. An interesting thing happened because of this introduction. Generations of gay and lesbian Latter-day Saints learned through lived experience that the institution of marriage itself holds intense benefits—physical, social, mental, emotional, and even spiritual. The institution of marriage is a healthy and stable way for humans to be configured. As the dominant narrative about mixed-orientation marriages collapsed, causing for many the collapse of their own marriage, it was these couples, not the modern church, who picked up the pieces and did the work to correct the damage. After reflecting upon their mixed-orientation marriages, many of these couples conclude that despite sorrow, discomfort, and—ultimately—divorce, the blessings and benefits of the institution of marriage still clearly appeal to them. Many who exit a mixed-orientation marriage are eager to marry again. In the hope of new beginnings, they crave to love within the highest ideals of fidelity, devotion, sacrifice, and family—but this time, according to their orientation. Being in a mixed-orientation marriage is a terrible way to have to learn the lesson that sexual orientation matters in a marriage.

When the dominant narrative of my generation collapsed, I may have guided my landing into family, friends, and an LGBTQ Latter-day Saint support community, but my membership in the Church was automatically directing me to make my spiritual home under the rainbow stained-glass ceiling. What awaited me there?

Capture.

As a teenage boy, as soon as I identified myself to my bishop, I was carefully captured and funneled into the second generation of gay men in the Church to abide by its special rules of belonging. Now that I was visible once again to the Church, I was facing my second capture, only this time, my belonging was subject to the rule of the newest generation: the single and celibate sexual minority. Generations of queer Latter-day Saints do not sit on a linear timeline with distinct boundaries. Because the lifespan of a dominant narrative is considerably shorter than that of a queer person, all four generations of sexual minorities are currently alive at the same time in the Church. I was from a collapsed generation bringing with me the lived experience of marriage that I had gained from my capture in a previous generation. However, most sexual minorities are being captured for the first time.

All youth and young adults in the Church are expected to refrain from sexual relations of any kind. This is an equal ask of all sexual orientations. But then, one day, amidst a feeling of living equally among one's peers, there is the capture. Marrying age is typically the moment of reckoning for the sexual minorities of the Church. This is when their inequality in terms of choice and opportunity as compared to their straight peers becomes a stark reality. At this juncture, the Latter-day Saint sexual minorities are carefully captured and funneled into the unofficial celibate order of the Church. There, they are taught the virtues of celibacy, how to manage the haunting absence of a companion, and celebrated for being able to do hard things.

To be sure, when a person chooses to be single, no matter their sexual orientation, it is a valid expression of self-determination. However, to demand celibacy of sexual minorities so that they may purchase the ability to remain in their spiritual home or see their families and heavenly parents in the eternities while their straight peers are tasked with no such thing is not only an act of prejudice, it is cruel. Practicing celibacy instead of marriage under the threat of no longer belonging creates anxiety and fear. Exaltation is the ultimate belonging.

Facing capture for a second time, I realized that in this ecosystem the Church had created for its LGBTQ population, mixed-orientation marriage had always been a "get out of jail free" card, passing me through the rainbow stained-glass ceiling conditionally, under constant threat that if I failed, I would be demoted to the celibate order. And now I was facing just that—not because I had failed but because the dominant narrative about my generation had failed. One of the things I highly value in my life is my membership in The Church of Jesus Christ of Latter-day Saints. It is my spiritual home. It has had a profound impact on my life and values. Even from my very beginnings, it changed the course of my life. My birth mother was not Mormon, and had she not used Relief Society Social Services for my adoption, I might have never even been a member. It was the first great blessing by the hand of Providence in my life, even before I was born. My belonging and belief in the Church was so dear to me that I remained publicly silent for many years about my sexual orientation. I had healing to do with my children, whom I love more than life itself, and I could not be distracted by the social wars. But the appearance of the exclusion policy changed the course of my life. This was the moment I chose love over prejudice.

Now, the orbit of my priesthood leaders surveilling my life to determine my marital status was tightening. I held the same burning belief and testimony in the gospel of Jesus Christ and the restoration out of the closet as I did while I was in the closet. None of that would change on the day I married Matthew, only my marital status. But just that one change would change everything. It was impossible for me as a Latter-day Saint to stand my queer body authentically in front of the Church and expect the dignity of belonging either on earth or in the heavens when I made the same self-determined choices as my straight peers: to marry according to my orientation and build a life together with another in fidelity and love.

I was on a direct collision course with an impenetrable rainbow stained-glass ceiling. Now, engaged to Matthew after years of experiencing the haunting absence of a companion, I could hear the approaching footsteps of prejudice coming for me. Its mission was to capture me or, if I resisted, excise me from the faith. Yes, it is a fearful thing to lose something you love dearly. But it was time to stop running. It was time to turn directly towards those footsteps and look the ugliness of my pursuer directly in the eye: I do not consent to my capture. I will be bought and redeemed, owned by the precious blood of Christ (1 Peter 1:18-19).

I will not be owned by prejudice.

THE BLESSING OF WAVES

We did not expect a Road to Jericho when we
   grasped the iron rod,
You named us Latter-day Lamanites,
And in this othering,
Made us a "those people."

No!

We are your people!
We are you!
Covenant born,
Sealed into the great houses of Zion.

Yet from the great and spacious building
Policies and words
Rain down upon us like arrows
As we humbly press forward.

We continue to struggle
To stand
In holy places while shielding
Our bodies with outstretched arms.

Our flame of testimony flickers,
As fellowship's air draws out.
Made servants,
And told to hide in plain sight.

It is unclear if we are given or driven to the margins,
But this we know:
We are your children and we asked for bread.
When you gave us a stone, we didn't expect it cast at us.

We will always be with you, see us!
We continually wash upon your shores as waves,
Born to our families to bless you
When you did not realize you were in need of blessing.

And the blessing of waves shapes shorelines
And tides bring life
To the everlasting lands
Of the kingdom of God.

CHAPTER 20

Under a Lemon Tree

> Love is the greatest force in the universe. It is the heartbeat of the moral cosmos. He who loves is a participant in the being of God.
>
> Martin Luther King, Jr.

The year 2019 was an unusually busy time to be president of Affirmation. Many significant events were happening in the queer/Latter-day Saint intersection. Yet, 2019 would be the year of the family for me. Matthew and I had a wedding to plan. After we proposed to one another on a sun-filled January mountain, we immediately started working out the details of our big day. One thing was certain: we wanted a backyard wedding in our desert oasis surrounded by the towering trees. A spring wedding would be too soon because we would have family and friends coming in from all parts of the country. And summer? No one gets married outdoors in a Phoenix summer. Backyard grass dies, and plants—hanging on for dear life—wither and brown. Considering guests, temperatures, and foliage, we decided a November date would be perfect.

At the west end of our backyard stands a mature eighteen-foot lemon tree. It is the largest of the six backyard citrus trees, striking in size and shape. With a massive, bifurcated trunk, it had been shaped and pruned over the years to bear the weight of fruit and bough. Its dark green foliage dotted with yellow lemons in winter is visually striking. It would be there, under the stunning boughs of this lemon tree, where we would exchange our vows in marriage. I immediately began some preparatory work with that lemon tree so it would be dressed and ready for our wedding day. It needed to be stripped of its remaining winter fruit, then pruned and shaped before spring. With this advanced preparation, the tree would be full of new fruit by fall, leaves densely filling the carefully pruned spaces—a beauty to behold. In the middle of my pruning, I received a text from my stake president. He wanted to come over for a visit and asked if bringing the bishop with him would be okay as well. After comparing schedules, we made an appointment to meet.

We started the visit by talking about my work in Affirmation. My stake president shared that he had a nephew who had come out as transgender, and, as his uncle, he was struggling to understand. As we talked about resources available to families concerning the transgender experience, I was reminded that the blessings of LGBTQ children are distributed equally among the families of Zion. God is no respecter of persons in such blessings. As we talked, I noticed my stake president could not stop looking at my engagement ring. He finally said, "I see you have a ring on. Brother Kitchen, has there been a change in your marital status since we last talked?" I told him I was engaged but not married. The mood changed in the room, and he reiterated that marriage to a man would make me an apostate of the faith, and he would have no choice but to excommunicate me.

"Lucky for you, you don't have to make that decision today," I curtly noted. I stewed on this for a few weeks. Nothing about me, my family, my testimony, my love of the Savior mattered. It was all about my marital status.

Not only did Matthew and I need to decide on a wedding date, but who would marry us and who would stand with us during the ceremony. Matthew wanted to ask his mentor turned longtime friend, Julia, to be his best woman. I thought about how to include my best friends, Heidi and Emily. I shared with Matthew that I was thinking about having Emily be my best woman and then asked how he would feel if we invited Heidi to marry us.

Both Matthew and I knew that Heidi was a master of words. She writes like she composes music—words, like notes, intentionally placed, but with that intangible gift of direction and theme that turns theory into art and beauty. "There is another reason I propose Heidi to be our officiant," I continued. "Because of the exclusion policy, when we marry, our marriage certificate will also be my excommunication certificate. The same words that will pronounce us husbands will at once pronounce me an apostate. I want to look upon the gentleness of love in my best friend's face as she speaks the words that will join us as husbands so that I may be reminded of the joy in that moment and not the sorrow." Matthew looked at me and took my hand. He was aware of the momentous choice before me in my spiritual home. The moment I chose love, the power center in the Church would only see me as choosing apostasy.

Likewise, Eden presented two contradictory trees with momentous choices, one life and the other death. Our first parents were commanded to not eat of the fruit of the tree of the knowledge of good and evil, for in that day, they would surely die. Yet they ate. And it was in that very act of transgression—necessary for all of humanity to exist and experience joy—that Adam and Eve became heroes in the Latter-day Saint story. This was not original sin but an essential transgression in the great plan of happiness.

It is with great sacrifice that queer Latter-day Saints make an essential choice when they stand before the tree of marriage, knowing that in the day they partake, they will be driven from their Eden. When we choose love in such a system, it becomes the binding of Isaac as we watch our Fathers in council raise the blade above our heads—pronouncing us separated from God for the eternities—as we frantically look for the ram in the thicket that never appears. It is there in the power imbalance, bound in the space between altar and blade, that we become as Job in Edward L. Greenstein's translation, proclaiming, "I am fed up. I take pity on 'dust and ashes!'"[1]

The "dust and ashes" that Job refers to is humanity—our humanness in the same context as when Abraham presented himself to God in that way (Genesis 18:27). Job pities humanity when people are made to suffer at the hands of power, as he had been. Patrick Reardon observes that Greenstein's translation of Job leads to the question of how humans should react to the suffering they must undergo, whether righteous or corrupt. "Is surrender to God the best method? Or anger? Bitterness? Defiance? Anyone seeking to live a full human life must come up with some answer to those questions,"[2] he argues. But this only scratches the surface. Reardon contends that no matter how we

---

1. Greenstein, Edward L. "Job's Response To The Deity (42:6)." In *Job: A New Translation*, 185. New Haven and London, Connecticut, United Kingdom: Yale University Press, 2019.
2. Reardon, Patrick T. "Book Review: 'Job: A New Translation' by Edward L. Greenstein." Patrick T. Reardon, November 30, 2019. https://patricktreardon.com/book-review-job-a-new-translation-by-edward-l-greenstein/.

answer those questions or how we imagine Job answering those questions, "the key thing is that Job, throughout this ordeal, remained a good person who never denied God." Reardon then asks, "Is defiance in the face of God the same thing as denying God?"³

To this, I answer an absolute "No!" If the story of Job explores our mortal experience as dust and ashes, then it provides the pathway forward when we experience unjust suffering at the hands of power. While same-sex marriage is seen as defiance in the face of God by the modern church, it is not denying God—even as married gay and lesbian Latter-day Saints are shown the door, testimony and belief intact.

Excommunication does not define married gay and lesbian Latter-day Saints, but it will most certainly define the Church. Anytime one cleaves a queer family in two and prunes out the queer children of God from their great and eternal family trees, it most certainly will define the face of God as one of trauma. Such a characterization of God is a great lie. God is not a God of trauma. God is a God of love. And it is this love I choose to exemplify in my own life—even in the face of injustice at the hands of power—to love another. And in such choices, we become the heroes in our own story and in our own families. With Matthew's hand in mine, he looked me in the eye and said, "I think it's a wonderful idea to ask Heidi to marry us. Let's do it."

On our engagement day, I sent Emily and Heidi a message sharing our happy news, inviting them to be a part of our special day. Emily responded, "Joy! My heart! So happy for this important

---

3. Reardon, Patrick T. "Book Review: 'Job: A New Translation' by Edward L. Greenstein." November 30, 2019.

day and so grateful to be invited to be a part of it!" She immediately entered best woman mode, wanting to know our wedding colors and venue. Her sense of beauty and decorum is impeccable. It wasn't long before she set me up a Pinterest page to start sharing pictures and formulating ideas about the big day's esthetics.

Unbeknownst to me, my invitation to Heidi to marry us had provoked a great internal wrestle, causing her to spend the better part of 2019 in the agony of indecision. After copious congratulations, Heidi concluded, "As for performing the ceremony, I'm deeply conflicted. On the one hand, this is the greatest honor I can think of, and I have so much I would love to offer in this capacity! Of all the accolades the world has to bestow, this is the one I covet, to know that I have meant so much to my friend that he wants me to share this day in this way. On the other hand . . ." The question Heidi held in her other hand was that if same-sex marriage was apostasy, would she—as a faithful, active, temple-recommend-holding Latter-day Saint—be guilty by association? Would church leaders consider her promoting apostasy by officiating a same-sex wedding? Would she be vulnerable to discipline? Matthew and I had asked Heidi to marry us under the oppressive weight of the exclusion policy. The exclusion policy was a scorched earth policy not only directly targeting same-sex married couples but their children as well. The burn then extended up into the branches of the great houses of Zion, extracting same-sex married couples from their parents and siblings out of their eternal family tree.

The existential fear that this caused was not just limited to the families of the Church who had queer children. The scorching of the exclusion policy was so far-reaching in its eternal implications that it bore an extra-familial threat as well. The policy was barely three years old, and much was still unknown as to how it would be implemented with faithful Latter-day

Saints who perform, encourage, pay for, or arrange for same-sex marriages. After much discussion between the three of us, our exchange ended on this note:

> **Nathan:** I know I may have asked something that is deeply conflicting. What are friends for, but to be surprising and ask each other uniquely challenging questions?
>
> **Heidi:** I feel like an abject coward next to you. You have had to ask yourself a far more terrible question. I admire your courage and want you to know I am always here for you.
>
> **Nathan:** This will be a moment I want to have a most loving and trusted friend as you—with much care and love—speak the words that will at once join me to the love of my life and deliver me into apostasy. You understand the complexities of this moment. And so, this is why I am asking you, as my lifelong friend, to escort me through this pivotal moment. It is much more than simply standing in front of Matthew and me to pronounce us husbands. It is a sacred event that I don't want just anyone to speak into existence.

In the hours after our engagement, Matthew worked through his family list, and I worked through mine, sharing our news. When I called my parents and siblings, it was a completely different experience than when I came out to them seven years earlier. This time, it was unequivocal joy within the boughs of the Kitchen family tree. Everyone immediately said that they would be there. The significance of this moment did not escape me. We had done the work over the years to gather one another up in love and support. As the year progressed, our family group chat teemed with messages about travel dates, plane tickets, car rentals, and hotel rooms. Everyone wanted to know what they could do once they got here to help with last-minute tasks and setup. This insistence on helping get things ready is the kind of practical love the Kitchen family is known for.

The most tender moments were with my children as we shared our news. For my three sons, who lived with me in Arizona and had gotten to know Matthew, this was the exciting moment when he would officially join the household. My son at Utah Valley University would fly down for the wedding, and as the wedding day approached with my newborn grandson in the NICU, my daughter would be with us in spirit on that day. My children experienced the collapse of the mixed-orientation marriage dominant narrative. They experienced their parents' divorce. They experienced the exclusion policy. Nevertheless—their Eden in dust and ashes—they rose. And in this rising, we rose together as a family into healing. In November, we would sit together under the boughs of another kind of tree—the house of Kitchen-Rivera—grown from a rock and now flourishing on our family's Peak of Champions.

Heidi called me on November 25, a little before 9 p.m. and five days before our wedding. She was sitting in her thinking place, cross-legged outside the funeral door of her stake center, surrounded by the now barren butterfly bushes. She realized it was past time to register with the State of Arizona if she was going to do this thing—and she was still in high internal conflict. This had been a ten-month wrestle with an angel, and the night was just as dark as when she had started. Her voice trembled as she surmised, "I have given this much thought and consideration, and I don't know that I can do this."

She explained that even though same-sex marriage was no longer considered apostasy in the Church now that the exclusion policy had been rescinded in April, everywhere she turned—church statements, leaders, family—she was still getting conflicting answers to her questions. The threat of discipline was still very real in her world by the butterfly bushes that night. In church discipline, she would lose her position as an accompanist at the private, LDS-oriented school where she worked. When it hires church members, they must be members in good standing. "After that, how many of the neighborhood mothers would continue sending me their piano students?" she asked rhetorically. The journey of a faithful Latter-day Saint ally can be intense when they are asked to act for and on behalf of those in the margins they champion. I recognized her wrestle as an ally. Spiritual and economic consequences were my very real wrestle as I was coming out, navigating my fear of the unknown. But I would never press a friend to do something that felt dangerous to them. Heidi's support of Matthew and me and my marriage did not hinge on her marrying us. When I got off the phone, I shared the news with Matthew. Having known Heidi since our freshman days at BYU, I knew this about her. She never made decisions lightly. She was thoughtful and comprehensive in judgment. But what I did not realize at that moment was I had mistakenly heard her declaration of "I don't know if I can do this" as a "no." God was not done with Heidi yet. Standing before the looming trees within her own Eden, she retired to bed in an attitude of full-on prayer. Daybreak was just moments ahead after her ten-month wrestle with an angel.

The following morning, as I was making inquiries among friends and family about finding an officiant for our wedding, Heidi texted me: "Woke up last night, anxiety resolved. Did this with confidence." She then sent a picture of her newly granted credentials, authorizing her to marry Matthew and me in Arizona. She quipped, "If you had said to me, sitting in front of the rostrum in Colloquium when we were freshmen in 1986, that I would one day preside over the wedding of you and your boyfriend . . ." I chuckled and replied, "The future would shock us all. I wasn't ready to hear my future then either."

It was dawn along the river where Heidi had wrestled an angel for almost a year. Jacob had named this riverbank anciently after his wrestle with an angel. This was Peniel, the face of God (Genesis 32:24, 26-30).

Matthew and I were married under a lemon tree in our backyard on November 30, 2019. All time stopped that bright Fall afternoon as I faced Matthew, standing tall and proud before God, surrounded by family and friends, making a public commitment to the man I dearly loved and chose to marry. I recognized this moment as love. This was belonging. This was family.

After we exchanged our vows, we clasped hands and looked to Heidi. At that moment, as she pronounced the words that would bind us together in marriage, she showed us the face of God. She had been there, the place of the great wrestle. This had been the place Matthew had been as well. And undeniably, I had been there.

I had been there.

For Matthew—

My dearest mooring in all the world,
Exists within the person I said "Yes" to
Under a lemon tree
The 30th of a November past.

Now arm in arm,
I would vow a thousand November 30ths
Again and again,
As we travel our life together
Towards our eternal home
To stand as one
Under the boughs of love.

CHAPTER 21

The Hunted

> **Elder Neil L. Andersen of the Twelve:** Do not rush to excommunicate same-sex married couples all at once. We don't want to rush to do this. It will make it look like a witch hunt.
>
> **Elder L. Whitney Clayton of the Seventy:** But eventually they will need to be excommunicated.
>
> From the notes of President Walt Wood, a member of the Mesa Mountain View Stake Presidency.
> Directions for executing the November 5th exclusion policy at the local level, given at a regional training meeting for bishops and stake presidencies.
> Mesa, Arizona
> January 2016

Three months before our wedding, I received a text from my newly called stake president. My old stake president, who had watched over me through the enactment and then the recension of the exclusion policy, had been released. My new stake president was an attorney at a well-known local firm. I knew him well as we had been in leadership together back when we were in the same ward ten years ago. In the years since, he rose through the ranks and had been called as the new stake president earlier that year.

In his text, he casually recalled "the good times" we had together when I was in his ward. He asked if he could come over to catch up. I knew in my gut that this visit he painted as a social call would be anything but. Having walked the halls of church government for many years, I understood the system, thinking, and motivation of the men who govern. I had not only witnessed it, I participated in this machine. I was acutely aware of the modern church's administration, assertion, and protection of power. Despite this, I felt that at the beginning of this relationship, I needed to take my stake president's stated intentions at face value if we were to build trust with each other.

I talked with Matthew about the upcoming visit. I asked him if he would mind not coming over that evening. I shared with him that I wasn't ready to bring him front and center into an inflamed moment in Mormon history over marriage equality that was now about to play out in my life on a local level. I wasn't ready to bring him into a situation with many unknowns. My stake president needed to earn the privilege of meeting and getting to know Matthew.

A few days before the meeting, I felt a spiritual prompting to assemble a support team. This small band of friends graciously agreed to be available that night for me. As the appointment time approached, Matthew sent an encouraging text. I alerted Heidi, Emily, and Laurie that I was about to go into my meeting with the stake president. I put on some Paul Cardall hymn arrangements and asked God in prayer that his Spirit would accompany me in my home during the meeting.

Ten minutes after the appointed hour, there was a knock on my door. My stake president stood with a man I did not know very well from my stake. I invited them in with a handshake. I directed both men to the loveseat and sat opposite them in the recliner. To this seating arrangement, my stake president immediately said, "Move over," pointing to the adjacent couch, "I'll sit there," pointing to where I had just sat down. Desiring to be accommodating during these first moments of our encounter, I obliged his aggressive request and moved to the side couch. My stake president was now in the center of the room, which my literary brain immediately identified as foreshadowing.

He then began recounting the time I came to his home ten years earlier to train him to be the "best second counselor in a new bishopric." He said he appreciated that and realized the wealth of information I had to pass on. "You were such a treasure in our stake. I looked up to you." He continued, "I was surprised to hear you had separated and divorced. What did your wife think when she learned you were gay?" I drew a hard-line boundary at this question. He was leading me to engage in hearsay. I told him that, as husband and wife, we had much to discuss and work through during those days and that we did then and still treat that period with tenderness and confidentiality. He continued to press, "Oh, come on, there must have been animosity. How are things today? Do you get along? Do you fight with each other? Surely you still have some hard feelings you would like to share."

I knew this tactic, and I was not going to take the bait. I was unsure why he was trying to stir up unhealthy drama between me and my former spouse, especially now that we had healed enough from the absolute trauma of a mixed-orientation marriage dissolution to have a working relationship. Moreover, he was not invited into those respected spaces we existed in as husband and wife, our vulnerable conversations, and our partnership in figuring out what this meant to our marriage and children. He did not deserve entry into our twenty-three-year-old institution of marriage, and I certainly was not going to let him recast it now as a train wreck. I told him my former spouse and I had an amicable relationship and worked well in co-parenting our children.

Seeing he was not making headway, he asked me about Affirmation. I was relieved because this was a subject that I was excited to talk about. I shared with him the details of my visit to BYU and spoke about our suicide prevention efforts within Affirmation. I shared that when I met with the Presiding Bishopric, discussing the various ways Affirmation cares for LGBTQ members around the world, the First Counselor in the Presiding Bishopric, Bishop Davies, leaned forward in his chair and said, "You know what you are doing? You are ministering just as President Nelson has talked about. Keep it up."

Rather than engage, my stake president bluntly said, "I'm really not here to talk about Affirmation. I'm here to talk about you." He asked me when my wedding date was. I told him November 30. He shook his head and responded, "You realize that you will be committing a very serious sin in the eyes of God when you marry." I reminded him that the Church no longer considered same-sex marriage an act of apostasy.

"But it is still a serious sin," he asserted, "and you need to know that I will follow the handbook to excommunicate you once you marry."

"Why?" I questioned, "As president of Affirmation, I have the chance to see many stakes around the world where the stake president will not hunt down and excommunicate the same-sex legally married couples in his stake."

"You want me to ignore the handbook and counsel from the brethren?" he asked indignantly.

"I am only asking you to follow your conscience in your care and love of same-sex married couples in your stake like other stake presidents do."

Silent at my request, he asked why I wasn't attending church. I told him that it was not safe to do so because it put me in the orbit of my Arizona priesthood leaders who were surveilling me, waiting to excommunicate me once I was legally married. "Nonsense," he said. He insisted he would be the first to wrap his arms around Matthew and heartily welcome us to church. I replied that this act might welcome us into the physical space, but the underlying culture of exclusion behind those smiles was far from welcoming.

He asked if I still wanted to be a member of the Church. I told him absolutely that I did and had a testimony of the restoration and the gospel of Jesus Christ. I had a great belief in the sealing power between me and my children. He sat back, arms folded, and said, "Ah, I see—that's it. You're in it just for familial reasons." I was astounded by his disrespectful assessment, the manner in which he casually diminished the sacred depth and breadth of my faith and experiences built over a lifetime in the Church.

He asserted that he could not see that I held any respect for the gospel or how I could have a testimony because I was choosing to marry a man, contrary to the teachings of modern-day prophets. I told him that was an unfair judgment. "I hold one of the most basic tenets of Christianity," I explained. "I have hope. I exercise hope that the children of God will someday be ready to accept LGBTQ people as full and equal persons in the Church." Without comment, he continued, "Even if the Church changes sometime in the future and allows same-sex marriage, and I suppose that it may, what you are choosing to do at this moment is against the will of God." For him, obedience in the "right now" was the basic tenet of a testimony, which I was choosing to ignore. I was taken aback that my very conservative stake president had just conceded that the Church may very well accept same-sex marriage sometime in the future. Unfortunately, the hope of a better tomorrow is nothing for LGBTQ Latter-day Saints today who are navigating "in the now." Such hope in a future change does not excuse the discrimination by people who have the power to make such a change today.

"Mormons are really good at looking at their visible minorities in the Church and telling them in their pain of exclusion that one day in the future, things will change," I noted. "However, The Book of Mormon teaches that 'men are that they might have joy', not joy at some future point in time, but joy in this life and joy right now." I bore testimony that what I do in Affirmation is minister to LGBTQ Mormons who are caught in this zone of exclusion and rejection while the Church is waiting for some future event of inclusion. "There is real pain and suffering right now in the margins, and this is where the work of Christ is. This is my space of ministry."

He asked me why I even wanted to marry a man: "Is it just so you can have sex?" I corrected him: "Getting married is not just about sex." He paused, smiled, and said, "But in fact, yes, it is." His assertion astonished me. I shared that even in a mixed-orientation marriage, I learned about the great benefits and safety of marriage. Of all people, gay men in a mixed-orientation marriage know that marriage is not just about sex. To reduce the institution of marriage down to the act of sex was an offensive and misguided characterization. He then asked me if I thought I could be married to Matthew and live the law of chastity by not having sex with him. By now, I was angry at the inappropriate questioning and that he was so obsessed with sex. I redirected him by asking a question in return, "In your opinion, can two men who live in total fidelity within the bonds of legal marriage live the law of chastity?"

"No," he emphatically snapped. He leaned back in the chair and continued, "I wish you wouldn't marry. You will be better off not married. You can get all the support you need from the members of your ward and stake." He continued, "You know Tom Christofferson, the gay brother of Elder Christofferson?

"I know Tom very well. I know him personally," I replied.

"Come be the Tom Christofferson of our stake, leave Affirmation, and use your leadership skills to bless our stake instead of using them to lead Affirmation."

Over the years, I had heard about priesthood leaders weaponizing the stories of Deseret Book-published gay authors such as Tom, Ben Schilaty, and even Charlie Bird. Now in my own home, it was my turn to experience this phenomenon firsthand. No matter how many times these authors voice that their story is not to be used as a template for other gay people's lives—and they articulate this position constantly—because the Church has given them its platform as a way to showcase the dominant narrative (it's the only way any gay person will get to be on such a platform), it always is. Always.

It hit home, now more than ever, that it is not the voice of the gay men on its platforms that is powerful to the modern church. It is the inequality they represent that is valuable to the modern church. My stake president was in my living room, weaponizing Tom's story as a template for my life. It was an unsafe feeling, and it felt like a betrayal. Instead of my stake president inviting me to be like Tom Christofferson, why wasn't he inviting me to be like Jesus Christ?

My face got hot, and I said, "I bet you do not counsel the young men and women of our stake not to marry and just live their lives instead in service to their ward and stake members."

"Of course not," he answered, "because they are not gay." He leaned forward in the chair and pointed his finger at me, "Look, the president of Affirmation cannot be married and still be a member of the Church. You are a very powerful and influential man. I knew this from the days you were still leading in our stake. Now, you lead over ten thousand people in Affirmation. We cannot have the president of Affirmation be married to a man and also still be a member of the Church."

When he said "we," it suddenly dawned on me what was happening. I paused, then asked him point-blank, "President, have you received direction from the brethren to come here to tell me this?" He smiled, looked over at the guest he brought with him, and said, "I am visiting you tonight by my choice." This didn't really answer the question. It felt like a skilled deflection.

Defending the good name of Affirmation to my local leader, I explained, "Affirmation exists to create safe spaces of love and hope for LGBTQ people. We do not take any positions on doctrine. We focus on the 'one' who needs burdens lifted, we mourn with those who mourn, and we comfort those in need of comfort." My stake president raised his voice and reiterated that he could not allow me to be a member once I married and would follow the handbook to remove my membership once my wedding day occurred. By now, we had both gotten a bit heated. I was experiencing the ecclesiastical arm of the Church rip past the institutional voice and mission of Affirmation to get to Brother Kitchen. The stake president's silent companion over on the loveseat looked very uncomfortable.

In this exchange it was now evident my stake president knew nothing about the complexities and nature of mixed-orientation marriages. He knew nothing about the lifesaving mission of Affirmation. I questioned if he cared to understand marriage beyond being a rote duty for exaltation. Wondering if any kind of calibration or counsel from his leaders up the line might be helpful in his ministry to me, I said, "If you are truly here of your own volition, you should really talk to your area authority and Salt Lake for a little background on Affirmation before you go excommunicating the president of Affirmation for getting married." To this, he turned his whole body in my direction, "Brother Kitchen, you must follow the law of the Lord, not the law of the land in this matter." He looked me squarely in the eye and forcefully said, "As your stake president, I invite you not to marry."

Time suddenly stopped. The Spirit immediately descended upon me like fire. It was literally as if the center of my chest was on fire. In this action, the extreme tension in the room was pushed and then held to the edges. And in this space, peace. I shook as I heard the voice of the Spirit speak directly to me, as clearly and audibly as one man speaks to another.

I can count on one hand the times the Spirit has spoken to me in clear, audible words. One of those was when I was sixteen. I was in bed before sleep, reading from The Book of Mormon about Christ's appearance to the Nephites after his resurrection. As I read the words of Jesus blessing the little children, the Spirit rested upon me, and I heard him speak, telling me that Christ loved me and knew me personally as he did the little children in Third Nephi. It was overwhelming to hear the voice of the Spirit that summer night as I sat in my bed awash in tears. I knew at that moment that God and Christ lived. It was a sacred moment for me, and has been a witness to the truthfulness of the gospel ever since.

Now, at the stake president's invitation not to marry Matthew, the Spirit entered the room and spoke to me once again: "This invitation is dangerous, and he is wrong to ask this of you. This invitation is not the will of God for your life. Do not heed his words. This is not the path God wants you to take." I was momentarily struck silent. Those unexpected words were so strong and so powerful. In disbelief at the disconnect between the voice of the Spirit and my stake president's invitation, I sought clarification from my stake president, "President, just let me clarify: you are inviting me not to marry?" He smiled, stammered, and said, "Well, yes."

The Spirit powerfully enveloped me a second time with what again felt like fire: "This is not true. This is not an invitation from God." He then showed me in vision a seventeen-year-old Nathan coming out in an Illinois bishop's office, the invitation issued me to be obedient, go on a mission, and marry a woman in the temple, and everything would "be alright"—followed with glimpses of the consequences throughout my life of the effects of that decision, both the sorrow and the joy, to follow my bishop's invitation. Then, for a third time, the Spirit spoke, "Do not accept this invitation. It is not from me. Do not live the rest of your life alone and bound to the opinion of this man. I have spent a lifetime preparing you. Now, go forward with no fear. Your marriage is blessed in me. You and your children are protected in me."

President Nelson had prepared me for this moment. In his first address at General Conference as prophet, President Nelson stood at the pulpit and asked, "How can we find answers to questions that perplex us?"[1] He reiterated that if Joseph Smith's experience in the Sacred Grove taught us anything, it was that "the heavens are open and that God speaks to His children."[2] He invited the members of the Church to bring our questions to God and then listen. He admonished us to write down the impressions that come to us. Record your feelings and follow through with actions that you are prompted to take. As you re-

---

1. Nelson, Russell M. "Revelation for the Church, Revelation for Our Lives." *Liahona*, May 2018. https://www.churchofjesuschrist.org/study/liahona/2018/05/sunday-morning-session/revelation-for-the-church-revelation-for-our-lives.

2. Nelson, Russell M. "Revelation for the Church, Revelation for Our Lives." *Liahona*, May 2018.

peat this process day after day, month after month, year after year, you will grow into the principle of revelation.

President Nelson's entire talk about the sacredness of personal revelation was affirming and familiar to me as a queer Latter-day Saint. I had prepared myself from the moment of Elder Scott's stake conference address, seeking wisdom while asking God—in heart, closet, and grove—to receive and follow through with actions I was prompted to take. For ten years, I had been growing into the principle of revelation, line upon line, making difficult decisions; so the night of my stake president's visit, the voice of the Spirit was not a stranger to my soul. In this spiritual growth into revelation, I realized that personal revelation was not involved when I was a young man coming out to my bishop. The spirit of fear was my companion that night, as a tsunami of relief washed over me when I left my bishop's office. It was a "performance in exchange for safety" moment, where obedience to the recipe of exaltation would guarantee results. As a teen, I felt an overwhelming sense of duty, fear, resolve, and relief—all valid emotions, but not the Spirit. Experience has shown me that living the gospel is not at all like following a recipe card in the kitchen. If Adam and Eve had followed the recipe of the Garden of Eden, they would still be there, and we would not be here. Personal revelation is required to make sense of what is written, and as any good chef will tell you, the secrets of a perfect dish are not found on a recipe card.

The forces of dominant narratives and policies create seemingly contradictory choices for LGBTQ Latter-day Saints in the modern church. In such contradiction, no guidance exists when queer Latter-day Saints claim the opportunities and privileges of their straight, cisgender Latter-day Saint peers. The rainbow stained-glass ceiling is a fearful thing, and it is undiscovered country navigating out from under its shadow, requiring personal revelation to guide our way. When we, as LGBTQ Latter-day Saints, make decisions for our lives, to stand in places that feel safe and healthy for us, to come unto Christ even as we are being rebuked for approaching as our authentic selves, and to stand with another in authenticity and love—it is our daily personal revelation that guides us to the place which God for us prepared. This is our privilege. President Lorenzo Snow called it the "grand privilege of every Latter-day Saint . . . that it is our right to have the manifestations of the Spirit every day of our lives."[3]

As LGBTQ Latter-day Saint people, we hold sacred our personal revelation in the face of dominant narratives and policies threatening to take our answers from us and judge them evil. To this, President Nelson promised, "Regardless of what others say or do, no one can ever take away a witness borne in your heart and mind about what is true."[4]

At that moment, I had received all the answers I needed in my living room. I knew it, and I knew God knew it. I had an undeniable witness about what was true in my heart and mind. I could not ignore this experience with the Spirit. This was a cherished and protective personal revelation, an experience I could not deny. I had received irrefutable and powerful confirmation that God approved my path and smiled upon my upcoming marriage to the most wonderful man I have ever known. Any fears I had of spiritual violence upon me or my children were swallowed up in Christ.

---

3. The Church of Jesus Christ of Latter-day Saints. "Strengthened By the Power of the Holy Ghost." *Teachings of Presidents of the Church: Lorenzo Snow*, January 1, 2011. https://www.churchofjesuschrist.org/study/manual/teachings-of-presidents-of-the-church-lorenzo-snow/chapter-4-strengthened-by-the-power-of-the-holy-ghost.

4. Nelson, Russell M. "Revelation for the Church, Revelation for Our Lives." *Liahona*, May 2018.

This was my gift from the Holy Ghost that I had prayed for earlier that evening. I knew the stake president had felt the Spirit as well. I could see it in his demeanor. I had learned as a missionary how to recognize when the Spirit entered the room. A friend who works with my stake president called me later and asked me what in the world went on in my meeting because the stake president said it was one of the most spiritual experiences he has had. And it should be, but it will be many years until he understands why.

I stood and invited the men out of my home. It had been an intense meeting culminating in a visit by the Spirit. The poor companion to the stake president looked as if he had been hit by a truck. As I escorted them to the door, the stake president said, "I'd sure like to get to know you better. I'd like to take you to lunch and be friends outside of a stake president relationship." I was silent. These felt like half-hearted words. He stopped at the door on his way out and pointed at my prominent wall hanging of Doctrine and Covenants 109: "Establish a house of prayer, fasting, faith, learning, glory, order, a house of God." He then turned and pointed to my display of wall hangings: "Serve with Valor" and "Return with Honor." He shook his head and commented, "You are doing good things here." Again, I was silent as I shepherded them out the door and into the night outside.

After they left, the emotions of what had just happened hit me, and tears flowed freely. I went to my desk and wrote down this experience so I could remember the exchange and the words of the Spirit to me. This was my personal revelation, as sacred as the word of God I knew and loved in the standard works. As I did so, my support system came back online. Matthew drove over and offered his love and support in the aftermath of a pastoral system that seemed so foreign to the Christianity he knew. Heidi and Emily sent their copious words of wisdom and comfort. By this time, I had melted away in tears, almost inconsolable after this confrontation with the ugliness of prejudice and the threat of spiritual violence that occurred within my home. Finally, Laurie's voice summarized this experience with the greatest empathy. She had traveled this road before and understood clearly what was happening. She tenderly wrote:

> I fully understand when the church that you love and served unnecessarily paints something so positive in your life as wrong, so wrong that they feel they must erase you. But God is not in this spiritually violent act. I understand how it feels when they tie your prominence in Affirmation (earned from hard, selfless work on behalf of others) to the reason they must disenfranchise you. This is not the gospel of Christ; their fruits betray them.
>
> Furthermore, I understand the very real grieving that you do experience as you mourn these actions and I mourn at your side. However, I assure you that no administrative action on the part of these men can ever separate you from the love of God or the blessings, relationships, and hoped-for promises that you cherish through your faithfulness to God and the covenants you made with him. No institution has that authority.
>
> I and many hundreds who understand these things proudly stand with you and Matthew and rejoice in the life commitment you will make. And I believe our heavenly parents smile upon your goodness, fidelity, and love to each other. As always, I am here to talk.
>
> Love, Laurie

These were my angels on this side of the veil.

CHAPTER 22

Unto Dust Thou Shalt Return

> 19 In the sweat of thy face shalt thou eat bread, till thou return unto the ground; for out of it wast thou taken: for dust thou art, and unto dust shalt thou return.
>
> Genesis 3:19

I knew what was coming next. Not because I was told but because I knew from experience, having been inside the system of power and church government. I knew that I must be brave for what was coming for me. The wheels of power were now in motion. Marriage was the trigger that prejudice had been patiently waiting for since 2015. You don't just turn prejudice away with silence at the door and into the night. It is not done with you until it asserts its dominance and displays its power. Over the following weeks, I pondered continually, seeking guidance from the Spirit about what I would do next.

My immediate "next" was moving Matthew out of his apartment and into our home. All the heavy furniture the Arizona Mormon network had so graciously carried up three flights of stairs was to be sold, and the buyers would get to maneuver it back down to ground level. This left the boxes and books. Lots and lots of books. Matthew claimed that he would purge his books before every move he made and after every degree he earned. That was a lot of purging points, but to my untrained eye, we were still hauling the equivalent of a great Alexandrian library over to the house. Day after day, Matthew, the kids, and I would bring books by the box full, carefully arranging them, stack after stack, along the long breakfast bar that divided the kitchen from the great room. Each time I would carry a box of books from the car, I would feel an increasing pain just behind my sternum. This pain had been low-grade present for over six months now. Ultrasounds and doctors diagnosed me as being a gassy fifty-one-year-old. An ignominious diagnosis of age, I thought. Slowly, the pain became more and more noticeable, especially after I ate.

On the last Sunday of January, Matthew and I were in the cultural hall at the stake center, attending my youngest son's Eagle Scout court of honor. During the ceremony, I could not find a comfortable position to alleviate the pain in my abdomen. I blamed it on the hard metal chairs. As the week wore on, the pain intensified. On the last Friday in January, when it was time for the kids to go to their mom's, I shooed them out the door, turned to Matthew, and said, "I need to go to the hospital." It was there, in an out-of-the-way cubicle in a midnight waiting room—anticipating CT results at any time—that the clot in the vein that drained my bowels achieved the size to stop the flow of blood. The sudden ischemia was overpowering. I doubled over in the most intense pain I had ever experienced in my life as my bowels began to die. I do not remember much after that point, but I could hear Matthew out in the waiting room, yelling up and down the halls that we needed help immediately. The staff were dismissive at first, but he continued to yell, not taking "no" for an answer. In all the years I had known Matthew, I had never heard him yell. Not even raise his voice. But that night, above the pain, his distant, persistent voice was as loud and clear as any "I love you" I had ever heard uttered. The Emergency Department came alive. Given morphine, heparin, and a diagnosis—I was admitted upstairs for a week-long stay of treatment and gut rest as a myriad of specialists tried to piece together why I had developed such an extremely rare blood clot. Thankfully, everything had been caught early enough, before bowel death and before my death.

That week, my hospital room became Matthew's home base, keeping me company as he sat with his trusty Mac, answering his history student's emails, studying, and eating the hospital food. He was sure to be there each morning during doctor rounds to ask questions and be a second pair of ears, writing down visit summaries and instructions. After teaching his classes, he would return, and we would talk and laugh into the night. He would be sure to check the weather to get back home in time to cover the outdoor plants before our night freezes. I thought about the words of my stake president, inviting me not to marry Matthew. His invitation to endure a lifelong haunting absence of a companion rang hollow in the face of my lived experience. Care in both sickness and health is just one of the privileges of marriage. Matthew and I shared countless other experiences that gently reminded me of the great blessings that come into my life from finding and committing to the right person, both in personality and orientation. After sharing a home base with Matthew in a hospital room during my recovery, I realized that home was not a place but *the* place where we were together. Surrounded by the hundreds of thousands of people in my hometown, in a state surrounded by millions, and in a country surrounded by a wide world of billions, I was somebody's person. And he was mine. And that is what matters.

When I got home from the hospital, the texts from my stake president resumed. He wanted to get me alone in his office now that I was married. I would always ask him what his intentions were. Although I knew full well what they were, I wanted him to be honest about his agenda. No one should ever walk into a power imbalance without transparency and honesty. His unwillingness to be forthcoming and his attempts to isolate me in his office were met with my invitation to come to my home and meet Matthew or grab a bite to eat in public. I remembered his interest in these things when he visited my home before my marriage. After a few weeks of these exchanges, this text arrived: "Nathan, I want to invite you to participate in a membership council. Is there a date in the coming month that you are available?" Finally, his intentions were clear. My stake president was ready to excommunicate me as promised now that I was married. I didn't doubt that he was devoted to his duty, or even that he thought he was showing love to me. I also knew that he was determined that it would be his love that prevailed.

It is amazing the clarity that a hospital stay for a life-threatening blood clot brings. Ever since my high school seminary days, I have been drawn to the teachings of Lehi to his son, Jacob. God created all things, both the heavens and the earth, "And all things that in them are, both things to act and things to be acted upon ... Wherefore, the Lord God gave unto man that he should act for himself" (2 Nephi 2:14, 16). I lived most of my life being acted upon because I was a gay man in the Church—from the scared seventeen-year-old boy sitting in tears confessing his homosexuality to his bishop, to my current stake president's struggle to excommunicate me for marrying the love of my life. Lehi teaches that our first parents were proactive in the Garden. Presented with forbidden fruit, they exercised the human right to choose—and in this act, they fell. But this action brought not loss but wisdom. Our first parents fell that men might be, and men are, that they might have joy (2 Nephi 2:25).

I cannot deny what the Spirit spoke to me about my marriage the night my stake president invited me not to marry. I cannot deny that the Spirit blessed my upcoming marriage with Matthew in the face of my stake president's words. My lived experiences are the fruits of my tree of knowledge in my own Eden. And like my first parents, I have partaken and know it is time to leave. This leaving is not a loss but wisdom. Eden is not where I will find joy in my life with Matthew. Eden is not my salvation, but in the end, it is Christ, and Christ alone, who will accomplish my exaltation.

The gospel of Jesus Christ is bigger in time and more inclusive in vision than any one person, administration, or policy. In time, people, administrations, and policies return to the dust, but Christ has risen from the dust, eternal in his love and care. And I know that through Christ, and Christ alone, I will rise from the dust alive in him. This is whom I follow and whom I will put my trust in. I can and will follow him in dignity and grace, arm in arm, with my beloved Matthew, for God had given us to each other.

I often wonder if our first parents left Eden with the poise and certitude that they had made the right decision. I believe they had. They knew that their act would lead to joy, and I believe they knew exactly what they were doing.

As do I.

By marrying Matthew, I had just met power in a power structure that would take from me the very things I held dear and had a testimony of. The modern church was now coming to violently prune me out of my eternal family tree under the premise that what it loosed on earth would be loosed in heaven (Matthew 18:18). I was but a small, internal cog in the modern church's powerful tussle with civil rights and politics—relying on its doctrinal premise, dominant narrative, and policies concerning queer people to assert its power in this world. To the modern church, I was but a child of God practicing an errant ideology—one that was so serious that it was considered apostasy in church law just ten months previously.

Power now demanded that I be corrected at the peril of my very soul or thrown out if I would not comply. By now, the only way I could comply was to turn away from love, divorce Matthew, and submit myself to being captured in the modern church's newest dominant narrative about queer people. Like its predecessors, this dominant narrative was not stable and would change. Why build life's foundation on such sand? I had already trustingly done so once before. I would not be force-fed fruit from a tree that prejudice had authoritatively pronounced as good but that I *knew* was bad. I knew the nature of the fruits of dominant narratives and policies concerning the queer children of God because of my unique vantage point as president of Affirmation and its forty-three-year institutional history. Closer to home, I knew the nature of these fruits because I had been captured in a dominant narrative years before, giving prejudice so many years of my life, only to see the construct collapse as I watched the modern church move on, leaving me and my family sitting in its wreckage.

It doesn't matter what version the dominant narrative is in now, it will still exact as many years as it can from a queer person before its prejudice can no longer sustain it, and it either moves on or evaporates through revelation. Power, especially in a religious context, refuses to be called prejudice and soundly rejects the notion that its prejudice and acts of prejudice are anything but love administered.

This was a moment I needed to look past the modern church to see my fellow saints gathered at our Waters of Mormon. The modern church is the hierarchy and bureaucracy of church government, administration, and political machinery. It is what historian D. Michael Quinn calls the Church's era of wealth and corporate power.[1] Separate from the hierarchy and bureaucracy is the human element of the Church. As the children of God, we are the church. As the body of Saints, we are God's people, not the modern church's people. We are the ecclesia; we call out to one another to gather in communion in the body of Christ. I knew in my heart that no matter the administrative action of separation that the modern church took, the ecclesia would continue to call out to me—both my fellow Saints and my family—and, with love, commune with me and claim me as their own. This care for one another is at the heart of our baptismal covenants that we made with God to take upon ourselves the name of Christ. As a power structure, the modern church was part of the Apostle Paul's "nothing" that could separate me from the love of God that was in Christ Jesus (Romans 8:38-39 NIV).

As a queer member of The Church of Jesus Christ of Latter-day Saints, I was party to a power imbalance so severe that I was powerless to prevent its spiritual violence—just stand by as I watched this system administratively remove my membership,

---

1. Quinn, D. Michael. *The Mormon Hierarchy: Wealth and Corporate Power*. Salt Lake City, Utah: Signature Books, 2017.

void my baptism, and unseal my children from me. It was the act of ultimate bureaucratic eternal isolation, severing all official records of my ties with the Saints and the heavens. Through ritual and symbolism, it illustrated eternal separation. The modern church may claim power over me, but as a queer person, I would now stand to claim my power over the system. To accomplish this, I would need to confront the system in a way that was meaningful to me, in a way that the system itself understood and drew power from: ritual and symbolism. I wrote out my statements of belief as a queer child of God facing unjust power—my defiance of prejudice in the face of God, not my denial of God. This would not only help me clarify the significance of this moment but also be the thesis for what I had planned next:

- I believe in the restored gospel, but to live it as a member in good standing, power dictates that I cannot believe in myself or live it as an authentic queer child of God.

- I am full—filled to the brim, cup-runneth-over full—of inherent self-worth. I am worth getting excommunicated for.

- I have a testimony of the restored gospel of Jesus Christ, but I do not have a testimony of prejudice.

- I subscribe to making covenants with God and keeping commandments, but I do not subscribe to making concessions to human prejudice.

- I yearn to be a part of a loving, supportive community of Saints, but I will not be a part of discrimination.

- I love to hear the word of God spoken by prophets, but I will not stand for harassment and the misrepresentation of queer people, myself included, from the pulpit.

The moon was rising in the east as I parked my car on the side of the road in one of the remaining rural neighborhoods that pepper the town of Gilbert. I stepped out of my vehicle and noted my direction. With no streetlights, the moonlight guided me as I made my way along the dusty shoulders of the road toward the home of my stake president. Large old-growth trees surround his property. It is a walled fortress with a keypad for entry through an iron gate. Standing under a tree on the roadside, I squarely faced his house and reflected on all the events that had brought me to that moment. I cast the dust from my feet, brushing my shoes with my hands and wiping their soles as I spoke the words from my heart.

I then drove to the stake center and parked next to the stake offices. Most of my time serving as a stake leader happened on this side of the building. However, just opposite the stake offices were the bishop's offices, where I spent seven years serving in two bishoprics. I walked directly to the front of the building and faced the chapel. I now symbolically faced the power structure of the modern church—the church government that delivers LGBTQ policy and takes it back again. As I stood on a large rock decorating the landscape, I again spoke the words I had recited at the house of my stake president:

> I stand at your threshold, having previously given my testimony of the holiness of my marriage and the equality of LGBTQ people in the body of Christ, and have been rejected by you. You have received me not and instead seek to violently cast me from the fellowship of the Saints.
>
> Therefore, in the name of Christ, I leave you, and in this leaving, I leave you a cursing instead of a blessing.

I shake off the dust from my feet as a testimony against your policies, legalism, prejudice, exclusions, stubbornness, and hard-heartedness.

I weep for the Church that she must continually watch her children reject and persecute their LGBTQ siblings. I weep that the brethren cast their siblings, who wear the coat of many colors, into a pit and sell them for silver as did the children of Israel with Joseph.

I shake the dust from my feet concerning you and your house and will trouble you no more.

I bent down, shook the dust from my shoes, and wiped their soles clean on the grass, as one wipes their feet on a mat before entering the house. I felt such an enveloping sense of relief and happiness. There were no tears, no regrets. Just a peace and stillness in my soul. I then drove to the neighborhood park, took the bowl of warm water I had prepared earlier at the house, the towel, and oil, and walked to a secluded bench. There, I completed the dusting of the feet, removed my shoes, washed my feet with water, and anointed them with oil.[2]

I reflected that in this moment of symbolism, in the face of impending spiritual violence, I had acknowledged the power structure that I was in. I acknowledged the power I had lost. And now, I had just acknowledged the power I was reclaiming: my agency, my voice, and my sense of control in this situation. Important for me, I symbolically claimed something in the face of power that I already innately knew was mine but had not yet owned: my own narrative. For the first time in my life, I let go of the dominant narrative and fully embraced mine.

---

2. Belnap, Daniel L., "'Those Who Receive You Not': The Rite of Wiping Dust off the Feet," in *By Our Rites of Worship: Latter-day Saint Views on Ritual in Scripture, History, and Practice*, ed. Daniel L. Belnap (Provo, UT: Religious Studies Center; Salt Lake City: Deseret Book, 2013), 209-260. https://rsc.byu.edu/our-rites-worship/those-who-receive-you-not-rite-wiping-dust-off-feet

I returned home, and Matthew was in bed, reading a book. He looked up over his glasses and greeted me. He knew I had gone out that evening on a personal errand. He was intrigued as he watched me fill a bowl with water and gather a towel and oil. But how can one explain this Mormon of all Mormon things to someone who has never been Mormon? But somehow, he innately understood. He gave me the space and the grace without question because he knew whatever I needed to do was important to me. And it was.

I leaned over, kissed him, and said, "Thank you." He smiled, and in his smile, all was right in the world. The future was so bright. We had a lifetime of mountains to climb and vistas to share, just waiting for us. I told him I had one more thing to do before bed. I walked to my computer, opened the completed QuitMormon electronic packet containing my scanned notarized resignation from The Church of Jesus Christ of Latter-day Saints, and pressed "Send."

CHAPTER 23

Change without Change

> So often the contemporary church is a weak, ineffectual voice with an uncertain sound. So often it is an archdefender of the status quo.
>
> Martin Luther King, Jr
> "Letter from a Birmingham Jail"
> April 16, 1963

As I rounded the corner into 2020, the significant changes in the queer/Latter-day Saint intersection in 2019 already felt like a high-speed run around a Mario Kart track: oil slicks, banana peels, turtle shells, and a little out of control. Now was not the time to rest. The modern church had just drifted into lap two and hit mini-turbo. In February, I received a text from the Church Communication Department giving Affirmation a heads-up that the Church was taking down its Mormon and Gay website and replacing it with two new ones: "Same-Sex

Attraction"[1] and "Transgender."[2] In effect, this ended its savvy multiyear public relations campaign, which began in the aftermath of California Prop 8. I know that part of this was to get rid of the word "Mormon" to follow President Nelson's initiative to use the proper name of the Church,[3] but this elimination was more than just scrubbing the word Mormon from use. The modern church's growing concern about LGBTQ identity was starting to surface. Religious freedom has a much easier time protecting discrimination against ideologies than it does people.

Dropping "gay" and naming the new site "Same-Sex Attraction" was a step backward. Same-sex attraction is not an orientation. The message this new heading was broadcasting was that gay, lesbian, and bisexual children of God are dealing with an attraction—feelings—not a sexual orientation identity. This verbiage was an example of change without change, a veiled attempt to use the same line of thought utilized in the Miracle of Forgiveness generation that homosexuality is a temptation without saying as much. It is helpful when you come across the word "attraction" in these kinds of discussions to mentally replace it with "temptation." Doing so makes it easier to see what the modern church is attempting to assert in its argument.

Exaltation is earned through behavior. All children of God must participate in the behavior of entering a one-man/one-woman marriage to receive the blessings of exaltation. This is

---

1. The Church of Jesus Christ of Latter-day Saints. "Same-Sex Attraction." Same-Sex Attraction: Kindness, Inclusion, and Respect for All of God's Children. Accessed July 27, 2024. https://www.churchofjesuschrist.org/topics/gay.

2. The Church of Jesus Christ of Latter-day Saints. "Transgender." Transgender: Showing Christlike Love to All of God's Children. Accessed July 27, 2024. https://www.churchofjesuschrist.org/topics/transgender.

3. Nelson, Russell M. "The Correct Name of the Church." *Ensign* 48, no. 11. November 2018. https://www.churchofjesuschrist.org/study/ensign/2018/11/sunday-morning-session/the-correct-name-of-the-church.

second nature to do if you are a person oriented to opposite-sex behavior. It is awkward and a struggle (or even repulsive) to do if you are a person oriented to same-sex behavior. Rather than acknowledging and including different sexual orientations, the modern church instead focuses on the "struggle." The struggle comes from Latter-day Saint sexual minorities trying to fit a square peg into a round hole provided by the hosts of the Restoration. They are struggling in a system not built for them. To deflect the truth that it is the system not the queer person that is the problem, the modern church authoritatively blames the struggle on "same-sex attraction," leading to what it has classified as unapproved behavior.

Furthermore, attraction is seen to be amenable to correction through repentance and conversion therapy. Although many queer minors are protected from conversion therapy by law, it is important to note that an industry of conversion therapy still exists for adults. In addition, religiously guided mixed-orientation marriages are a form of long-term conversion therapy. Although you will find this nowhere in the official teachings of the Church, members and leaders—including General Authorities—will still today tell sexual minorities to find an opposite-sex spouse and get married. We saw this with David Archuleta who revealed such pressure from the Church's General Authorities.[4] These religiously motivated invitations rooted in the prejudice of the doctrinal premise about queer people are dangerous and wrong.

As I perused the new same-sex attraction site, I noted it highlighted videos and stories of two mixed-orientation mar-

---

4. Osunsami, Steve, Dominick Proto, and Carson Blackwelder. "David Archuleta Details 'Faith Crisis' After Coming out in the Mormon Church." *Good Morning America*, November 18, 2022. Accessed July 27, 2024. https://www.goodmorningamerica.com/culture/story/david-archuleta-details-faith-crisis-coming-mormon-church-93505214.

riages and one lone gay single young man. He shared that when he realized he "genuinely lacked the ability to have a real, complete relationship with a woman,"[5] he adapted his expectations for the future and sought ways to live a happy and meaningful single life. This struck me with sadness. The Church really is preparing its young, wide-eyed, trusting sexual minorities how to cope with being chronically single for a lifetime. How can you effectively sell this perpetual discipline that has no parallels to the blessings of marriage or the love of another? It is apples to oranges. More like apples to dung beetles.

Contrast this message to the one President Oaks gave to the Church's young adults, instructing straight Latter-day Saints on the absolute importance of marriage and counseling them not to delay it. To this, his wife, Kristen, observed, "Life becomes better as our marriage becomes connected to something greater than ourselves and closer to our Savior. We want that for you."[6] The Church is barring queer Latter-day Saints from having, if they so choose, the opportunity of a "life made better" through marriage according to their orientation by making marriage equality "unavailable" to them in their spiritual home. The Same-Sex Attraction site is loudly broadcasting that if a mixed-orientation marriage doesn't work for you, then the Church will help prepare you to live a life of loneliness and to be happy alone.

I affirm this young man's courage to share his story with us on the Church's Same-Sex Attraction website. He reminds me of myself as a young gay man in both conviction and resolve

---

5. The Church of Jesus Christ of Latter-day Saints. "Andy's Story." Same Sex Attraction. Accessed July 27, 2024. https://www.churchofjesuschrist.org/topics/gay/videos/andys-story.

6. Oaks, Dallin H., and Kristen Oaks. "May 2023 Worldwide Devotional for Young Adults with President and Sister Oaks." The Church of Jesus Christ of Latter-day Saints. YouTube, May 22, 2023. Accessed July 27, 2024. https://www.youtube.com/live/wull4cTXUTk?si=jSLTBCgYGb2xa8hB.

in the golden age of mixed-orientation marriage. However, his voice is being used as a messaging tool to officially advertise the happy single and celibate trope to support the current dominant narrative about queer people, using a single snapshot of a gay young man's life. Contrast this with the overpowering message running 24/7 to straight Latter-day Saints to get married pronto and become something greater than their single selves. This is an example of religious prejudice.

When I went through the Church's new Transgender site, the first thing that struck me was that, unlike the Same-Sex Attraction site, it contained no videos or testimonials. No transgender Latter-day Saint spokespeople. There is nothing at all to depict or model transgender Latter-day Saints navigating the transgender experience in the Church like there is for gay and lesbian Latter-day Saints on the Same-Sex Attraction page. It is not hard to figure out why. Any form of transitioning is against church policy, so we won't see any examples of transitioned transgender Latter-day Saints experiencing their gender and gender euphoria on a church website. Socially and medically transitioned, active, testimony-bearing transgender members of the Church filled with the Spirit are not hard to find. They are just not useful to the modern church to reinforce its dominant narrative about transgender people.

It was not a coincidence that the Mormon and Gay website disappeared, and the Same Sex Attraction and Transgender websites appeared when they did. That same month, the Church released the first portion of its new General Handbook online. One of the newly included items was the 2019 recension of the exclusion policy. Most notably, a completely new section on transgender individuals was included. Elder Anthony D. Perkins, executive director at the Church's Correlation Department, commented that this was a welcome addition because of the increasing number of questions coming from bishops and stake presidents asking, "What can a transgender person do? What are the guidelines?"[7] As Affirmation's leadership read through the new handbook additions, it was apparent that although this new section contained positive messages, it cast a dominant narrative about transgender people that was not true, including the assertion that gender equals biological sex at birth.

As a healthcare professional, I will be the first to admit that none of us are infallible in the work we have been trained to do, even those who assign sex at birth. Further, birth sex equaling gender works for most humans, but not all. You cannot claim a fallen mortality—tilling about thorns and thistles while experiencing the frailty of flesh and blood—yet expect that somehow everyone's genitals and chromosomes survived the Fall and are 100% reliable at determining our future. We are not reading tarot cards here. We must have the grace to allow those who live in the dysphoria of any faults in this process the dignity of self-determination to correct such errors nature or others made when they were born into this world. We are here to overcome the world (Doctrine and Covenants 64:2), not be bound to it for the eternities.

A person can know in their heart the measure of their creation—the truth that their gender is not the same gender that was affixed to them at birth by a sex assignment. Acknowledging this truth is not a sin: "The Church does not take a position on

---

7. Stack, Peggy Fletcher, and David Noyce. "LDS Church Publishes New Handbook with Changes to Discipline, Transgender Policy." *The Salt Lake Tribune*, February 19, 2020. https://www.sltrib.com/religion/2020/02/19/lds-church-puts-new/.

the causes of people identifying themselves as transgender."[8] But, as the doctrinal premise asserts, when a transgender person presents themself at the judgment bar of God, they can only present as their sex assigned at birth if they are to be judged worthy of exaltation. This flies in the face of the prophet Samuel, who declared that God looks upon the heart—not the countenance, the height, or outward appearance (1 Samuel 16:7).

Laurie led Affirmation's rapid response team in a statement concerning the new transgender section in the handbook, noting, "narrowly defining gender as the biological sex at birth negates the lived experience of transgender individuals."[9] She emphasized that identity is a sense of self that is in the mind, in the heart, and in the soul that transcends physical biology, whatever that may be. Placing transgender persons in situations in which they are misgendered causes significant mental, emotional, and physical harm. "There is no valid reason for such harm to be knowingly caused among such a vulnerable population at the intersection of their faith."[10]

As the waves of queer generations roll along in the modern church like the tide, the doctrinal premise that the queer person in their authenticity cannot be exalted remains constant

---

8. "Church Policies and Guidelines" Section 38.6.23. In *General Handbook: Serving in The Church of Jesus Christ of Latter-day Saints*. Accessed July 27, 2024. https://www.churchofjesuschrist.org/study/manual/general-handbook/38-church-policies-and-guidelines#title_number118.

9. Affirmation: LGBTQ Mormons, Families & Friends. "New Church Handbook Provides Some Clarity but Minimizes LGBTQ Identities." Affirmation, February 19, 2020. Accessed July 27, 2024. https://affirmation.org/new-church-handbook-provides-some-clarity-but-minimizes-lgbtq-identities/.

10. Affirmation: LGBTQ Mormons, Families & Friends. "New Church Handbook Provides Some Clarity but Minimizes LGBTQ Identities." Affirmation, February 19, 2020. Accessed July 27, 2024. https://affirmation.org/new-church-handbook-provides-some-clarity-but-minimizes-lgbtq-identities/.

and, horrifyingly, its exclusion expands as the brethren learn more about the queer children of God. Getting to know queer Latter-day Saints better does not lead to equality in privilege and opportunity. Such familiarity only helps the power center better understand what it needs to change to more effectively exclude us from exaltation while calling it "belonging." It is change without change.

More change without change was in store. February was not done with us yet. On the nineteenth, *The Salt Lake Tribune* broke the story that BYU "had quietly removed from its Honor Code the section titled 'Homosexual Behavior',"[11] The infamous homosexual clause was now completely gone. The Honor Code used to specifically call out homosexuality by name, declaring that homosexual behavior not only included sexual relations between members of the same sex but all forms of physical intimacy that give expression to homosexual feelings. Now it simply read, "Live a chaste and virtuous life, including abstaining from any sexual relations outside a marriage between a man and a woman." Nowhere did it say anything about homosexual romantic behavior.[12]

Students immediately went to the Honor Code Office to seek clarification. They were informed that both heterosexual

---

11. Tanner, Courtney. "BYU Students Celebrate as School Removes 'Homosexual Behavior' Section from Its Online Honor Code." *The Salt Lake Tribune*, February 19, 2020. https://www.sltrib.com/news/education/2020/02/19/byu-appears-remove/.

12. The Church of Jesus Christ of Latter-day Saints. "Church Educational System Honor Code." Wayback Machine - Internet Archive: Church Educational System Honor Code, Archived February 19, 2020. Accessed July 27, 2024. http://web.archive.org/web/20200219225501/https://policy.byu.edu/view/index.php?p=26.

and homosexual BYU students could now equally participate in chaste hand-holding, kissing, and even dating for fun or companionship. In other words, when queer students claimed the same privilege and opportunities as their straight peers in chaste public displays of affection, it was no longer an Honor Code violation. The line that no one could cross, queer or straight, was engaging in sexual relations outside a one-man/one-woman marriage. Everyone would be punished equally if that occurred. As the day wore on, queer students cautiously began to hold hands on campus, and two even stole a kiss in front of the Brigham Young Statue in the shadow of the administration building. As a BYU alum, I chuckled, "What is the world coming to? I never thought I would live to see the day. Ernest L. Wilkinson must be rolling in his grave. Good for BYU and good for queer BYU students."

Later that afternoon, BYU sent out a mysterious tweet, "In speaking with Honor Code Office Director Kevin Utt this afternoon, we've learned that there may have been some miscommunication as to what the Honor Code changes mean. Even though we have removed the more prescriptive language, the principles of the Honor Code remain the same."[13] Having recently met with Kevin Utt, he didn't strike me as a slouch. If the new Honor Code confused the Honor Code Director, it had most certainly confused BYU students. This seemed like an optimal moment for the administration to explain themselves. But no additional explanation or clarification came that day—just the mysterious tweet.

The next morning, reporters began contacting me for clarification and comment. Not wanting to speculate or propagate

---

13. BYU (@BYU). "In speaking with Honor Code Office Director Kevin Utt this afternoon, we've learned that there may have been some miscommunication as to what the Honor Code changes mean." X, February 19, 2020, 3:31 PM. https://x.com/BYU/status/1230258699693723648

rumors, I messaged Ben Schilaty at the Honor Code Office. He told me that as of that morning, no further direction or clarification had been provided them. Ben confirmed that indeed, it was no longer an Honor Code violation for same-sex BYU students to kiss, hold hands, and even date for fun or companionship if the intention of these actions was not to get married. This seemed an amazing moment, which an Honor Code Officer verified, and I began returning calls to news organizations. By day two, the Honor Code Office continued to hold to its interpretation while the administration stayed silent. CNN shared with me that when they reached out to BYU for clarification, they were referred to the original mysterious tweet with no further comment. By now, the campus was in complete chaos.

Soon the press turned from reporting the Honor Code change to reporting the absolute confusion and trauma queer BYU students were experiencing as they were caught in the opacity of this new Honor Code. Eight days after the message about the Honor Code, Nico Lang with VICE told me that BYU was still referring the press to its original mysterious tweet as its only comment. What in the world was happening at BYU? Who was in charge here? This opacity of an Honor Code Office in conflict with the administration was proving to be incredibly harmful to queer students. Violating the Honor Code can result in suspension and even expulsion. With stakes this high, students need to know what is expected of them. This illustrated the precise scenario that worried the visiting CAMWS classicists just four months earlier during our meeting with the Honor Code Office.

Approaching the last week of February, I noted queer BYU student anxiety and confusion steadily rising. I messaged Laurie and asked if she would write an op-ed with me to submit to *The Salt Lake Tribune*. I felt that queer BYU students needed to hear from their peers and feel the support from the wider LGBTQ Latter-day Saint community at this moment. George Pyle, editor at the opinion desk, warned us that the line for publication was long because it was the middle of a Utah legislative season.

While our piece languished in the queue, BYU tweeted out a letter on March 4 from Elder Paul V. Johnson, the Commissioner of the Church Educational System, finally clarifying the matter. He quoted the Family Proclamation then affirmed the doctrinal premise: "Same-sex romantic behavior cannot lead to eternal marriage and is therefore not compatible with the principles in the Honor Code."[14] Even though it had been removed from the written word,[15] the old "homosexual behavior" clause remained in force as an unwritten rule. BYU students began to protest immediately. Queer students and their student allies said, "Enough." Frantic, I emailed Pyle, asking if we could have twenty-four hours to modify our op-ed to respond to Elder Johnson's letter. He told us he would make room in online and print editions. The BYU Honor Code had just become priority news.

In our op-ed,[16] Laurie and I noted that the rollout and rollback of the updated Honor Code were not only unprofessional but highly irresponsible and dangerous, placing vulnerable LGBTQ students squarely in harm's way. We affirmed that all students have the right, regardless of sexual orientation, to enjoy chaste, affectionate public behavior without any fear of reprisal. Student sexual minorities are worthy of the same rights, protections, and freedom of loving expressions that are afforded

---

14. BYU (@BYU). "Today this letter from Elder Paul V. Johnson, Commissioner of the Church Educational System, regarding the updated Honor Code was sent to students and employees at all CES schools." X, March 4, 2020, 11:14 AM. https://x.com/BYU/status/1235267296970473472

15. After Elder Johnson's letter, the Church Educational System inserted the following clarification into the new Honor Code: "Living a chaste and virtuous life also includes abstaining from same-sex romantic behavior." https://policy.byu.edu/view/church-educational-system-honor-code.

16. Kitchen, Nathan, and Laurie Lee Hall. "Commentary: Unwritten Rules Can Cause a Lot of Harm at BYU." *The Salt Lake Tribune*, March 5, 2020. https://www.sltrib.com/opinion/commentary/2020/03/06/commentary-unwritten/.

their heterosexual peers. This was not a matter of BYU's sexual minorities seeking relief from the law of chastity. They only sought the same opportunity to enjoy a fullness of joy and expression during their university years that their heterosexual peers were encouraged to have—not by way of exception, but by inclusion. Finally, we observed that gender identity was still not addressed in the new Honor Code. As such, these students faced higher ambiguity and greater safety concerns than their sexual minority peers.

Amid this absolute chaos at BYU-Provo, my eye was on a remarkable event happening across the Pacific, 3000 miles away. Sarah Bowers, president of Affirmation's Pacific Region, had just overseen the organization of an Affirmation chapter to serve as the off-campus support for BYU-Hawaii students. The newly installed student leaders met with administrators at BYU-Hawaii to inform them about Affirmation's mission and vision and how the chapter would benefit the community. In these meetings, the BYU-Hawaii administration assured students that it would not be an Honor Code violation to assemble in such a manner as an off-campus group. With anxieties relieved, Affirmation Hawaii welcomed 100 people to their first gathering in Laie, providing a much-needed community for queer BYU-Hawaii students.

I noted the transparency that queer BYU-Hawaii students were afforded when they interfaced with administrators, while queer students at BYU-Provo were disoriented by the opacity and lack of communication in the Honor Code change. This would not be the last time this contrast between the two BYUs would manifest itself.

The week following the CES clarification letter, protests and demonstrations at BYU–Provo spread to Salt Lake, BYU–Idaho, and even out to Manhattan.[17] As the protests and media coverage continued relentlessly, Lisa Deaderick with *The San Diego Union-Tribune* contacted me, asking for an interview.[18] In her emailed questions, she asked if I thought there was an ability for religious organizations to become more welcoming to LGBTQ members while also maintaining an opposition to same-sex romantic relationships. I had to think long and hard about this. All religious organizations that oppose same-sex romantic relationships indeed have room to be kinder and more civil towards their LGBTQ members. However, whether these efforts are perceived as welcoming by LGBTQ members is entirely up to the LGBTQ person. To maintain an opposition to same-sex relationships, religious organizations must create a separation, a segregation in both the physical space and the theological realm that justifies discriminating against sexual minorities. How welcome an LGBTQ person feels in such an environment depends on their level of tolerance for the inequality inherent in such a system.

As I sent my response off to Deaderick, I reflected on the whirlwind of February changes we experienced in the queer/Latter-day Saint intersection. These changes turned out to be nothing more than a weak, ineffectual voice doing little else than strengthening the ties that suspend the rainbow stained-glass ceiling over the heads of queer Latter-day Saints. It was

---

17. Pierce, Scott D., and Peggy Fletcher Stack. "New Yorkers Rally in Support of BYU's LGBTQ Students." *The Salt Lake Tribune*, March 7, 2020. https://www.sltrib.com/news/2020/03/08/new-yorkers-rally-support/.

18. Deaderick, Lisa. "Religious Organizations Need to Include LGBTQ Community in Efforts to Be More Loving and Accepting." *The San Diego Union-Tribune*, March 22, 2020. https://www.sandiegouniontribune.com/2020/03/22/religious-organizations-need-to-include-lgbtq-community-in-efforts-to-be-more-loving-and-accepting/.

a month of playing with words, making semantical alterations without changing substance. It seemed that February's goal was to obfuscate the modern church's unwillingness to change, thereby remaining an archdefender of the status quo.[19] By now, I was ready for a vacation.

The first weekend of March, in the middle of the BYU student protests, Matthew and I took the kids to the Bay Area for spring break to visit his mom and see the sights. Monday morning, we parked at the Golden Gate Bridge on our way to Muir Woods so we could walk the bridge. I noticed a huge cruise ship slowly passing under us as we reached the bridge's center. It was a stunning visual. Ever since we had arrived in California, we continually heard the news of a Princess Cruise ship circling just off the coast, ordered to stay offshore because passengers and crew were exhibiting signs of COVID. And now it was directly below us.[20]

COVID, in the early days of the pandemic, was a terrifying illness, highly transmissible, unstoppable by medication, and untreatable once your breathing became labored. Hospitals overseas were overwhelmed, and mortality rates were high. If you contracted COVID, death was a very real possibility. No one—from the State of California to the federal government— was prepared for the scale of exposure a cruise ship presented. Up to this point, COVID seemed a faraway problem. Yet as we stood on that bridge as a family, watching this huge ship slowly enter the United States, escorted by a half dozen Coast Guard boats on its way to the Port of Oakland to begin quarantine pro-

---

19. King, Martin Luther. "Letter from a Birmingham Jail." African Studies Center - University of Pennsylvania, April 16, 1963. Accessed July 27, 2024. https://www.africa.upenn.edu/Articles_Gen/Letter_Birmingham.html.

20. Graff, Amy. "Grand Princess Cruise Ship Carrying Coronavirus Patients Arrives in Oakland." SFGATE. March 9, 2020. https://www.sfgate.com/bayarea/article/Grand-Princess-San-Francisco-Oakland-Golden-Gate-15117411.php.

tocols for the 3000 people on board, COVID suddenly had a tangible feel to it. This seemed an ominous sign. What were the chances of standing on the bridge to witness this solemn event at that exact moment? I turned to my children and said, "You have just witnessed the pandemic come to America."

CHAPTER 24

When the World Shut Down

> God be with you till we meet again;
> Keep love's banner floating o'er you;
> Smite death's threat'ning wave before you.
> God be with you till we meet again.
>
> Jeremiah E. Rankin
"God Be with You Till We Meet Again"

There at Muir Beach on the last day of spring break—my sons mesmerized by the meandering rivulets of Redwood Creek as it flowed into the Pacific while Matthew and I stood hand in hand at water's edge—it was peace and happiness all at once. My sons soon discovered they could be masters of sand and flow, working together to channel new pathways for the creek in its final journey to the ocean. Watching my children build together in the sand, I had forgotten that the BYU protests were still going strong. I had forgotten about the Princess Cruise ship under the Golden Gate Bridge. I had even forgotten about the previous day's Zoom board meeting that I conducted on the shore of San Francisco Bay, during which board members began to voice their concerns about the spread of COVID in their own countries. Now, with our children on the edge of the Pacific, I was also standing on the edge of another ocean that would exercise immense power and dramatically shape the shoreline of family and Affirmation: A worldwide pandemic. Over the next two years, I would draw from this time of peace and happiness, this respite at Muir Beach at the edge of two oceans.

***

During our drive back home from California, we listened intently to the rapidly evolving news of soaring infection rates, shutdowns, social distancing, and stay-at-home orders across the United States. We arrived to find an Arizona in panic. Like a wildfire, the world had shut down over the course of a weekend with unprecedented speed. The collapse of the food supply chain was immediate. As a Mormon household, our shelves were well stocked with abundant toilet paper, paper towels, and laundry detergent before our spring break trip. When we were dating, Matthew would chuckle at my habit of keeping months and months worth of commodities stocked in the house. With conviction, I would always reply, "This is a Mormon thing. You'll just have to get used to it." But I had neglected food staples in the pantry leading up to spring break. What would have been a regular post-vacation grocery store trip resulted in me driving all over the valley, store after store, only to be greeted by empty shelves. Nothing kicks in the anxiety of "hunter-gatherer dad mode" more than knowing you have children and a spouse at home to feed.

I learned that the local Walmart received food delivery trucks on Friday mornings, so I spent my Fridays in line, everyone masked and six feet apart, for a chance to be one of the first people in the store when it opened. People were let in by groups to comply with social distancing requirements, so front-of-the-line positioning was essential. Upon entering, it was a game of Supermarket Sweep. Within thirty minutes, the shelves were bare of all pantry essentials until the following Friday.

During that first week, Arizona's governor ordered all healthcare facilities closed except for emergency care. Luckily for patients, toothaches, abscesses, and broken teeth are rare. For the dentist, they are essential to treat when they happen, but they are not a primary economic driver in a dental practice. I called each of my staff with the difficult news that we would all be without a job for the foreseeable future. I kept on-call hours, only going into the office to treat emergencies. Dentists are already hypervigilant about infection control, but in this new normal, full-on personal protective barriers now covered my entire body. Each encounter with a patient felt like I was dressed for a moon landing, but I was not in a position to take COVID lightly. I was in constant contact with oral aerosols, the primary mode of transmission for the coronavirus. Even with all my protective gear, I was still vulnerable from the unknowingly infected. In those early stages of the pandemic, the virus was in its most virulent and deadly form. Death was always a possibility after an encounter with an infected patient. This was constantly in the back of my mind as I provided emergency care.

The healthcare community didn't know how long the virus could survive outside the aerosol cloud. I had to assume every surface after a patient encounter, dentist included, harbored a live virus. Every time I returned home after emergency care, I would quarantine myself as I undressed and then stand under the shower for as long as the water ran hot, scrubbing each part of my body multiple times, competing for hot water with the washing machine that was disinfecting my scrubs in sanitary mode.

I rested at the kitchen table the last Friday in March after a successful early morning food run. The effects and dangers of the pandemic on my family and Affirmation finally hit me. It was evident that the global shutdown was not going away anytime soon. As a leader of a nonprofit that brings people into community, I was mindful of two things: first, the organization's financial health, whose lifeblood is donations. Second, and most importantly, the people we served. Affirmation was founded on the principle of friends caring for friends. It is what we do, and we have perfected the system over the decades. Lose sight of your queer peers in an LGBTQ organization, and the loss of institutional trust becomes devastating. The worldwide COVID pandemic brought immense challenges to both these areas in Affirmation.

As the economic realities of the shutdown began to sink in, I confronted the uncomfortable realization that my dental practice and Affirmation had fixed costs that were accruing daily. Surprisingly, the fixed cost pressure for my practice was not as great as it was for Affirmation. Yes, without patient flow, revenue was non-existent. But with the governor's order in place, creditors offered forbearance for financial obligations. Additionally, payroll—the biggest expense for a dental office—was now at zero. Even in the face of the unknown, the "doctor side" of me was at least flying in a holding pattern while I was not in operation. But Affirmation was still very much in operation. The most pressing anxiety was the financial obligation with the Utah Valley Convention Center to hold the September 2020 International Conference. A worldwide pandemic causing economic and social shutdown was not on anyone's radar when we signed the contract in 2019. A substantial second payment was due in four weeks, and the management company would not entertain releasing us from our contract under the force majeure clause, citing that this would all be over by fall. Most importantly, Joel McDonald was just getting settled in as our new director of operations. It was critical to have him working if we were going to successfully bring the entire world of Affirmation online during a pandemic.

Cash flow in a nonprofit is not just about money flowing out of the organization to fund its mission. Inflow is essential. Without that, you will bleed out in no time flat. Donations for March had dried up, and major donors indicated they were pausing contributions until the economic picture became clearer. Already, nonprofits nationwide were beginning to fold due to pandemic economic pressures. Stomach in knots, I stared out the window, trying to manage this growing anxiety by watching Matthew read his book out on the back porch. Without income and the ability to gather Affirmation together in person, would I be the president standing at the helm as the ship went down? "Don't be ridiculous," I told myself, "Stop the navel-gazing, pull your britches up, and lead. You are not alone. Keep moving forward with your team." This was the time to keep going. It was time to get to work.

Nobody knew what a "pandemic Affirmation" looked like. It was up to the executive committee to cast a vision for what was next for our community. At our next meeting, I laid out the circumstances before us. We were five months out from the 2020 International Conference date. The Centers for Disease Control was now forecasting that the worst of the pandemic was still ahead of us. The United States had closed its borders to all travel, even with our closest neighbors, Canada and Mexico. Jairo doubted any travel between Latin America and the United States for the conference would be possible in September.

With the logistics required to execute an International Conference as well as all the advance travel planning of both international and domestic flights to Utah, I could not see how we could, in good conscience, hold an in-person International Conference that year. The risk was too great for the health of our members, and it would be mismanagement of Affirmation's money to rent facilities for a thousand when we could not even guarantee a hundred would be able to gather with us in Provo. Not one to be hampered by circumstances, Laurie counseled that we must not cancel or postpone the conference. This was a time to rise in our leadership to meet the challenges of this perilous and unprecedented time. Indeed, this was a time to use out-of-the-box thinking and all the technology, creativity, and means available to us to carry out a conference that meets the specific needs of our communities in this worldwide pandemic.

We moved forward earnestly. For the first time in the history of Affirmation, we would hold an International Conference online. It seems commonplace today in a post-pandemic world to meet online, but in 2020, this was breaking new ground. Many features that made large-scale virtual conferences a reality had not yet been invented for public use. United in our direction, we began pressing forward to make this a success. I immediately moved to acquire Paycheck Protection Program funds to retain Joel. Then, I entered intense negotiations with Utah County over the clause in our contract allowing cancellation due to extraordinary unforeseen circumstances—both successful ventures that eliminated our economic pressures.

When the world shut down in March, the executive committee directed the leadership of Affirmation's regions and chapters to follow all local, state, and national recommendations and restrictions where they resided. Almost daily, I would get reports detailing the decisions of local leaders as they followed this direction: "Brazil has suspended all regional meetings for the next two quarters." "Mexico has postponed their annual conference from August to November." "Colombia canceling all meetings in the principal cities of Bogotá and Cali." "The United States is discontinuing all chapter activities until further notice." The news continued until the entire world of Affirmation's in-person programming had ceased. It was surreal to watch the operations of Affirmation go dark around the world.

Building community in isolation was uncharted waters for Affirmation, which is known for a robust social component in our work. Joel brought considerable technical expertise to the table as we moved the entirety of Affirmation into virtual space. As an organization, we had to figure out the technology and then introduce this virtual space as Affirmation's primary meeting place. The goal was to keep people together in community and feeling supported while in isolation. It was Joel's job to make sure this plane could fly.

We kept a master schedule of these worldwide meetings, and I attended as many as possible. No matter where an Affirmation group was meeting, the level of care people exhibited with one another exceeded my expectations—meaning, I didn't really have expectations, only hope. Having never experienced a virtual Affirmation, I didn't know what to expect as we met together through screens. In this leap of faith, I unexpectedly experienced community in the virtual spaces of Affirmation. The experience was just as strong as the day I walked into the lobby of the Palmyra Inn in 2015.

I began to crave attending these virtual meetings. Through a window the size of a laptop screen, the world became small, the distance erased. I felt the genuine love and concern from my Affirmation peers in parts of the world I would have never been able to visit in person during our pre-pandemic days. Week after week, these were my virtual Waters of Mormon. The common attribute of each meeting was the spontaneous visiting that took place after the program. It turns out—just as it was for in-person gatherings—programming gets everyone together, but it is the personal interaction at the end that keeps the connections going long past the meeting. As the weeks of the pandemic rolled along, virtual meetings, music performances, book readings, talent shows, conversation hours, and Sunday firesides became the staple of Affirmation life in 2020. In these spaces, we not only shared in one another's joys but also grieved together over the loss of family and friends taken from this life too soon by the virus. The vision of community in the virtual space had been realized, and we held steady, holding each other through the summer and into the fall.

So much was happening within Affirmation during our exodus to virtual space that it had not crossed my mind that 2020 was an election year for Affirmation. My two-year term was coming to a close. In June, Laurie messaged me. She did not plan to serve another term. She had been in an executive committee ever since she and her partner, Nancy, had been together, and they were going to be ready to do other things. "I commit to you that I will finish serving with integrity," she concluded. "Please know the great love and admiration that I feel for you. Laurie Lee." I put my work down and messaged her back. I thanked her for her remarkable service in Affirmation. Like her great architecture that dotted the stakes of Zion, her contributions to Affirmation would be felt for many years. Recalling the first conversation we had two years earlier where we hatched our plan to serve together, I asked Laurie, "If it is agreeable with you, I would like to have one last vulnerable conversation about the state of Affirmation. It will help organize my thoughts as I consider my own intentions about running again."

I set my phone down, put away my work and retired to the bedroom where I openly wept at this news. I find no fulfillment in friendships that are shallow or superficial. I have little patience for those who are not genuine or principled. I crave meaningful relationships and thrive when daily collaboration, authenticity, and a shared sense of purpose build a rich history of accomplishments and camaraderie. This is what it was like to work with Laurie. Her work and service were extremely meaningful and effective. We had accomplished much together in that difficult outward-facing year of 2019 as we stood in the queer/Latter-day Saint intersection to confront a barrage of newly articulated narratives and policies. We stood united in the vision of what a virtual Affirmation would look like in the face of a pandemic. We made a good team. Such a relationship in any leadership configuration is rare, so I understood how special this time had been. If I chose to run for another term as president, all this would be missed in ways that would change how I would need to operate in an executive committee without her presence. Seeing that I had gone missing from my desk, Matthew found me on the bed and gently asked what had happened. I pulled my phone out and read Laurie's message to him. "I'll be fine after a while," I told him, "I could not be more supportive of Laurie and Nancy. But for now, I just need space to mourn this loss. It's a me thing. You know me." And he did. He knew that I needed to experience the multifaceted layers of emotion embedded in this moment. It is how I experience this world. I cannot fathom living a life that is not rich in meaning.

The next evening over Zoom, Laurie and I had one last vulnerable discussion about Affirmation, a bookend discussion to the one in 2018 that started it all. This was not an exit interview but a conversation between friends who had the privilege of serving together for a season in a work we both firmly believed in.

❦

Matthew and I talked extensively about what we wanted our future to look like. Like Laurie and Nancy, Matthew only had known me as a senior leader in Affirmation with two time-intensive roles. We reflected on how intense 2019 was in the business of LGBTQ Latter-day Saint change. The intensity didn't go away in 2020, only focusing inward, gathering Affirmation into virtual space during a pandemic. I shared that I felt I had more to give, more to build, more people to help, more work to strengthen an Affirmation in pandemic mode—but I wanted to know what Matthew felt. We had been charting our course together since our very first date as we lay on the grass in the backyard looking at the stars overhead. This time would be no different. Over the next few weeks, we discussed Matthew's recent decision to begin a new career direction, starting ASU's nursing program in January. We carefully considered each of my children and where they would be in life over the next two years. After considering all the variables facing us, Matthew took my hand and gently concluded, "I know the joy that service in Affirmation brings you. You have my support if you decide to run again." This was not just a decision that affected only me; it involved the entire family. I did not take this for granted.

As I began to assemble a candidate executive committee for the upcoming election, I wanted it to represent the diversity found within Affirmation as well as constitute a team that would inspire the creativity and energy required to lead a worldwide organization of our peers. Jairo would be the cornerstone of this new arrangement. He is one of the most talented consensus builders I know. Under his leadership, the extremely active and passionate Latin America area grew, even during the pandemic. Fortunately, he indicated that he would serve another two years if we were elected. As I thought about who might join us as the new vice president, my mind gravitated to Rebecca Solen. I first met Rebecca at Affirmation's opening social at the Encircle house the night before she delivered the opening keynote at the 2019 International Conference. There, on the staircase in Encircle's living room, she shared her story and her family's journey as she transitioned after her congressional run for the U.S. House. Her passion and clarity of purpose struck me. I knew that the rise of the transgender moment in the queer/Latter-day Saint intersection was far from over, and to have her voice in this moment was a key piece to leading Affirmation. I called Rebecca and asked if she might consider running with me and Jairo in the upcoming Affirmation presidential election. I asked her jokingly—but not really—if she spoke Spanish. Jairo did not speak English, and I did not speak Spanish. Our relationship was destined for Google Translate and interpreters, so to have a bilingual speaker in the executive committee would be a dream for both of us.

"Unfortunately not," she said, "but I do have a master's in international relations for what it's worth."

"This kind of a degree in an international organization? You're hired!" Deep down, I hoped it would become a reality for Affirmation to have her on board. After a few days considering my invitation, Rebecca called with her answer: "I'm in. I'm all in. Let's do this."

Full steam ahead amid 2020, Affirmation launched its first virtual International Conference. I was proud of our conference planning team as we traversed new ground. I always pressed Joel for what seemed technologically impossible in scale and logistics as we built the framework for such a large international virtual event. Joel called it building the airplane while we were flying it. Indeed, it was both exhilarating and a bit terrifying. Part of creating this experience was to hold the sessions as a series of short programming snacks over several weekends—a technique we picked up from other organizations who had learned by experience that continually holding people in front of their screens for hours on end was insufferable for attendees. As the conference progressed, Joel shared attendance numbers and the countries people were tuning in from. We had an overwhelming number of participants join us who would not have been able to come to Utah for an in-person conference. In this forced opportunity the pandemic handed us, the excitement and energy of a gathered international community was available to all. I knew it would forever change Affirmation and how we thought about gathering people together in community.

Emotions high during the last conference session, I spoke directly from my heart before we signed off. I observed how remarkable Affirmation's first virtual conference had been: "We have met as friends, taught each other as friends, and tonight we leave as friends." I reminded us to resist the urge to divide ourselves within our community, especially along spiritual belief lines. "Let us affirm one another's accomplishments and unique journey as a celebration of the self-determination of the LGBTQ person. Division causes chaos. We cannot move together toward understanding, justice, and equality as a divided house," I noted. "Today, more than ever, we are moving forward on a crest of increased visibility, changed hearts, and recognized rights. We stand on the shoulders of giants who have gone before us in the Affirmation community—and make no mistake about it: there are giants among us today." It was surreal addressing a worldwide community sitting alone in my study, our connection made possible by a billion zeros and ones. But this was not a moment of isolation. In hope, I looked forward to the day we would again be together. Until then, I knew in my heart we still had a distance to go, our "pandemic Affirmation" band. I looked deep into my screen and wished for everyone's continued health and safety: "May God be with you till we meet again."

STATE OF EMERGENCY

In the back of your mind is a room
Where you stash your fears and unknowns
About a virus.
And you are vulnerable
Even clothed in mask and smock—
Shielded, as you heal another's pain.

Uncertainty reigns—
People dying
No vaccine
No treatment
Hospitals at capacity
Tents for morgues

The ever-present question,
"Is this the day it happens?
Is this the day I begin to die?"
Is not ignored, but managed
During each encounter
Inside an aerosol cloud.

To treat their pain, there you are
Intimate inches away
From their eyes
Relying on you, watching.
Watching your eyes for feedback
That they will be alright.

Your eyes become the answer,
Unspoken,
Trained to be part of healing—
Projecting care,
And competence,
And dignity.

But behind those eyes,
Imperceptible,
In the room at the back of your mind,
Where you have stashed the fear
Of your own mortality,
Is the thing you hold—

The thing you hold
As you do the things
You love to do—
To care for your neighbor,
To heal a fear,
While holding your own,

Knowing

That if today is the day
You begin to die,
There are others, who
Are just as strong,
To care for you
As you have done unto others.

CHAPTER 25

Of Sand and Stone

> In the end, only three things matter: how much you loved, how gently you lived, and how gracefully you let go of things not meant for you.
>
> Gautama Buddha

With the last Affirmation board meeting of 2020 in the books and Christmas done, it was time for Matthew and me to get out of town! I was not sad to see 2020 in my rearview mirror. The pandemic was lasting much longer than originally forecast, keeping Affirmation firmly in virtual space. Virtual fatigue was starting to set in among our members, matching the general malaise happening in a world growing weary of pandemic restrictions.

Thankfully, the pandemic had focused the modern church's attention away from the queer/Latter-day Saint intersection. Things had been remarkably quiet on that front. In all this, one positive development about the pandemic had just occurred.

COVID vaccines were now available in the United States. It felt like I was coming to the end of a long night. I would be able to go to work and not fear sickness or perhaps even death. Notably, my work in this space would continue for two more years. In November, I was elected for a second term as president of Affirmation. I was excited to work with Jairo and Rebecca in planning Affirmation's return to in-person programming. But that was work for 2021. At this moment, I was looking forward to adventure!

Matthew has a little yellow Prius. It is distinctive and fun. To keep us out of the poorhouse, we tool around the Southwest in his car rather than fire up the Tahoe, burning through a tank of gas just getting to the edge of town. We have taken that little yellow Prius places Priuses should not go. We have sunk it axle-deep in mud in the middle of the San Carlos Apache reservation, driven it over boulders at a 45-degree angle to an old decommissioned dam in the middle of nowhere Arizona, and parked it under the towering Rain God Mesa in Monument Valley in the middle of a thunderstorm.

On the last day of 2020, we piled into the yellow Prius and headed out to the Buckskin Mountains in the desert of Western Arizona to explore the old abandoned copper mines. These mountains are exactly the stereotypical landscapes you see in the old Wile E. Coyote and Roadrunner cartoons, with towering jagged red cliffs, perilous canyons, and barren plateaus spotted with the occasional lonely cactus. Trekking mile after mile under the wide sun-centered skies, the unending desert views from each peak on the hiking trails remind me of the seemingly insignificant scale that my human frame occupied in this immense land that was lifted in the Triassic and folded in the Mesozoic.

This vast scale of geology and time made it all the more remarkable when I reached a summit in this lonely environment and was suddenly greeted by the Colorado River coursing through the desert. It was a magnificent and breathtaking sight. With all its water, the mighty river can seem out of place as you stand there amid sand and stone. This water originated a thousand miles away, in a completely different climate high in the Rocky Mountains, yet is responsible for much of the geography and the presence of people in the desert southwest. I could feel the life-giving, transformative power of the river. It is the one thing that tames this desert and sustains millions of people in the Southwest. As I watched the river, I was struck by the life-giving, transformative power of another great force I witness daily: the great network of LGBTQ mentors and peers.

As I wondered about the future, I sat on a rock overlooking the absolute power of the Colorado River. Pandemic or not, I understood that Affirmation was an important part of many LGBTQ people's river of support. Such a river is just as transformative and powerful as the Colorado River is to the American Southwest. Affirmation's mission is to create communities of safety, love, and hope. In the face of the pandemic, we gathered these communities into virtual space. Now, with vaccines available and better-understood treatments for infection on the horizon, I was beginning to feel the weight of the pandemic lift from the shoulders of Affirmation. Full incorporation of our communities back into real-world space would be slow. This would require the collective help of our community, and now was the time to put out the call for assistance to harness the power of this great LGBTQ river in preparation. In my call for volunteers, I reflected on the power of rivers in our lives. "You have the ability to be a transformative power and sustain our queer peers in times when they feel insignificant in the personal deserts that surround them."[1]

---

1. Kitchen, Nathan. "Be a Part of the Life-Giving Work of Affirmation in 2021." Affirmation, January 2, 2021. Accessed July 27, 2024. https://affirmation.org/transformative-power-you-2021/.

As 2021 rolled along, the pandemic's easing was not uniform worldwide. Latin America was still under stay-at-home orders, with online meetings the only option. COVID restrictions mandated Affirmation UK and Ireland hold their regional conference online. In the United States, we began the soft launch of in-person activities with two June events. For the first, Affirmation marched at Salt Lake City Pride, carrying our banner from the steps of the State Capitol down to Liberty Park. This marked the first time we had been able to gather in the United States since the pandemic began. For the second, Affirmation participated in the first-ever Pride event in Rexburg, Idaho, the home of BYU-Idaho.

The flight to Rexburg was in two legs; the first was to Salt Lake City, where we would board a puddle jumper to Idaho Falls before driving the last stretch to arrive just in time for the opening luncheon. Once in Salt Lake, we found our Idaho Falls gate and took a seat, looking out the huge terminal windows. From this vantage point, I could see the city in the distance, the Motherland, as Matthew would say. Feeling a gentle notification ping in my pocket, I pulled out my phone. Here, in view of the center of the kingdom of God on Earth, I read my email:

Dear Nathan Raymond Kitchen,

Resignation finalized. Your resignation from the church has been confirmed! Congratulations!

We sincerely thank you for the opportunity to serve you.

Mark & Ryan
Quitmormon.com

I don't care how many exclamation points are in a resignation confirmation letter. For me, it cheapened the gravity of this situation as a queer person. In my own spiritual home, I had been surveilled for years, experiencing continual check-ins by my priesthood leaders to ascertain my marital status. On the happiest day of my life, as I joined myself publicly in love and fidelity to my dear Matthew, I was hunted down to be dismembered from the faith with the cold precision of a butcher severing a limb from a carcass. As a gay married Latter-day Saint, I had become the most dangerous game in a dangerous game of hunted vs. hunter. It was a game where I could not outlast the prejudice. There was simply not enough time to outlast the prejudice.

I set my phone down and stared out onto the runway. I needed a moment to process this before I shared it with Matthew. The only emotion emanating from my soul was the injustice of it all. Just a month earlier, President Nelson had delivered a Mother's Day message in which he talked about experiencing the "haunting absence of a companion" after his first wife died.[2] In her passing, he realized how much her strength had bolstered his own. He did not have to endure this haunting for long before he remarried again. I asked myself, "Why are we insisting that the queer children of God spend life and the eternities haunted by the absence of a companion when we don't even expect our prophets to endure such a thing?"

During my attempted capture into the single and celibate generation, I was presented with the rules of engagement.

---

2. Nelson, Russell M. "I love Mother's Day, but I realize that many women don't share my enthusiasm." Facebook, May 9, 2021. https://www.facebook.com/russell.m.nelson/posts/i-love-mothers-day-but-i-realize-that-many-women-dont-share-my-enthusiasm-some-f/3956143364453070/

Unlike marriage, where both parties vow to build a life together, the vows of the single and celibate life were a one-sided covenant. The members of my ward and stake would now be my companion, yet in a non-binding, non-obligated, "if we have time" kind of way. I knew how terrible we were as a church at home teaching, visiting teaching, and now, ministering. None of that just magically changes because someone is a single celibate gay. Our fellow members all have their own families, jobs, and activities. They are busy building a life together, experiencing the very real blessings of love and stability in marriage. As a single and celibate gay Latter-day Saint, I would forever be a guest in the families that people were building a life with. In religiously-mandated queer celibacy, a ward family, a stake, and local leaders are a poor substitute for marriage and the wellbeing that marriage bestows upon humans. Relying on the hospitality of other people's marriages only makes me the beggar for companionship in this scenario, where the single celibate vow becomes a vow of poverty of connection. This marriage of a queer person to their ward, to their stake, and to their church leaders becomes some sort of weird nun-like arrangement. But, instead of being the bride of Christ, I would be the bride of the Church—looking forever to the members and leadership for companionship that a spouse would usually provide, while being expected to give marriage-level commitment to the Church in return. I knew this was a counterfeit companionship. It is a companionship that dries up like cheat grass on the summer Utah hills, dead and a dangerous fire hazard to the soul.

My mind then wandered to that day nine months ago when I received the text from my stake president inviting me to a membership council. After reading it, I slammed my phone down on the table. Like Job, I was "fed up." It was a moment where I was expressing defiance, not capitulation. If God were really in the middle of this—all about power—not morality and justice—

then I would not condone it through acceptance.³ Staring at my phone while fighting back the intense rush of helplessness and injustice, I was acutely aware that two different stake presidents had already pronounced the verdict of a membership council in my living room if I were to marry again: excommunication. I had been a dead man walking for the past five years.

I determined that in my final moments as a queer member of the Church, I would apply the great wisdom of Lehi. I was, after all, on earth to act, not be acted upon (2 Nephi 2:14, 16). It was time for one final bit of action for the hunted. It would be by my own hand that my membership would be terminated. This action would be a conscious taking back of power in a system of extreme power imbalance. I determined that the silence I had sent my stake president out the door with on the night of his visit would continue in this process. My resignation would do a silent end run around the stake president by using Quitmormon's third-party representation in this matter. When confronted by the injustice of the power structure of his day, even Jesus remained silent in the face of his accusers (Matthew 27:12).

When I took my resignation letter to get notarized at the local UPS store, I intended to do it alone during my lunch hour, as if it were an everyday lunchtime errand. I didn't get but two steps out the door before I started shaking uncontrollably. I could not do this alone. Even holding the unsigned papers sent my stomach into knots at the injustice of it all and the sadness of what was being lost against my will and wishes. I called Matthew and asked if he would stand with me as I notarized the document. He dropped what he was doing and, within twenty minutes, was by my side, standing shoulder to shoulder with me

---

3. Greenstein, Edward L. "Introduction." In *Job: A New Translation*, xxi. New Haven and London, Connecticut, United Kingdom: Yale University Press, 2019.

in front of a UPS notary public about to go on their lunch break. I flinched at the sudden loudness of the notary's ink stamp as it forcefully pounded the document. It was just as startling as an unexpected gunshot. What an anticlimactic ending, to be in a utilitarian commercial establishment to say goodbye to my membership in the Church that I had held dear since the earliest days of my memories, the Church I had proselytized for in the mission field and served and believed in with all my heart, might, mind, and strength.

With the Quitmormon attorneys handling the termination of my membership with the Church's attorneys at Kirton McConkie, I assumed this would be the end of the matter. However, one month later, I came home from work to a Post-it note on my front door. It was a notice from the post office that they had attempted to deliver a certified letter from my stake president. As I looked at the Post-it note, rolling it between my fingers, I realized I had been caught in a bureaucratic nightmare. Kirton McConkie had created such a delay in processing resignation requests that my stake president had no clue what was happening and had begun the local wheels of church law. Having served in presiding councils in my ward and stake, I knew what protocol demanded next. The post office would attempt delivery two more times. Because I would not sign for it, the post office would return the unaccepted certified letter unopened to sender. The stake president would then consider that sufficient notice and convene a membership council in absentia. All this would happen way before my stake president received word from headquarters that my resignation had been received. I was not going to let them excommunicate me while communication of my resignation sat in limbo at the Church's law firm for months. Knowing that a resignation is effective immediately once it is signed and sent to the Church, not when the Church finally acknowledges the resignation, I penned a quick letter to my stake president informing him of the termination. I sent it via certified mail to his law firm, tracking it to the acceptance signature. Seeing him receive a certified letter I had sent him in response to the certified letter he had unsuccessfully attempted to send me was a grim irony.

And then it was finished. All communication ceased. The years of monitoring, visits, texts, checking in to see if I had married a man—finished. Both the hunter and the hunted satisfied that they had prevailed. But I know that in this game, no one is the winner—absolutely no one. This is the moment that prejudice wins. Prejudice is so pernicious that it wounds everything it touches: the target, those who wield its power, and the society that tolerates its presence. If Zion is truly built on equity and justice, then prejudice is that antithetical force that rots Zion into its basest form. Building Zion is a collaborative venture. We cannot approach Zion in isolation. Rooting out prejudice from our hearts begins when we call out to our neighbor and tell them we want them with us, to be a part of us, to belong with us. I was reminded of the maxim: "True belonging doesn't require you to change who you are; it requires you to be who you are."[4]

I felt the gentle touch of Matthew's hand on mine. It brought me back to the present. He saw that I was lost in thought and asked me if everything was okay. I attempted to gather my words. As I met his gaze, I could feel the familiar opening of trauma as I held this news. Matthew was familiar with this look. He had witnessed the toll this process exacted as I was being hunted.

---

4. Brown, Brené. "The Quest for True Belonging." In *Braving the Wilderness*, 40. Random House, New York, 2017.

Earlier that year, I would wake up in night terrors, calling out for help, finding Matthew there to calm me. Yet time and again, in my dreams, the chase and feeling of helplessness would continue just as vividly as it had played out in real life. He recommended I speak with a therapist to heal the parts of me still wounded. It was finally EMDR therapy that allowed my soul to rest. The night terrors stopped, and I could once again sit in the chair in my living room that my stake president had occupied the night he invited me to cancel my wedding and not marry the love of my life or else suffer the consequences of spiritual death.

As I faced Matthew in the Salt Lake City airport, every version of me in this long process of nearly six years was now sitting at once, all together, in that airport chair: That scared father of five, holding his children close in the aftermath of the exclusion policy, listening to his son exclaim, "Why do they want to do this to us?" That father full of resolve as he gathered his children, year after year, under a palo verde tree growing from a rock on The Peak of Champions, holding his family together as forces worked to tear it apart. That Nathan standing in front of Matthew as Heidi pronounced the words that at once joined him in marriage and in the same breath pronounced him an excommunicate from his faith. That Nathan standing before a UPS notary public, eyes so blurred by tears in that moment of loss that he couldn't make out the document in front of him, the pounding of the notary stamp announcing a resounding finality that still rang in his ears. Every single one of these Nathans gently squeezed Matthew's hand and read him the email. Matthew caressed my cheek as I noted today's date: June 26. Today was the sixth anniversary of the Obergefell ruling, decreeing marriage equality the law of the land. I told him I found it poetic that the notification came on this day. "I love you dearly and would marry you a thousand times over—I am that confident in the correctness and goodness of our union before God. I firmly believe that love wins in the end. And if love hasn't won yet, it isn't the end."

After boarding our plane, I looked at the email one last time before shutting off my phone. I recognized that this was but one of the countless experiences of exclusion and rejection that queer people encounter every day. As we rose through the sky, leaving Salt Lake behind, I realized the symbolism in that moment of leaving. I could now let it go. This confirmation was the final piece in this tortuous journey of expressing my faith within my spiritual home as a queer child of God. I was entangled no longer with my hunter. It was a moment of closure, leaving behind the legal system of church government, the politics, the administrative hierarchies, and scores of unwritten rules—all landmines for queer Latter-day Saints.

Like the arrow of time—where death is at the feather and life is at the point—with Salt Lake in my rearview mirror and Matthew at my side, life lay before us. Hope now charted our course as we flew through the skies. And coming with me was all the good I had accumulated over a rich lifetime within my spiritual home—my faith, my Latter-day Saint heritage, my belief, my family, and most importantly, Christ. Life was no longer grounded in sand but stone. I was now on a direct course, flying true, directly into the arms of my loving heavenly parents.

CHAPTER 26

The Hosts

> Let all who are in need come and eat!
>
> Rav Huna
> B. Ta'anit 20b

At the October 2020 General Conference, Elder Quentin L. Cook mentioned a concept with far-reaching implications for queer Latter-day Saints, "In our doctrine we believe that in the host country for the Restoration, the United States, the U.S. Constitution and related documents, written by imperfect men, were inspired by God to bless all people."[1]

The idea of the United States being the host nation of the Restoration is not unique to this talk. At the next General Conference, President Oaks taught, "Without a Bill of Rights, America could not have served as the host nation for the

---

1. Cook, Quentin L. "Hearts Knit in Righteousness and Unity." *Ensign* 44, no.11, November 2020. https://www.churchofjesuschrist.org/study/liahona/2020/11/15cook.

Restoration of the gospel."[2] A decade earlier, Neal A. Maxwell pointed out that President Gordon B. Hinkley loved America, "the host nation for the restored kingdom," yet he did not insist on Americanization as part of implementing the gospel in other nations.[3] The theme of this messaging is twofold. First, the Restoration had to happen in a nation, and in 1830, the United States was the nation in a position to host this event. Second, we may have a host nation for the Restoration, but the brethren do not insist that other nations become America or behave American to receive or enjoy the full blessings of the gospel of Jesus Christ.

Consider the other hosts of the Restoration. In 1830, heterosexuality was the host sexual orientation of the Restoration, and cisgender was the host gender identity. Just as the gospel expanded to people beyond the borders of the host nation, the gospel today has expanded to people of various sexual orientations and gender identities. The concept of hosts is layered for Latter-day Saints. The United States is the host nation of the Restoration, and in turn, the Restoration hosts the children of God. Both hosts have important host duties. Today, just as we find pockets of American exceptionalism in the culture of the Church, we are squarely confronted by heterosexual and cisgender exceptionalism in the ongoing Restoration of the gospel of Jesus Christ. Those called to continue the host duties of the Restoration still insist that being heterosexual and cisgender is a part of the implementation of the gospel for other sexual orientations and gender identities. It forms the doctrinal premise

---

2. Oaks, Dallin H. "Defending Our Divinely Inspired Constitution." *Liahona*, May 2021. https://www.churchofjesuschrist.org/study/liahona/2021/05/51oaks.

3. Maxwell, Neal A. "President Gordon B. Hinckley: The Spiritual Sculpturing of a Righteous Soul." *Ensign* 12, no. 1, January 1982. https://www.churchofjesuschrist.org/study/ensign/1982/01/president-gordon-b-hinckley-the-spiritual-sculpturing-of-a-righteous-soul.

today about queer people. This lack of hospitality from the host creates division in our spiritual home, as LGBTQ people are continually cast as outsiders unless they conform and perform to the host's acceptable sexuality or gender identity.

As I listened to Elder Cook speak of a "host country," I was reminded of the great responsibility expected of the hosts of the Restoration. This responsibility includes doing the work and having the wisdom to overcome the prejudice and discrimination that was inherent in the host nation during the Restoration. We are witness to the Church's work to overcome the host nation's prejudice that slavery had fostered. A key part of this is openly acknowledging the Church's own racial prejudice as it grew and learned, cradled in the arms of its host nation. In his October 2020 conference talk, Elder Cook provided some of the self-reflection required as the Church undertakes this reckoning, "We are not under the illusion that in the past all relationships were perfect, all conduct was Christlike or all decisions were just."[4] Being a host means that when you know better, you do better. Currently, the Church's work is to do better and wipe away racial prejudice from the hearts of Latter-day Saints that has been held and propagated by those called to carry on the host duties of the ongoing Restoration. As this critical change continues, the work advances to eradicate another prejudice from the hearts of the great houses of Zion, to which our heavenly parents are continually sending their queer children to live. These queer children are being sent into what church leaders proclaim is the "greatest generation"[5] of Latter-day Saints

---

4. Cook, Quentin L. "Hearts Knit in Righteousness and Unity." *Ensign*, 44, no. 11, November 2020.

5. Ballard, M. Russell. "The Greatest Generation of Young Adults." *Ensign* 45, no. 5, May 2015. https://www.churchofjesuschrist.org/study/ensign/2015/05/general-priesthood-session/the-greatest-generation-of-young-adults.

in the history of the Church. Such a heavenly birthright illustrates how important the queer children of God are, yet at the moment, the hosts of the Restoration deny these queer souls the ability to approach their heavenly parents in authenticity, privilege, and opportunity in the equality that their straight/cisgender peers enjoy.

God choosing a host nation, a host sexual orientation, or a host gender identity to get the ball rolling in a new dispensation doesn't mean there are no other nations, sexual orientations, or gender identities in the world. For better or worse, these chosen hosts were what was available at the time. Like Elder Holland lamented, "Imperfect people are all God has ever had to work with. That must be terribly frustrating to Him, but he deals with it."[6] Our hosts of the Restoration in 1830 were what God had to work with. God had to start somewhere. And using them in this way does not mean they are more favored than their fellow children of God—present or future. It does mean, however, that these hosts are responsible for propelling the Restoration past their own understandings, imperfections, and limitations. Interestingly, each time a host tries to exclude a people from coming to Christ—be it Gentiles, children, Black people, or any number of others—they are corrected.

The work now is for those who inherited the host duties of the Restoration to be inclusive of their fellow LGBTQ Saints and realize that past words and actions towards queer Latter-day Saints have been harmful—even deadly—for some in the modern church. The Restoration is much bigger than the host nation that cradled it. It is so much bigger than the host gender and sexual orientations of the Restoration. Caught in a web of poli-

---

6. Holland, Jeffrey R. "'Lord, I Believe.'" *Ensign* 43, no. 5, May 2013. https://www.churchofjesuschrist.org/study/ensign/2013/05/sunday-afternoon-session/lord-i-believe.

cies and dominant narratives, queer Latter-day Saints can sometimes come to believe that the Restoration belongs exclusively to others, but that is a grave error. This is Christ's Restoration, and his gospel exists independent of its hosts. Elder Holland reminds us that despite being surrounded by imperfect people, Christ is the only perfect actor in the plan of salvation.[7] Even when we as a queer people center on him in mortality, we do so in an enclave nation at the Waters of Mormon, where prejudice and acts of prejudice are still parts of the human heart in this world that surrounds us, requiring Christ to purify and heal. Others may balk at our queerness, but Christ, in his perfect atonement, experienced queerness with us in Gethsemane so that he might understand us (Doctrine and Covenants 88:6). This was not a moment of shame for him but a recognition of who we are as beloved queer children of God. Just as bringing the gospel of Jesus Christ to other nations does not Americanize them, one cannot bring the gospel into a queer person's life and reasonably expect to heterosexualize or cisgender them.

Today, our hosts hold the queer children of God under the rainbow stained-glass ceiling, where they experience a deliberately limited gospel. As a queer people, we know full well what happens above this ceiling, for we have been taught all our lives what exaltation looks and feels like. This holding is a comprehensive plan of exclusion. The great struggle of our day is mistaking prejudice for love and using the law of the Lord to exclude LGBTQ people from the law of chastity, marriage, and gender self-determination, as well as from their eternal families and their heavenly parents. To the question of queer spiritual equality, defenders of a status quo Restoration first insisted that we did not exist. Responding to this, we became visible. In the face of such visibility, they attempted to erase us, and

---

7. Holland, Jeffrey R. "'Lord, I Believe.'" *Ensign* 43, no. 5, May 2013.

so we stood up for ourselves. Finally, in the face of resistance, we are now treated as a "belief," an "ideology," or a "faith crisis." Instead of making our queerness a human experience, it is made a religious experience. This is because that is how religion first experienced us. And this experience is filtered through the straight/cisgender lens of our initial hosts of the Restoration.

Since its launch into space, the Hubble telescope has been producing images of stars with four points because all incoming light on its way to Hubble's main mirror bends past four crosshair struts holding the secondary mirror in position. Once the James Webb telescope became operational, it sent back images of stars with six points. These striking six spikes of light result from diffraction from the overlapping of the hexagonally-segmented mirror and the secondary mirror.[8] As humans, we depend on these mirrors, these lenses into space, to see these faraway stars. Stars do not inherently have four points or six. Light emanates from these stars in all directions. Fundamentally, seeing spikes in stars is not a problem if we understand these are artifacts of our human-made lenses. But what if we don't? What if our reality is founded upon artifacts? If we think the image is reality and don't account for diffraction and flares, we build an idea of reality on something that isn't really there.

Within Mormonism, we are a 2SLGBTQIA+ community with a shared experience, navigating a plan of salvation not built for us. The hosts of the Restoration tell us the system is not broken—we are broken. Looking at queer people through the struts of the heterosexual/cisgender lens, queer sexual orientation or gender identity is seen as attraction, behavior, or choice. Using these metrics as the basis to forbid queer people

---

8. Novak, Sara. "Why Do Stars Look So Pointy in James Webb Space Telescope Images?" *Astronomy Magazine*, May 18, 2023. https://www.astronomy.com/space-exploration/why-do-stars-look-so-pointy-in-james-webb-space-telescope-images/.

from participating in the very rites and blessings that not only solve religion's earthly problem of concupiscence or gender dysphoria but which are essential for exaltation is like going into Eden and cutting down both trees to keep our first parents forever in the garden. It ruins the plan of salvation. Without queer spiritual equity and justice, the plan of salvation is ruined for queer Latter-day Saints and their families, leaving us to remain under the rainbow stained-glass ceiling in life only to receive one of the many consolation prize heavens in death, away from our families and heavenly parents for all eternity.

In the ongoing Restoration, we have been seeing queer Latter-day Saints through various telescopes during our 200-year-old history. Dominant narratives have been created by seeing things in queer people that really aren't there. The different and changing points encountered over time as the Church sees us are, in reality, artifacts that result from bending the light of a queer soul through the struts of the straight/cisgender lens. It is time to show the hospitality of the ongoing Restoration to queer Latter-day Saints. It is time to see us as God sees us: Queer children of heavenly parents, artifact-free and filled with God's light, illuminating the heavens in all directions.

When considering the many areas in the ongoing Restoration where LGBTQ Latter-day Saints are not shown hospitality, three readily come to mind. The first is General Conference. Once, Peggy Fletcher Stack asked me in an interview if Affirmation leaders watch General Conference to monitor for anti-LGBTQ speech. I candidly replied, "I watch General Conference to be spiritually edified."⁹ Unfortunately, I sometimes do encounter rejecting words during General Conference that grieve the Spirit. In an authoritative attempt at "othering," conference speakers sometimes make judgments and advance misconceptions about LGBTQ people and their families that simply are not true. I know they are not true because I know my LGBTQ peers, and I see Christ in them.

Many LGBTQ Latter-day Saints who hear prejudice from the pulpit—no matter how dogmatically justified, beautifully articulated, or sincerely held—experience a great deal of trauma from such words. A lot of this is the cognitive dissonance experienced from hearing very true words one minute and then being confronted with incorrect assertions about gender identity and sexual orientation the next. But this is the nature of prejudice. Prejudice can comfortably live alongside some of the greatest truths and ideals humans hold dear.

As president of Affirmation, I would send out little message snacks dispersed here and there during General Conference weekend. This way, my peers knew Affirmation was aware of what was being said, would feel us stand up for them on any egregious parts, and then hear an affirming voice as they practiced their own self-care. These messaging snacks would revolve around seven common themes I had identified that LGBTQ Latter-day Saints universally encounter from our hosts in the ongoing Restoration:

- You are not responsible for theological shortcomings taught over the pulpit about LGBTQ people. Your existence is not to blame for another's prejudice.

---

9. Stack, Peggy Fletcher, and David Noyce. "'Mormon Land': Affirmation Leader Discusses the Challenges LGBTQ Latter-Day Saints Face around the World." *The Salt Lake Tribune*, September 9, 2020. https://www.sltrib.com/religion/2020/09/09/mormon-land-affirmation/.

- Do not pick up and carry the burden laid at your feet that it is your fault as a queer person for not ending up with God or your family in the eternities. You exist in a system not made for you and currently refuses to make room for you.

- LGBTQ people are entitled to meaningful and powerful revelation to lead their lives by the Spirit. This revelation is valid.

- The Restoration of the gospel began with a question. God appreciates questions. Jesus taught in questions. Christ loves questions so much that he made continuing revelation a feature in his Church just for questions. As an LGBTQ person, be wary of those who are intimidated or angered by your questions.

- As an LGBTQ person, you are whole, equal, and complete. Christ requires a broken heart and a contrite spirit. He does not require a broken you.

- You are surrounded by thousands upon thousands of supportive voices both within and outside the Church who want to see you have the same opportunities as your straight/cisgender peers.

- The trifecta of LGBTQ prejudice, harassment, and discrimination is still ugly, even if it is clothed in the brilliant and glorious vestments of the restored gospel of Jesus Christ.

A second area where LGBTQ Latter-day Saints are not shown hospitality is in the temple. As I scroll over the years of pictures of Affirmation's in-person regional conferences around the world, one common theme appears. If the conference is near a temple, Affirmation members will often go to the temple grounds, tour the outside, and take a group picture out front. To some, it seems odd that people who are rejected from entering are drawn to the temple. On the contrary, doing so makes perfect sense. Queer Latter-day Saints and former Latter-day Saints are reclaiming symbols. The temple is important to each queer person for a myriad of reasons. It is the House of the Lord and symbolizes the house of our people. Temples for queer Latter-day Saints of faith are full of the potential energy of godliness. Whether or not we are allowed entry to realize such potential energy converted into kinetic energy within our lifetime is unknown. But this much I know, it is not us as a queer people who are limiting such a conversion.

Despite Laurie Lee Hall's breathtaking temple designs beloved by both members and prophets—physical icons of a church connecting heaven to earth—she was removed from her position as the Church's chief architect of temples for no other reason than she was a transgender woman. Laurie brought her talents, discarded by the Church, to build and connect LGBTQ souls, their families, and friends who take shelter under this house she helped build in Affirmation. Laurie recalled the attempts by the modern church to eliminate her name, her voice, and her connection to any of her work or service within the Church after she was forced from her employment because she was transgender.[10] As her community of the queer children of God, we remembered her when others would not.

Laurie was the architect of the temple in my hometown, where I sat excluded in its waiting room as my daughter was

---

10. Kitchen, Nathan. "The Most American Religion's Transgender Temple Architect." Affirmation, December 18, 2020. Accessed July 71, 2024. https://affirmation.org/the-most-american-religions-transgender-temple-architect/.

upstairs getting married. Laurie made that space for me, not knowing me but knowing what that space needed to accomplish for those like me who sat there. Most tenderly, when my son returned home from the Gilbert temple after receiving his endowments, he reminded me that he sat in a temple Laurie had designed and built. I had spent that morning alone on my couch, stung by the separation of the queer family woven deeply into the fabric of temple worship. As he gave me a hug, I instantly felt tears and swelling of love for the Church's transgender architect, my friend, and now my colleague. A part of her—this space she created as a transgender woman—stood as a proxy for me to be with my son when I could not. Laurie had not been erased from our memory as a family. On that weekend my son received his endowments, Laurie's design and spaces were a symbol to my family that pointed us past the exclusions of our day and to the safe space of Christ's eternal love. It was the very fulfillment of the hope of the architect that their designs may uplift, inspire, and function—ultimately enhancing our lived experiences in this life.

A third place queer Latter-day Saints are not shown great hospitality is queerness in the scriptures. Finding ourselves as a queer person in the scriptures is challenging when we have no clear way to find ourselves within the plan of salvation. Arch defenders of the status quo stand ready to bat us down as we rise above the interpretive lenses of the hosts of the Restoration. In her book *Queer Mormon Theology*, Blaire Ostler shares the queer theology hidden in plain sight within our Latter-day Saint scripture and teaching. It remains stubbornly hidden but so refreshing as more and more queer Latter-day Saints begin to find themselves in the scriptures and then instruct us all for our profit and learning.

In July 2020, I taught the Dialogue Gospel Study that follows the "Come Follow Me" curriculum. Covering Alma's born-again experience (Alma 36-37), I likened this to what happens when a queer person confronts the prejudice of a dominant narrative and then rises from underneath its capture to experience a fresh view about God, themselves, and their place as authentic queer children of God in this world. I first talked about what it meant to be born again in the context of being born of God. This process involves Christ, for there is no repentance without Christ. As with Alma's experience, Christ is in the middle of it all. How we intersect with Christ is a tender and sacred experience, the very essence of being born of God. And it is sacredly subjective. Objective steps of repentance—no matter how worthy the list, no matter how authoritative the person giving you a list—don't make you whole. It is Christ that heals you. Christ is not our jailer; Christ is our liberator (Acts 16:25-31). By focusing on Christ, not lists, repentance becomes a Christ-centered rethinking. It is the divine that heals you. It is the love of Christ that burns in your heart that comforts and transforms you. I observed that queer people in the Church have also been given objective lists on how to be an acceptable queer in the kingdom. Many queer people focus on policies rather than on Christ for salvation. In all this, the focus is on brokenness. Queer salvation is not in brokenness. Our brokenness is swallowed up in Christ. And it is at this realization that we comprehend that our souls will not be left in hell, or as Alma said, that he would not be "banished and become extinct both soul and body" (Alma 36:15). Christ overcomes this and is at the center of it all. It happens to each of us subjectively and is essential in our declaration that we are born of God. I then paused in the lesson, broke the fourth wall, and addressed my queer peers directly: "As an LGBTQ Latter-day Saint, you are not broken, for as an LGBTQ Christian, only your heart needs to be. You may stand tall in the great heritage of Saints who gift a broken heart and a contrite spirit" (3 Nephi 9:19-20). Such is the privilege of every Christian in every age.

As I concluded, I bore testimony that despite being a marginalized population in the Church—even refugees from the faith—LGBTQ members continually have deep and meaningful experiences with Christ that are just as sacred and just as spiritually intense as Alma's experience when he was born again. Queer people have the same intensity of love for the gospel that we see in the general Latter-day Saint population; they just demonstrate it in a system that was not built for them. They do it as they pioneer through the scriptures to find themselves within the pages. It did not take much for me to positively include queer people in a "Come Follow Me" lesson. In our personal ministry, extending this same hospitality as we teach from the scriptures is an empowering, Christlike attribute that blesses all who have ears to hear.

Today, queer Latter-day Saints come seeking the hospitality of the hosts of the Restoration. We have traveled from our heavenly home to sojourn with the Saints. Yet, today, the seed of Abraham has yet to practice his radical hospitality where "Hospitality to travelers is greater than welcoming the presence of the Shekhinah—the presence of God."[11]

---

11. Talmud Shabbat 127a

CHAPTER 27

A Light on a Hill

> 14 Ye are the light of the world. A city that is set on an hill cannot be hid.
> 15 Neither do men light a candle, and put it under a bushel, but on a candlestick; and it giveth light unto all that are in the house.
> 16 Let your light so shine before men, that they may see your good works, and glorify your Father which is in heaven.
>
> Matthew 5: 14-16

In February 2021, the Equality Act, which aimed to add LGBTQ people to the 1964 Civil Rights Act, passed the Democratic-controlled House and headed to the Republican-controlled Senate. The day after its passage, Utah Representative Chris Stewart introduced competing legislation, the Fairness for All Act. The *Deseret News* reported that Stewart's bill would "boost protections for people of faith."[1] I sighed. Are queer people not people of faith? I was weary of the continual drumbeat that queer people could only belong to the "people of faith" club if they subscribed—as a part of their covenants as a Latter-day Saint—to the conditions of their own discrimination and inequality. Despite the Fairness for All buzzwords of "win-win," "equal protections for all," and "equality and fairness," many queer people of faith inherently know that any Fairness for All legislation means enhanced protections for prejudice and discrimination under the rainbow stained-glass ceiling.

My queer peers in the civil arena were doing remarkable work advancing LGBTQ rights in a pluralistic society. Their voice is so strong and reasoned that it has been taken seriously by the modern church for many years as one to communicate and negotiate with. Since my wheelhouse as president of Affirmation was building community within the queer/Latter-day Saint intersection—where the voice of the queer Latter-day Saint is captured by dominant narrative and policy, protected by religious freedom—I wanted to make a "cry from the intersection." I wanted to provide a point of view on the dominant narrative currently steamrolling the conversation about the Equality Act. I penned an op-ed in *The Salt Lake Tribune*, highlighting the institutional church's outward-facing historical tussles in politics, social issues, and government matters. I posited that by ignoring LGBTQ rights today, the modern church forgets lessons learned from the past and perpetuates discrimination and exclusion of LGBTQ people in a misguided effort to protect itself.

---

1. Dallas, Kelsey. "Latter-Day Saint Leaders Join Other Faith Groups Sharing Support for Stewart's LGBTQ Rights Bill." *Deseret News*, February 26, 2021. https://www.deseret.com/indepth/2021/2/26/22297987/chris-stewart-reintroduces-bill-to-expand-lgbtq-rights-religious-freedom-utah-equality-act/.

Recalling that President Nelson had urged each of us to abandon attitudes of prejudice against any group or individual, I emphasized that while this was essential, it was a process that took time. "Minorities cannot wait, nor should they wait, for prejudice to be wiped from the hearts of a people before they experience equality. The truth is, equal opportunity and equality actually come before acceptance, and they must come protected by anti-discrimination laws. It takes institutional courage to accept LGBTQ equality while still working to abandon prejudice. Latter-day Saint families with LGBTQ children are counting on this kind of courage from the church."[2]

The day my op-ed was published in *The Salt Lake Tribune*, Affirmation's contact at the Church Communication Department texted me, informing me that they were coming out with a public statement that the Church was not supporting the Equality Act. I shared with them that my op-ed supporting the Equality Act written from a queer-centric Latter-day Saint perspective had just been published at *The Salt Lake Tribune* that morning and sent them the link. Later that afternoon, they asked if we could have a face-to-face meeting over Zoom the upcoming Friday, March 5. Their boss wanted to join and speak with me. They had obviously now read my op-ed.

Since the Office of Public Affairs dissolved, Religious Freedom has been in the room with Affirmation. This frustrated me. It was my continual reminder to join the two-handed conversation between the modern church and the LGBTQ community if we wanted to be heard. I was continually struggling to amplify

---

2. Kitchen, Nathan. "Nathan Kitchen: Time for the LDS Church to Accept LGBTQ Equality." *The Salt Lake Tribune*, March 2, 2021. https://www.sltrib.com/opinion/commentary/2021/03/02/nathan-kitchen-time-lds/.

the experience of the queer Latter-day Saint as something other than unfaithful, angry, or attacking amid the cacophony of the dominant narrative.

A good part of our meeting was spent educating me on why the Fairness For All Act was superior to the Equality Act—that this was the middle ground forward, balancing rights for everyone. Despite the presentation, I was still not inspired by Fairness for All, seeing it as a way to encourage and foster internal prejudice and discrimination within the spiritual home of LGBTQ Latter-day Saints, making LGBTQ exclusion a morally acceptable prejudice. Morally acceptable prejudice leads to harassment and discrimination, and to accept it seemed an unprincipled action for an organization such as Affirmation to take, considering our mission to create safe and affirming spaces for LGBTQ Latter-day Saints. As I attempted to communicate the challenges within the unique place queer Latter-day Saints occupy in their spiritual home, I could see that these seeds were falling on barren ground. Those hired by the Church to dialogue about political matters on a playing field of good faith negotiations and constructive politics did not have the ears to hear about the lived experiences of queer members navigating their intersections with the Church, let alone do anything about it. Such things were not in their wheelhouse, just as LGBTQ politics were not in mine. As we talked past each other for most of our meeting, I tried not to let my eyes glaze over. I felt powerless watching a huge, extremely well-funded political machine describe their lobbying efforts to strengthen their religious freedom to better discriminate against their own LGBTQ members. But then, we got to the good part.

Our Friday meeting's singular focus on federal legislation surprised me, given the absolutely earth-shattering event that happened the night before at BYU-Provo. The previous day was Rainbow Day at all the BYU campuses. These happen twice a year, in the fall to coincide with National Coming Out Day and in the spring to coincide with the March anniversary of the 2020 BYU Honor Code rollback fiasco. On Rainbow Day, students and allies wear rainbow colors as a visible sign of love and support for queer students and faculty at all Church Educational System schools.

The day began normally enough. I sent out a message of support from Affirmation with a picture of me and the rainbow-colored shoes that carried me through the World Pride march: "You have a whole bunch of people who are proud of you and love and support you in so many ways." What I was really waiting for was the eight o'clock hour that evening. A few days earlier, one of the organizers at BYU-Provo contacted me to give me a heads-up about what queer student leaders were planning at the end of Rainbow Day. They wanted to keep it confidential until it unfolded, but wanted queer community leaders to know so we could be prepared for the reaction. Even in my wildest imagination, I had no idea how stunning this would be.

As we reached the appointed hour, I kept my phone close. And then my contact sent me the first picture. The Y on the mountain overlooking BYU was lit top to bottom in bright, brilliant rainbow colors—piercing the darkness with red, orange, yellow, green, blue, and purple light. It was spectacular. It took my breath away. As a BYU grad and president of Affirmation, fully understanding the gravity and visibility of this moment, I could not hold back the tears. "Well, rise and shout, the Cougars are out!" I said in ugly cry voice as I showed Matthew the pictures starting to come in. I immediately shared the lit rainbow

Y into the four corners of social media: "LGBTQIA+ BYU and CES students, you ARE the light unto all that are in the house!"

That massive white block letter Y towers prominently over Utah Valley up on the mountainside, a reminder of the Lord's University below. It has done so for generations, a symbol of the pride and identity of Brigham Young University. A white Y, it turns out, is a blank canvas primed and ready to project colored lights like a projector screen in a campus classroom. That night, in rainbow colors, we were unmistakably reminded that sometimes Latter-day Saints are queer. All of Utah Valley turned to the mountain that night, looking up at the icon they had grown accustomed to in their everyday lives in a completely new light. The following day, I received a message from the mother of a twelve-year-old young man in Utah Valley who had just come out. She asked me to thank those responsible for lighting the Y in beautiful rainbow colors: "My twelve-year-old needs to see that there are many people in the community who see and love him just as he is!"

Seeing that it was time to kick the elephant in the Zoom room out into the middle, I commented: "I am sure you are aware of what happened at BYU when LGBTQ students lit the Y in rainbow colors." Indicating they had, I pointed out the terse, highly problematic communication that BYU-Provo issued about Rainbow Day on Twitter: "BYU did not authorize the lighting of the Y tonight."[3] Continuing the scolding, university spokeswoman Carri Jenkins told the *Deseret News*, "It appears it was lit by individuals on the Y with colored lights. The Y is BYU prop-

---

3. BYU (@BYU), "BYU did not authorize the lighting of the Y tonight." X, March 4, 2021 8:22 PM. https://x.com/BYU/status/1367676851343085571.

erty, and any form of public expression on university property requires prior approval. We intend to make certain that members of our campus community understand this."[4] A more perfect Dolores Umbridge response could not have been written.

Clamping down on "any form of public expression" was precisely what BYU had done a year earlier during the 2020 Honor Code changes. The rhetoric about the lighting of the Y ripped open every trauma and emotion from a year earlier when queer students were made to understand that homosexual romantic public expression, like a rainbow Y, was not approved. The messaging that night over social media and to the press was tone-deaf and inflammatory. I asked my hosts at Church Communication if this was representative of the message the Church wanted to broadcast about its values and practices, especially towards LGBTQ Latter-day Saints. The tone of the message reminded me of the terse press release the Church had issued in 2008, venting its displeasure at Affirmation for holding a press conference about the lived experiences of gays and lesbians within the Church. That tussle cooled relations and delayed any communication between Affirmation and the modern church for five years before it was reopened. What might last night's messaging damage? I asked if they had read President John S. K. Kauwe's response to the Rainbow Days events on Hawaii's campus. They had not.

For Rainbow Day at BYU–Hawaii, Affirmation BYU student leaders held an activity to paint colorful pictures and rainbow

---

4. Walch, Tad. "Group Lights BYU's 'Y' on Mountain with Rainbow-Colored Lights." *Deseret News*, March 4, 2021. https://www.deseret.com/faith/2021/3/4/22314855/group-lights-byus-y-on-mountain-with-rainbow-colored-lights-provo-lgbtq/.

rocks to let queer students know they were loved and supported. As the Affirmation Hawaii student leaders handed out rainbow rocks across campus, their fellow students proudly carried them around, placed them outside their dorm windows, and made them visible on-screen during Zoom classes. Faculty members put the student's colorful pictures on their doors and windows.

As Hao Le, president of Affirmation Hawaii, was handing out rainbow rocks, she messaged President Kauwe and asked if he wanted a Rainbow Day rock, an act of Aloha. Not waiting for a response, she gathered a couple of her fellow student Affirmation members and headed to the president's office. As they approached, they saw President Kauwe walking out the door. Not wanting to miss him (Hao told me he walks *really* fast), they ran after him. When they caught up with him, they excitedly told him about Rainbow Day and presented him with their simple but meaningful hand-painted rainbow rock. Hao asked President Kauwe if he would make a simple post of support and love on social media like other BYU-Hawaii professors were doing. These messages were helping make the campus a safe place for all students. She told him that the student leaders of Affirmation Hawaii had deeply appreciated working directly with the administration on LGBTQ+ issues over the past year. However, without an affirming message from BYU-Hawaii, "we still live in fear." Later that evening, President Kauwe posted a picture of Hao's rainbow rock on Instagram and included a beautiful, affirming post acknowledging Rainbow Day, appreciating the diversity found on the campus.

I pulled up President Kauwe's Instagram post and read it to the Church Communication Department. In it, he expressed his love to every student at BYU-Hawaii, pointing out that they came from more than 60 countries and many different walks of life. He reminded the student body, faculty, and administration that "[t]ogether we continue to work to develop a campus where each student strives to honor their covenants and commitments, where each student exhibits Christ-like love for themselves and those around them, and where each student feels safe and loved."[5] Instead of ignoring the presence or work of LGBTQ students on that special day, he concluded: "I want [to] thank each student, especially those who expressed love and felt loved today, for working to build that campus through communication, cooperation, and respect."[6]

Navigating back to my Zoom screen, I looked at my hosts and noted that President Kauwe's message was a master class on how to give a trauma-informed response. Nothing in his post was contrary to gospel principles, yet he had just made LGBTQ students feel seen and loved. It hit all the notes. This was the tale of two responses from the BYUs. In just a few tweets, BYU-Provo created tension, division, and a power struggle with its queer students, whereas in a single post, BYU-Hawaii had created a feeling of community.

Lighting the Y was not a protest. It was the gift of visibility. It was queer BYU students who did not feel seen, showing themselves to BYU and the world for one very cold, dark hour on a mountainside—one hour of visibility in the 8,670 hours of a year. This is an example of why Elder Christofferson's "two-hand" model does not work to describe the location of queer Latter-day Saints. If the queer part has to be ignored or erased as a condition of participation in the faith-inspiring part, you are going to get a queer Latter-day Saint population who will find ways to be seen and heard. It is critical to understand that the existence of visible queer people in faith-inspiring communities

---

5. Kauwe, Keoni (@keoni.kauwe) "I love every student at BYU-Hawaii. We come from more than 60 countries and many different walks of life." Instagram, March 4, 2021. Accessed July 27, 2024. https://www.instagram.com/p/CMBtds2hKwM/?igsh=ZzlsZmxnMG02eDh1.

6. Kauwe, Keoni (@keoni.kauwe) Instagram, March 4, 2021.

is not an act of protest. Visibility is not a protest. And the harder a power center tries to suppress the queer spirit, the stronger queer visibility will brilliantly pop out from around the edges.

At the close of Rainbow Day, BYU-Hawaii had a message that faced its LGBTQ students. Its queer students felt loved and seen. BYU-Provo's message looked right past its LGBTQ students as if they were invisible, instead facing the public as it Tweeted from the hip. It did not have to be this way. Even if BYU-Provo felt it needed to issue a statement, it could have been almost identical to BYU-Hawaii's, taking a page out of Elder M. Russell Ballard's playbook to "understand what our LGBT brothers and sisters are feeling and experiencing."[7] Instead, BYU-Provo's response that evening projected the kind of trash talk we would expect from an ego-bruised basketball player who just got dunked on. No one got dunked on. The take-home message to my hosts? Be like BYU-Hawaii.

With time running short in our Zoom meeting, the Communication Department asked if I would send them a copy of President Kauwe's Instagram statement so they could share it at headquarters as an example of better public communication moving forward concerning LGBTQ issues. As I attached it in an email, my thoughts turned to the LGBTQ BYU students who had lit the Y. The university's threat to make certain that members of the campus community understood the seriousness of the unauthorized display of a rainbow Y was ominous. I expressed my deep concern that the LGBTQ students who lit the Y would now be hunted down by the Honor Code Office and brought in for disciplinary action and possibly expulsion from the university. I told my hosts that this was not right. The BYU Police Department confirmed that no crime was committed:

---

7. Ballard, M. Russell, "Questions and Answers." BYU Speeches, November 14, 2017. Accessed July 27, 2024. https://speeches.byu.edu/talks/m-russell-ballard/questions-and-answers/.

"Flashlights don't meet the elements of vandalism."[8] Punitive action by the Honor Code Office for something that was not a crime or prohibited explicitly by the Honor Code would ruin the lives of these BYU students for absolutely no reason, making such action appear as animus towards queer students. Not only would such action be devastating, but it would be seen as "punching down," striking a blow to the Church's relationship-building efforts with the LGBTQ community. I formally requested on behalf of Affirmation that these students not be hunted down and brought in for discipline. I was promised they would take this request "up the line."

Let's not ruin lives over flashlights.

---

8. Gonzalez, Sydnee. "LGBT Students and Allies Light the 'Y' in Rainbow Colors." *The Daily Universe*, March 4, 2021. https://universe.byu.edu/2021/03/04/lgbt-students-and-allies-light-the-y-in-rainbow-colors/.

CHAPTER 28

The Family Will Endure

> 12 And as I partook of the fruit thereof it filled my soul with exceedingly great joy; wherefore, I began to be desirous that my family should partake of it also; for I knew that it was desirable above all other fruit.
>
> 13 And . . . I cast my eyes round about, that perhaps I might discover my family also.
>
> 1 Nephi 8:12-13

Now, at the end of June, with Affirmation's summertime programming coming to a close, it was time to finish organizing September's International Conference. At the beginning of the year, Affirmation's board considered the many unknowns that still existed with the worldwide pandemic. Even though vaccines were available in the United States and community gatherings were cautiously starting up again, this was not the case throughout the world. COVID was still a real danger for most Affirmation members outside the United States. Inbound international travel was still heavily restricted, and there was no prediction of when that might change. Additionally, global forecasts predicted a surge of COVID infections in the fall. Weighing the risks to our members with our mandate of community building, Affirmation's board plotted a course to hold the International Conference virtually in 2021 with an eye to meeting again in person in 2022. I had my marching orders. I was excited to get building.

If only 2021 could have just been about managing COVID. Turns out, the lighting of the rainbow Y had deep implications for the general population of queer Latter-day Saints. It seemed the modern church saw that action as a direct threat by a rising power—one that had just assaulted its beloved icon on a mountainside that symbolized its very identity. It moved to assert its dominance.

At the end of August, Elder Jeffery R. Holland, apostle and former president of BYU-Provo, stood and addressed BYU faculty and staff. He recalled how special he felt as a seven-year-old when he first saw that huge block "Y" on the mountainside, "white and bold and beautiful."[1] He reminisced how special BYU had been to him for sixty-nine years. He then shared a letter from an unnamed concerned citizen expressing that "some people" felt abandoned and betrayed by BYU. These people believed that some faculty did not support the Church's doctrines and policies, even criticizing them publicly. They went on to lament that BYU now appeared to be like any other university their sons and daughters could attend, indicating that several

---

1. Holland, Jeffrey R. "The Second Half of the Second Century of Brigham Young University." BYU Speeches, August 23, 2021. Accessed July 27, 2024. https://speeches.byu.edu/talks/jeffrey-r-holland/the-second-half-second-century-brigham-young-university/.

parents no longer wanted to send their children there or donate to the school.

I noted that this was not a new sentiment by any means. Over the past twenty years, I consistently listened to my conservative Arizona friends express that they would not send their children to BYU-Provo because it was too liberal. They would only send them to BYU-Idaho, where the "gospel is pure and the university true." Even when I was in high school in Illinois, I received pushback from people in my ward for going to BYU-Provo because "they teach evolution there, and that goes against God."

I found it curious that Elder Holland drew on an anecdotal story—"We don't get too many of those letters"[2]—to establish how things were going to be from now on at "the BYU" about all the queer stuff. He told the story of the temple builders in Nauvoo who, amid the hostility of their Illinois neighbors, worked with a trowel in one hand and a musket in the other. Drawing a comparison, he argued: "Today, scholars building the temple of learning must also pause on occasion to defend the kingdom."[3] He quoted President Oaks, who used this story several years ago to call on BYU faculty to handle both trowels and muskets: "I would like to hear a little more musket fire from this temple of learning."[4] Elder Holland referenced notable firefights at BYU since that time, and indicated that those who fired their muskets sometimes didn't always aim at those hos-

---

2. Holland, Jeffrey R. "The Second Half of the Second Century of Brigham Young University." August 23, 2021.

3. Holland, Jeffrey R. "The Second Half of the Second Century of Brigham Young University." August 23, 2021.

4. Holland, Jeffrey R. "The Second Half of the Second Century of Brigham Young University." August 23, 2021.

tile to the Church. A couple of stray rounds "went north of the Point of the Mountain,"[5] hitting the brethren at headquarters.

I gasped at this violent metaphor. Never mind that LGBTQ people were the target in his speech. In this scenario, it was the brethren who felt fired upon. This reminded me of when the Saints in southern Utah used revolvers to protect the polygamous brethren walking the grounds of the St. George Temple, targeted for capture by US Marshals hostile to the practice of polygamous marriage.[6] Now, 140 years later, the Saints were again asked to take up arms against a perceived threat to marriage and family in the Church. Only this time, instead of revolvers towards US Marshals, it was muskets towards LGBTQ people.

Elder Holland paused, possibly cognizant of the violence he was illustrating: "Let me go no farther before declaring unequivocally my love and that of my Brethren for those who live with this same-sex challenge and so much complexity that goes with it."[7] I winced at his assertion. I recalled that the spiritual violence of the exclusion policy was also excused by the brethren through love. After recounting the hours of weeping that the brethren undergo as they consider how "unkind" and "crushingly cruel" the world is to LGBTQ people, he took direct aim at them: "Be careful that love and empathy do not get interpreted as condoning and advocacy."[8] He declared that love and empathy can become "friendly fire," where instead of defend-

---

5. Holland, Jeffrey R. "The Second Half of the Second Century of Brigham Young University." August 23, 2021.

6. Woodbury, Grace Atkin, and Agnus Munn Woodbury. "Wilford Woodruff On the Underground." Manuscript. In *The Story of Atkinville: A One-Family Village*, 29. 1957. Washington County Historical Society. https://wchsutah.org/documents/woodbury-atkinville-book2.pdf.

7. Holland, Jeffrey R. "The Second Half of the Second Century of Brigham Young University." August 23, 2021.

8. Holland, Jeffrey R. "The Second Half of the Second Century of Brigham Young University." August 23, 2021.

ing the faith, it wounds students and the parents of students who are "confused about what so much recent flag-waving and parade-holding on this issue means."⁹ This comment revealed the intentions of Elder Holland's remarks. He was defending his white Y against flag-waving, parade-holding, and flashlight-bearing. The lighting of the Y in rainbow colors was seen as a direct attack on the family and marriage, another in a decades-long line of skirmishes between the modern church and the LGBTQ civil rights movement. He then made his final call: "My Brethren have made the case for the metaphor of musket fire, which I have endorsed yet again today."¹⁰

I instinctively jumped out of my chair, heart racing. I recognized what I was experiencing. It was the adrenalin-pumping anticipation of inbound trauma. I spent a year on call during my residency at the hospital at the University of Iowa. This was the same feeling I had when the hospital operator would page me in the middle of the night, jolting me out of bed, alerting me that trauma was inbound to the Emergency Department via ambulance. Elder Holland's speech was a 911 emergency for queer Latter-day Saints and their families. They now had a physical metaphor of violence that matched the spiritual violence they were already experiencing on an eternal scale. The doctrinal premise that queer people, in their authenticity, cannot be exalted was already roiling the great houses of Zion. Now, they had just been told that to be faithful to the doctrine of the Church, they must not only be faithful to a dominant narrative about their queer children built from prejudice, but they must defend it. Faced with the premise of eternal rejection that such thinking demands, Elder Holland's speech exacerbated the sim-

---

9. Holland, Jeffrey R. "The Second Half of the Second Century of Brigham Young University." August 23, 2021.

10. Holland, Jeffrey R. "The Second Half of the Second Century of Brigham Young University." August 23, 2021.

mering existential anxiety about the survivability of their own family in the eternities. So many people were hurt, confused, angry, and frightened. Most felt unsafe. I carefully considered my responsibility as president of Affirmation to build communities of safety, love, and hope. Those three attributes were missing from Elder Holland's speech and the conversations that followed. I thoughtfully penned a presidential response, not to Elder Holland but to the families of Zion.

Protect Your Queer Children Under the Boughs of Love

Elder Holland reiterated in his speech to BYU faculty and staff that it is a serious sin for sexual minorities to participate in the blessings, stability, and safety of fidelity, family, and love within the bonds of marriage as their straight peers do. To teach otherwise requires a violent defending of the faith (insert musket metaphors here).

"Acceptable" sexual minorities must instead live their entire life as celibate singles, outsiders among their pair-bonded straight peers in a church that values fidelity, family, and love. Elder Holland stated BYU is prepared to lose professional affiliations and certifications over this issue, and he will personally go to his grave defending against marriage equality. This is PTSD: "bury the foundation of the Salt Lake temple because an army is marching upon us" talk. In actuality, queer joy and equality are something deeper and ever so tender to talk about within our families in Zion.

You can posture all you want, threatening to bury the very foundations of BYU, but there is no gay army marching upon the church requiring muskets and fire. Instead, in homes across Zion, LGBTQIA+ children are born daily to families entrusted by their heavenly parents to care for these beautifully perfect, queer children of God. They are born into the covenant. They are not invaders of the covenant.

You cannot build walls and fortresses to keep them out, for they are already a part of us, already a part of the sealed network of Saints. But you can use musket fire to drive them out from among you, from their spiritual home and from their families, through exclusionary positions and rejecting behavior. You can teach them that they are different from their straight peers, so they must carry the burden of difference, like a mark. Marks are a very Mormon thing, and they find support throughout modern-day scripture as a way to "other" family. Once othered, you can feel justified to withhold blessings and opportunity. It is a design flaw in our orthopraxy, and it even colors how we obey the second great commandment.

This is where we must begin as families in Zion. We must begin to talk about what it truly means when we say, "Families are forever," and then in the same breath, "All are alike unto God." Why do the scriptures teach that God's people are prosperous when their laws are formed according to equity and justice?

If you are lucky enough, you will be one of the thousands upon thousands of families in the church who have a queer child. Parents must begin the conversations under the Tree of Life, as a type and a shadow of Lehi and Sariah, on how they will not leave their queer children behind to be driven into the mists of darkness or fired upon from the great and spacious building.

Unashamedly bring your authentic and completely whole queer children to stand with you under the boughs of Love.

Dig past the early Western frontier language of our young faith of siege, muskets, armies, and isolation. Dig past the posturing, the fear, and the othering. Dig past it all and dig to uncover your family foundation to build a house that shelters your queer children. You are living in a home-centered, church-supported era, and this holds just as true for homes with queer children. Insist that the church supports your home that you have built. The house you build will shelter them. You are not under siege, for in this world that Elder Holland admits is incredibly hostile to queer people, you are a sacred refuge for your queer children. Do not feel ashamed or intimidated that you want your queer children to have all that you have, including loving relationships built upon fidelity and blessed by God.

The Tree of Life is expansive, and so many queer Latter-day Saints are pressing forward towards it. Unfortunately, now able to make the same choice as their straight, cisgender peers to partake in legal marriage, they must shield themselves from musket fire and endure the speeches, finger-pointing, and scoffs from others who are angered by this new choice. Parents, keep calling to your queer children as they press forward in faith and authenticity. Build a house of love and refuge.

Begin today to have a family plan to meet under the boughs of Love.[11]

---

11. Kitchen, Nathan. "Protect Your Queer Children under the Boughs of Love." Affirmation, August 28, 2021. Accessed July 27, 2024. https://affirmation.org/protect-your-queer-children-under-the-boughs-of-love/.

The Church has worked out eternal family rejection once before in its history. Jaxon Washburn illustrated this during a road trip in the summer of 2022 to visit religiously significant sites while on a semester break from Harvard Divinity School. He wrote in a Facebook post that when he reached Palmyra, New York, he stopped at the General John Swift Memorial Cemetery, the final resting place of Joseph Smith's eldest brother, Alvin. Jaxon reflected that it is difficult to overstate the immense impact that Alvin's death had on the trajectory of Joseph's life and the Mormon Restoration as a whole. He recalled Mormon Studies scholar Sam Brown wrote that Joseph did not mince any words expressing that he would rather have died than Alvin. Brown observed, "Coming of age in the culture of holy dying, the Mormon prophet never fully recovered from Alvin's death. Though it would be overly simplistic to attribute all of Smith's religious activity to Alvin, this death cast a long shadow over Joseph Jr.'s career."[12] Alvin's tragic death was made especially bitter when the Smith family was told by their church community that Alvin's fate was hell because he had not been baptized. Later, Joseph and Emma lost their first-born son, whom they named Alvin after Joseph's brother. The thought of the eternal loss of the Alvins in Joseph's life was unbearable. Jaxon had lost his father to death several months prior. Still grieving for his father, he noted that the abiding grief from the loss of the two Alvins "would eventually be swallowed up by the tenor of the Mormon cosmos in its promises of a universal salvation, vicar-

---

12. Brown, Samuel Morris. "Death, Dying, and the Dead. 'Melancholy Reflections': Joseph Smith and Holy Dying." Chapter 1. In *In Heaven As It Is On Earth: Joseph Smith and the Early Mormon Conquest of Death*, 35. New York, New York: Oxford University Press, 2012.

ious ritual practices on behalf of the dead, and families sealed together through the eternities."[13]

As I read Jaxon's heartfelt account, I realized that the desire for the family to endure created an arc of divine justice and love in this dispensation. Reunion in exaltation is the hope rooted deep into the earliest days of the Restoration. Death is the ultimate exclusionary practice, and the Restoration solved it through love. Joseph loved his brother Alvin. He loved his son Alvin. This kind of love is a godly love. Such love is now the queer Mormon's arc towards kinship, slowly bending towards ultimate reconciliation in the ongoing Restoration. We are a religion where we do not leave our children, brothers, sisters, siblings in hell, queer or not. This is the gift of the Alvins. And we can do it again.

But what can the families in Zion do in the meantime as the brethren take their time tending to the doctrine? Just a few days after Elder Holland's musket fire address, I received a letter from the Office of Seventy informing me that the First Presidency had canceled the temple sealing between me and my former spouse. Unlike the first time where I vomited all over my driveway at the earthly cancellation of my marriage through divorce, I was much more reflective in this moment, my emotions much more subdued. I had been through a lot since then. I now had the experiences of many Nathans over what seemed like many lifetimes to draw from. The letter explained that children born in the covenant or sealed to their parents are assured the right and privilege of eternal parentage, declaring: "Such blessings, including your eternal family relationships, will be deter-

---

13. Washburn, Jaxon. 2023. "My heart raced upon reaching Palmyra, beginning to close out the second day of my summer religious road trip." Facebook, February 23, 2023.

https://www.facebook.com/jaxonjwashburn/posts/pfbid0KRFmaGCGX-U6Px7jd8uBvxMrF7ektLARHnvS4vUWf2fzJ2yNv5LtKLxptrjoQiRbHl.

mined by our wise and loving Heavenly Father after we have completed our mortal probation."

I was struck by what this letter was conveying. Despite what the institutional church does to queer people, queer families, and families with queer children, God is the final decider of our eternal family relationships. We can, and should, use this to our advantage. Today, when Latter-day Saints are asked to abandon their queer child or spouse and leave them behind in the eternities, it is time to utilize the "Loving Heavenly Father Clause" like a great parent of the universe would. Joseph Smith observed that while humans are busy judging and condemning one another without mercy, God—the great parent of the universe—looks at the human family with great care and parental regard: "He views them as His offspring, and without any of those contracted feelings that influence the children of men."[14] Parents, lean into your own parental regard and choose your queer children. As queer Latter-day Saints, exhibit great care and choose your queer spouse or partner. These choices are godly choices because this is how our heavenly parents choose to interact with their children. We can choose and nurture inclusive families on Earth in complete trust that a loving Heavenly Father will make it right in the next.

Why cause harm to one another and suffer in this life in family tension, exclusions, estrangements, and separations over rejecting your queer children or experience the haunting absence of a companion, hoping that such unhappiness and harm will be resolved in the next life under the "Loving Heavenly Father Clause?" Walt Whitman said, "Happiness . . . not in another

---

14. Smith, Joseph. "Chapter XXXV." In *History of the Church of Jesus Christ of Latter-Day Saints*, edited by B.H. Roberts, 4:596. Salt Lake City, Utah: The Church of Jesus Christ of Latter-day Saints, 1908.

place, but this place, not for another hour but this hour."[15] This is how the "Loving Heavenly Father Clause" should work. As Lehi said, we exist to have joy. We experience joy surrounded by our family and loved ones in this life. Use the "Loving Heavenly Father Clause" to your advantage and resolve to enjoy an inclusive and affirming family in this life with your queer children, spouse, or partner—and then place your trust in your heavenly parents that they will recognize such goodness as an eternal family relationship in the next. Joseph Smith taught, "The purposes of our God are great. His love unfathomable. His wisdom infinite, and His power unlimited; therefore, the Saints have cause to rejoice and be glad."[16] Rejoice in the choosing of your queer children! Be glad as you choose to marry the love of your life in a way that your heart opens towards love! The "Loving Heavenly Father Clause" will work in your favor despite any "contracted" feelings in mortality that influence the children of men.

In responding to Elder Holland's "Musket Fire" speech and in digesting my letter from the Office of Seventy, my role in Affirmation and my personal life intersected and I felt the tension. As queer Mormons, we watch as the tears of an institution and the tears of our parents compete. The tears of the institution break our bodies as it fits us into a plan of salvation like a bed of Procrustes. The tears of our parents and families bathe us in love. More and more of our parents and families are scooping us up into the boughs of the great houses of Zion to protect us and hold us close, shedding tears as they frantically throw off great sheets of kudzu from their branches.

---

15. Whitman, Walt. "A Song for Occupations." In *Leaves of Grass*, 274. New York, New York: Random House, 2001.

16. Smith, Joseph. "Chapter X." In *History of the Church of Jesus Christ of Latter-Day Saints*, edited by B.H. Roberts, 4:185. Salt Lake City, Utah: The Church of Jesus Christ of Latter-day Saints, 1908.

The modern church can indefinitely go head-to-head with what it sees as the ideology of queerness because it is a holy war to keep queerness out of its doctrine. In contrast, the parents and families of Zion are struggling to keep their own flesh and blood alive within their families in this life and the next. When our parents and family show forth the very care and parental regard to their children and family as our heavenly parents do to theirs, it is an act of godliness. The moral of this great story of the universe is told by the Gods: The family will endure.

As every member of Affirmation does, I brought my intersections with me to our September International Conference. My experiences seemed monumental to me. I also understood that the intersections my peers brought with them were equally monumental and important. None of us have the power to overcome institutional eternal family rejection. None of us have the luxury of being stationary on our trails in life. But we have the power to build communities of safety, love, and hope and then bring our loved ones along with us on our journey. We cannot navigate one another's intersections for them, but we can stand with them in joy and affirm their choices and destinations.

At our closing session, I once again sat in front of my laptop screen as I did in 2020: alone in my study, facing my peers from every corner of the world. I was struck by the gravity of the intersections we brought to one another and the privilege it was to run to our peers, receive their stories, and lift them. I realized more than ever the role of the supportive communities of Affirmation. I spoke from my heart, from my intersections, and cast the hope of community. I shared that one of my favorite hymns is "Come, Come, Ye Saints." The first words we sing in this hymn encourage us to have no fear in our journey, but joy. This can seem difficult to do at times because many of the spaces we encounter in our journey as LGBTQ persons appear to be unsafe and uninviting. But this hymn gives us an important clue about how to make our journey successful and find joy as we live our lives. The clue is in the lyrics. We do not sing this hymn in the singular person. There is no "me" or "I" in this hymn. Instead, we sing using the plural pronouns "us" and "we." We sing this hymn as the hope of an entire community. The secret to finding joy in our journey as LGBTQ people is to be surrounded by a community of peers, mentors, friends, and family. Making the journey through this life by ourselves is isolating and confusing. Being a part of a supportive community is one important way we can find joy in this life. Knowing that we are connected to others who have had similar experiences and affirm the personal choices we make about our lives and spirituality is lifesaving. Filled with the hope of community, I leaned into my screen and concluded:

> I want you to know that I am grateful you are a part of Affirmation. I am so glad you are here. God desires that you might stand proudly in the places you want to stand, that feel safe and healthy for you. And like the hymn promises, together, "We'll find the place which God for us prepared."[17]

May God be with you till we meet again.

---

17. Clayton, William. "Come, Come, Ye Saints." In *Hymns of The Church of Jesus Christ of Latter-Day Saints*, Hymn 30. Salt Lake City, Utah: The Church of Jesus Christ of Latter-day Saints, 1998.

OUR FAMILY PROCLAMATION

At the Tree of Life
Standing under boughs of love
No one left behind

CHAPTER 29

In the Temple with an Apostle

> We dance round in a ring and suppose,
> But the Secret sits in the middle and knows.
>
> Robert Frost

In September 2021, my friend, Tom Christofferson, sent me an invitation on behalf of the Church to attend a special tour of the Mesa Temple for LGBTQIA leaders, with a light supper and conversation to follow. He had been working behind the scenes to help facilitate this event during the open house for the newly renovated Mesa Temple in October before it was rededicated in December. Generally, the first week of a temple open house is reserved for VIP tours for the press, political leaders, community leaders, and religious leaders of different faith traditions. To my knowledge, this was the first time the Church specifically dedicated one evening during its VIP week for LGBTQ people. I was excited to represent Affirmation at this event and was looking forward to touring the temple and seeing the changes.

When my family moved to Arizona, the Mesa Temple was our temple. I spent many hours there doing temple work for my ancestors and baptisms for the dead with my children. Every time I would go in the summer, I had a special spot I liked to sit in the terrestrial room, right next to the giant AC returns mounted in the wall. The gentle, constant flow of frosty air over my body was the best representation of heaven in all of Arizona on a hot summer night. In 2018, the temple closed for three and a half years for extensive renovations. The open house and rededication of the temple were a big deal for all of Mesa. The Mesa Temple is one of the oldest temples in the Church. It is a beloved temple with a history woven directly into the community of Saints. Everyone was anticipating the moment it would be finished. When I confirmed that Matthew and I would be delighted to be there, Tom indicated that his purpose in all this was to provide an opportunity for "more senior church people to find LGBTQ people they can bond with." I was excited about this prospect of relationship building.

On the evening of October 12, Matthew and I arrived at the church building across the street from the temple. The west foyer was set up as the staging area for arriving guests, and the building was swarming with security, church employees, and volunteers. It all had a sense of importance but also a sense of familiarity. The check-in tables were the classroom tables we see every week during Sunday School and primary. The folding chairs were the same metal ones I had been setting up and taking down ever since I was a deacon. It felt like home, with a ward activity vibe. I miss that.

Outside, a team of golf carts efficiently whisked checked-in participants to the new visitor's center across the street from the temple grounds. Matthew and I rode over with the managing director of the temple department, who was curious about our story and about Affirmation. I appreciated that one-on-one time and hoped the evening would continue in such a way. As Matthew and I entered the visitor's center lobby, I stopped in the doorway. It was teeming with people. It took me a minute to get my bearings. I had not expected such a crowd because Tom had billed the evening as a more intimate event. Recognizing me, Troy Williams, the Executive Director of Equality Utah, grabbed my arm and pulled me in. "Welcome to the show!" he said with a smile. He then calibrated my expectations for the evening. As I mingled, Tom shared with me that Elder Jack N. Gerard had decided to jettison the original idea and instead create an opportunity to host the Church's strategic partners from the LGBTQ community.

Looking around the lobby, I saw that it held a diverse representation of well-known local and national LGBTQ community leaders and organizations, many of whom flew to Arizona to participate in this event. As far as I could tell, I was the only faith-based leader in a room full of LGBTQ community leaders who were doing business with the Church in the civil arena. Soon, we were directed into the theater, where Elders Rasband and Gong of the Quorum of the Twelve warmly greeted us. Flanking the apostles were several of the Seventy. As Elder Gerard opened the program, I was struck by the familiarity the General Authorities had with many of these queer community leaders, calling them by name and even sharing inside jokes—a privilege only earned through prolonged engagement over time. It was a completely foreign moment to witness this power dynamic with queer community leaders compared to how the brethren engage with queer Latter-day Saints in-house.

Elder Rasband asked that we take a moment to introduce ourselves and our organizations to one another. I was sitting on the front row with Matthew, and Elder Rasband pointed to me, "Let's start here." I stood, faced my peers, and said, "Hi, my name is Nathan Kitchen. I am the president of Affirmation: LGBTQ Mormons, Families & Friends. I am here tonight with my husband, Matthew Rivera." The audience immediately began applauding. I smiled and waited for the clapping to die down so I could introduce Affirmation.

"Affirmation is a refuge for LGBTQ Mormons to land, heal, share, and be authentic. We are a place for those who feel marginalized in their spiritual ho—"

"Aaaaaaaaand thank you," Elder Rasband interrupted before I could put the period on "home."

Feeling buoyed by the recognition of Affirmation from my queer peers in that room, I had momentarily forgotten that this night was now under the "two-hand" rule. Tonight, from one hand, the Church was talking to the LGBTQ community on the other. It was not a time to acknowledge the margins within the Church. The Church's right to rule those margins was what it sought protections to do in its work with the LGBTQ community.

After our introductions, the brethren presented a compelling look at the work of the Church and the purpose of temples before showing the temple open house video. It made me proud and frustrated at the same time. I straddle two worlds. The ideas presented were absolutely beautiful. However, the Church uses a different dictionary with different meanings assigned to the words that encapsulate these lovely ideas. Unless you are fluent in both dictionaries, a non-native speaker of Mormon can miss the exclusion hidden in plain sight. Words like marriage, family, man, woman, belonging, heaven, eternal life, sealing, worthy, connection—and even joy—all come with queer exclusions in Mormon vernacular. For those who are fluent in both dictionaries, listening to these words enthusiastically come at you all at once in such a short period of time—like I was at the temple open house—there comes a point where it begins to sound like queer exclusion being worn as a badge of honor.

After the presentation, the brethren announced that the group was so large they would split us in two, and Elders Rasband and Gong would each personally lead a group on our temple tour. I was beyond excited that Matthew and I were assigned to Elder Gong's group. The ideas and processes of Elder Gong's father, Walter Gong, a famous educational theorist, were used in my freshman year Honors Colloquium at BYU. Walter Gong's methods of learning how to learn were so transformational in my life that I still use his process today to capture ideas from another's point of view, expand and liken them to my life, and then teach others. As we walked to the temple, Tom Christofferson caught up with Matthew and me, calling out, "Husbands!" He excitedly put his arm around me and said, "It was a remarkable moment when you stood and introduced Matthew as your husband. This is the first time at an event such as this that the senior brethren have encountered a man introducing his husband. That was so lovely to hear. More of this needs to happen!" I smiled and then became astonished at how this could be true. The brethren really do need more opportunities to meet and get to know same-sex married couples with Latter-day Saint heritage in the faith-inspiring spaces of the Church. The difficulty of doing this so that such a venture feels safe for queer Latter-day Saints desperately trying to avoid both eternal exclusion and those with the power to make that a reality is the real barrier that prevents this from happening more often.

From the moment we entered the temple, Elder Gong was a gracious host, prepared and knowledgeable. And it was oh, so familiar. Yet that night—for the first time in my life—I encountered the temple authentically with my husband. We traveled from the basement baptistry to the top floor during the tour, stopping at every room. I loved the changes to the temple and the things that were kept the same but refreshed. Every step of the way, Elder Gong was prepared with interesting facts about the Mesa Temple that I had not heard before. This was the ultimate tour guide experience. When we entered the terrestrial room, we were invited to sit while he talked with us. I lamented that the HVAC system had been changed. The giant returns that used to bathe me in frosty air were no longer in the walls next to the seats. As we sat facing the veil, Elder Gong talked about this room and the next room, the celestial room. The fabric of the veil was not in place, so to our nonmember "never been in a temple before" friends, it looked like we would just be passing through a bank of narrow archways to get to the next room. But I knew what this entryway symbolized.

After Elder Gong taught about the celestial room, he invited us to stand and enter. Matthew and I were near the back of the crowd, so we stood side by side for a few minutes as we watched our peers file through the archways. I knew the veil's significance, how couples who come to the temple to be sealed in marriage will first traverse this gateway together through ceremony and, hand in hand, enter the celestial room together, a symbol of entering eternal life—the ultimate exaltation with God, spouse, and family. When it was our turn, I tenderly clasped Matthew's hand, tears streaming from my face, and took him through the veil into the celestial room.

As Matthew and I held hands on an elegant celestial room couch, surrounded—every inch—by the symbolism of eternal life and the presence of God, it was not lost on me that the faith of my fathers, mothers, grandparents, and ancestors currently has no room for Matthew and me—nor our children—as a family for either time or eternity. Liam's words in the Kirtland temple at Affirmation's 2011 conference gently rested on my mind, "Don't you think, if they could just see us—if they could just see us here, don't you think they would change their minds?" That was twelve years ago. Since then, the exclusion policy had come and gone. Marriage equality was now the law of the land. The dominant narrative of the celebrated "celibate and single" sexual minority was now larger than life within my spiritual home, and the rainbow stained-glass ceiling remained unmoved. The status quo still reigned. No, it was no longer important that the brethren see me, for I knew with certainty that God saw me.

After some time, Elder Gong shepherded us out of the celestial room and down the stairs to one of the sealing rooms to conclude our tour. He seated us on both sides of the altar in front of the massive mirrors on each opposing wall. It was a remarkable sight to see queer people reflected in a sealing room, stretching off into infinity in both directions, without end. In this setting, Elder Gong shared what happens in a sealing room—where a man and a woman would be sealed in marriage to one another for the eternities. As he spoke, I felt the immediate presence of tension beginning to emanate from my peers. I was taken aback as it continued to swell within the room. Everyone was polite, but by the time Elder Gong finished, I felt like I could have cut it with a knife. I swallowed as I scanned the room, taking the unspoken temperature of my colleagues. I had never felt tension or discomfort in a sealing room before. This was absolutely brand-new territory for me. It was a sealing room filled with successful, self-determined, married, transitioned LGBTQ community leaders. Some had gone head-to-head with the Church about LGBTQ rights, while others had worked with the Church to pass local and state non-discrimination ordinances. Still, others had served communities that the Church also had an interest in serving. It was a room full of organizations with which the Church wanted to build a relationship—and now we had all just been reminded that LGBTQ people who claim the opportunities and equality of their heterosexual/cisgender peers have no place in that sealing room. It was the capstone moment of exclusion that many had already started noticing earlier in the tour.

Elder Gong then asked if there were any questions. Reading the room, I thought this a rather brave thing to do. A board member for the Southwest Center for HIV/AIDS, one of the largest healthcare organizations for the LGBTQ community in Arizona, immediately raised his hand and remarked, "You have brought us all into this glorious sealing room, yet here, along with the other rooms in the temple, there is no place for gay couples." He pointed out how exclusionary it was that the open house signage around the temple frequently referred to a man and a woman. I quickly reviewed my own trip through the temple that night. If I had seen signage, it didn't cause a blip on my radar. I was Mormon-blind to those signs. But to my queer peers encountering the inside of a Latter-day Saint temple for the first time—and by extension, the queer/Latter-day Saint intersection—this signage was problematic and exclusionary.

Elder Gong seemed a bit surprised and remarked, "Our understanding tonight was that we were going to be authentic with one another, and skipping rooms and changing our signage or script for your group because it might cause offense would not be authentic." He explained that earlier, the brethren met and discussed modifying the tour for our group but decided against it. "You received the same tour as our Muslim groups and our Jewish groups. We decided it was most respectful to give you the same tour with the same signage that everyone sees, and if that caused you offense, that was not our intent." Sitting at the edge of the sealing room, my brain was trying to process all this at a million miles an hour: the setting, the tension, the question, the answer. The LGBTQ community had just asked the same question that LGBTQ Latter-day Saints have been asking the brethren for decades: where is our place?

The Church has been giving queer Latter-day Saints the same tour through the plan of salvation and the Restoration that everyone else gets. Yes, that is equality, but the plan of salvation only becomes realized through the rites of temple worship. The purpose of temples is not touring. The purpose of temples is for the Saints to enter and participate in sacred and saving ordinances. While queer Latter-day Saints are given a tour through the plan of salvation in our gospel instruction, we are barred from equitably *participating* in the plan of salvation, making the law unjust in application. Just as a difference exists between touring and participating, a difference exists between equality and equity. Equality is about uniform access to opportunities and resources. Equity is about adjusting for individual differences and needs to achieve a fair and just outcome. To be clear, queer Latter-day Saints are not asking that the plan of salvation or the Restoration be modified for us so we won't be offended. We are asking to be accommodated in these spaces so that we can fully participate in every room of the Restoration and not have the plan of salvation prematurely terminate for us as we press forward towards the Tree of Life. That is equity.

Currently, President Oaks argues that queer Latter-day Saints are being treated *equally* in the Church. Immoral conduct in heterosexual or homosexual relationships is treated equally. Temple marriage is available to all equally. Relief Society is available to all women equally, and the priesthood is available to all men equally. Every ordinance is available to all children of God equally. To cast equality in such a facially neutral manner hides the unjust and discriminatory application of heterosexual and cisgender qualification. This becomes readily apparent when queer Latter-day Saints attempt to access these "equal opportunities" while claiming the same actions of sexual orientation and gender authenticity that their straight/cisgender peers do. In attempt after attempt to access the entire plan of salvation only to be denied, queer Latter-day Saints are the importunate widows of the ongoing Restoration, asking for access to the Bread of Life. Yet, every time, we are given a stone. A passage from The Book of Mormon emphasizes the importance of equity and justice. The eight years before Christ appeared to the Nephites was a time of great peace and order. There was nothing in all the land to hinder the people from prosperity because they had formed their laws according to equity and justice (3 Nephi 6:4). The Book of Mormon is plain on this matter, "Among the Lord's people, equity and justice must always prevail."[1]

Sensing that I was deep in thought processing some serious Mormon calculations, Matthew reached for my hand as Elder Gong offered this stone: "Tonight, we have offered our authentic self to you. It was done in love, and we hope you can understand that it was offered in love." I was struck with deep sadness. This was but another example of the love that is proffered queer Latter-day Saints by the modern church, just as the exclusion policy was justified as having been offered in love. As we said our goodbyes, filing out of the sealing room and into the night, I reflected on the words of Elder Gong. In his argument, if the LGBTQ community felt the exclusion of

---

1. McConkie, Joseph Feilding, Robert L. Millett. "Righteousness Brings Peace." In *Doctrinal Commentary on The Book of Mormon. Vol. 4. Third Nephi through Moroni*, 1151. Salt Lake City, Utah: Bookcraft, 1987.

the sealing room, it was morally acceptable because the Church meant no offense. In the spirit of Elder Christofferson's "two-hand" metaphor, the Church was just one hand talking to the other. It was given in love. After all, once the tour ends, everyone parts ways, where the Church is located in one direction and the LGBTQ community in another. Elder Gong's exchange with the LGBTQ community avoided the elephant in the sealing room: The location of queer Latter-day Saints. As a church, we have been beating around the bush for decades on this issue. But between the two hands of the LGBTQ community and the modern church, the secret sits in the middle and knows: The queer children of God are not others.

They are us.

CHAPTER 30

The Gentleness of Love

> How silently, how silently
> The wondrous gift is giv'n!
>
> Phillips Brooks
> "O Little Town of Bethlehem"

The prophet Lehi had a dream that caused him to rejoice. He shared with his family that in his vision, he saw a tree whose fruit filled his soul with indescribable joy when he ate it. He felt a strong desire to share this fruit with his family. Desiring to understand his father's dream, Nephi inquired of the Lord and was swept up into an "exceedingly high mountain" (1 Nephi 11:1). There, the Spirit taught him the nature of love by telling him the Christmas story. Nephi saw the Christ child in the arms of his mother, Mary. This was the condescension of God, which John the Beloved spoke about: "For God so loved the world that he gave his only begotten Son . . ."(John 3:16). Once shown the Christmas story, Nephi understood the meaning of the tree in his father's vision and declared it "the love of God which sheddeth itself abroad in the hearts of the children of men, the most desirable above all things" (1 Nephi 11:22). The Spirit replied, "Yea, and the most joyous to the soul."

I am continually struck by how poignantly the Christmas story teaches us about love. It is a story—most joyous to our soul—of the gift of God's love for us. Each time I reach the third verse of "O Little Town of Bethlehem," and sing, "How silently, how silently the wondrous gift is giv'n!"[1] I feel—feel deep down into my bones—the gentleness of sheer love, silently, gently, given to the world the night Jesus was born.

The work and the glory of God to bring to pass the immortality and eternal life of all humankind (Moses 1:39) is enveloped in this love. As an eyewitness to the love of God in the flesh, John the Beloved invites us to participate in the work and glory of God: "Beloved, if God so loved us, we ought also to love one another" (1 John 4:11). You are the "Beloveds" to whom John is speaking. You are empowered to love because God first loved you. The invitation of Jesus to "Come, follow me" (Matthew 4:19) is not some theoretical exercise. It is a practical, flesh and blood, corporeal journey where we take upon ourselves the very name of Christ and become the physical manifestation of his love as we follow in his footsteps and go about doing good in this world. "Come follow me" is made alive by incorporating the gentleness of love within our daily discipleship.

Christ is love (1 John 4:8). We know that Christ was given in love. Therefore, we practice love by living the love of Christ, bearing such love as the fruits of our personal discipleship. What this practice looks like is different for everyone because, on our particular road, we may encounter any number of others

---

1. Brooks, Phillips. "O Little Town of Bethlehem." In *Hymns of The Church of Jesus Christ of Latter-Day Saints*, Hymn 208. Salt Lake City, Utah: The Church of Jesus Christ of Latter-day Saints, 1998.

on our way: be it the hungry, the thirsty, the stranger, the naked, the sick, the imprisoned—the least of these, as Jesus would say (Matthew 25:35-45). In our mortal journey, we not only encounter "others on our way," but we also encounter those who have been "othered" as well—those who bear some sort of mark that separates them from the power centers and opportunities of either society or religion. Jesus spent much time during his mortal ministry with those who had been othered. It is with the marginalized, the refugees, and the "others" that faith is made alive through love. Faith without action is dead. Faith with action is eternal (James 2:17-23). The action of those who follow Christ is to be the face and hands of Jesus Christ; in so doing, we become eternal, made alive in Christ. We are not asked to judge our neighbor, to exclude our neighbor, to erase our neighbor, to fear our neighbor, to "other" our neighbor—for it is to the "others" that we run, to greet, and to lift.

There is no room in the gentleness of love for a Rameumptom (Alma 31:12-22, 32:1-3), for are we not all sinners and "fall short of the glory of God"? (Romans 3:23). We all are weary peers walking together, equally reliant upon God to sustain us no matter where we were born, whom we were born to, the color of our skin, our gender, our gender identity, our sexual orientation, whom we marry, our ability, or disability. In the end, it is the love of God that welcomes each of us home, and it is our bearing of his gentle love that helps others along the way.[2]

A friend of mine, April Green, is the Relief Society President of a peninsula ward on the shores of Puget Sound. She delivered

---

2. Jones, Mabel. "He Sent His Son." In *Children's Songbook of The Church of Jesus Christ of Latter-day Saints*, Song 34. Salt Lake City, Utah: The Church of Jesus Christ of Latter-day Saints, 1989.

a sacrament meeting talk about community and belonging so powerful that I have pondered it continually since I first heard it. She declared, "We were made for belonging!" She read a passage from *This Here Flesh*, "Maybe you've heard it said that you need to learn how to be alone before you can be with someone. I say you have to learn how to be with and a part of something in order to know how to be alone."[3] Out of a deep anchoring in community, we are free to explore the solitary. April continued that there is no "me" without "we." We cannot reach our true potential without embracing the full community that we all belong to, the community of the family of God. Only when even the smallest link is securely interlocked is the chain unbreakable. I was struck by what she was proposing. The health and wellbeing—even the survival—of the community of Saints depends on the unbrokenness—the wholeness—of each interlocking link, no matter how small. April concluded her thoughts by recalling the two great commandments to love: Love God and love your neighbor as yourself (Matthew 22:38-39). She explained how these two commandments are symbolized in the configuration of the cross: the horizontal relationships we have with each other and the vertical relationship we have with God. "You can't have one without the other."

As the children of God, we are the horizontal relationships with one another. Elder Christofferson illustrated horizontal relationships with the Church on the one hand "and LGBT persons on the other."[4] Horrifyingly, in the modern church, these two hands of the horizontal arms of a Christofferson Christ are nailed down, painfully secured and immobile, stretched as far apart from one another as possible on the horizontal plane on a

---

3. Riley, Cole Arthur. "Belonging." In *This Here Flesh*, 70. Convergent Books, New York. 2023.

4. Sistas In Zion, 2018. "*Elder Christofferson's address to the NAACP livestream.*" Facebook. May 18, 2018.

symbolic legalistic cross. When we separate the Church from the LGBTQ person in this manner, we crucify Christ afresh. But we do not worship a Christ nailed to the cross. For in his resurrection, his hands are free from nail and tree. As a community of Saints approaching Zion, it is in the resurrected Christ that we are his outstretched arms on that horizontal plane. These arms are outstretched, not because they have been nailed down. They are outstretched so that we may have the widest reach as we bring them together in a mighty embrace of the queer children of God.

We cannot forget that the heart of Christ also lies on this horizontal plane. In a horizontal embrace of the queer children of God, we create a wholeness at the heart of the family of God. There, we find ourselves cradled at the heart of Christ. It is the heart of Jesus that is love—the greatest and most gentle of all. We are the outstretched arms of Christ. What we value in these freely mobile, horizontal relationships with our LGBTQ siblings in Christ becomes the answers for God's people. These are the positive, peaceable things of the kingdom to value.

I have always loved the way Jesus presented how to love our neighbor. When he says to "love thy neighbor as thyself" (Matthew 22:39), he teaches that we love our neighbor to the extent that we love ourselves. But what do we do when we feel this capacity to love ourselves is small or non-existent? Sometimes, we encounter moments when we feel unlovable—perhaps broken, imperfect, or unworthy. These are moments when we feel that we are not whole. What or who defines wholeness?

A few years ago, I had my piano tuned by someone I consider a master of his craft. I found him by chance in the local grocery store parking lot. His vehicle had a decal advertising his profession. As we talked while I loaded groceries into my car, I learned he had retired to Montana and visited town once a year to stay with family. While here, he tuned pianos during the day to pass the time while his grandchildren were at school. I asked him to please come over. While past tuners would bring an assortment of electronics and tuning forks, he just brought his ears. He looked at my piano and said, "I know just what your Yamaha needs. She needs a bright treble and a deep, gorgeous bass." He proceeded to tune intervals and octaves, runs and chords, not to a tuning machine, but to each other. Within thirty minutes, he had freed my piano, and I could hear something magical resonating from the strings. When he was done, he took a tuning machine out of his pocket, not to check his work but to show me his craft. He told me tales of years past, tuning for famous pianists in famous places. "The secret," he said, "is to tune the mid-piano dead on, the higher octaves just above center pitch, and the lower octaves just below center." Master musicians frequently ask him to stretch the octaves, and this tuning technique is what they mean by that. "Even though a piano has eighty-eight keys, the piano is a single instrument, not eighty-eight separate instruments," he observed. "It's how the notes work with each other, not how they sound individually." The master tuner told me he usually never tells his clients these facts because they cannot comprehend why a perfectly tuned piano is not a beautifully tuned piano. "Why pay for an 'out of tune' piano tuning?" a novice would say.

 He left me much to think about. How often do I strive to tune each individual note in my life to perfect pitch? Such exacting precision may make each part of me pitch perfect, but like the piano, I am a whole instrument. My life is of stretched octaves and beautiful harmonics, not because I am perfectly tuned, but because I am beautifully tuned. We can be whole when our parts are not perfect. And this, I discovered, is what the Master prefers. You can participate in love just as you are.

Christ has given us two great commandments that contain three admonitions to love: God, our neighbor, and ourselves. This is the invitation to participate in the gentleness of love in both the horizontal and vertical arms of our relationships. It is our gentle bearing of this love within community that brings us all along into the arms of our heavenly parents. Exaltation is a family matter; we get there with each other. Let us not leave others behind. Together, we'll find the place which God for us prepared as we wend our way with joy. Together, we can be brave in our journey, for it is a journey where LGBTQ people may face the eternal rejections of a sealing room, face the removal of blessings and membership for claiming marriage equality, and face the restrictions upon our church membership for transitioning. It is a journey where LGBTQ people will be denied equity in the law of chastity and denied accommodation as the queer children of God within the plan of salvation, conditioning worthiness based upon covenants inaccessible to queer people but second nature for straight and cisgender people. But at this time we will also witness on an eternal scale what happens when the prejudice of dominant narrative and policy meets the very power of the gentleness of love. Love wins.

At the Waters of Mormon, Alma beautifully taught that the second great commandment comes alive through loving our neighbor in community. It is love that will greet the queer children of God when our journey is through. There, the "Loving Heavenly Father Clause" will bless our horizontal relationships that we established and nurtured one with another on Earth, melting away prejudice and discrimination under the greatness of the gentleness of love that is in Christ Jesus.

CHAPTER 31

Smoke and Oakum

> I have different responsibilities when I teach people who follow Latter-day Saint doctrine than I have when I speak as a representative of the Church on what positions the Church ought to take in society as a whole... don't judge a private sermon by public issues.
>
> President Dallin H. Oaks
> University of Virginia, 2021

I was now coming into the last year of my presidency. I marked 2022 as a resurrection year for Affirmation, raising us out of virtual space. During the pandemic, Affirmation experienced a large influx of new growth as people sought community amid physical isolation. By now, many participating in Affirmation had only experienced our communities virtually. A virtual Affirmation had its benefits—and as leaders, we noted them— but a virtual Affirmation cannot replicate the power of the in-person format. The personal connection people experience in flesh-and-blood community is transformational. It is the magic woven into the center of Affirmation's DNA, present since its organization in 1977.

The world was now open. If resurrection was our theme, then our goal was to remember the effectiveness of our face-to-face meetings. The strategy was to begin holding a slate of in-person conferences and gatherings worldwide, each with senior-level leaders attending, reminding our peers the Affirmation way of creating community. The capstone event in this process would be the in-person International Conference in September. Amid our preparations, my twin grandsons were born. It was a tense moment, for they came into this world at just over twenty-eight weeks. Though premature and small, they were healthy and active. Doctors advised us that they would be in the NICU for several months. This addition to our family's boughs of love was the joy that propelled me into 2022.

True to form during this moment of the ongoing Restoration, the modern church was continuing to throw obstacles directly into the middle of the queer Latter-day Saint experience. Each time it does this, you can almost feel the collective tilt of the intersection as thousands of queer Latter-day Saints navigating this intersection throw their wheels in unison to avoid collision. One such event set the stage coming into the new year.

Two months previously, President Oaks stood in the Rotunda Building at the University of Virginia and delivered what felt like an executive's summative reflection of a life's work. President Oaks has devoted his life to spearheading the political and legal anti-LGBTQ initiatives of the modern church, setting the internal tone towards LGBTQ Latter-day Saints within their spiritual home. The tone for any organization is set at the very top, and this tone had been running like smoke and oakum into our corners of the vineyard for decades. For many years, we have been getting hints about the modern church's strategy concerning LGBTQ people, and his speech that night connected the dots for me, explaining what I had been feeling and witnessing in bits and pieces. Hawaii's Baehr case; The Family Proclamation; California Prop 8; the Utah Compromise; amicus briefs in the Gavin Grimm, Obergefell, and Bostock cases; the exclusion policy; Fairness For All; the Equality Act; the love and law of the Lord press conference; the rainbow stained-glass ceiling; the celebrated single and celibate generation; the current BYU Honor Code: The modern church's position on all these matters made sense in light of President Oaks' speech in the Rotunda where he revealed his agile legal mind.

He began by confirming in great detail the existence of the modern church's tactic to divorce the larger LGBTQ community from LGBTQ Latter-day Saints. He outlined the Church's external/internal strategy of negotiating with the LGBTQ community under the rules of human law and ruling LGBTQ Latter-day Saints under divine law. The Church's management of its LGBTQ population remains in force and unmolested by the government "when it does not violate what Jesus called 'Caesar's law'."[1] His candor stunned me. I had pretty much figured this out over the past few years working amid the practical effects of what I had dubbed the "Great Divorce" political strategy in the lived experiences of LGBTQ Latter-day Saints—and here he was saying it out loud. The "gentleman's game" of politics the Church heavily participates in with those in the civil arena does not exist within the Church. Constructive politics and good faith negotiations between the men in the red chairs

---

1. Oaks, Dallin H. "President Dallin H. Oaks' Speech at the University of Virginia." newsroom.churchofjesuschrist.org, November 12, 2021. Accessed July 28, 2024. https://newsroom.churchofjesuschrist.org/article/president-dallin-h-oaks-speech-university-of-virginia.

and LGBTQ Latter-day Saints are not an option. A negotiating table is not a thing. Unfortunately for LGBTQ Latter-day Saints, if you're not at the table, you're on the menu.

Having a "dust and ashes" Job moment at the injustice President Oaks was laying out in the Church's long-game LGBTQ strategy, my jaw dropped at what he did next. He revealed the weakness of this multi-decade "Great Divorce" strategy. It turns out that this strategy is not an insurmountable, untouchable power for LGBTQ Latter-day Saints after all. President Oaks noted that this strategy was made possible by religious freedom. He observed that preserving religious freedom ultimately depends on public appreciation and support for First Amendment freedoms of religious conscience, association, and free exercise. In turn, "appreciation and support depends on the value the public attaches to the positive effects of the practices and teachings in churches, synagogues, mosques, and other places of worship."[2] In other words, it's a symbiotic relationship between churches and the public. This relationship has burned the Church before. As he spoke, I remembered that First Amendment freedoms and religious liberty protections failed the Church a hundred and fifty years ago in the case of polygamy, and the Church has a very long institutional memory of that trauma. The public attached no value to the effects of the practices and teachings of the Church on polygamy. Consequently, the federal government walked right through the front doors, reached for the Church's doctrine on family and marriage, and shut the early practice down by exerting every pressure it could bring to bear.

The Church's experience of the public's power in this symbiotic relationship explains why it views civil rights movements as it does. The Church sees civil rights movements as the tail

---

2. Oaks, Dallin H. "President Dallin H. Oaks' Speech at the University of Virginia." November 12, 2021.

wagging the dog, the citizenry's fickle movements of social discontent that threaten to devalue—if not upend—sacred tradition and sincerely held beliefs about how to view and treat other human beings. What is it about civil rights that threatens churches? Civil rights walk right into the middle of prejudice in a pluralistic society and hold open a space of safety and privilege under the law for vulnerable classes of people. It does so because prejudice takes a long time to leave a human heart on its own, if it ever does. Because of civil rights, protected classes do not have to wait for inclusion, opportunities, rights, and privileges until the last vestiges of prejudice leave society.

When civil rights are allowed to stand and work within society, they challenge and then change the overall narrative surrounding prejudice and equality. Within this change, people begin to find no value in the teachings and practices of a church that continues to traffic in prejudice and inequality of other human beings. This feature is what makes civil rights a danger to the status quo. Even with strong religious freedoms firmly in place, when a society that once tolerated exclusionary theologies in its churches rethinks and repents of its prejudice and acts of prejudice, change happens in churches. This is the kind of change that civil rights movements and laws make in a society. The privileges of equality and opportunity may be soundly rebuffed at the heavily fortified religious freedom gates, but they are gently carried in through the hearts of the members. President Oaks acknowledged that no amount of religious freedom can withstand this change in society's values. The preservation of the status quo in the modern church concerning queer prejudice, harassment, and discrimination depends on the value that the public and, by extension, its members attach to the effects of the dominant narrative and policies about LGBTQ people.

With religious freedom spectacularly failing the Church once before in its practice of polygamy, it is wary of the efficacy of existing religious freedom guarantees to protect its sincerely held religious beliefs about LGBTQ people. This is why we see such a politically active church: instead of leaning in on existing protections that it knows it already has, it is anxiously working to obtain and strengthen more and more protections as it works to carve out a place in the law to protect itself from the citizenry. It is imperative to note that attaching no value to a particular practice or teaching in one's church is not the same as advocating for removing First Amendment freedoms of religious conscience, association, and free exercise. It is not the same as wanting to see the undoing of religion. Religious freedom is essential to a free society and is worthy to be defended. However, religious freedom can be co-opted into becoming an unwitting partner in perpetuating immoral prejudice and acts of prejudice among human beings. And this is where a society, especially the society of Saints who are building Zion with their families, must be vigilant that religious freedom serves the interests of "equity and justice" (3 Nephi 6:4).

Religious freedom is not going anywhere, nor should it. But the practices and beliefs it protects are subject to change over time according to what the members of the Church value. Religious freedom guarantees the right of religious bodies to teach and practice their beliefs, even if people outside these communities judge them prejudicial. If a religious community no longer chooses to practice or believe a certain way, or considers the continued holding of such beliefs immoral, religious freedom will just as vigorously protect its right to make those changes.

In President Oaks' revelatory speech, we have the key to effectively engaging this two-pronged "Great Divorce" strategy. The first key is to greet LGBTQ civil rights as a political matter and meet the Church out on the political playing field. The second, and most important, is to greet the injustice of the theological and corporeal exclusion of the queer children of God within the Church as a moral issue—and to do so with the tenacity of an importunate widow. After all, these are not only our fellow Saints, but our own children, parents, and family.

Externally, do not be afraid to meet the modern church in the political arena on the matter of queer equality. The divorce of the LGBTQ community from the LGBTQ Latter-day Saint is not a spiritual practice. It is a political strategy. You do not have to do this alone. Many LGBTQ organizations that traverse this playing field would welcome your help. Political advocacy aside, never forget the power of your vote. Guaranteeing civil rights improves the temporal health, safety, and security of LGBTQ people in civil society. When this civil society then meets on Sundays to worship, they bring these values into the pews. Interestingly, the Church encourages its members to be involved in politics and vote,[3] even in the matter of LGBTQ civil rights.[4] After the disaster of mobilizing the pews during Prop 8, the modern church has virtually swept politics from the pews and dumped them into the civil arena. As long as you keep politics out of the pews and meet the modern church out on the political playing field, your membership and belonging will be just fine.

---

3. The Church of Jesus Christ of Latter-day Saints. "Political Neutrality and Participation in the Church of Jesus Christ." newsroom.churchofjesuschrist.org, June 1, 2023. Accessed July 28, 2024. https://newsroom.churchofjesuschrist.org/official-statement/political-neutrality.

4. Stack, Peggy Fletcher, and Robert Gehrke. "Balancing LGBT, Religious Rights Won't Be Easy, Mormon Leaders Concede." *The Salt Lake Tribune*, March 2, 2015. https://www.sltrib.com/news/mormon/2015/03/03/balancing-lgbt-religious-rights-wont-be-easy-mormon-leaders-concede/.

But what about internally? The tools available to affect societal change are unavailable inside the Church. But this does not mean that we are powerless. Jesus teaches us by parable that the continual questioning of the importunate widow gets results (Luke 18:1-8). It is good to remember that the widow relentlessly approaches a judge who initially rejects her pleadings. Yet through her consistent entreaties, she eventually wears out the judge, and her request is granted. By following her example, we employ the very thing that began the Restoration: questions (Joseph Smith—History 1:13). It is no longer enough just to acknowledge that a rainbow stained-glass ceiling exists in the Church through which LGBTQ people cannot rise. It is time to question why the rainbow stained-glass ceiling is there in the first place. Start asking this question at every chance. Why are we capturing and holding our queer children in a celibate state for life, never to have the opportunity within Zion to experience the love, fidelity, devotion, sacrifice, and family found in marriage—and to do so according to their orientation? Why are we allowing the erasure of transgender members of the Church, placing restrictions upon them, and even withdrawing their membership for simply living their gender in authenticity and honesty? Why do we value the act of eternal rejection of our beloved queer children? Why do we accept their exclusion from the sealing room, the celestial room, their eternal family tree, and the very presence of God when they claim the equality and privilege of their heterosexual/cisgender peers? Why do we not want them by our side, able to equitably participate in the same opportunities and privileges that the general population in the Church has? We have heard the theological answers to these questions ad nauseam over the pulpit. However, capturing people into an ideology that is founded in a doctrinal premise that queer people in their authenticity cannot be exalted has real-world, practical effects that cause the families in Zion harm, revealing the prejudice and animus in this entire system.

As our beloved, non-queer ecclesia, keep asking for bread. Despite receiving bucketfuls of stones, keep asking for bread. And in your asking, work within your sphere of influence in the Church to create as much safety, love, and hope within the spiritual home of LGBTQ Latter-day Saints as possible. Notably, you are not there to hold LGBTQ Latter-day Saints in a place if that place doesn't feel safe or healthy for them. Sometimes, church spaces are safe and healthy, and sometimes, they are not. That is for the queer person to determine, not you. Your job is to provide the breathing room and space for LGBTQ Latter-day Saints to figure out what to do and where they need to be in this world in the face of some very intimidating prejudice and acts of prejudice.

You will be met by resistance as you do this because it is easy for power to conflate the pleadings of an importunate widow with advocacy. Your ministry of direct care of LGBTQ people within the walls of Zion will be judged as activism. You will be met with scolding from the unjust judge. Brother Ahmad S. Corbitt, first counselor in the Young Men general presidency, has already reminded the Saints, "Change in the kingdom of God is not accomplished in the same way as change is in, say, government."[5] This is absolutely true, and President Oaks has shown the way. Understanding the modern church's strategic differences between government and the kingdom of God laid bare in a Virginia Rotunda allows each of us to effectively minister to the queer children of God from the weak position in a power imbalance. Because of religious freedom, no one is

---

5. Toone, Trent. "Brother Ahmad S. Corbitt: How Activism against the Church Can Blind, Mislead 'Valiant' Souls." Church News, November 1, 2022. https://www.thechurchnews.com/leaders/2022/11/1/23424931/brother-ahmad-s-corbit-activism-discipleship/.

coming to help from the outside—not the government, not our LGBTQ community leaders—no one is coming. It is up to us to gently carry in this change through our hearts. Jesus approves of the importunate widow.

※

The first Affirmation regional conference I attended outside the United States in 2022 was with Affirmation Mexico in Mérida. Between sessions, Matthew and I had time to explore the city. It was a hot and humid afternoon as we walked to the historic center of Mérida, so we stopped at a corner store to buy ice cream before finding a bench to sit in the Plaza Grande.

The Plaza is a remarkable open space in the middle of the city. In 1526, Francisco de Montejo petitioned Charles V, King of Spain, to conquer and colonize the Yucatán. His request was granted, and he was given the mandate to bring the indigenous peoples of the New World "to our Holy Catholic Faith."[6] The Mayan people proved more tenacious and resistant to colonization than the Spaniards had anticipated. In 1542, Montejo's son, El Mozo, finished his father's conquest and led a successful mission into the heart of the Yucatán, where he established Mérida on top of the ruins of the Mayan city Ichkanzihóo. He reserved a large plot of land in the center of the city to be the Plaza Grande. Fulfilling the king's mandate given to his father to bring the Catholic Church to the indigenous people, he designated the land to the east of the Plaza for a cathedral to be the seat of the bishopric of Yucatán. This was the first cathedral built on the mainland of the Americas. The cathedral plot was

---

6. Chamberlain, Robert S. "The Early Career of Montejo and His Patent for the Conquest of Yucatan, 1514-26." In *The Conquest and Colonization of Yucatan: 1517-1550*, 20. Washington, D.C.: Carnegie Institution of Washington, 1948.

not vacant. The giant Mayan Pyramid, Yajam Cumu, built hundreds of years earlier, occupied the designated plot. Slowly, the great Mayan temple was disassembled, stone by stone, and then those same stones were reused to build the new and imposing Mérida Cathedral. Masonry Magazine notes that this cathedral was meant to be massive from its initial inception. It was to stand as an imposing symbol representing "tangible evidence of Christianity's power and dominance over the local culture. It was a towering reminder of who was now in charge."[7] Nothing, it would seem, conveys power better than an empire dismantling your temple and then using the pieces to build its own. For 200 years, a large Mayan stone monument stood on the land west of the Plaza, directly across from the Mérida Cathedral. In the early 1700s, the governor of Yucatán demolished it to build the Palacio Municipal de Mérida, the seat of government.[8] This building stands today bearing a salmon-colored neocolonial façade spanning the length of the street. It is a stunning seat of power in the Yucatán.

As Matthew and I ate our ice cream together on a green painted park bench on the Plaza Grande, the symbolism of it all struck me. As a queer person, I was sitting directly between two imposing symbols of power: government and religion. To my left, "Government" not only regulates queer marriage laws but provides a level of everyday control right down to the restrooms we can use, the healthcare we can access, and the sports we can play. To my right, "Church" controls our pathway to God. It teaches that in our wholeness, we cannot belong and are not

---

7. Blake, Indi. "Marvelous Masonry: Mérida Cathedral." Masonry Magazine. Accessed July 28, 2024. https://masonrymagazine.com/Default?pageID=1665.

8. Castillo, Sergio Ceballos. "Historia del Palacio Municipal de Mérida." El Blog de Mérida en la Historia, July 5, 2020. Accessed July 28. https://meridaenlahistoria.com.mx/2016/05/historia-del-palacio-municipal-de-merida/.

worthy of the presence of God. It has the audacity to configure our own families both on Earth and in the heavens, threatening eternal separation from God and from those we love if we choose love on Earth.

As queer people, we exist in the shadows of these immense power centers looming over our lives. These powers that surrounded me in the Plaza Grande existed long before I was born and will continue long after I die. What can we do in the face of such power? We sit in the Plaza Grande and eat ice cream with those we love. We gather in our friends and family to enjoy the wide-open spaces within the beautiful city center of our life. With integrity, we do not allow our queer bodies—temples of God—to be dismantled to become a symbol of empire. With tenacity, we run as fast as we have strength (Mosiah 4:27) to diligently eliminate the inequality and injustice that lies within our power to change, and then give God the burden of what we cannot do, grounded in the utmost assurance that God will take care of the rest (Doctrine and Covenants 123:17). With hope, we hold the "Loving Heavenly Father Clause" tightly in our hearts. And with love, we find queer joy in the Plaza Grande of God.

CHAPTER 32

The Stench of Lazarus

> 39 Jesus said, "Take away the stone." Martha, the sister of him who was dead, said to Him, "Lord, by this time there is a stench, for he has been dead four days."
>
> John 11:39 (NKJV)

At the end of January 2022, Rebecca sent me a message: "My family needs me more than Affirmation needs me." Executive duties in an LGBTQ global nonprofit are rewarding but prove complex in many time zones, cultures, and languages. It was time to pass the baton and focus on her family. This was a difficult decision for her. She was anxious about making this change before her term was over. Even though family and self-care come first in my book, it couldn't stop my sadness. I would miss working with her terribly. We led Affirmation through a pandemic and kept it on the rails. We would have stories for a lifetime. I messaged back, "Your work and voice have been so good for Affirmation. I completely understand and support you and what's next for your family. This isn't 'goodbye'. Matthew and I plan to visit next time we are in Washington."

Rebecca wanted to write a farewell note to the board and Affirmation members. After reviewing the event calendar, we decided the best time for this announcement would be after I returned from a presidential commitment in Utah in mid-February. I was presenting at the Humanities Symposium at Utah Valley University.

A few months earlier, the Humanities Department at UVU contacted me and asked if I would come to campus and speak. The organizer had read several of my op-eds in *The Salt Lake Tribune* written during my presidency, and indicated he was particularly excited for the students to have the opportunity to learn about me and Affirmation. He asked if I would address the topic of "Homosexuality and the LDS Church." I was honored and excited to receive such an invitation. Two huge items relevant to this topic were rattling around my brain: My experience with Elder Gong in the Mesa Temple and President Oaks' University of Virginia speech. These experiences were rooted in the very foundation that the November 5th exclusion policy had been: the modern church's continued tussle with the LGBTQ civil rights movement. The immediacy of this moment struck me. The students would get the opportunity to learn about these long-standing issues in the context of current events cresting in the queer/Latter-day Saint intersection. In accepting UVU's invitation, I noted that I would push the boundaries of the topic to include all queer people since this was the population Affirmation serves in its intersection with the modern church. As I constructed my presentation, I centered on this question:

What are the practical effects of dominant narrative and policy on the LGBTQ population in the Church?

President Nelson teaches that the Restoration is ongoing.[1] We sing that the Restoration breaks like the morning, dawning at the speed of light, majestically rising on the world.[2] In the matter of LGBTQ people, when the Restoration is weighed down by prejudice and discrimination, the Restoration slows down from light speed to baby steps. When the Restoration is slowed in this manner, the aging of queer people does not slow down. A slow Restoration means that LGBTQ Latter-day Saints grow old while suspended indefinitely in an abjectly unfair state of stasis founded in prejudice. Prejudice in the spiritual home of queer Latter-day Saints means capture under the rainbow stained-glass ceiling. For the sexual minorities of the Church, this means joining the lifetime holding tanks of the single and celibate monastic order of the Church, asking that they never join with another in the highest ideals of love, fidelity, devotion, sacrifice, and family.[3] For transgender and non-binary Latter-day Saints, this means the inability to experience their gender or transition without restrictions or removal of their membership, possibly inducing a chronic state of managing gender dysphoria throughout their life. These are the expectations of queer Latter-day Saints until others receive further light and knowledge. How long do you, as a church, ethically and morally hold your LGBTQ children there? How long can you ethically and morally tell them to be patient and wait? You can sit with them, weep with them, and celebrate them, but in the end, only the

---

1. Stevenson, Gary E. "The Ongoing Restoration." BYU Speeches, August 20, 2019. Accessed July 28, 2024. https://speeches.byu.edu/talks/gary-e-stevenson/the-ongoing-restoration/.

2. Pratt, Parley P. "The Morning Breaks." In *Hymns of The Church of Jesus Christ of Latter-Day Saints*, Hymn 1. Salt Lake City, Utah: The Church of Jesus Christ of Latter-day Saints, 1998.

3. Obergefell v. Hodges, 135 S. Ct. 2584 (2015)

straight/cisgender person is free to move about the Restoration, while LGBTQ people are restricted to the margins.

The rainbow stained-glass ceiling is a tomb. We must stop entombing queer Latter-day Saints. Reduced to an ideology in a system structured by prejudice, LGBTQ people in the Church become the Lazarus of our day (John 11:1-45), damned in progression, still as death, unable to move any further in the mortality of our spiritual home, waiting on others to either roll away the stone by revelation and call us forth or pass to the other side where God will have to pick up the work of equity and justice that his children would not do in his name on Earth. An ineffectual church stands outside the tomb and calls out platitudes and encouragement through the stone door, day after day, as the queer children of God gather the stench of Lazarus. But, like Martha, you are mistaken about what is happening within this tomb.

As the queer children of God, we will not languish in the tomb forever. LGBTQ people were not born for baby steps; we were born to run, to rise. We were born with inherent self-worth and inalienable human rights. Spirituality is a human right. LGBTQ people are born every hour into the families of the Church. Understand that in the Church, you are surrounded by LGBTQ people who are whole and equal persons in the sight of God and consider the Church their spiritual home. Unable to kickstart the Restoration, LGBTQ people are not helpless hostages. We hold one of the most powerful gifts of the Restoration: personal revelation. Personal revelation is the check and balance of the contracted feelings and fallibility of the hosts who are called to drive and administer the Restoration in our day.

We exist to have joy. This is our birthright as the children of God. Our first parents taught us that marrying and creating a family was worth being driven from the garden over. Shadrach,

Meshach, and Abednego taught us from the furnace that claiming our authenticity of self in the face of power is a protective measure presided over by angels (Daniel 3:16-28). Despite many profiles of courage in the scriptures of maintaining personal integrity and choosing joy, the current "ask" of LGBTQ Latter-day Saints is that we instead just patiently hold in the tomb under the rainbow stained-glass ceiling while we faithfully accumulate the stench of Lazarus. No! Personal revelation empowers us to claim our authenticity in the face of prejudice and acts of prejudice, not to wait for baby steps or to be acted upon. Let the ongoing Restoration catch up with us! Rejecting prejudice is not a matter of having a weak faith. It is silly to say that being authentically queer equals having a faith crisis. The queer children of God are not faithless or unspiritual. Like all people, we navigate towards joy, not the darkness of a tomb. When the day comes that the stone is finally rolled away, the church will not be met with the stench of Lazarus. The church will not be met by Lazarus. Instead, it will find this tomb empty. For this was not a tomb of Lazarus after all, but a space as freeing as the tomb of Joseph of Arimathea from which the queer children of God have already risen to walk the path of joy and progression that God has laid out before them. The Church will need to run to come find us.

As long as the rainbow stained-glass ceiling remains unshattered, you will continually be wishing your queer children goodbye. It doesn't matter how sincere your well-wishes are or how tearful the goodbyes. Collectively as a church, you are as the children of Israel who have stripped us of our identifiable coat of many colors and separated us from our spiritual home, selling us for silver, and then misrepresenting to our Father why we have gone missing. It does not have to be like that. We do not have to wait until Egypt to embrace.

I held these thoughts in my heart through weeks of writing and rewriting. As I flew to Utah the third week of February, I considered what lay ahead at UVU. This would be a moment I would introduce Affirmation to an academic audience, stand up for my queer Latter-day Saint peers, and express that I found no value in the practices and teachings of the Church concerning queer Latter-day Saints. Identifying and disavowing queer prejudice in the modern church without sounding like I wanted to burn it all down would be a difficult needle to thread. The complexity owed in part to how the modern church's covenant path requirements of "faith" and "belief" were tethered at the moment to sincerely held religious beliefs rooted in prejudice and acts of prejudice, against which no one can have a rational discussion about the treatment of queer people in the Church without being cast as "unfaithful" or "a barking dog snapping at the heels."[4]

I realized that this would be a moment to draw upon my experience of having difficult but ethical conversations with my patients about their health. This would be a time to speak objectively about the experiences of queer Latter-day Saints, shine a light on the intersection, and then inspire hope and queer joy. Without the firsthand data and stories that I had accumulated from the queer/Latter-day Saint intersection as president of Affirmation, I could not have spoken to the topic with any amount of insight or wisdom. Now, because of my circumstances, I was a holder of things most do not see beyond their own experiences, their own gender identity, sexual orientation, or their geographic location. I have seen the queer/Latter-day

---

4. McConkie, Bruce R. "The Caravan Moves On." *Ensign* 14, no. 11, November 1984. https://www.churchofjesuschrist.org/study/general-conference/1984/10/the-caravan-moves-on.

Saint intersection from a vantage point not many get to experience. My peers had elected me to this unique position, and my duty was to be a reliable reporter of my experiences there.

PowerPoint and notes in hand, I felt a mixture of resolve and nervousness when I arrived at UVU. I was ready to show love to all my queer peers no matter where they stood on the faith spectrum while showing little patience for power structures that litter our intersections with obstacles and hazards. I purposely arrived an hour early to center myself. I found my way to the Bingham Gallery in the Fulton Library, where I sat before the Roots of Knowledge, a massive floor to ceiling stained-glass mural, one hundred and fifty four feet long with eighty immense panels intricately depicting a sweeping view of the progress of human innovation, creativity, and the pursuit of learning over time. It was breathtaking in beauty and symbolism.

The beginning frame depicts the Tree of Knowledge, connecting heaven and earth. Directly to its right was the Tree of Life, where our first parents are sheltered under its boughs. Together, these two trees extend their roots and branches throughout each panel, coursing through history towards the final frame where root and bough converge to form, floor to ceiling, one great tree—the Tree of Hope for Humanity. This tree "symbolizes the transfer of knowledge and wisdom to the subsequent generations"[5] who will carry the light to illuminate the world into the future. Standing before this towering tree of glass and light, its sweeping message spoke to my soul and circumstance. I whispered, "In the end, it's about hope, isn't it?" I closed my eyes and took a deep cleansing breath. Then, carrying the weight of inspiration great art can spark, I walked to the auditorium and entered a packed hall, the subsequent genera-

---

5. "Visitor Guide." Resources | Roots of Knowledge | Utah Valley University. Accessed July 29, 2024. https://www.uvu.edu/rootsofknowledge/resources/index.html#brochure.

tions, where I delivered my thoughts in the great hope I had just glimpsed in glass.

At the end of my presentation, I explained that when we survey the queer/Latter-day Saint intersection, it is not about the intersection. It is about the navigator. Celebrate the navigator, not their captors, and not the seas full of underwater hazards. Celebrate the hope that the continual wave of beautifully perfect queer children born to Latter-day Saint families will find refuge and protection in their homes, shielded from a spiritual culture of muskets and fire. Casting hope into this intersection, I exclaimed: "To all my queer peers who are navigating to their joy towards love, guided by the Spirit in personal revelation through these waters of prejudice, I affirm you. I celebrate you. No toil or labor fear as you wend your way. I cheer for you that you will find the place which God has prepared for you!"[6] Then, recalling the signs at the end of the World Pride march in New York City—and remembering the fate of stationary pioneers—I earnestly concluded: Don't stop! Keep going!

---

6. Kitchen, Nathan. "Unashamed Authenticity: UVU Humanities Symposium Presentation." Affirmation, February 18, 2022. Accessed July 28, 2024. https://affirmation.org/unashamed-authenticity-uvu-humanities-symposium-presentation/.

CHAPTER 33

Sprint to the Finish

> God of the neighborhood, De Mejorada, give protection
> to the band that comes to eat at the temple.
>
> > A written blessing painted on a
> > table at the GastroBarrio El Templo at
> > Affirmation Mexico's conference in Mérida

Affirmation needed a vice president. As I talked with Jairo about the vacancy, we were flummoxed about where to turn for that additive voice in the executive committee. We needed help gathering the world of Affirmation back up into corporeal space. We could not do this by ourselves. We eventually tabled the issue for a few days to consider our options.

The following day, over breakfast, I contemplated how to move forward. Affirmation needed a proven community builder. This was a time to put our shoulder to the wheel. Heading into my second bowl of cereal, Laurie's partner, Nancy, messaged me about a dental question. After chatting about teeth and gums, the conversation naturally turned to Affirmation. I shared that my most pressing concern was filling the vice president position. Nancy replied, "If you need help, I volunteer my girl." Momentarily stunned by the possibilities couched in her words, my spoon went clattering to the floor. It was a watershed moment. One thing I learned about Laurie in my experience working with her was that she meant what she said, and she meant what she said the first time. Her words are delivered like fully rendered architectural plans—such a great executive skill. So, back in 2020, when she shared that she would not be part of a second-term executive committee to focus on her life with Nancy, it was the finality of stone tablets delivered from Sinai in my world. But it was here, strewn about teeth and gums, that Nancy's words flooded my mind with a sliver of light and possibility. If I have one talent, it is to hold to hope. I messaged Laurie and asked if we could meet over Zoom. This, it turns out, would be our final vulnerable conversation about the state of Affirmation, a series of conversations we had started as fellow board members in the summer of 2018. By conversation's end, I understood the heart of love and leadership that Laurie carried. This buoyed my soul tremendously. She would return to serve alongside Jairo and me for the remainder of my term as president.

Jairo, Laurie, and I had ten months—sprinting to the finish—to create abundant opportunities for Affirmation members to be with one another around the world. As the year progressed, I kept a tally of the in-person local meetings, pride events, and regional conferences to help us gauge our success in our mandate to finally shake the COVID cobwebs out of our psyche. This wasn't about numbers or scale. This was about meaningful connections made. To see Affirmation back in the saddle and off our screens was to see an influx of people seeking Affirmation's communities. This showed me that we were headed in the right direction.

As the executive committee member assigned to oversee the United States and Canada, I had one chapter I had always wanted to visit in my area, but the pandemic made it impossible—until now. My youngest son was graduating high school in May. Senior trips are a tradition in our family, and he set his heart on Hawaii. With the stars aligning under the immense heavens, this facilitated a very serendipitous opportunity to meet our Affirmation Hawaii leaders in person. I was beyond excited.

To the casual observer, nothing special was happening at the Seasider Snackbar at BYU-Hawaii that March morning of 2022. It was just another lunchtime where a group of friends had pushed a few tables together to visit over sandwiches, chow fun, and ice cream. Our Affirmation Hawaii leaders reported how Rainbow Day had gone the previous week and excitedly shared their plans for upcoming gatherings and activities. Their energy and spirit lifted me in my work on the international stage. This was the flesh and blood representation of the Tree of Hope depicted in stained glass at UVU. Sitting in a college cafeteria with the future of the work I was currently engaged in was humbling yet ever so hopeful. These were the ones who would carry our collective knowledge and wisdom to the subsequent generations to light the Zion of the future. I was so proud of them. I still am.

On our last night in Hawaii, Matthew and I waded into the ocean at Waikiki Beach at sunset. We stood hand in hand to watch the sun dip below the horizon as gentle Pacific waves rolled past us toward the shore. Now in 2022, I was on the other side of the Pacific from where I had stood hand in hand with Matthew two years earlier at the beginning of COVID. No longer facing an unknown ocean on the shores of Muir Beach, this moment signified the beginnings of what was next for us. No matter where Matthew and I stand, no matter what we face, we will do so hand in hand in love. Love is an experience to which I assign great value.

***

When I called the International Conference Committee together after I returned to Arizona, I reiterated the vision to reboot Affirmation's worldwide in-person programming. The capstone of our regional events would be our International Conference in October at the Salt Palace in Salt Lake City. Our members and leaders would be coming in from around the world and the United States, together again after almost three years. This would be an important one. In addition to that meeting, two other major conferences at the end of the year were on my radar. In September I would be with Affirmation Mexico in Mérida, and the following month I would be in Madrid for Affirmation's Continental Europe conference. I would be with Jairo in Mexico and Laurie in Spain. During this final moment out in the field for the executive committee, I would be with two of the greatest souls I have ever worked with in this life. I cherished each moment with Jairo and Laurie. Each time I observed their interactions with others in Affirmation, I realized afresh the beauty and strength they demonstrated in their leadership.

As the immigration officer stamped my passport upon landing in Mérida, I noted that Mexico was my first stamp in my empty passport book, a symbol that life does not always work out how you had planned. I applied for my first passport when I was elected president of Affirmation. I aspired to get out among my peers in Affirmation, wherever they were assembled. And then COVID happened. My pre-pandemic travel agenda as president of an international organization may not have been realized, but the journey that materialized was exactly what it needed to be for Affirmation.

On the final day of the Mexico conference, we traveled to the coast at Progreso to take in the sights and feel the sea. As the sun set, I stood with Matthew on the long fishing pier, Muelle de Pescadores. We shared the dramatic sunset, clouds streaming across the Gulf of Mexico, catching the reds and oranges of a September sky. My mind turned to a significant obstacle that had appeared in Affirmation's path concerning our International Conference. A few weeks earlier, I learned that Faith Matters had just booked space in the Salt Palace to hold its inaugural conference, the same venue and weekend as ours. Theirs would be a huge, well-funded conference. I wondered why we had not been seen. We had been heavily advertising and promoting our conference for six months.

I was continually receiving messages from Affirmation's LGBTQ members and our allies. They felt torn between which event to attend. In the Mormon world, the communities that Affirmation and Faith Matters serve overlap. I anticipated this scheduling conflict would cause a significant drop in our attendance and a drop in focus as people ran between conferences. Frantic, I reached out to their conference organizer, and we discussed possibilities for collaboration to accommodate shared interests. I noted that their programming day on Friday ended in the afternoon. Buoyed by the positive conversations with their Executive Director, the Affirmation board invited Faith Matters to be with us Friday evening for dinner and our opening plenary session. That evening would be very special for us as LGBTQ Mormons, our families, and our friends. We wanted to draw our circle to include them and come to the faith's margins. We heard back that their board would not advertise this invitation anywhere in their programming. My heart sank. Even though there was no time conflict on their end, they declined to acknowledge our invitation to be with us at our Waters of Mormon nonetheless. Attendance at our International Conference was now an additional obstacle on my plate, a continual stressor until the night of our opening session.

Now, on the shores of the Gulf of Mexico, my mind was racing a million miles an hour. I thought of our Affirmation band that had gathered in Mérida and the faith they showed as they bravely stood in the face of rejection. Each exhibited extreme courage as they looked prejudice directly in the eye as the hands of connection that once held them close in their spiritual home loosened and let go. Their faith mattered. I then thought of Faith Matters' space in the Latter-day Saint landscape. Faith Matters is a community of Saints organized to be a companion on the journey of faith through expansive conversations about the restored gospel of Jesus Christ. It is led by many prominent Latter-day Saints known for being thought leaders in Latter-day Saint spirituality. When I visited their website to learn more about their mission, it boldly exclaimed, "All who are involved with Faith Matters share a deep commitment to the restored gospel tradition."[1] Their mission helped me understand why we

---

1. Faith Matters. "About." Wayback Machine - Internet Archive: Faith Matters.org/about. Archived August 19, 2022. 20:10:37. Accessed July 28, 2024. http://web.archive.org/web/20220819201037/https://faithmatters.org/about/

Faith Matters has since revised its mission, removing its stated "deep commitment to the restored gospel tradition," now communicating that it is "inspired by Elder BH Roberts' admonition to us all to take part in the ongoing Restoration." It now declares: "We do not shy away from difficult topics," and "We believe in casting a wide gospel net to embrace a wide diversity of people and thought, from within and from outside our faith." However, Faith Matters' wide gospel net and embrace of diversity still seems to frustratingly exclude the difficult topic of queer people of faith with Latter-day Saint heritage who stand outside of the current dominant narrative boundaries of the Church. I am hopeful that the Faith Matters community will grow into its wonderfully inclusive mission and come to the margins to see and explore the depth, beauty, and faith of the queer Latter-day Saint refugee found in the complete queer tapestry of the Restored Gospel of Jesus Christ. Current Faith Matters "About" page accessed July 28, 2024. https://faithmatters.org/about/

had not been seen. Even though queer people have been a part of the Church since its founding, the concept of an "LGBTQ person" was not around at the beginning of the Restoration. If a characteristic of a faith that matters is to have a deep commitment to the restored gospel tradition, LGBTQ people are obviously not "old" enough to be a part of that tradition. We are anything but tradition.

Is the only legitimate faith one approved by the faith tradition? Should it be? If it is, is it then faith or just being faithful to tradition? This is the Richard Bushman question of our day, "Is there room in the restored gospel for multiple queer faith experiences?"[2] Where is the place for our Affirmation band in Zion? If we cannot see LGBTQ Latter-day Saints in any other way than what is spun by the current dominant narrative that the modern church is teaching about queer people—which, by way of reminder, is not true—queer Latter-day Saints become frustratingly invisible to tradition. When confronted by this dichotomy between what the modern church thinks about LGBTQ people and what LGBTQ people know about themselves, Latter-day Saints will tend to ignore the matter entirely in Latter-day faith spaces because it is an uncomfortable, dissonant topic to sit with. Only our queer peers under the rainbow stained-glass ceiling will get attention because they are the easiest and least complicated to love. When no room is made for us in theology or kingdom, the practice of LGBTQ exclusion in one's personal discipleship is made acceptable.

In the Restoration, "faith" had been replaced with "faithful" for the queer children of God. For the modern church, it is "faithfulness" that matters. A world of difference exists between a "faithful queer Latter-day Saint" and a "queer Latter-

---

2. "Richard Bushman States the Dominant Church History Narrative Is False." YouTube, July 14, 2016. https://youtu.be/uKuBw9mpV9w?si=m9XFw4i4o7ojfXxJ.

day Saint of faith." For queer people, the word "faithful" runs the queer person through the judgmental lens of the ever-changing dominant narrative built from prejudice and misunderstanding. The label of "faithful" is virtue signaling to others that the power structure's dominant narrative finds you to be a safe, acceptable queer in the kingdom. Despite my testimony of the restored gospel, I was not judged a "faithful" Latter-day Saint because I was married to my husband, Matthew. But I reject this adjective as a modifier for my life. I am a queer person of faith. Faith is not a modifier. Faith is a noun, the object in my life that is eternal. Joseph Smith taught that faith is power.[3] Faith is the power by which all things are created.[4] Faith returns you home to your heavenly parents. Faith overcomes the barriers that prejudice presents. Faith is the first governing principle of power in the gospel of Jesus Christ (Articles of Faith 1:4).

"Faithful" entangles me in the facially neutral rules that manage the queer population in the Church. "Faith" focuses me directly on God the Father and Jesus Christ. "Faithful" is a label applied to queer people as an external validation based on the judgment of others. "Faith" is my identity that stands independent of human judgment. "Faithful" is a friend of queer prejudice. "Faith" is my liberator. It is not faithfulness that matters; it is faith that matters. There is power in being a queer person of faith. As a queer person, do not be ashamed to claim such. As a queer person, reject the label of "faithful," for it is our scarlet letter that binds us in prejudice and perpetuates a tradition of division within our spiritual home. As a principle of power, your

---

3. Doctrine and Covenants, 1835, Section 1:13. p. 7, The Joseph Smith Papers, accessed July 28, 2024, https://www.josephsmithpapers.org/paper-summary/doctrine-and-covenants-1835/15

4. Doctrine and Covenants, 1835, p. 11, The Joseph Smith Papers, accessed July 28, 2024, https://www.josephsmithpapers.org/paper-summary/doctrine-and-covenants-1835/19

faith is yours, and it is portable through any waters you navigate in mortality.

Night had now enveloped the Gulf, and I let go of my thoughts for the evening. Our friends in Affirmation Mexico had gathered at pier's edge and called out to Matthew and me to walk with them to the bus station. It was time to return to Mérida. On our way, we walked past the Faro de Progreso sending its light out into the Gulf. For me, this was the work of Affirmation, a lighthouse in the queer/Latter-day Saint intersection signaling the seas with piercing light so that others may know where to safely land. It is community building at its finest, surrounded by the best of God's children.

***

Back in the United States, the day finally arrived! This was my eighth Affirmation International Conference and the last of my presidency. I needed to bring so many items to the International Conference that flying to Salt Lake was impractical. After two virtual conferences, I had forgotten how much "stuff" was needed to put on an in-person conference. I drove all day Wednesday and stayed the first night with Heidi. She had been my home base since 2015 whenever I was in Utah for Affirmation events. It was a moment of peaceful familiarity when I dragged my suitcase through her front door after the eleven-hour drive. Her living room is the closest thing to a celestial room outside of an actual temple. During my Affirmation stays over the years, I spent many hours in that room calling down the Spirit, pondering, gathering strength, writing addresses, and napping. This was me coming in for a rest during the work of Affirmation.

As in the pre-COVID days, I reserved the day before our conference to build relationships with the press and our community partners. This time around, I was accompanied by Laurie and Melissa Malcolm King, one of our board members. I had appointments lined up all day, meeting with The Salt Lake Tribune, recording a Mormon Land interview,[5] having lunch with the AP before heading down to Provo to meet with the student leaders of the RaYnbow Collective before ending the day talking with the leadership of USGA over pizza and root beer about the state and safety of queer BYU students. As I drove Laurie and Melissa Malcolm home, we talked about the conspicuously absent organization on our list we had not made time to visit. For a decade, Affirmation always made time to go to headquarters to dialogue with our contacts at the Church. Our current pairing with religious freedom in the room turned out to be frustrating for both parties, with no one able to build a needed relationship of trust conducive to productive dialogue surrounding the queer Latter-day Saint experience. After my UVU presentation in February, The Department of Government and Community Relations sent me a scolding email about my presentation. I noted that for the first time, their email had a large bold header in red, "Confidential—for Church Use Only." I was not interested in communications that were expected to be restricted. When I share the experiences of the LGBTQ Latter-day Saint intersection, good and bad, if someone takes offense, that was not my intent, for, like Elder Gong taught, I offer such things in love.

Friday night, as I made final preparations at the Salt Palace for our opening session, my three sons were on the FrontRunner to Salt Lake from Orem. Matthew had just landed and was making

---

5. Stack, Peggy Fletcher, and David Noyce. "'Mormon Land': Affirmation Leaders Discuss Diversity, Dallin Oaks and the Future for Queer Latter-Day Saints." The Salt Lake Tribune, October 12, 2022. https://www.sltrib.com/religion/2022/10/12/mormon-land-affirmation-leaders/.

his way from the airport to the convention center by TRAX. At the top of the hour, when I saw Matthew and my sons enter the great hall, I beamed ear to ear as I called out to them to come join me at our table. This was my first time at an Affirmation International Conference with my husband and children. This blending of family with Affirmation symbolized triumph. If an angel had come to me as I stood in that autumnal sacred grove in 2013 and lifted my chin to show me this moment, I would not have believed it. I would have been astonished without comprehension, denied the vision, declaring it not true.

Conducting the opening session, Laurie welcomed everyone to the 45th annual International Conference. She reminded us that it had been three years since we had last been together and invited us to stand and hug one another: "We need to express love again! We are a loving people, and this is why we are back together!"[6] To stand and embrace was the sign of peace we all needed. I was so proud of the work we had accomplished. This was the final piece of the great resurrection of Affirmation back into corporeal space. As I turned to watch the crowd as we hugged and greeted one another, I saw the hall full. We had done it. We had filled this space as a community, and my heart could rest in the fact that we had successfully created this special place for our LGBTQ peers, their families, and friends. We had kept the lower lights burning through the pandemic, and now the whole of Affirmation was landing into our communities, which had been built by the generations and now passed to the next to carry the hope of us all.

---

6. Affirmation. "Friday Plenary, 2022 Affirmation International Conference." YouTube, October 13, 2022. Accessed July 28, 2024. https://youtu.be/JAMdh5oNhaY.

The weekend flew by. Sessions, workshops, and connections were happening at lightning speed. As I took to the stage Sunday to close the conference, the hope of the Nathan sitting alone in his study conducting the past two International Conferences in front of his laptop, anticipating the day we would meet again in person, was now realized. Gratitude filled my soul at the significance of this moment. For a season, I had the privilege to build communities of safety, love, and hope for my fellow navigators of the queer/Latter-day Saint intersection. Together, we walked out from under the trauma of the exclusion policy era and towards joy. A new light was now shining on the queer/Latter-day Saint intersection, the light of queer joy.

I stood before the body of Affirmation and announced our closing song. This was the moment to transmit the tradition of our closing session to the upcoming generations. "In Affirmation, we close our conference a bit backward from other meetings you may have attended," I began. "We will first have a closing prayer, and then we will end by singing, 'God Be with You Till We Meet Again'.[7] This is a moment where we reflect on everything we have heard and experienced this weekend together as friends. It is a moment where we sing our heartfelt blessing to one another that God will keep us safe, protected in joy and love, during the next year until we meet again." I paused, taking in this final moment's meaning before continuing. "To know that your mentors and peers surround you is protective and empowering. To symbolize this, I ask that you all stand and form one giant circle around the room, clasping hands in one unbroken chain so that we may greet one another face to face as we pronounce our blessings upon each other in song."

---

7. Manwaring, George. "God Be with You Till We Meet Again." In *Hymns of The Church of Jesus Christ of Latter-Day Saints*, Hymn 152. Salt Lake City, Utah: The Church of Jesus Christ of Latter-day Saints, 1998.

I closed my notes and looked out into the hall and into the faces of many I knew and loved in this beloved community. Overcome by the moment, I choked back tears as I concluded, "For my last conference as president of Affirmation, it will be my honor to accompany you on the piano as we sing our blessing to one another." I made my way to the piano as the room configured into a single, unbroken circle, every link connected. I really did mean this. It was my absolute honor to be able to accompany my friends in Affirmation on the piano in our final song of blessing, just as it had been my absolute honor to accompany my friends as president of Affirmation during the previous four years in the building of communities of safety, love, and hope—and in the blessing of queer souls.

CHAPTER 34

The Lifting of Samuel

> All we have to decide is what to do with the time that is given us.
>
> Gandalf
> *The Lord of the Rings: The Fellowship of the Ring*

Matthew and I left Sky Harbor Airport for Madrid the second week of November for Affirmation's conference in Spain. As I stood at the panoramic terminal window and watched our plane pull up to the gate, I felt a gentle notification ping from my phone. It was from Google Photos reminding me that on that day, nine years ago, I was in an autumnal Sacred Grove in Palmyra. The contrast of circumstances struck me. That was the day I felt prompted to leave my continuing education course in the Catskills and drive directly to the Sacred Grove. I had the most difficult life decisions ahead of me, and I needed a space to ponder and pray. I sought God as my partner in what was next in life. My faith drew me to the grove that late autumn afternoon, alone and isolated—and full of questions. My joy level then: 0.

Today, I was boarding a plane with Matthew as the president of Affirmation, to attend the Continental Europe conference. As I stood at the gate, the meaning of this moment flooded my mind. Being a part of Affirmation's supportive communities during these eleven years was transformative. It was lifesaving and life-giving for me and my family. The communities of Affirmation lifted me up and held me when I felt I could not stand—when I could not breathe—as I made decisions and met the full force and power of a dominant narrative about queer people in my spiritual home that simply was not true. Affirmation did not allow me to make important decisions alone in isolation. My joy level today: 11.

Our time in Spain reminded me how special and unique Affirmation conferences are. Our home base for the conference was an old nunnery turned hotel in the municipality of Cercedilla, nestled in the Sierra de Guadarrama. I was impressed that no matter where we go in this world, the queer spaces our leaders build and the programming they lead are always focused on wholeness and joy. After the conference, Matthew and I shared a beautiful sunset at the royal garden in Madrid as the largest formation of geese I had ever seen flew overhead in a seemingly never-ending "V." They were noisily announcing my place in the family of things, reminding me of the joy in my life. There, at sunset, I felt an overwhelming sense of gratitude for the pressings in life, that final push through an autumnal grove, to be standing with my husband under the boughs of love.

I returned from Spain on Monday evening and was back to work the next day. By the time clinic hours were done, I was exhausted and ready to catch up on my sleep. As I was leaving the office, I received an email from Peggy Fletcher Stack. She asked if I had a statement reacting to the Church's public support of the Respect for Marriage Act that codified the recognition of same-sex marriages just as long as there were religious exemptions. This was breaking news: "We need a comment ASAP. Thanks!" Her request came when all the other leaders on our rapid response team were in the air, smarter than I by taking an extra day in Madrid before flying home. My last press statement as president of Affirmation would happen alone. But after four years working shoulder to shoulder with the executive committee and knowing the mind of the vice presidents that such familiarity affords, I wasn't really alone.

I put my car keys away and opened Word. As the sun began to set, I penned Affirmation's statement about an event our previous generations during California Prop 8 would have thought absolutely unthinkable: the Church supporting a law supporting marriage equality. I wished I could have been happily surprised, but my forced relationship with the modern church on religious freedom political matters and "Fairness for All" legislation brought clarity of mind to this moment.

As I wrote, I noted Affirmation's appreciation for the Church's work with the LGBTQ community. I offered our wholehearted congratulations to our LGBTQ leaders in the civil arena who had worked tirelessly to move the Respect for Marriage Act forward. Over the decades, civil rights leaders in the LGBTQ community have done incredible work securing rights and protections for LGBTQ people. They were bringing the Church right along with them in this progress. I anticipated that the thrust of all those providing sound bites for this article would focus on the Church and its actions. In my statement, I was interested in articulating the implications of this new development in the relationship between the modern church and its own queer population. Affirmation has stood on this ground for almost a half-century, building communities for those navigating this intersection with the Church. It harms queer Mormons not to be seen and acknowledged in their intersection. If there were to be a voice for the visibility of the queer Latter-day Saint experience at this moment, it would need to be supplied by Affirmation. The Church's religious freedom strategies ignore the internal reality of the rejection and othering of LGBTQ Latter-day Saints within their spiritual home—especially for those who participate in marriage equality and gender self-determination.

While typing away at my computer, I was struck by how similar this moment felt to the times I had sat alone in a dark office, staring at a computer screen, casting hope into a "pandemic Affirmation" during our virtual International Conferences. Tonight was also about casting hope into the queer/Latter-day Saint intersection. Channeling the spirit of David O. McKay, I concluded, "Every hour, an LGBTQ child is born into a Latter-day Saint home. They are a perpetually renewing internal resource within the church and a population that one cannot ignore indefinitely by only opting to act in the civil arena. It is time for the church to get serious and start putting the same extensive time, attention, and resources into their own LGBTQ members and their families as they have done with outside LGBTQ groups. No amount of religious freedom success can compensate for failure within our spiritual home."[1, 2]

---

1. Kitchen, Nathan. "Nathan Kitchen: There Is a Disconnect between LDS Church's Outreach and How It Treats Its Own Members." *The Salt Lake Tribune*, November 17, 2022. https://www.sltrib.com/opinion/commentary/2022/11/17/nathan-kitchen-there-is-/.

2. Kemsley, Tamarra, Peggy Fletcher Stack, Emily Anderson Stern, and David Noyce. "In a Stunning Move, LDS Church Comes out for Bill That Recognizes Same-Sex Marriage." *The Salt Lake Tribune*, November

As I drove home that night, I reflected that I was old enough to have lived through the intense marriage equality fights of the California Prop 8 days, the Obergefell ruling declaring marriage equality the law of the land, the appearance of the exclusion policy, its recension, and now the Church's support of the Respect for Marriage Act. I was the president of Affirmation during the last two. I thought of my colleagues who led in the intersection for the first three events. I was but a part of the great chain of leaders who stood for a season, elected by their peers, to cast hope and affirmation into the world. I was the 25th president of Affirmation, each elected by their peers to lead for a season. I thought about the teams they assembled who stood shoulder to shoulder with them to affirm, protect, and amplify the queer children of God. I thought about my team and the privilege of standing with Jairo, Laurie, and Rebecca to accomplish the work of the intersection relevant to our day.

When I was a young boy, the paintings of Arnold Friberg were printed in the copies of The Book of Mormon. They were epic—every Nephite and Lamanite a fitness model. Even the old men had muscles, including a ripped shirtless Abinadi standing before King Noah's jaguars. To this day, the Book of Mormon stories I remember best are those depicted in those paintings. Most striking was Samuel the Lamanite, standing on a massive Mesoamerican stone wall, arms outstretched as he prophesied, untouched by the arrows flying around him from the Nephite archers. Samuel was on that wall for three chapters worth of prophesying. Samuel not only prophesied that Jesus would be born in five years, but he angered the Nephites when he told

---

15, 2022. https://www.sltrib.com/religion/2022/11/15/lds-church-comes-out-federal/.

them they were "encircled about by demons and seek for happiness in doing iniquity" (Helaman 13, chapter heading). People do not like it when they are told they are not doing it right. Hence, the stones and arrows. God protected Samuel on that wall amid the arrows, and he remained unscathed. Seeing they could not take him down by shooting at him, the Nephites went to grab him off the wall. At that moment, Samuel "did cast himself down from the wall, and did flee out of their lands . . . and behold, he was never heard of more among the Nephites" (Helaman 16:7–8).

Michael Austin observes that Samuel came from outside the center of the social hierarchy of his day. In Latter-day Saint scripture, two kinds of prophets exist: those who "lead a Church organization and exercise authority as a function of their institutional position" and those who "come from the margins and speak with an urgency inspired by their vision and an authority derived only from the power of their voice."[3] Nephi, the institutional prophet who led from the center of the church's social world, ignored Samuel's words. When Jesus visited the New World and asked to inspect the Nephite records, he saw that Nephi had not included the words that Samuel preached from the wall. Jesus told Nephi to "fix it."[4] Samuel was a prophet who came from the margins, and Jesus taught that such words are just as important for the record of God's people.

This has parallels to what is happening in the queer/Latter-day Saint intersection today. The presidents of Affirmation are by no means the prophets of Affirmation, which is not the

---

3. Austin, Michael. "Samuel the Lamanite and Who We Call a Prophet #BOM2016." By Common Consent, a Mormon Blog, October 5, 2016. https://bycommonconsent.com/2016/10/05/samuel-the-lamanite-and-who-we-call-a-prophet-bom2016/.

4. Austin, Michael. "Samuel the Lamanite and Who We Call a Prophet #BOM2016." By Common Consent, a Mormon Blog, October 5, 2016.

comparison to be considered. However, consider that every few years, Affirmation hoists a new president onto the wall to stand for a season and produce a few chapters in the ongoing LGBTQ Latter-day Saint intersection, speaking from the power of their voice. This is not a solitary effort, for presidents bring with them a team of leaders to get things said and done amid the stones and arrows of prejudice, harassment, and discrimination. People tend not to like it when we stand to declare those things that are hurting queer Latter-day Saints. Experiencing a reproving at times with sharpness from a queer leader in the LGBTQ Latter-day Saint intersection produces indignation in Zarahemla.

Presidents are the public face of Affirmation, charged with representing the organization as its spokesperson. In this responsibility, presidents tend to hear the stones and arrows whistle by their ears. I have stood on that wall more than once, amazed that I had not been directly hit. Like Samuel, Affirmation presidents are from the margins and hence often not taken seriously by the modern church, by non-queer Latter-day Saints, and sadly, sometimes not even by our allies. We speak from the power of our voice and the power of our collective lived experiences. Any Affirmation president worth their salt will amplify as many queer voices as possible, sending those stories out as copiously and rapidly as Samuel's prophecies came out of his mouth to the Zarahemla side of the wall. At some point, Jesus will ask those in Zion why those stories were not seen as important enough to record in their hearts. Why were the queer children of God not seen? He will tell them to fix it.

As the body of Affirmation, we know that standing on the wall is hard, so we ensure that this moment is seasonal. The hoisting of Samuel and bringing down of Samuel from the wall are extremely healthy actions for the organization's wellbeing and that of its presidents. To the people inside the walls of Zarahemla, it appears as if the outgoing president casts themself down from the wall and is never heard from again. But seriously. Who wants to go back to a people who were shooting arrows and casting stones at you while you were doing the Lord's work? The LGBTQ people on the margins of their faith have a different perspective. The outgoing president is coming down on *our* side of the wall. Emeritus presidents are given a much-needed rest as the lifesaving community building continues. Queer people have a life outside of wall-standing. It is highly possible that Samuel was never heard from again in Zarahemla because he was returning to a spouse, a family, and a community that brought him joy. He had a life down off the wall. It brings me great sadness that there even must be a wall. One thing is certain: LGBTQ people didn't build it.

As I pulled into the driveway after my long day, I marveled that when Paul Mortensen was elected the first president of Affirmation after its founding in 1977, I was only a ten-year-old boy, still sitting in the boughs of the cherry trees of my childhood home. I wondered how many quiet acts by others over the decades had made my own road easier to follow—teams of LGBTQ people I would never meet or know but who loved and cared about the future me to prepare and leave the landing and healing spaces that I encountered when I was ready to come out. This is the unseen power of supportive communities. Generations of LGBTQ Mormons had built something special for me. In my life, through it all, I was never alone. These leaders participated in quiet acts of love in the horizontal relationships of this life, building community to secure a chain of connection with one another. Love is not linear on this horizontal plane. Love is an arc. The arms of this horizontal arc gently bend together in embrace, love forming one unbroken circle of connection. The end of my story as president of Affirmation was the beginning of the story for another, someone sitting in their own boughs preparing for a life of joy and wonder. It is this ever-circling of love that enfolds the great generational communities of queer people. It is a circle that draws in our family and friends who will walk with us, the queer children of God, as we find the place which God has prepared for us.

Matthew greeted me at the door. I had told him I would be home late to finish some Affirmation business, and he instinctively knew what this meant. As we embraced, I realized I wasn't just tired because I was recovering from an international flight and a long day of patients. I was tired because I had been sprinting for the past four years. In those years, I had the honor to run as fast as I could toward people I loved dearly: my LGBTQ peers and their families who were navigating their intersection with the Church. I was all in, propelled by an almost boundless enthusiasm for Affirmation, its mission, vision, and, most importantly, the communities it builds and sustains. The wisdom in Laurie and Rebecca's voices now sat top-of-mind: "My family needs me more than Affirmation needs me." Indeed. I have fought a good fight. I'll continue fighting, but now I need to live.

Part of the genius of Affirmation is that we take turns leading this beloved community of our peers. It is not just a community of one voice but the voice of many. Its leadership is not just one person but a group effort. We have a president for a season who is willing to bring along a team and ride the crest of current events. We know from experience that this is not easy to do or maintain over time in this pressure cooker of an intersection. But we have others who are right behind us to come to take a turn for a while and advance this beloved community. When I was elected president, Joshua Behn, ten years and five presidents before me, shared, "Us old timers have a saying: Affirmation becomes exactly what it needs to be for each subsequent generation who needs it." This is a significant amount of trust our queer elders have placed in the rising LGBTQ generation for the perpetuation of an organization that has been a critical part of LGBTQ Mormon life for almost a half-century. But it is also the strength of Affirmation that it makes space for new leaders and engages new generations to tackle the cutting-edge concerns within this rapidly changing queer landscape that they are personally experiencing. The other reason Affirmation only holds its president for a season is founded in queer wisdom and experience. Affirmation understands that once you have come out, once you have transitioned—and achieved wholeness—you now have a life to live in that wholeness. It is unfair to keep your shoulder chained to the wheel or make you feel obliged as if it were. Placing our hope in the rising generation has propelled Affirmation along for generations, each new wave becoming exactly what it needs to be for those seeking its communities of safety, love, and hope. This "lead it then live it" practice allows us to give back to our beloved community in gratitude, make the road easier for those who follow, and then go and live thankful for a life of wholeness and queer joy.

To every queer person navigating their intersection with the Church, you are not alone! I want to shout this from the rooftops! You have peers who care immensely for you and for what you want to achieve in this life. You often do not see the generations gone before who have created the space in which you now live. You stand on the shoulders of giants as you reach for the heavens.

It was now December. My term would end on the 31st at midnight. Affirmation was ready to hoist a new president onto the wall. As I prepared to hop down after the absolute privilege of serving as its president for four years, I penned a farewell message. A month earlier, my words from the wall went to the Zarahemla side concerning the Church's support for the "Respect for Marriage Act." This time, my words would be delivered to those on the other side of the wall, to my LGBTQ friends and colleagues preparing to welcome me back on the ground in our beloved community. It was my farewell letter, not to Affirmation, but to the wall. As I concluded, I observed that occasionally, I hear queer leaders and allies say that they do what they do because they feel called to this work. Some cast it as their mission in this life to enter into this space where queer people are courageously navigating their personal intersections with the Church. Recalling the past four years helping lead Affirmation out from under the trauma of the exclusion policy and COVID, I turned my thoughts to the ultimate attribute that would sustain us as a people in the dawning of this new era of queer joy:

> Calls and missions are noble indeed; however, I am here in this space because I love you. It makes all the difference to me, as a queer person, when someone tells me that they are in this space to help because they love me. Four years ago, I entered this space as president of Affirmation because I loved you. I could do so because I was first loved by you, my community of mentors and peers. I am grateful for your trust and the opportunity you have given me to take a turn for a season leading this great organization.
>
> Queer joy will always be found within the boughs of Affirmation when we are rooted in love.
>
> Thank you all,
> Nathan[5]

---

5. Kitchen, Nathan. "Reflections and Farewell from Affirmation President Nathan Kitchen." Affirmation, December 18, 2022. https://affirmation.org/reflections-and-farewell-from-president-nathan-kitchen/.

AFTERWORD

> The great movements of history so frequently find their origins in the minutia of family. We are leaders of lands and peoples, and yet it is family that moves us.
>
> > King Charles VI of France to King Henry V of England upon learning that the terms of his surrender would include Henry marrying his daughter, Catherine, so Henry's posterity would inherit France and England.
>
> The King

In the entryway of my house hangs a scripture, a beautifully lettered piece of art that greets us in our comings and in our goings. It reminds us to establish a house of prayer, a house of fasting, a house of faith, a house of learning, a house of glory, a house of order, a house of God (Doctrine and Covenants 88:119). This is the house that my children and I chose together to become the place where we would start again in the aftermath of divorce. This is the house, mutually chosen, to be our place of stability, where we would come in for a landing until all wheels were on the ground.

This is the house where we renewed our strength and courage to confidently branch out into this world, enveloped in the love that emanates from this place. This is the house where we sat together around the family dinner table and welcomed Matthew in. This is the house where we stood together as a family the afternoon Matthew and I were married in its backyard—under a lemon tree, our Arizona boughs of love. We have established a house, one of the great houses of Zion, filled with the love of Christ that sheddeth itself abroad upon the hearts of the children of God (1 Nephi 11:22). Establishing a house is a family matter. Together, we stretch our arms wide along the horizontal plane of our relationships to welcome others in through love, inclusion, and hospitality. It is an ever-growing house where we welcome all those born to us, those who join us in marriage, and our neighbors who surround us.

The collapse of the Church's dominant narrative of my generation about sexual minorities and mixed-orientation marriages blew me out of the water. It kicked the legs out from under me and all those who loved me. As a husband and a parent, this was not a solitary disaster. It affected an entire family. It was incredibly disorienting and traumatic for all of us. Religiously guided mixed-orientation marriage leaves behind so much trauma and sadness in its wake across multiple decades, touching multiple lives. For me, my greatest trauma was watching my children face loss and the unknown. No matter how much I was present for them, I could not help. I could not take upon myself the pain and sadness they felt.

All through this trauma, my phone kept sending me "On This Day" photo reminders, serving up pictures of me and my children before the separation and divorce. I finally had to shut these notifications off for my mental and emotional wellbeing. I could not bear to look at them. Each time I did, I was reminded of the sadness and instability I felt during that time. It was also a painful reminder of the sadness and instability my children felt. I held an incredible amount of grief, guilt, and responsibility in this shattering of their Eden. During my last year as president of Affirmation, I decided I was ready to see "On This Day" photos. I knew that to finish my healing, I needed to give myself the grace to remember my children without attaching trauma to them.

The first photo my phone served up hit me hard. I wanted to shut it off, shut it out. Memories flooded in, and the swelling emotions began tearing up my insides. It was a simple photo of my little children playing a game of "Simon Says" out in the backyard the summer I had come out to myself. I looked at each of my children in that picture, and I saw the innocence and joy in their faces. They had no idea what was about to happen in their young lives—the unexpected journey of sorrows that lay ahead as life fell apart and then re-formed around them. Tears ran freely now. It had been fifteen years since I had taken that picture yet in this brief moment, I relived all the trauma sandwiched in between. But this time, I didn't shut my phone off. I sat with this picture and confronted these heavy waves of memory. I named the nameless, assigning meaning to my wordless emotions that I had avoided for years. I penned a poem to my children. I needed to express this. I needed to acknowledge what had happened. This was my moment to wrestle with an angel so that I might see the face of God in all the seasons of my life, especially those when I felt helpless and abandoned.

TO MY CHILDREN

Loss of a thousand losses
When our happily ever after endings end
Before the ever after—
Before lies became truth.

What might have been becomes what is now.
Where I have only begun to allow
Machines that store my data
To serve up daily memories

Of us.

Pictures frozen in time
When we were young
Before the loss of a thousand losses
And we saw one another for the first time.

And over time,
We came to know
Our "lived happily ever after" story
Has a "loved happily ever after" ending.

As I internalized what I had just written, my heart reminded me of the words that hung at the entrance of my house. We may have traveled through fire and flood as a family but we prevailed like that mighty desert tree growing from a rock on The Peak of Champions. We built our house from dust and ashes. For the first time, I had the realization that this wasn't just a story about me reaching for my children. All this time, my children had also been reaching for their father. Not only had I been building a place for them, they had been building a place for me. And in this reaching, our hands tenderly met, and we pulled each other in tightly, reclaiming one another in love.

During my final days as Affirmation's president, most of my free time was spent preparing for the International Conference. This was not a time to rest when I arrived home from work. One September evening, I had a lengthy to-do list that would occupy the entire evening. I called Matthew on my way home and told him I was "coming in hot." This describes the intensity of nights like this, for when I open that front door under the weight of all I need to do, I feel like a meteorite bouncing across the atmosphere, setting me aflame at 3000 degrees. It's not always like this, but it was that night. Matthew works the night shift at St. Joe's. Typically, on the nights he works, we have, at best, thirty minutes together before he heads out to the hospital. I was late coming home that Monday night, so our time together at the house would be brief in my comings and in his goings.

I landed at my desk, still in scrubs, surrounded by papers and notes, just as he was walking out the door. He paused and touched my shoulder, "Be sure to take care of yourself tonight. Be sure to eat some good food. I love you." Matthew can convey deep affection and love in just a moment of eye contact and a gentle touch, one of his superpowers. This superpower is life-giving. It is the kind of recharge I will never take for granted. He is an anchor in the house we have established, my dearest mooring. He is a foundational element that my children welcomed in, and they insisted he stay. Having him in our boughs of love strengthened our immediate family and brought immense joy and acceptance throughout our extended branches.

My parents sent two packages to our house the first year we were married, one addressed to Matthew and the other to me. Each had a Father's Day gift and a personal note wishing us a happy Father's Day. This was no small recognition. In my family, this one affirming act from my returned senior missionary, temple presidency parents was the equivalent of hoisting nine million pride flags at their house, illuminating it in rainbow lights 24/7— all while shooting off a glitter cannon from their front porch on the hour, every hour all month long. But this is the thing. My parents are, and have always been, understated. They are the examples of the humility and grace I continually strive for in my own life. Sending a Father's Day gift to their son's husband is the quiet affirmation reminding me that we are in the "loved happily ever after" moment within our family boughs.

I understand the love of my heavenly parents through the love of my earthly parents. I am especially lucky because I have both adoptive and birth parents who participated in giving and receiving me in love. My heavenly parents also gave me in love, and with great parental regard, they are waiting to receive me in love when my journey is through. Enveloped in this gift of belonging in the boughs, I experience love in community within the wide expanse of my family tree. Matthew and I have been scooped up into these boughs, off the ground, where the law lurks in an attempt to modify and balance the love that it encounters. I was born too early in a church not ready for me. The hosts of the Restoration of yesterday and today were not ready for me. My three grandchildren were also born too early into this world. However, their community was ready for them. They were gently cared for in a NICU prepared for their early arrival. No such lifesaving courtesy exists for queer Latter-day Saints born too early into a church in crisis on its way to renewal. Instead, they are met with the inhospitality of rejecting words, actions, exclusions, and segregation within their spiritual home.

Surrounded by my children and now grandchildren, on my journey through life, I think about another in the branches of my family tree, Ann Jewell Rowley. I echo her words in the darkest hours of her handcart trek to Zion in 1856: "I always thought I shall be the happiest person if I could reach Zion, with all my children alive." And she did. I hold this same hope, the great hope that every pioneer holds as they press forward to the promised land. I will reach Zion, arm in arm with Matthew, with all my children alive.

Putting the handcart pioneers out onto the plains late in the season on their journey to Zion always felt to me like putting gay and lesbian Latter-day Saints out onto the trail of mixed-orientation marriages. In both cases, you have Latter-day Saints who want to get to Zion, obey and sustain their leaders, and demonstrate faith in every footstep. Yet leaders who know the dangers—or should know the dangers—either encourage everyone along or do nothing to counter the misplaced enthusiasm for such a trek, knowing the conditions of the trail ahead. The dominant narrative in the modern church about mixed-orientation marriages that spanned two generations of gay and lesbian Latter-day Saints turned out to be a "handcart experiment." My family, the Rowleys, were a part of the original handcart experiment in the 1850s, getting the Saints from Europe to Salt Lake City as inexpensively as possible. As members of the Willie Handcart Company, their great hope was to be with the Saints in the Salt Lake Valley, and they put their trust in church leaders to help get them safely there. What happened next was one of the more tragic moments in church history. The companies were caught in the bitter freezing conditions of an unforgiving early winter, fueled by the relentless winds of Wyoming. *The Rowley Family Histories* reveal that, "Hunger and fatigue stalked the company by day. By night, the specter of death visited those who were weakened and poorly protected."[1]

Today, it is not just gay and lesbian Latter-day Saints who were (and still tacitly are) sent off with their mixed-orientation marriage handcarts with the promises they will get to Zion if they have enough faith. Sexual minorities are continually being committed to the Mormon Trail of lifelong celibacy and singleness, commanded that they may never marry according to the way their heart opens towards love. At the same time, the Church counsels against any form of transitioning, just push and pull through the dysphoria mile after mile, after mile, after mile unseen in the wagon wheel ruts of binary sex assigned at birth.

These things have been happening since the beginning of the modern church, and what are the fruits of this handcart experiment? As a collective queer population in the Church, we are in Wyoming, in a blizzard, on the frozen banks of the Sweetwater. We have been and still are being sent off with handcarts and faith, and at this moment in the modern church, we are all witnesses to the queer children of God stalled out on the plains freezing under a dominant narrative built from prejudice that is collapsing upon our heads. It is a disaster. It cannot be sustained. The danger for queer Latter-day Saints is real and present—unsustainable around the issue of sexuality, gender identity, and marriage. As an entire church, as the body of Christ, we can't stay in this queer handcart experiment. The question debated today about the handcart pioneers of 1856 is: "How could good men of great individual faith have risked the lives of so many others so imprudently?"[2] This is the question I

---

1. Richardson, Frank D., and Deane Johnson Cook, eds. "The Camp Rolled On." In *Rowley Family Histories*, 53. Fruit Heights, Utah: StoryWorks Publishers, 1992.

2. Christy, Howard A. "Weather, Disaster, and Responsibility: An Essay on the Willie and Martin Handcart Story." *BYU Studies* 37, no. 1, January, 1997.

ask about the treatment of queer Latter-day Saints in the modern church: How can good men of great individual faith risk the lives of so many others so imprudently?

The history of the modern church is littered with good men and women with great individual faith who sincerely believed that mixed-orientation marriages, family rejection, electric shock therapy, conversion therapy, lifelong celibacy, trans erasure, never transitioning, and theological segregation were the safest routes to go and the most loving advice they could proffer. Even if we give those in the past a measure of grace that they were products of their time, we no longer live in that time. Knowing that there are currently companies of trusting queer Latter-day Saints stalled and dying out on the queer Mormon Trail because of this "loving" advice should be enough data to eliminate today's extraordinary management and exclusion of queer Latter-day Saints. It is time to stop this queer handcart experiment and bring them in off the plains in full authenticity and equality into both the kingdom of God and their own eternal families.

In the last week of 2022, Matthew and I piled into the yellow Prius and headed to Southern California. We were going to Long Beach, where, after fifty-four years, I would meet my birth mother for the first time since we said our goodbyes at Cottonwood Hospital in Utah in 1968. I was excited and a bit nervous, but in awe that our goodbyes would turn into hellos, symbolizing the love present even in absence. Because of her,

---

https://byustudies.byu.edu/article/weather-disaster-and-responsibility-an-essay-on-the-willie-and-martin-handcart-story.

I understood love's power and influence on an entire lifetime. Love really is the greatest of all.

On the way, we stopped at the University of California, Riverside, where Matthew earned his Ph.D. We visited his downtown haunts, where he would go with friends to eat and study. We then took a walk over to the Downtowne Bookstore off Main. The bookstore had a small "Mormon" section where a copy of Spencer W. Kimball's book, *The Miracle of Forgiveness*, was prominently displayed. I momentarily froze as I met an old nemesis. This was the publication that started it all in my queer story, as it had for many in the early queer generations. In those beginnings, it seemed to wield absolute power. Its old ideas continue to echo in the halls of the Restoration today, still bringing about much anguish and heartache. To unexpectedly meet it now—an out-of-print paperback on a lonely used bookstore shelf for $6.50—it looked small, pathetic, and powerless. A shell of its former self. How could such a small thing have caused such great harm? Is this the book that shook the earth and made the kingdom tremble?

I plucked it off the shelf and took it to the register. I purchased it so other queer people would not be contaminated by its presence. I shared with the owner that this book had caused immense trauma and harm to LGBTQ Latter-day Saints. Not being Mormon, she indicated that this was valuable information. She would not stock *The Miracle of Forgiveness* on the shelves again. As Matthew and I left the bookstore, it wasn't as much about taking a harmful book out of circulation as it was about reclaiming my power. It was poetic to encounter this book that shaped the beginning of my story and now disempower it at the end of my story as president of Affirmation. Continuing our journey toward Long Beach, I reflected that I was still giving *The Miracle of Forgiveness* too much power by framing this moment in this way. This book was not the beginning of my story. I was hurtling seventy miles an hour on I-10 towards the beginning of my story. Soon, my birth mother and I would hold one another in a long, tearful embrace—goodbyes turning into hellos and sorrow into joy. I would show her what I had become in this beautiful life she had given me. Hers was the flesh and blood influence that started it all, the story of my life. Hers was the love that invited others in. Love was the miracle of my life. It was love that profoundly shaped my life, and it is within my boughs of love that I am with Matthew, enfolded safely in my shepherd's care, with grandbabies in my arms and children by my side—the hope for the future of the house Kitchen. I am surrounded by my parents, who first beckoned me to this tree, with brothers, sisters, grandparents, and their grandparents—our parents throughout all generations of time—all in the interconnecting boughs of love that rise unbroken to my heavenly parents.

As we parked our little yellow Prius in front of my birth mother's house, I took a deep breath as I held Matthew's hand. I had butterflies in my stomach. I reflected that in my journey from those cherry tree boughs of my childhood, I had now accumulated a lifetime of words that have slowly revealed the gentle love flowing through these immense branches of my family tree, hearts connecting and turning towards one another, infinitely expansive as the seemingly endless orchards behind my childhood home. This is the love in our great house, blossoming and kudzu-free, filled with the light of ten thousand sacred groves.

Within my heart, I now held the words, the experiences, the wisdom—counted in the gentle chirps of life—brightly confirming, as never before, the love that has always been present in my life. I understood the joy of my birthright. I am a beloved queer child of God—given and received within the boughs of love.

LOVE, RETURNED

The older I get, the more I wonder.

Wonder, with eyes and soul wide open,

In a God who returns tenfold

What was given long ago.

Goodbyes now hellos; departures, arrivals.

And hope, reality.

Yet the mystery of love endures.

"How can it deepen and grow in absence?

Just tell me the reason, the method, the plan."

The Spirit then breathes a gentle, "Hush."

For love's not explained but experienced.

We live the universe in real time, upon the crest of happening—

Witnesses of light, as love's red shift turns blue.

Oh, the mystery! What is cast upon the waters, returns!

Love arrives magnified.

What once was ours is discovered anew, not lost but always with us.

We are God's children, beholders of such wonder.

The wonder when arc becomes circle—and love, returned.

ACKNOWLEDGMENTS

While president of Affirmation, I lived at the absolute crest of current events in the queer/Latter-day Saint intersection. Never before had I been in a position that was so singularly focused on the present. Like a healthcare provider, I was on call. But instead of a hospital, it was an intersection, and the topic was change. I served Affirmation during the busy President Nelson administration when change for queer Latter-day Saints and their families was not only a regular occurrence, but the consequences of those changes were often nothing short of monumental. Sometimes, I had minutes to respond, like when a reporter was asking for an immediate comment for a breaking story. Other times, I only had a night to compose commentary and reassurances to my fellow queer peers who were hurting—seeking assurance and affirmation in the face of intimidating words spoken or rejecting actions taken by leaders in our spiritual home. This demand for immediacy is a crucible that forges the skills of quickly delivering meaningful and relevant commentary and essays as the words spill directly out of your head, onto the page, and into the wounded hearts of your friends.

From this crucible, BCC Press took a chance on me, willing to mentor me as I shaped the short-form world I lived in into the realm of books. I will be forever grateful to Michael Austin, who listened to my book pitch and encouraged me to begin this process and not let my experiences fade from the consciousness of Mormon thought. I am indebted to my developmental editor, Adam McLain, who helped me slow down and extract the story that needed to be told from my many experiences. It was a gift to have a queer editor. He not only worked from a place of empathy for the queer experience, but his knowledge, professionalism, and kindness inspired me. I am grateful for my line editor, Lori Thompson Forsyth. Her meticulous work and enviable writing skills cleaned up the manuscript and clarified sentences that would have been a stumbling block for a reader. I loved our bonus sidebar conversations in the margins of Google Docs, broaching the heady aspects of feminism, queerness, and grammar as we went through the polishing process. Many thanks also go to Anna Taylor, who provided valuable copy edits, and to D Christian Harrison for his stunning cover design. I also thank Cece Proffit and Conor Hilton, whose tireless, behind-the-scenes work at the Press lifted this project to completion. I would also like to thank Tyler Marz, Seventy, Community of Christ, Formation Ministries Specialist, who graciously reviewed the chapter where I write about Community of Christ, making edits to ensure accuracy in my vernacular and fidelity to their tradition.

To my friends and colleagues, Jairo Fernando González Díaz, Laurie Lee Hall, and Rebecca Solen, who stood shoulder to shoulder with me in Affirmation's executive committee, I love you. This time we had together, running as fast as we could towards our peers to lift and serve, will mark one of the most fulfilling and joyful moments in my life. You gave me the strength and courage to do what we needed as we took a turn leading this great organization. Most of all, I acknowledge every person who is part of the beloved community of Affirmation. In the spirit of the apostle John, I love because you first loved me. You held me when I felt I could not stand—when I could not breathe—as I made some of the most difficult decisions in my life about me and my family. You were that lifesaving and life-giving community of friends where I could land, heal, share, and be authentic.

To my dear husband, Matthew: Thank you for being my "at home" editor, cheerleader, and proofreader. Writing, and writing well, is your world, and I am grateful you unselfishly shared your talents with your STEM husband. You always knew what a writer needed and intervened when the process of words and thoughts began to overwhelm me. Writing this memoir unexpectedly opened parts of me that were hard to revisit, reacquainting me with all the emotions I lived a lifetime ago before things got better. But you knew this power that memoir writing has upon an author. For two years, whether at home, the library, or a café, you would often just come and silently sit with me for hours with your books to read as I wrote. Your intentional, gentle presence was reassuring, a reminder of the love in my life. Adventures lie ahead, and I cannot wait to experience them with you.

To my children—we made it. I love you dearly and am grateful that we reached our "loved happily ever after" moment. You make my life so joyful, and I am proud of each of you. To my grandchildren and great-grandchildren, to the posterity that will continue through the generations, your grandfathers are waiting for you under the boughs of love.

NATHAN KITCHEN (he/him) served as president of Affirmation: LGBTQ Mormons, Families & Friends from 2019 through 2022. Before his term as president, he sat on Affirmation's board of directors and co-founded Fathers in Affirmation, a peer support group for queer fathers. In 2024, he received the Mortensen Award, the highest honor Affirmation can bestow on an individual member for leadership and service within the queer Latter-day Saint community. He is currently the chair of the board of directors for Flourish Therapy, a leading nonprofit that provides culturally competent and affordable care for LGBTQIA+ individuals, families, and friends.

Nathan served a full-time mission for the Church of Jesus Christ of Latter-day Saints in Alabama, graduated with a B.S. in Zoology from BYU-Provo, earned his Doctor of Dental Medicine from Southern Illinois University, and completed a general practice residency at the University of Iowa Hospitals and Clinics. He is currently in private practice in Mesa, Arizona. He has been a speaker at BYU-Provo, Utah Valley University, and Eastern Illinois University about the queer/Latter-day Saint intersection and how to better support the queer Latter-day Saint experience. He is also a certified QPR suicide prevention trainer.

Nathan is the proud father of five children and grandfather of four grandchildren. He lives in Gilbert, Arizona with his husband, Matthew Rivera. In his free time, Nathan likes to travel with his husband, read a wide variety of books, and, of course, hold grandbabies!

www.ingramcontent.com/pod-product-compliance
Lightning Source LLC
Chambersburg PA
CBHW050256010526
44107CB00033B/1404/J